THE HISTORY
OF ROME

Theodor Mommsen

a new edition by

Dero A. Saunders &

John H. Collins

Meridian Books

THE WORLD PUBLISHING COMPANY

CLEVELAND AND NEW YORK

A MERIDIAN BOOK

Published by The World Publishing Company
2231 West 110th Street, Cleveland 2, Ohio
First Meridian printing (Greenwich Editions) August 1958.
Fourth printing (Meridian Books) January 1965.
Copyright © 1958 by The World Publishing Company.
Library of Congress Catalog Card Number: 58-12948
Typography and Design by Elaine Lustig
Printed in the United States of America   4WP165

INTRODUCTION

One of the highpoints of Mark Twain's European tour of 1892 was a large formal banquet at the University of Berlin given in honor of two of the nineteenth century's scientific giants, Rudolph Virchow, one of the founders of modern biology, and Hermann von Helmholtz, perhaps Europe's greatest scientific mind since Newton. Mark Twain was an honored guest, seated at the head table with some twenty "particularly eminent professors"; and it was from this vantage point that he witnessed the following incident:

"When apparently the last eminent guest had long ago taken his place, again those three bugle blasts rang out and once more the swords leaped from their scabbards. Who might this late comer be? Nobody was interested to inquire. Still, indolent eyes were turned toward the distant entrance; we saw the silken gleam and the lifted swords of a guard of honor plowing through the remote crowds. Then we saw that end of the house rising to its feet; saw it rise abreast the advancing guard all along, like a wave. This supreme honor had been offered to no one before. Then there was an excited whisper at our table—"MOMMSEN!" and the whole house rose. Rose and shouted and stamped and clapped, and banged the beer mugs. Just simply a storm! Then the little man with his long hair and Emersonian face edged his way past us and took his seat. I could have touched him with my hand —Mommsen!—think of it! . . . I would have walked a great many miles to get a sight of him, and here he was, without trouble or tramp or cost of any kind. Here he was clothed in a Titanic deceptive modesty which made him look like other men. Here he was, carrying the Roman world and all the Caesars in his hospitable skull, and doing it as easily as that other luminous vault, the skull of the universe, carries the Milky Way and the constellations."

It is doubtful whether any other European intellectual figure of that day could have been thus honored in the

presence of such men as Virchow and Helmholtz, and certainly none could have deserved the honor more than
Mommsen. For Theodor Mommsen (1817-1903) was
the greatest classical historian of his century or of ours.
His only rival in any century was Edward Gibbon, whose
monumental *History of the Decline and Fall of the Roman Empire* complements rather than competes with
Mommsen's superb description of the Roman republic.
Mommsen had, moreover, the advantage over Gibbon in
the extent and validity of the basic historical data (such
as the vast collection of Roman inscriptions, which
Mommsen himself later edited) at his disposal, and in the
advance of the scientific and critical method in historiogra-
phy, to which Mommsen made fundamental contributions.

The finest fruit of this toil was Mommsen's *History of
Rome,* published in some 2,000 pages in 1854-56, which
is of greater scholarly value today than Gibbon's *Decline
and Fall,* yet yields little to Gibbon in its power of direct
and forceful expression. Not until he was 86, the year before his death, did Mommsen receive the Nobel Prize for
Literature; yet the honor merely set an official stamp on
the judgment made decades earlier by the world of letters. The terse tribute of the *Encyclopædia Britannica* is
unequivocal: "Equally great as antiquary, jurist, political
and social historian, Mommsen lived to see the time when
among students of Roman history he had pupils, followers, critics, but no rivals. He combined the power of
minute investigation with a singular faculty for bold gen-
eralization and the capacity for tracing out the effects of
thought on political and social life."

Such a tribute, especially from a source so unsparingly
critical as the *Britannica,* automatically raises the question, Why is Mommsen's name and work so little known
in the English-speaking world today? That question will
be explored more fully later in this introduction. For the
moment, however, suffice it to say that the editors of this
volume are convinced that it is due to an unhappy set of

extraneous circumstances; and in support of that conviction we have spent a great many hours in the preparation
of this work.

The Man

Theodor Mommsen was born in Garding, Schleswig-
Holstein, on November 30, 1817—within a year, inci-
dentally, of the birth of two other towering nineteenth century figures, Karl Marx and Otto von Bismarck.
Mommsen, the son of a Lutheran pastor, spent his child-
hood in a bookish atmosphere; but there are no surviving
anecdotes of youthful precocity, and it was not until he
was at the University of Kiel in 1838-1844 that his powers of research and organization, as well as his brilliant
literary style, began to develop conspicuously. At Kiel he
first came in contact with men of outstanding intellect,
among them J. G. Droysen, the famous historian of
Greece and of Alexander the Great.

At Kiel Mommsen threw himself into the study of
jurisprudence (which in Germany meant the study of Roman law), and his later legal and historical masterpiece,
the *Römisches Staatsrecht* ("Roman Constitutional
Law") was the ripe harvest of a lifetime of study. He
also found himself in the thick of student political agitation, in which questions of liberalism and democracy, na-
tionalism and separatism, the future of Germany and the
future of Europe, were passionately discussed.

However, before the revolutionary wave of 1848 swept
the youth of Germany into intense political activity,
Mommsen received a research stipend which he used for
an extended trip through Italy. There he began the serious collection and study of ancient inscriptions. Previous
extensive collections had been made, and Otto Jahn, one
of Mommsen's professors at Kiel, was a leading authority on the subject. But there had been no massive systematic effort to collect, reproduce, edit, and publish them

all. This truly gigantic task, requiring the co-ordination of many scholars, became one of Mommsen's major activities in later life; and the monumental *Corpus Inscriptionum Latinarum* ("Collection of Latin Inscriptions"), which today occupies six feet of folio-size shelf space in every leading historical library, is the enduring result.

Mommsen's Italian years were thus crucial to his intellectual development. His knowledge of Rome broadened and deepened, and personal contact with the massive remains of the ancient world was stimulating in the highest degree. One recalls the famous passage from Gibbon's autobiography: "It was at Rome, on the 15th of October, 1764, as I sat musing amidst the ruins of the Capitol, while the barefooted friars were singing vespers in the Temple of Jupiter, that the idea of writing the decline and fall of the city first started to my mind." Mommsen has left us no autobiography, and his inner intellectual life is perhaps less known than that of any other comparable figure in his century. Yet it is surely reasonable to assume that the sight of the ruins of the Capitol raised emotions in him similar to Gibbon's.

Returning to Kiel in 1847, Mommsen found, like many another young genius, that the world was not yet ready to reward the high reputation he enjoyed in special circles. He went back to an obscure teaching position in a girls' private school in Altona, in the province of Schleswig-Holstein. That province was a focal point of the revolution of 1848. Though nominally Danish, the overwhelming majority of the population were German by language and sympathy, and the province was held under Danish rule by the most tenuous of threads. In the excitement of the day a provisional government was established, declaring independence from Denmark with the ultimate objective of joining the German confederation.

One of the provisional government's leaders was Theodor Olshausen, a friend from Mommsen's student days at Kiel, who recognized his potential as a publicist and sharp political thinker. He persuaded Mommsen to take the editorship of the newspaper *Schleswig-Holsteinische Zeitung,* which appeared from April through July of 1848. Although the revolution failed, and Schleswig-Holstein remained under Danish control until 1866, these busy months brought Mommsen into the closest contact with practical politicians, and showed him the real world of politics in a way that he could never have learned from books.

But Mommsen was not born to be a journalist. His friend and teacher Otto Jahn recommended him to the Ministry of Culture in Saxony, and he began his life as a German scholar with an appointment as a special Professor of Law at the University of Leipzig. True, his early university life was not wholly placid: in 1851, after two years of teaching and study at Leipzig, he was dismissed in "disgrace" along with his sponsor Otto Jahn and another well-known scholar, Moritz Haupt. It was a flick of the tail of reaction. With the collapse of the 1848 revolution came the revenge of the outraged government, and Mommsen lost his job as one who had associated with the "wrong" people—in short, as a security risk. But there were other and less benighted universities in Europe, and the dismissal from Leipzig was quickly followed by an invitation from the University of Zurich, where Mommsen went in 1852.

The "History of Rome"

Despite its unhappy ending, the Leipzig period was the seed-time of the great work on which Mommsen's world reputation was founded—the *History of Rome.*[1] The Leipzig publisher Karl Reimer had met the young professor, heard some of his lectures, and had become con-

∎

1. Originally published in German as the *Römische Geschichte*—literally, "Roman History."

vinced that he was the man to write a popular though soundly scholarly history of Rome, to rival Ernst Curtius' *History of Greece* then in preparation. He approached Mommsen with a contract, and the man and the opportunity fused.

One after another, in 1854, 1855, and 1856, the first three volumes appeared. Their success was immediate and increasing. Never before in Germany, and rarely in any country, had a professional scholar written with such vigor and life, such grasp of detail combined with a wide vision, such self-confident mastery of a vast field of learning. The work was literally epoch-making in two major aspects. It astonished and shocked professional scholars by its revolutionary treatment of the misty beginnings of Rome, sweeping away the old legends of the kings and heroes and along with them the elaborate critical structure deduced from those tales by Barthold Niebuhr, whose reputation as the grand master of Roman history was then sacrosanct. It replaced the critical work of Niebuhr with a far more penetrating criticism and a profounder body of inference.

But beyond the circles of specialists, a second feature of the work was still more arresting. In the third volume, as Mommsen reached the final period of the republic, with its rich and varied mass of source material, he wrote with a fire of imagination and emotion almost unknown in a professional history. Here was scientific learning with the stylistic vigor of a novel by Scott or Hugo, giving the lie to countless jokes about the pedantic dullness of German professors. In the same decade Macaulay in England was turning out the similarly lively volumes of his *History of England,* which outsold the novels of Dickens. But Macaulay's work, though like Mommsen's based on an enormous learning and written in an equally brilliant style, has not stood the hard judgment of time, and is no longer widely read. Mommsen's *History of Rome* can never be superseded in this sense. His philosophical sweep, his depth of penetration, his solidity of judgment will continue to make his work a permanent classic regardless of the rise of new interpretations, new schools of thought, new historical discoveries.

This quality of permanence in Mommsen's work is one that he shares with no more than one or two historians of modern times. By its very nature a history becomes outdated. The patient labor of thousands of scholars continually re-examines old points of view and finds new or neglected evidence. Every age must rewrite the history of its past, as new political, social, and economic theories constantly evolve. No historical work can stand forever as the "definitive" treatment of its field. But there are a few —a very few—infused with a vision that later students will ever find fruitful and stimulating, however they may disagree with details and with points of view. Such a work is Gibbon's *Decline and Fall,* and no other history of the past two hundred years except Mommsen's is solidly in this class. One possible contender might be Macaulay's *History of England,* and another is surely Michelet's *History of France.* But no other product of the classic age of great historians, the nineteenth century, is even in the running. Carlyle's *History of the French Revolution* will long be read as literature, but it cannot seriously be called a history.

Those who read this book will discover Mommsen's style for themselves, but a few words are in order about his viewpoint and personal participation in his history. Mommsen's attitude is not that of the cold judge "above the battle." His emotions are powerfully engaged; indeed, it is precisely this engagement that makes his history so vivid and exciting. In the last convulsive struggle of the late Roman republic, out of which the republic perished and the empire arose, Mommsen sees the figure of Julius Caesar as the heroic agent of destiny. The republic, having become degenerate and oppressive for the vast mass of the Mediterranean peoples, could not be reformed and did not deserve to be saved. Hence, its destroyer, Caesar, the instrument of historical necessity, is for Mommsen "the entire and perfect man"—though this does not for a moment prevent Mommsen from recognizing and chronicling Caesar the rake, Caesar the conspirator, and Caesar the groundbreaker for later centuries of absolutism. Caesar's opponents—in particular his three most famous opponents, Pompey, Cicero, and Cato— seem to Mommsen foolish, petty-minded, and sterile. His contempt of Cicero in particular refuses to let him recognize even Cicero's literary genius.

But despite these strong personal feelings, Mommsen is never deliberately guilty of suppressing evidence. His scholarly conscience is ever stronger than his loves and hates, and thus there is no genuine misleading of the reader. Mommsen's opinions and judgments are there for all to see; but being sharply differentiated from the facts he presents, they do not undermine the reader's ability to make independent judgments.

In only one important aspect of the last century of the republic, at least in the opinion of most twentieth century scholars, did Mommsen fall into serious error. This is in his description of the Roman "party" system. Mommsen frequently speaks of "the democratic party" and "the oligarchic party" as if there existed in Rome of 100-50 B.C. organized political movements with clearly recognized programs and organizations. In Mommsen's account the "democratic movement" began with the brothers Gracchi, became more and more ideologically organized, and finally found a leader in Caesar. After striving with little success to promote the "democratic program" by political agitation, Caesar finally turned toward military force. Securing the major command in Gaul in 58 B.C., he singlemindedly pursued the objective of "democratic reform," now with military backing.

The historical research of the past 50 years has greatly weakened this picture of a "two-party system" vaguely resembling the "right" and "left" of modern European politics. There was no such clear political division in the late Roman republic. A hard core of senatorial families, legitimately called "the aristocrats" or the "oligarchy," practically monopolized by family position, wealth, and marriage alliances the chief offices of the state. These men may be said to have formed a "party" in the sense that they had at least a common outlook—stubborn conservatism. They contended among themselves for personal position and "honors," forming cliques and intrigues in what amounted to a private game. Their one unifying principle was "no innovations, no change." Their greed and misrule often aroused sporadic and sometimes massive and desperate opposition. But the opposition was never organized into a party with the unity and purposiveness implied by Mommsen's terms "the democracy" and "the democratic leaders." From time to time more or less able demagogues made use of popular discontent to promote their private ambitions; and of these demagogues Caesar was, of course, the ablest and greatest. But there was no clear political tradition running from the Gracchi through Marius to Caesar, as there is a political tradition running from Thomas Jefferson through Andrew Jackson to Franklin Roosevelt.

The Roman opposition to the senatorial oligarchy, or "optimates," came from dissatisfied and ambitious men of senatorial rank and families, whose tactics were not based on a "democratic" or even a "popular" ideology. Contemporary sources speak of certain politicians as *populares,* and in the older histories—as in Mommsen—this term is interpreted as meaning "popular leaders." A closer analysis of this expression in context shows that these men were merely aristocrats pursuing personal ends, and the only thing "popular" about them was the *method* which they used to promote themselves. They sought by agitation among the lower classes to bring pressure on the Senate, but not with the aim of a general programatic reform.

The later years

With the publication of the third volume of the *History of Rome* in 1856, Mommsen's fame became international. He moved from Zurich to Breslau in 1854, and in 1858 settled in Berlin as a member of the Prussian Academy of Science, carrying with him in his mind the plan for the editing and publication of the *Corpus Inscriptionum Latinarum,* which was to be supported by the Academy. The first volume appeared in 1863. Meanwhile Mommsen had joined the faculty of the University of Berlin. Until the close of his long life in 1903 he made Berlin his home, turning out an astounding series of books and special monographs, and growing into the legendary learned professor whom Mark Twain met in the last decade of the century.

Yet his life was hardly that of the buried recluse. His house in Charlottenburg must have been at least lively, since there were sixteen Mommsen children. A story still firmly believed in Germany today is that he met an urchin on one of his walks and, after a short conversation, inquired, "And what is your name?" "Helmut Mommsen," came the reply.

The three volumes of the *History of Rome* covered the period to the end of the great civil war and the establishment of the "new monarchy" of Caesar. The original plan had envisaged an additional volume on the history of the emperors, perhaps down to Justinian and certainly as far as Diocletian. But it was never written. Instead, in 1886 a *fifth* volume appeared, entitled *The Provinces of the Roman Empire,* leaving the definite public impression that the missing fourth volume would yet be published. A much discussed "mystery" of Mommsen's career is why it never was, and no very convincing explanation has ever been given. The curious reader may find various suggestions in Professor Gilbert Highet's recent book *The Classical Tra-*

dition, and in the first volume of Mr. Toynbee's famous *Study of History.*

After the Franco-Prussian War of 1870 and the unification of Germany under Bismarck, Mommsen's voice was often raised on contemporary political questions, about which he grew increasingly liberal as he grew older. In 1881 he was elected to the Reichstag, where he joined the so-called "Radical Party" in sharp conflict with Bismarck. (He denounced Bismarck's policy of a protective tariff as a "swindle.") In a personal altercation in the Reichstag Bismarck declared, "I can only assume that the profound studies this learned man has made in the time that lies two thousand years behind us have entirely blinded his eyes to the sunlight of the present day." Later Bismarck even brought Mommsen to trial for libeling the government, but the historian was triumphantly acquitted.

In educational matters, where he spoke with great authority, his influence was consistently on the side of freedom, humanity, and scholarly integrity. He denounced antisemitism with savage vigor. At 84, at the very end of his life, he wrote a fiery essay on university instruction and religion in which he declared that the lifeblood of a university was the untrammeled search for truth, *"die voraussetzungslose Forschung."* The selection of university teachers on religious grounds, he felt, was an axe laid at the root of the tree—the tree of integrity on which depend "our self-respect, our social honor, and our influence upon youth."

In the 1880's and 1890's the honor and deference paid to him were perhaps unique in the world; but there are many signs that he was troubled with the emerging Germany, and that he foresaw in some dim sense the tragedy of the following century. When in 1902 he received the Nobel Prize and the wave of applause began, he held his hand up for silence and, gazing at his audience with his piercing eyes, remarked, "No applause, my friends—the times are too grave."

According to his will his private papers, which would have enabled a satisfactory biography to be written, were impounded for thirty years. Then, when the ban on publication was lifted in 1933, the environment of Hitler's Germany was such that no attempt was then made to use the documents, and the bulk of them were destroyed in the Berlin bombings of 1944. They had, however, been examined and partly copied by Professor Lothar Wickert, who is now preparing a full-length biography.

One suggestive and interesting document, first published in 1948, was the note accompanying his will that provided for the disposition of his papers, and enjoined his family to "prevent as far as possible the publication of a biography." After thirty years, if anyone were still interested, a biography might be written. But the most moving sentences of the document were these:

"In spite of the outward signs of success, I have not achieved in my life what I ought. Accidental circumstances have placed my name among historians and philologists, although my education and probably also my talents were not sufficient for these studies; and a painful realization of inadequacy in what I have done, that I have seemed more than I was, has been my constant companion through life, and ought neither to be concealed nor displayed in a biography. I have never had and never wished political position and influence; but in my inmost being, that is, with the best that was in me, I have always been 'a political animal,' and have wished to be a good citizen. That is not possible in our nation."

The plan of this work

To tell how this volume was constructed is also to tell why it was attempted. As editors and classical enthusiasts, we felt that the single overwhelming work on the

Roman republic deserved the attention and respect that it had received in Mark Twain's time, rather than the blank looks with which at least 99 out of every 100 American college graduates today would greet the very name of Theodor Mommsen. His work was obviously passing into limbo when the last available English edition, the four-volume Everyman Library set, went out of print in the mid-1950's. Even the recent reprinting in the United States did not seem to us sufficient to overcome the obstacles which have hindered Mommsen's work from receiving at least the same kind of popular appreciation as Gibbon's *Decline and Fall.*

The first of those obstacles is now history, but worth noting for that very reason. For all of Mommsen's enormous vogue in Germany and on the continent, we do not doubt that he was less popular among literate Englishmen merely because England already had (in Gibbon) a certified Grade A genius among classical historians—and this despite the overwhelming likelihood that at this very moment Gibbon and Mommsen are delightedly comparing footnotes in a quiet corner of the Elysian Fields. This instinctive British attitude toward the redoubtable German was not mollified by Mommsen's sharp criticism of England during the Boer War, although he was far more temperate than many a leading Englishman.

We freely admit that the preceding paragraph is speculative, but some of the other obstacles to an appreciation of Mommsen are unquestionably real. Any work of 2,000-odd pages tends at most to be admired and respected today rather than read. Much of the early part of the *History of Rome* is rendered dubious by the inadequacy of the historical materials—although, despite new archeological data subsequently unearthed, only the boldest authorities dare to disagree with Mommsen's general approach to the city's early history. Nevertheless, since all Roman history prior to 250 B.C. is a debating ground for scholars, we felt that we could safely eliminate almost the

first third of the *History of Rome* from a one-volume
work intended for nonspecialists.

Further, goaded by the necessity for maximum com-
pression, we decided regretfully to eliminate the very important, exciting, and well-documented 100 years from
250 to 150 B.C., a period which saw Rome's victory over
Carthage in the Punic wars and the establishment of Roman supremacy over much of the Hellenic world. This we
have done partly because we had to, but also because we
felt that the period from 150 to 45 B.C., from Tiberius
Gracchus to Julius Caesar, witnessed the final overwhelming tragedy of the republic and was therefore the period
of keenest interest to the modern reader. If anyone doubts
the pertinence of this period to our own time, we urge
that he reflect upon the unnerving similarities between the
political strategy and tactics of Gaius Gracchus and those
of Franklin Roosevelt.

We concluded very early in the work that still further
eliminations could be made, notably Mommsen's occasional chapters dealing with art, religion, and culture,
which do not always sustain the excellence of the political
and military history. We also found it both desirable and
possible to eliminate several chapters dealing largely or
wholly with military campaigns in Gaul and in the East,
substituting for them brief italicized "bridge" passages
to tell in capsule form what happened and what effect it
had upon the political deterioration of Rome itself, which
is the central subject. And finally, even within the chapters which are included we have found it possible to de-
lete occasional sections which seem to us superfluous elaboration of an adequately clear general statement. Each
omission in this last-named category is marked by a footnote; the other footnotes comprise mainly brief definitions of Roman words and phrases which may be unfamiliar to the general reader, and which are more fully
defined in the Glossary. The only omissions not marked by
footnotes (and we warn any literary detectives among our

readers that they are extremely rare throughout this volume) are sentences or phrases deleted because they contain classical or nineteenth century references which might be obscure to the modern reader, but where a footnote marking the deleted passage would have required more space than was saved by the omission.

By these multiple surgeries we have reduced by more than half a chunk of Mommsen which runs nearly 1,000 close-packed pages in the *Everyman* edition; and yet we feel that the reorganized remainder has complete unity and cohesiveness. In fact, at one point along the way we seriously considered including a few noteworthy sections from other parts of the *History of Rome,* such as Mommsen's gripping description of Hannibal's march across the Alps. But in its final form the present volume seemed to have such internal coherence that we could not bring ourselves to clutter it with extraneous addenda.

Selecting what to include, however, was a trifling matter compared to the editing job on what remained. The *History of Rome* was, for its day, well translated by Dr. William P. Dickson, a divinity professor at the University of Glasgow. A continental writer once remarked that "translations are like women—they can be either beautiful or faithful"; and Dickson was as fundamentally on the side of morality as might be expected of a Scottish divine. Moreover, Mommsen, who of course knew English among his other languages both ancient and modern, was a hard man with his translators no less than with his publishers. For this reason Dickson was perhaps even more faithful as a translator than he might have wished to be, and at best his colloquialisms are still those of mid-nineteenth century Britain. At times Mommsen in an excess of zeal would insist on an ill-chosen English equivalent, such as the word "burgess" for "citizen," or "client state" for "satellite state" or "protectorate." Mommsen also followed the then prevailing scholarly practice of giving each event two dates, one according to the Christian

era and one according to the legendary founding of the
city of Rome in 753 B.C. Thus the battle of Zama in 202
B.C. would be dated "552/202."

Whether through Mommsen's pressure or his own
scholarly preferences, Dickson followed Mommsen's par-
agraphing exactly; and Mommsen's paragraphs are often
a hundred lines long. Dickson also on occasion (though
not invariably) followed the Germanic sentence structure,
which a wag once described as "the sentence diving into
the river and coming up on the other bank with the verb
in its mouth"; and the fact that he did so only spasmodi-
cally gives the Dickson translation a curiously uneven
quality, with easy colloquialisms, old-fashioned Victorian-
isms, and weirdly constructed sentences incongruously in-
tertwined.

The only remedy here, it seemed to us, was complete re-
editing and revision of the translation. Therefore we went
word by word and line by line over every portion that was
to be included; modernized the punctuation; changed from
British to American spelling; cut interminable sentences
into two or more shorter ones; rearranged sentence structure; substituted modern for archaic phrasing; and made
two or more brief paragraphs out of each long one. Any
such drastic reworking always raises the question whether
the final result may be not only unfaithful to the original,
but downright wanton. We have sought to guard against
this by checking some hundreds of pages of our revised
English version against the original German text. At long
last, however, we became convinced that Dickson had at
least been supremely accurate; thereafter we contented
ourselves with editing from the Dickson translation,
checking back to the original German only in the case of
obscurities or where we suspected that Dickson might
have merely grazed the point.

This is not to involve Dickson, let alone Mommsen, for
any mistakes or shortcomings in the present volume. In
large matters or small, in conception or in detail, any

blame is ours alone. But we shall regard the risk as having been well taken if this volume serves to introduce a wider group of English-speaking readers to one of the noblest historians and intellects that ever walked upon the face of the earth.

Dero A. Saunders
John H. Collins
April, 1958

I

THE REFORM MOVEMENT
AND TIBERIUS GRACCHUS

For a whole generation after the battle of Pydna [1] *the* Roman state enjoyed a profound calm, scarcely troubled by a ripple here and there on the surface. Its dominion extended over three continents; the luster of the Roman power and the glory of the Roman name were constantly on the increase; all eyes rested on Italy, all talents and all riches flowed thither. It seemed as if a golden age of peaceful prosperity and intellectual fruitfulness must surely soon begin. The Orientals told each other with astonishment of the mighty republic of the West, "which subdued kingdoms far and near, so that everyone who heard its name trembled; but which kept good faith with its friends and dependents. Such was the glory of the Romans, and yet no one usurped the crown and no one glittered in purple dress; but they obeyed whomsoever from year to year they made their master, and there was among them neither envy nor discord."

So it seemed at a distance; matters looked differently at closer view. The government of the aristocracy was well on the way to destroying its own work. It was not that the sons and grandsons of the vanquished at Cannae and the victors of Zama [2] had utterly degenerated from their fathers and grandfathers; the difference was not so much in the men who sat in the Senate as it was in the times. Where a few old families of established wealth and hereditary political importance conduct the government, they will display in seasons of danger an incomparable tenacity of purpose and heroic self-sacrifice—just as in seasons of tranquility they will be short-sighted, selfish, and negligent: the germs of both traits are inherent in their hereditary character. The aristocratic rottenness had long existed, but the sun of prosperity was needed to

■

1. In 168 B.C., when the Romans crushed the power of Macedonia and consolidated the Roman dominion in the East.
2. Crushing of the Romans by Hannibal at Cannae (216 B.C.) preceded total victory over the Carthaginians at Zama (202 B.C.).

ripen it. There was profound meaning in Cato's [3] question, "What will become of Rome when she no longer has any state to fear?"

That point had now been reached. Every neighbor whom she might have feared was politically annihilated; and of the men who had been reared under the old order of things in the severe school of the Hannibalic wars, and whose words still echoed that mighty epoch so long as they survived, death called one after another away until at length the voice of the last of them, the veteran Cato, ceased to be heard in the Senate and the Forum. A younger generation came to the helm, and their policy was a sorry answer to the question of that veteran patriot.

In internal affairs the Romans were, if possible, still more disposed than in foreign affairs to let the ship drift before the wind: if internal government means more than the mere transaction of current business, there was in this period no government in Rome at all. The single thought of the governing clique was the maintenance and, if possible, the increase of their usurped privileges. The state did not have the right to get the best man for its supreme magistracy; rather, every member of the clique had an inborn title to the highest office of the state—a title not to be threatened by the unfair rivalry of his peers or the encroachments of the excluded. Accordingly the clique set as its most important political aim the restriction of reelection to the consulship and the exclusion of "new men." It succeeded, in fact, in obtaining the legal prohibition of the former about 151 B.C., and thenceforward contented itself with a government of aristocratic nobodies. Even the government's inaction in external affairs was doubtless connected with this policy of the nobility, exclusive toward commoners and suspicious of individual members of their own order. There was no surer means to keep commoners, whose deeds might become their patent of nobil-

---

3. Marcus Porcius Cato, "the Elder" (232-149 B.C.).

ity, out of the pure circles of the hereditary aristocracy than by allowing no one to perform any deeds at all. Even an aristocratic conqueror of Syria or Egypt would have embarrassed so mediocre a government.

It is true that there was no want of opposition, some of it even partly effective. The administration of justice was improved. The administrative jurisdiction which the Senate exercised either personally or by extraordinary commissions over provincial officials was confessedly inadequate; and the innovation proposed in 149 B.C. by Lucius Calpurnius Piso, for a standing commission to try the complaints of the provincials against the extortions of their Roman magistrates, had a momentous bearing on the whole public life of the Roman community. An effort was made to free the *comitia* [4] from the domination of the aristocracy. The panacea of Roman democracy was vote by ballot in the assemblies of citizens, introduced first for the election of magistrates by the Gabinian Law (139 B.C.), then for the public tribunals by the Cassian Law (137 B.C.), and lastly for voting on legislative proposals by the Papirian Law (131 B.C.). Soon afterwards the senators were also required by decree of the people to give up their command of mounted soldiers on admission to the Senate, and thereby to renounce their privilege of voting in the equestrian order.[5] These measures, directed to the emancipation of the electorate from the ruling aristocracy, may perhaps have seemed to the party which suggested them the first steps toward regenerating the state. In reality, they made not the slightest change in the impotence of the legally supreme organ of the Roman community, the citizenry. That impotence, indeed, was only the more obvious to all, whether it concerned them or not. Equally ostentatious and equally empty was the formal recognition of the independence and sovereignty

■

4. The electoral and legislative assemblies of the people. See Glossary.
5. The middle class of capital and business. See Glossary.

of the citizens by transferring their place of assembly from the old Comitium below the Capitol to the Forum (c. 145 B.C.).

But this hostility between the formal sovereignty of the people and the actually existing constitution was largely a sham. Party phrases were in free circulation, but of parties themselves there was little trace in important practical affairs. Throughout the republic's last century the annual public election, especially to the consulship and censorship,[6] was the real focus of political activity; but only in rare and isolated instances did the opposing candidates represent different political principles. Ordinarily the contests were purely between personalities, and it was a matter of practical indifference whether the majority of votes fell to a Caecilian or a Cornelian. The Romans thus lacked the great compensation for the evils of party politics—the spontaneous choice by the masses of the goals which they preferred—and yet endured all those evils solely for the benefit of the paltry game played by the ruling clique.

It was comparatively easy for the Roman noble to begin a political career as *tribune of the people* or as *quaestor,*[7] but the consulship or the censorship was attainable only by great exertions prolonged over the years. The prizes were many, but those really worth having were few: the competitors ran, as a Roman poet once said, over a racecourse wide at the starting point but gradually narrowing toward the end. This was right so long as political office was (as it was called) an "honor," and so long as men of military, political, or juristic ability competed for the ultimate prizes. But now the exclusiveness of the nobility did away with the benefits of

6. The two *consuls,* elected annually, were the executive heads of the state, while the primary function of the two *censors* was choosing new senators and removing unworthy ones from the rolls. See Glossary.
7. The *tribunes of the people* were the guardians of popular freedom; the *quaestors* were auxiliary officials acting for the two consuls. See Glossary.

competition, and left only its disadvantages. With few exceptions the young men of the ruling families crowded into the political arena, and their impetuous and premature ambition soon sought channels more effective than mere public service. The first prerequisite for a career came to be powerful connections. Therefore that career began not, as it once had, in the camp, but in the waiting-rooms of influential men. A new and genteel body of hangers-on began to do what had formerly been done only by dependents and freedmen, to come and wait on their patron early in the morning and appear publicly in his train.

But the populace was also a great lord, and desired its share of attention. The rabble began to demand as its right that the future consul should recognize and honor the sovereign people in every ragged idler of the street, and that every candidate should in his "going round" (*ambitus*) salute every individual voter by name and press his hand. The world of quality readily entered into this degrading canvass. The candidate cringed not only in the palace but also on the street, and recommended himself to the multitude by flattering attentions, indulgences, and civilities. A demagogic cry for reform was sedulously employed to attract public notice and favor, and was the more effective the more it attacked personalities. It became the custom for beardless youths of genteel birth to introduce themselves noisily into public life by replaying with boyish eloquence the part of Cato, proclaiming themselves state prosecutors against some man of high standing and great unpopularity. Thus the Romans permitted the courts and the police to become a means of soliciting office. The provision (or still worse, the promise) of magnificent popular amusements had long been the accepted route to the consulship, but now the votes of the electors began to be directly bought, as is shown by the prohibition issued about 159 B.C.

Perhaps the worst consequence of this continual courting of popular favor by the ruling aristocracy was the incompatibility of such begging and fawning with the position which government should rightfully occupy in relation to the governed. The government was thus converted from a blessing to a curse for the people. It no longer ventured to dispose of the blood and treasure of the citizens, as exigency required, for the good of their country. It allowed the people to become habituated to the dangerous idea that they were legally exempt from direct taxes even as an advance: after the war with King Perseus of Macedonia ending in 168 B.C. no further advance was asked of the community. It allowed the military system to decay rather than compel the citizens to enter the hated overseas service; and hard was the fate of officials who attempted strict enforcement of the conscription laws.

In the Rome of this epoch, the twin evils of a degenerate aristocracy and an infant democracy already cankered in the bud were joined in a fatal marriage. According to their party names, which were first heard during this period, the "Optimates" wished to give effect to the will of the best, the "Populares" to that of the community; but in fact there was in Rome of that day neither a true aristocracy nor a truly self-governing community. Both parties contended alike for shadows, and numbered in their ranks none but zealots or hypocrites. Both were equally tainted by political corruption, both were equally worthless. Both were necessarily tied to the *status quo,* for neither had a single political idea (not to mention a political plan) reaching beyond the existing state of affairs. Accordingly, the two parties were in such entire agreement that their ends and means dovetailed at every step, and a change of party was a change of political tactics rather than of political sentiments. The commonwealth would doubtless have gained if the aristocracy had introduced a hereditary rotation, or if the democracy had produced from within itself a genuine popular government. But these "Optimates" and "Populares" of the Republic's last century were far too indispensable to each other to wage internecine war; they not only could not destroy each other, but would not have done so if they could. Meanwhile the commonwealth, politically and morally more and more unhinged, was verging toward utter disorganization.

The crisis that sparked the Roman revolution arose not out of this petty political conflict, but out of the economic and social relations which the Roman government allowed, like everything else, simply to take their course. Thus the social infection, which had long been developing, was allowed to come to a head with fearful rapidity and violence. From a very early period the Roman economy was based on two factors, always interdependent and always at odds—the husbandry of the small farmer and the money of the capitalist. The latter, hand in glove with the great landholders, had for centuries waged a war against the small farmer, a war which seemed destined to end by destroying first the farmer class and then the commonwealth. But the struggle was broken off indecisively by the extensive distribution of new lands accruing to the state from successful wars.

In that same age, which renewed the distinction between patricians and plebeians under altered names, the disproportionate accumulation of capital was preparing a second assault on the farming system. It is true that the method was different. Formerly the small farmer had been ruined by loans of money, which practically reduced him to a mere steward of his creditor; now he was crushed by the competition of overseas, especially slave-grown, grain. The capitalists kept pace with the times. While waging war against labor and against personal liberty, as they had always done to the extent permitted by law, they waged it no longer in the unseemly fashion that converted the free man into a slave through his debts, but on the contrary with slaves regularly bought and paid for; the former usurer of capital appeared in contemporary guise as the owner of commercial plantations. But in both cases the ultimate result was the same: the undermining of the Italian farms; the supplanting of small farming first in part of the provinces and then in Italy by the farming of large estates; the concentration of these large Italian farms upon cattle, oil, and wine; and finally, the replacing of free laborers both in the provinces and in Italy by slaves. Just as the new nobility was more dangerous than the old patricians, because the former could not be set aside by changing the constitution, so the new power of capital was less controllable than that of previous centuries because nothing could be done to oppose it by changing the law of the land.

Before we attempt to describe this second great conflict between labor and captial, it is necessary to give some account of the nature and extent of the slave system. We do not now refer to the old, and in some measure innocent, rural slavery, under which the farmer tilled the field along with his slave, or, if he possessed more land than he could manage, placed the slave either as a steward or as a sort of share-tenant over a detached farm. Such relationships no doubt persisted (around Comum, for instance, they were still the rule in the time of the Empire), but only as exceptions in privileged districts and on humanely managed estates. What we now refer to is the system of slavery on a grand scale, which in the Roman state as formerly in the Carthaginian grew out of the ascendancy of capital. While the captives taken in war and the hereditary transmission of slavery sufficed to keep up the stock of slaves during the earlier period, this new system of slavery was, like that of America, based on the methodically prosecuted hunting of man. For owing to the manner in which slaves were used, with little regard to their life or propagation, the slave population was constantly on the wane, and even the wars that continually furnished fresh masses to the slave markets could not cover the deficit.

No country where this species of game could be hunted

remained unmolested; even in Italy it was by no means unheard of for the poor free man to be placed by his employer among the slaves. But the Negro-land of that age was western Asia, where the Cretan and Cilician corsairs, the real professional slave hunters and slave dealers, robbed the coasts of Syria and the Greek islands, and where the Roman taxgatherers emulated their feats by instituting manhunts in the satellite states and enslaving those whom they captured. This was done to such an extent that about 100 B.C. the king of Bithynia declared himself unable to furnish the required contingent of auxiliaries to the Roman army, because all his people capable of labor had been dragged off by the taxgatherers. At the great market in Delos, where the slave dealers of Asia Minor sold their wares to Italian speculators, as many as 10,000 slaves are said to have been disembarked in one morning and to have been sold before evening—a proof of how enormous was the number of slaves, and of how the demand still exceeded the supply.

It was no wonder. The Roman economy of the second century B.C. was based, like all the large-scale economies of antiquity, on the employment of slaves. In whatever direction speculation applied itself, its instrument was invariably man reduced by law to the status of a beast of burden. Trade was in great part carried on by slaves, the proceeds belonging to the master. Tax-gathering in the lower departments was regularly conducted by the slaves of the associations that leased them. Servile hands performed the operations of mining, of making pitch, and others of a similar kind. It early became the custom to send herds of slaves to the Spanish mines, whose superintendents readily paid a high rent for them. The vine and olive harvest of Italy was not conducted by the people on the estate, but was contracted for by a slave operator. The armed, and frequently mounted, slave herdsmen who roamed the great pastoral districts of Italy were soon transplanted to those provinces which were favored by

Roman speculation—Dalmatia, for example, had hardly
been acquired (155 B.C.) before Roman capitalists introduced there the rearing of cattle on a great scale after the
Italian fashion.

Far worse in every respect was the plantation system
proper, the cultivation of the fields by a band of slaves
sometimes branded with iron, who with shackles on their
legs labored in the fields under overseers during the day,
and were locked up together at night in their common
and often underground prison. This plantation system
had migrated from the East to Carthage, and seems to
have been brought by the Carthaginians to Sicily, where it
appears to have developed earlier and more fully than in
any other part of the Roman dominions. The Sicilian territory of Leontini, for example, where about 30,000 acres
of arable land were let out by the censors as Roman domain, was divided some decades after the time of the
Gracchi among not more than 84 lessees, making an average of 360 acres per lessee; and among these only one was
a Leontine, the rest being foreign, mostly Roman, speculators. We see from this instance with what zeal the Roman capitalists walked in the footsteps of their predecessors, and what extensive dealings in Sicilian cattle and
Sicilian slave-grown grain must have been carried on by
the Roman and non-Roman operators who covered that
beautiful island with their pastures and plantations.

Italy, however, still remained substantially exempt
from this worst form of slave-husbandry—although in
Etruria, where the plantation system seems first to have
emerged on the mainland, and where at any rate it was
most extensive forty years afterwards, it is quite probable
that plantations already existed. Yet Italian agriculture in
this age was still carried on chiefly by free laborers or at
least by unchained slaves, while larger undertakings were
frequently let out to contractors. The difference between
Italian and Sicilian slavery is clearly apparent from the

fact that the slaves of the Mamertine community, which lived after the Italian fashion, were the only slaves who did not take part in the Sicilian servile revolt of 135-132 B.C.

The abyss of misery and woe which engulfed this most miserable of all proletariats we leave to be fathomed by those who can bear to gaze into such depths. It is quite possible that, compared with the sufferings of the Roman slaves, the sum of all Negro suffering is but a drop. Here, however, we are less concerned with the hardships of the slaves themselves than with the perils which they brought upon the Roman state, and with the government's policy in confronting them. It was plain that this proletariat was not created by the government and could not be directly set aside by it, for this would have entailed remedies still worse than the disease. The duty of the government was simply (1) to avert by a vigilant police the direct threat of the slave population to property and life, and (2) to aim at restricting the spread of slavery as far as possible by the support of free labor. Let us see how the Roman aristocracy executed these two tasks.

The slave conspiracies and wars breaking out everywhere illustrate their management as regards police. In Italy the scenes of disorder which had been among the painful accompaniments of the Hannibalic war were now renewed; in one year (133 B.C.) the Romans were obliged to seize and execute 150 slaves in the capital, 450 in Minturnae, and 4,000 in Sinuessa. Still worse, as might be expected, was the state of the provinces. At about the same period the revolting slaves at the great market at Delos and in the Attic silver mines had to be put down by force of arms. The war against Aristonicus and his "Heliopolites" in Asia Minor was in substance a war of landowners against the revolted slaves.

But worst of all, of course, was the condition of Sicily, the chosen land of the plantation system. Brigandage, long a standing evil there, especially in the interior, began to swell into insurrection. Damophilus, a wealthy planter of Enna who emulated the Italian lords in the exploitation of his living capital, was attacked and murdered by his exasperated rural slaves; then the savage band flocked into the town of Enna and repeated the process on a greater scale. The slaves rose in a body against their masters, killed or enslaved them, and summoned to the head of their now considerable insurgent army a juggler from Apamea in Syria who knew how to vomit fire and utter oracles. Formerly named Eunus when he was a slave, as king of the insurgents he was styled Antiochus, King of the Syrians. And why not? A few years earlier another Syrian slave, who was not even a prophet, had in Antioch itself worn the diadem of the Seleucids of Syria. The Greek slave Achaeus, the brave commander of the new "king," traveled throughout the island; and not only did the wild herdsmen flock from far and near to the strange banner, but also the free laborers, who bore no goodwill to the planters, made common cause with the revolted slaves.

In another district of Sicily Cleon, a Cilician slave who had in his native land been a daring bandit, followed the example of Eunus by occupying Agrigentum. Then the leaders came to a mutual understanding, and, after gaining various minor advantages, at length succeeded in totally defeating the praetor Lucius Hypsaeus and his army (mostly Sicilian militia) and in capturing his camp. By this victory almost the whole island fell into the hands of the insurgents, whose numbers, by the most conservative estimates, are put at 70,000 men capable of bearing arms. The Romans found themselves compelled for three successive years (134-132 B.C.) to send consuls and consular armies to Sicily, until, after several indecisive and even unfavorable conflicts, the revolt was finally subdued by the capture of Tauromenium and Enna. The most resolute insurgents threw themselves into the latter town with the determination of men who despair of deliverance or pardon. The consuls Lucius Calpurnius Piso and Publius Rupilius lay before it for two years, and finally reduced it more by famine than by arms.

Such was the quality of the policing by the Roman Senate and its officials in Italy and in the provinces. While the task of getting rid of such a proletariat all too often transcends the power and wisdom of a government, its police repression is comparatively easy for any large commonwealth. It would be well with states if the unpropertied masses threatened them with no greater danger than from bears and wolves; only the timid, and those who trade upon the silly fears of the multitude, prophesy the destruction of civil order through slave revolts or proletarian insurrections. But even this easier task of restraining the oppressed masses was beyond the capacities of the Roman government, despite the general peace and the inexhaustible resources of the state.

This was a sign of its weakness, but not of its weakness alone. By law the Roman governor was bound to keep the roads clear and to have the robbers who were caught crucified, if they were slaves, for slavery is not possible without a reign of terror. In this period in Sicily a roundup was doubtless initiated by the governor, when the roads became too insecure. But in order not to disoblige the Italian planters, the captured robbers were ordinarily handed over by the authorities to be punished at their masters' discretion; and those masters were frugal people who, if their slave herdsmen asked for clothes, replied with lashes and with the inquiry whether travelers journeyed through the land naked. The result of such connivance was that on the subjugation of the Sicilian slave revolt the consul Publius Rupilius ordered all those who came into his hands alive—upwards of 20,000 men, it is said—to be crucified. It was no longer possible to spare capital.

The efforts of the government in supporting free labor, and thereby restricting the slave proletariat, promised fruits far more difficult to harvest but also far richer. Unfortunately, in this respect nothing was done at all. In the earlier social crisis the landlords had been required by law to employ free laborers proportionate to the number of their slaves. Now, at the government's suggestion, a Punic treatise on agriculture, giving instructions in the Carthaginian system of planting, was translated into Latin for use by Roman speculators—the first and only instance of a literary undertaking initiated by the Roman Senate!

The same tendency showed itself in a more vital question—indeed, *the* vital question for Rome—the system of colonization. It needed no special wisdom, beyond a mere recollection of the course of Rome's first social crisis, to perceive that the only real remedy for an agricultural proletariat lay in a comprehensive and regular system of emigration; and for this the external relations of Rome offered the most favorable opportunity. Until nearly the middle of the second century B.C., the continuous diminution of the small landholders of Italy was offset by the continuous establishment of new farm allotments. True, this was not done to the extent that it might and should have been done. Not only was the public land long occupied by private persons not recalled, but further occupation of newly won land was permitted. Other important acquisitions, such as the territory of Capua, though not abandoned to occupation, were leased to commercial operators rather than distributed to individual farmers. Nevertheless, allotments of land had given help to many sufferers and hope to all. But after the founding of Luna (177 B.C.) there is no trace of further distribution for a long time, with the isolated exception of the Picenian colony of Auximum in 157 B.C.

The reason is simple. After the conquest of the Boii and the Apuani no new territory was acquired in Italy except the unattractive Ligurian valleys. Therefore no land existed for distribution save the leased or occupied public land, the appropriation of which was, as might be expected, just as disagreeable to the aristocracy as it had been three hundred years before. The distribution of territory outside Italy appeared inadmissible for political reasons: Italy was to remain the ruling country, and the wall between the Italian masters and their provincial servants was not to be broken down. Unless the government was willing to set aside considerations of higher policy and even the interests of the ruling order, no other course was left for it but to remain a spectator of the ruin of the small Italian farmer; and precisely that result ensued.

The capitalists continued to buy out the small landholders, or, if they remained obstinate, to seize their fields outright—in which case, as might be supposed, matters were not always amicably settled. A particularly favored method was to evict the farmer's wife and children while he was absent on military service, and thus to make him comply with a *fait accompli*. The landlords continued largely to employ slaves rather than free men, because the former could not like the latter be called into the army. Thus they reduced the free laborer to the slave's level of misery. They continued to supersede Italian grain in the capital, and to lessen its value over the whole peninsula, by selling Sicilian slave-grown grain at a nominal price. In Etruria the old native aristocracy, in league with the Roman capitalists, as early as 134 B.C. had brought matters to such a pass that there were no free farmers left. It could be said aloud at Rome that the wild beasts of Italy had their lairs, but nothing was left to the citizens save the air and the sunshine, and that those who were called the masters of the world had no longer a clod to call their own.

The census lists of Roman citizens gave point to these words. From the end of the Hannibalic war (202 B.C.) down to 159 B.C. the number of citizens was steadily on the rise, mainly because of the continuous and extensive distributions of public land which occurred chiefly in the first twenty-five years of this period. After 159 B.C., when the census enumerated 328,000 citizens capable of bearing arms, there appears a regular decline to 324,000 in 154, 322,000 in 147, and 319,000 in 131—an alarming trend in a time of widespread peace at home and abroad. If matters went on at this rate, the whole population would end up either as planters or slaves, and the Roman state might ultimately, like the Parthian, buy its soldiers in the slave market.

Such was the condition of Rome when the state entered upon its seventh century of existence. Wherever the eye turned it encountered abuses and decay, and every wise and well-intentioned man could not but ask himself whether this state of things was not capable of remedy or amelioration. There was no lack of such men in Rome, but none seemed more called to the great work of political and social reform than Publius Cornelius Scipio Aemilianus Africanus (184-129 B.C.), the favorite son of Aemilius Paullus and the adopted grandson of the great Scipio, whose glorious surname of Africanus he bore not through mere hereditary right but by personal achievement. Like his father, he was a temperate man, thoroughly healthy in body, and never at a loss to choose the immediate and necessary course of action. As a youth he had kept aloof from the usual antics of political novices, such as attending in the anterooms of prominent senators and delivering forensic declarations. At the same time he loved the chase: after serving with distinction as a youth of seventeen under his father in the campaign against Perseus, he had asked as his reward the free run of the deer forests of the Macedonian kings which had been untouched for four years. He was also especially devoted to literary and scientific enjoyment. Through his father's care he had been early introduced to the genuine Greek culture, which elevated him above the tasteless Hellenizing then in vogue. By his appreciation of the good and bad in Greek character, and by his aristocratic bearing, this Roman impressed the courts of the East and even the scoffing Alexandrians.

His Hellenism was especially recognizable in the delicate irony of his discourse and the classic purity of his Latin. Though not strictly an author, like Cato he committed his political speeches to writing (like the letters of his adopted sister and the mother of the Gracchi, they were esteemed by later students as prose masterpieces); and he took pleasure in surrounding himself with the cream of the Greek and Roman intelligentsia, a plebeian crowd doubtless regarded with no small suspicion by his senatorial colleagues whose noble birth was their sole distinction. A man morally steadfast and trustworthy, his word held good with friend and foe. He avoided ostentatious building and speculation, and lived simply. In money matters he acted not only honorably and disinterestedly, but also with a humaneness and generosity that seemed the more singular alongside the mercenary spirit of his contemporaries. He was an able soldier and officer. He brought home from the African war the honorary wreath conferred on those who saved the lives of fellow-citizens at peril of their own, and he terminated as a general the war he had begun as an officer, though circumstances gave him no opportunity to try his military skill on really difficult tasks.

Scipio was not, any more than his father, a man of brilliant gifts (as indicated by his predilection for Xenophon, the sober soldier and correct author). But he was a man honest and true, who seemed pre-eminently suited to stem the incipient decay. All the more significant is the fact that he did not attempt it. It is true that he helped, when he had opportunity and means, to redress or prevent certain abuses, and he labored particularly at improving the administration of justice. It was chiefly through his aid that Lucius Cassius, an able man of old

Roman austerity and uprightness, was able to carry
against the vehement opposition of the Optimates his voting law, which introduced vote by ballot for those popular tribunals which comprised the most important part of
the criminal jurisdiction. In like manner, though he had
chosen not to take part in boyish impeachments, in his ma-
ture years he brought to trial several of the guiltiest of
the aristocracy. In the same spirit, when commanding before Carthage and Numantia, he drove the women and
priests out of the camp, and once more subjected the soldiers to the iron yoke of the old military discipline. As
censor (142 B.C.) he cleared away the smooth-chinned
coxcombs from the world of quality, and urged the citizens in earnest language to adhere more faithfully to the
honest customs of their fathers.

But no one—least of all Scipio—could fail to see that
increased stringency in the administration of justice was
not even a first step toward healing the organic ills that
burdened the state. These Scipio did not touch. His elder
friend, political mentor, and confidant Gaius Laelius (consul in 140 B.C.) had conceived the plan of resuming the
distribution of the Italian public lands which had not been
given away but had been temporarily occupied, and thus
relieving the visibly decaying Italian farmers; but he de-
sisted when he saw what a storm he was going to raise,
and was thenceforth named "the Judicious." Scipio was of
the same opinion. He was fully convinced of the greatness
of the evil, and with honorable courage he remorselessly
assailed it when he risked himself alone. But he was also
persuaded that the nation could be relieved only at the
price of a revolution similar to that which had accompanied the reforms of the third and fourth centuries B.C.,
and rightly or wrongly, the remedy seemed to him worse
than the disease. Thus with a small circle of friends he
held a middle position between the aristocrats (who never
forgave him for his advocacy of the Cassian law) and the
democrats (whom he neither satisfied nor wished to sat-

isfy), solitary during his life, and praised after his death by both parties as the champion of the aristocracy and as the promoter of reform. Down to his time, the censors on giving up their office had prayed the gods to grant greater power and glory to the state. The censor Scipio prayed that they might deign to preserve the state, and his whole confession of faith lies in that painful exclamation.

But where the man who had twice led the Roman army from deep decline to victory despaired, a youth without achievements had the boldness to step forth as the savior of Italy. His name was Tiberius Sempronius Gracchus (163-133 B.C.). His father of the same name (consul 177 and 163, censor 169 B.C.) was the model of a Roman aristocrat. The magnificence of his games (as aedile, 182 B.C.), not produced without oppressing the dependent communities, had drawn upon him the severe and deserved censure of the Senate. His intervention in the pitiful processes against the Scipios, who were personally hostile to him, gave proof of his chivalrous feeling, and perhaps of his regard for his own order; and his energetic action against the freedmen in his censorship evinced his conservative disposition. As governor of the province of the Ebro in Spain, he rendered a permanent service to his country by his bravery and integrity, and at the same time he raised to himself in the hearts of the subject nation an enduring monument of affection.

His wife Cornelia was the daughter of the great Scipio, the conqueror of Zama, who, simply on account of Gracchus' generous intervention, had chosen his former opponent as a son-in-law. Cornelia herself was a highly cultivated and notable woman, who after the death of her much older husband refused the hand of the king of Egypt, and reared her three surviving children in memory of her husband and her father.

Tiberius, the elder of the two sons, was of good moral disposition and gentle bearing, apparently fitted for anything rather than for an agitator of the masses. He belonged to the Scipionic circle, whose refined and thorough culture, both Greek and Roman, he and his brother and sister shared. Scipio Aemilianus was at once his cousin and his sister's husband; under him Tiberius, at the age of eighteen, had taken part in the storming of Carthage, and had by his valor acquired the commendation of the stern general. It was natural that the able young man should, with all the vigor and stringent precision of youth, adopt and intensify the views prevalent in his circle as to the pervading decay of the state, and more especially their ideas for relieving the Italian farmers.

It was not merely to the young men that Laelius' hesitancy to carry out his ideas of reform seemed rather weak than judicious. Appius Claudius, who had already been consul (143 B.C.) and censor (136 B.C.), one of the most respected men in the Senate, censured the Scipionic circle for having so soon abandoned the scheme of distributing the domain-lands; and the passionate vehemence which was the hereditary characteristic of the Claudian house seemed in this case to have been tainted with greater bitterness, apparently because he had come into personal conflict with Scipio Aemilianus in his candidacy for the censorship. Similar views were expressed by Publius Crassus Mucianus, the *pontifex maximus* [8] of the day, who was universally honored by the Senate and the citizens as a man and a jurist. His brother Publius Mucius Scaevola, the founder of Roman scientific jurisprudence, seemed not averse to the plan of reform, and his voice was of greater weight in that he stood somewhat aloof from the parties. Similar sentiments were held by Quintus Metellus, conqueror of Macedonia and of the Achaeans, but respected less for his warlike deeds than because he was a model of the old discipline and manners in both his personal and public life. Tiberius Gracchus was closely

---

8. Head of the official priesthood. See Glossary.

connected with these men, particularly with Appius whose daughter he had married, and with Mucianus whose daughter was married to his brother. No wonder he cherished the idea of furthering the project of reform, as soon as he should find himself in a position which would constitutionally allow him the initiative.

Personal motives may have strengthened this resolution. The treaty of peace which Mancinus concluded with the Spanish city of Numantia in 137 B.C. was in substance the work of Gracchus. The recollection that the Senate had canceled it, that the general had on this account been surrendered to the enemy,[9] and that Gracchus and other superior officers had escaped a like fate only through the greater favor which he enjoyed with the people, could scarcely put the proud and upright young man in better humor with the ruling aristocracy. The Hellenic rhetoricians with whom he was fond of discussing philosophy and politics, Diophanes of Mytilene and Gaius Blossius of Cumae, nourished within his soul the ideals over which he brooded. When his intentions became known in wider circles, there was no want of approving voices, and many a public placard summoned the grandson of Africanus to think of the deliverance of the poor people of Italy.

Tiberius Gracchus became tribune of the people on the tenth of December, 134 B.C., when the fearful consequences of the past misgovernment and the political, military, economic, and moral decay of the community were naked to all eyes. One of the two consuls of this year fought without success in Sicily against the revolted slaves. The other, Scipio Aemilianus, was employed for months in crushing rather than conquering a small Spanish country town. If Gracchus still needed a special summons to give

---

9. A curious Roman custom, dating from the disgraceful surrender at the Caudine Forks (321 B.C.), was to repudiate, on occasion, agreements made with the enemy by field commanders, and to offer a kind of moral compensation for the bad faith by surrendering the offending general and his principal officers.

effect to his resolution, he found it in this state of affairs
which filled the mind of every patriot with unspeakable
anxiety. His father-in-law promised assistance in counsel
and action, and the support of the jurist Scaevola, who
had just been elected consul for the coming year, might be
hoped for.

Accordingly Gracchus, immediately upon taking office,
proposed an agrarian law which was fundamentally a renewal of the Licinio-Sextian Law of 367 B.C. Under it all
the state lands which were occupied and enjoyed by the
possessors without remuneration (regularly leased lands,
such as the territory of Capua, were not affected) were to
revert to the state. However, there was the restriction
that each occupier should reserve 500 acres for himself
and 250 acres for each son (not, however, to exceed 1,000
acres in all) in permanent and guaranteed possession, or
should be entitled to claim equivalent compensation in
land elsewhere. Indemnification appears to have been
granted for any improvements executed by the former
holders, such as buildings and plantations.

The public land thus recaptured was to be broken up
into plots of 30 acres. These were to be distributed partly
to citizens and partly to Italian allies, not as their absolute property but as inalienable heritable leaseholds,
whose holders bound themselves to use the land for agriculture and to pay a moderate rent to the state treasury. A
commission of three men, who were to be regarded as ordinary and standing magistrates of the state to be annually elected by the assembly of the people, was to be entrusted with the work of recapture and distribution, to
which was later added the important and difficult function of legally settling what was public and what was private property. The distribution was thus designed to go
on for an indefinite period until the very extensive and
complicated Italian domains had been dealt with. The new
features in the Sempronian agrarian law as compared
with the Licinio-Sextian were (1) the clause in favor of

the hereditary possessors, (2) the leasehold and inalienable tenure proposed for the new allotments, and especially (3) the permanent regulatory commission, the lack of which had been the chief reason why the older law had become a dead letter.

War was thus declared against the great landholders, who, as three centuries before, found their major ally in the Senate; and once again a single magistrate stood up in defiance of the aristocratic government. The Senate began the conflict by means long sanctioned in such cases, by countering the innovation of one magistrate by the conservative power of the magistracy itself. Another tribune, Marcus Octavius, a resolute man convinced of the objectionable character of the proposed land law, interposed his veto when it was about to be put to vote—a step whose constitutional effect was to set aside the proposal. Gracchus in his turn suspended the business of the state and the administration of justice, and placed his seal on the public treasury. The government acquiesced: it was inconvenient, but the year would draw to an end. Gracchus, in perplexity, offered his law to the voters a second time. Octavius of course repeated his veto, and when his colleague and former friend pleaded with him not to obstruct the salvation of Italy, he replied that opinions differed as to how Italy could be saved, but that his constitutional right to use his veto against the proposal was beyond all doubt.

The Senate now attempted to open up a decent retreat for Gracchus. Two former consuls challenged him to debate the matter further in the Senate, and the tribune agreed with alacrity. He sought to construe the offer of debate as implying that the Senate had conceded the principle of distributing the public lands; but since this was not the case, nor was the Senate disposed to yield at all in the matter, the discussions ended without result. Constitutional means were thus exhausted. In former days men were not indisposed to let the proposal sleep for the current year, and to take it up in each succeeding one until the urgency of the demand and the pressure of public opinion overcame the resistance. But things were now at a higher tension, and Gracchus felt he had reached the point when he must either wholly renounce his reform or begin a revolution.

He chose the latter course. He came before the people with the declaration that either he or Octavius must retire as tribune, and suggested to Octavius that a vote of the citizens should determine which of them should be dismissed. Octavius naturally refused this strange challenge: the tribune's veto existed for the very purpose of giving scope to such differences of opinion among colleagues. Then Gracchus broke off the discussion, and asked the assembled multitude whether a tribune of the people who acted in opposition to the people had not forfeited his office. The assembly, long accustomed to approve all proposals presented to it, and for the most part composed of farmers who had flocked in from the country and were personally interested in the success of the law, gave an almost unanimous affirmative. At the bidding of Gracchus, Marcus Octavius was removed by the lictors from the tribunes' bench. Then, in the midst of universal rejoicing, the agrarian law was carried and the first allotment commissioners were nominated.

Those chosen were Tiberius Gracchus himself, his brother Gaius (who was only twenty years of age), and his father-in-law Appius Claudius—a family selection that heightened the exasperation of the aristocracy. When the new magistrates applied to the Senate for an appropriation to cover their equipment and daily expenses, the equipment outlay was refused, and twenty-four *asses* (one shilling) was set as a daily allowance. The feud spread, and became more envenomed and more personal. The intricate task of defining, recapturing, and distributing the public domains carried strife into every Roman community, and even into the allied Italian towns.

The aristocracy made no secret that, while they might acquiesce in the law because they had to, its officious author would never escape their vengeance; and the announcement of Quintus Pompeius, that he would impeach Gracchus on the very day he resigned the tribunate, was far from the worst of the threats hurled at the tribune. Gracchus believed, probably with reason, that his personal safety was imperiled, and he no longer appeared in the Forum without a retinue of 3,000 to 4,000 men—a step which drew bitter condemnation from the Senate, even from men like Metellus who were not averse to reform itself. If he had expected to reach his goal by passing his agrarian law, he now learned that he was only at the starting point. The "people" owed him gratitude, but he was a lost man if he had no further protection than the gratitude of the people, and if he did not continue indispensable to them by constantly arousing fresh interests and hopes through new and more comprehensive proposals.

Just at that time the kingdom and wealth of the Attalids had fallen to the Romans by the testament of the last king of Pergamus. Gracchus proposed to the people that the Pergamene treasure should be distributed among the new landholders for the purchase of the necessary implements and livestock; and he proposed, contrary to existing practice, that the status of the new province should be decided by popular vote. He is said to have prepared further popular measures for shortening the period of military service, for extending the right of appeal, for abolishing the exclusive prerogative of senators to serve as civil jurymen, and even for admitting the Italian allies to Roman citizenship. How far his projects actually reached cannot now be ascertained. This alone is certain, that Gracchus saw that his only safety lay in inducing the people to elect him again to the office which protected him, and that, to obtain this unconstitutional re-election, he dangled the prospect of further reforms. Where at first he had risked himself to save the commonwealth, he was now obliged to imperil the commonwealth for his own safety.

When the assembly met to elect the tribunes for the following year, the first divisions cast their votes for Gracchus. But the opposing party's veto prevailed in the end, at least to the extent that the assembly broke up without decision, which was postponed to the next day. For this second meeting Gracchus marshaled every resource. He appeared in public dressed in mourning, and commended to the people the care of his youthful son. Then, anticipating that the election would once again be disturbed by a veto, he made provision for expelling the adherents of the aristocracy from the place of meeting by force. On the second day of election the votes fell as on the first. Again the veto was exercised, and the tumult began. The citizens dispersed, the elective assembly was practically dissolved, and the Capitoline temple was closed. It was rumored in the city that Tiberius had deposed all the tribunes, and was resolved to continue his magistracy without re-election.

The Senate met in the temple of Fidelity, close by the temple of Jupiter. The bitterest opponents of Gracchus spoke in the sitting, and when Tiberius moved his hand to his forehead to signify to the people amid the wild tumult that his head was in danger, it was charged that he was summoning the people to grant him the crown. The consul Scaevola was urged to order the traitor immediately put to death. When that temperate man, by no means averse to reform in itself, indignantly refused the barbarous demand, the ex-consul and chief priest Publius Scipio Nasica, a harsh and vehement aristocrat, summoned those who shared his views to arm themselves as they could and to follow him. Few of the country people had come into town for the election, and the people of the city timidly gave way before men of quality with fury in their eyes and chair-legs as clubs in their hands. With a few attendants, Gracchus attempted to escape, but in his flight he fell on the slope of the Capitol, and was killed by a blow on the head from the bludgeon of one of his furious pursuers (Publius Satureius and Lucius Rufus afterward contested for the infamous honor) before the statues of the seven kings at the temple of Fidelity. Three hundred others died with him, not one by weapons of iron. When evening came the bodies were thrown into the Tiber, Gaius Gracchus vainly pleading that his brother's corpse might be spared for decent burial.

Such a day had never before been seen in Rome. The strife of more than a century during the first social crisis had led to no such catastrophe. The better men of the aristocracy might shudder, but they could no longer retreat. With no choice save to abandon a great number of their most loyal partisans to the vengeance of the multitude, or to assume collective responsibility for the outrage, they chose the latter course. They gave official sanction to the story that Gracchus had sought the crown, and justified this latest crime by the primitive precedent of Servilius Ahala.[10] In fact, they even formed a special investigating commission to ferret out Gracchus' accomplices, placing at its head the consul Publius Popillius, to put a kind of posthumous legal stamp on the murder by issuing bloody sentences against a large number of lesser persons (132 B.C.).

Nasica, against whom the multitude breathed special vengeance, and who at least had the courage to admit his deed openly and to defend it, was sent on an honorable mission to Asia, and invested during his absence with the office of pontifex maximus. Nor did the leaders of the moderate party dissociate themselves from these actions. Gaius Laelius took part in the investigations against the

■

10. A legendary figure of the first century of the Republic, whose assassination of Spurius Maelius for seeking the kingship by currying popular favor was a much-quoted example.

supporters of Gracchus; Publius Scaevola, who had tried
to prevent the murder, defended it afterwards in the Senate; and Scipio Aemilianus, when challenged publicly on
his return from Spain (132 B.C.) to declare whether he
approved the killing of his brother-in-law, gave the ambiguous reply that so far as Tiberius had aspired to the
crown, he had been justly put to death.

Let us endeavor to form a judgment on these momentous events. The appointment of an official commission to
counteract the dangerous diminution of the farmer class,
by the comprehensive creation of new small holdings from
the public lands owned by the state, was hardly a sign of a
healthy national economy; but it was, under existing conditions, well suited to its purpose. The distribution of the
public domain was, moreover, not a revolutionary issue.
It might have been carried out to the last sod without
changing the constitution or threatening the government
of the aristocracy. Nor could there be any complaint of a
violation of rights. The state was admittedly the owner
of the occupied land. The holder, as a possessor on sufferance, could not generally claim even a *bona fide* pro-
prietary tenure; and in the exceptional instances where he
could do so, he confronted the fact that under Roman law
mere possession could not invalidate the right of the state.
The distribution of the domains was not a negation but
an exercise of the right of property, and all jurists were
agreed upon its formal legality.

But the attempt to carry out the state's legal claims was
far from being politically warranted by the fact that distribution of the public lands neither infringed the existing constitution nor violated any right. These occupied
domains had undeniably been in heritable private possession, some of them for three hundred years. The state's
proprietorship of the soil, which by its very nature loses
the character of a private right more quickly than that of
the individual citizen, had in the case of these lands be-

come virtually extinct, and the present holders had universally come into their possession by purchase or other regular acquisition. The jurist might say what he would: to men of business the measure appeared to be an ejection of the great landholders for the benefit of the agricultural proletariat, and in fact no statesman could give it any other name. Less objectionable perhaps, but still not without hazard, was the arrangement by which the new allotments bore the character of inalienable heritable leaseholds. The most liberal principles in regard to freedom of dealing had made Rome great; and it was hardly in keeping with the spirit of Roman institutions that these new farmers were committed to cultivate their lands in a definite manner, and that their allotments were subject to revocation and all the cramping measures associated with governmental restriction.

Granted that these objections to the Sempronian agrarian law were of no small weight, they were still not decisive. The proposed eviction of the occupiers of the public lands was certainly a great evil, yet it was the only available means of checking a much greater evil directly destructive to the state—the approaching ruin of the Italian farmers. We can well understand why the most distinguished and patriotic conservatives, headed by Gaius Laelius and Scipio Aemilianus, heartily approved, in principle, the land distribution.

But if Tiberius Gracchus' aims appeared good and salutary to the great majority of discerning patriots, the methods which he adopted did not and could not meet with the support of a single man of note. The Rome of this period was governed by the Senate. Anyone who carried a legislative measure against the majority of the Senate made a revolution. It was revolution against the spirit of the constitution when Gracchus submitted the land question to the people. It was revolution against the letter when he overrode (and set the precedent for overriding) the tribunician veto—the corrective of the state machine—by deposing his colleague, which he justified with unworthy sophistry.

But it was not in this step that the moral and political mistake by Gracchus lay. There are no set forms of high treason in history: whoever provokes one power in the state to conflict with another is certainly a revolutionist, even though he may be at the same time a discerning and praiseworthy statesman. The essential defect of the Gracchan revolution, too frequently overlooked, lay in the nature of the existing popular assemblies. The agrarian laws of Spurius Cassius [11] and of Tiberius Gracchus had the same tenor and the same object, but the enterprises of the two men were as different as the former Roman citizenry which shared local spoils differed from the Romans who established the provinces of Asia and Africa. The former was a town community, whose members could meet and act together; the latter was a great state, in which the attempt to bring all the citizens into one great legislative body yielded a result as lamentable as it was ridiculous.

The fundamental defect of ancient politics—that it never developed from an urban constitution to that of a state, or (what is the same thing) from a system of primary assemblies to a representative system—in this case avenged itself. The sovereign assembly of Rome was what the sovereign assembly of England would be if all the voters of England, instead of sending representatives, should meet together as a parliament in an unwieldy mass, wildly agitated by interests and special passions, in which intelligence was totally lost; a body neither able to take a comprehensive view nor even to form a will of its own; above all, a body in which, with rare exceptions, a couple of hundred or thousand individuals accidentally picked

11. A probably legendary figure of the first period of the republic (c. 485 B.C.). He brought forward an agrarian law for the relief of the property-less citizens, was accused of aiming at royal power, and was hurled from the Tarpeian Rock.

from the streets acted and voted in the name of the whole citizenry.

But although these voting assemblies were attended, at least mainly, by Roman citizens, in the great popular meetings (*contiones*) everyone in the shape of a man— Egyptians and Jews, street-boys and slaves—was entitled to take his place and shout. Such a "meeting" certainly had no legal significance, for it could neither vote nor decree. But in practice it ruled the street, and already the opinion of the street was a power in Rome, so that it was of some importance whether this confused mass received the communications made to it with silence or uproar, and whether it applauded or hooted the orator. Not many had the courage of Scipio Aemilianus to face down the mob when he was hissed for his remarks on the death of his brother-in-law: "Ye to whom Italy is naught but step-mother ought to keep silent!" And when their fury grew still louder, "Surely you do not think I will fear those let loose, whom I have sent in chains to the slave-market?"

It was bad enough that the rusty machinery of the comitia should be used for legislation and elections. But when the masses—including in practice the *contiones*— were permitted to meddle in the government, and the instrument which the Senate employed to prevent such meddling was wrested out of its hands by the disregard of the tribunician veto; when this so-called citizens' assembly was allowed to decree to itself farms and equipment out of the public purse; when anyone able to command the streets for a few hours could impress on his projects the legal stamp of the sovereign people's will—then Rome had reached not the beginning but the end of popular freedom, and had arrived not at democracy, but at monarchy. For such reasons Cato and his followers in a previous age never brought such questions before the people, but discussed them solely in the Senate. For such reasons the men of the Scipionic circle, contemporaries of

Gracchus, described the Flaminian [12] agrarian law of 232 B.C. as the beginning of the decline of Roman greatness. For such reasons they allowed Tiberius Gracchus to fall, and saw his dreadful end as a kind of rampart against similar attempts in the future, while at the same time they carried out the land distribution his law had provided.

So sad was the state of things in Rome that honest patriots were forced into the horrible hypocrisy of abandoning the man and yet appropriating the fruit of his deed. For that reason too the opponents of Gracchus were in a sense not wrong, when they accused him of aspiring to the crown. That he himself probably had no such thought is a fresh impeachment rather than a justification. For so thoroughly pernicious was the aristocratic government, that the citizen who was able to depose the Senate and put himself in its place might have benefited the commonwealth more than he injured it.

Such a bold player Tiberius Gracchus was not. He was a tolerably capable, thoroughly well-meaning, conservative patriot who simply did not know what he was doing. In the belief that he was arousing the people he evoked the rabble, and grasped at the crown without being himself aware of it. But the iron sequence of events swept him irresistibly along the career of the demagogue-tyrant, until the family commission, the tampering with the public finances, the further "reforms" exacted by necessity and despair, the bodyguard from the gutter, and the conflicts in the streets betrayed the usurper more and more clearly to himself and others; and at last the unchained spirits of revolution seized and devoured the clumsy conjurer. The infamous butchery through which he perished

---

12. Gaius Flaminius, the greatest popular leader before the Gracchi, was tribune of the people in 232 B.C., and against bitter opposition by the Senate carried a law to distribute newly conquered territory in Picenum and Italian Gaul. He later commanded against Hannibal, and was killed in the disastrous ambush at Lake Trasimene (217 B.C.).

condemns itself, as it condemns the aristocratic faction which perpetrated it. But the glory of martyrdom that has embellished the name of Tiberius Gracchus came in this instance, as usual, to the wrong man. The best of his contemporaries judged otherwise. When the catastrophe was announced to Scipio Aemilianus, he uttered the words of Homer:

"So perish all who dare such deeds as he."

And when the younger brother of Tiberius seemed inclined toward the same career, his own mother wrote to him: "Shall our house have no end of this madness? Where shall be the limit? Have we not already enough to be ashamed of, in having confused and disorganized the state?"

So spoke not the anxious mother, but the daughter of the conqueror of Carthage, who knew and experienced a misfortune still greater than the death of her children.

II

THE REVOLUTION AND
GAIUS GRACCHUS

Tiberius Gracchus was dead, but his two works, the land distribution and the revolution, survived their author. Faced by the starving agricultural proletariat, the Senate might commit a murder, but it could not thereby kill the Sempronian land law. The law itself had been signally strengthened, rather than shaken, by the frantic outburst of partisan fury. The reform-minded aristocrats who openly favored the distribution of the public domains—headed by Quintus Metellus, who was censor about this time (131 B.C.), and Publius Scaevola—together with the followers of Scipio Aemilianus, who were at least not opposed to reform, gained the upper hand for a time even in the Senate, and a senatorial decree expressly directed the land commissioners to begin their labors.

According to the Sempronian law the commissioners were to be nominated yearly by vote of the people, and this was probably done. However, from the nature of their task it was to be expected that the same men should be elected again and again, and new elections in the true sense occurred only when a place became vacant through death. Thus Publius Crassus Mucianus, the father-in-law of Gaius Gracchus, was appointed in place of Tiberius; and after the defeat of Mucianus in 130 B.C. and the death of Appius Claudius, the business of distribution was entrusted to young Gaius Gracchus and two of the most active leaders of the popular party, Marcus Fulvius Flaccus and Gaius Papirius Carbo. The very names of these men attest that the work of recapturing and distributing the occupied public lands was pushed with zeal and energy, and proofs to that effect are not wanting.

As early as 132 B.C. the consul Publius Popillius, who had directed the prosecutions of the followers of Tiberius Gracchus, recorded of himself on a public monument that he was "the first to turn shepherds out of the public lands and put farmers in their stead." According to tradition, this land distribution took place all over Italy and everywhere increased the number of farms, for the purpose of the Sempronian law was to elevate the farmer class not by founding new communities, but by strengthening those already in existence. The wide extent of these distributions is proved by the numerous innovations in the art of land measurement that go back to the Gracchan distribution—for example, the placement of boundary stones. But the numbers on the franchise lists give the clearest evidence. The census published in 131 B.C., and probably taken early in the preceding year, counted only 319,000 citizens capable of bearing arms; whereas six years later, instead of continuing to fall off, the number rises to 395,000—unquestionably the result of the land commission's work. Whether it increased the number of farms among the Italian allied communities in the same proportion may be doubted, but what it did accomplish yielded great and beneficial results.

These results, it is true, were not achieved without injury to respectable interests and existing rights. The land commission, composed of dedicated partisans and absolute judge of its own work, went about its labors in reckless and even disorderly fashion. Public notices summoned everyone who could give information about the extent of the public lands. The old land registers became the commission's Bible, and not only were occupations revoked without distinction between new and old, but in various cases private property to which the holder was unable to prove his title was also confiscated. Loud and often well-founded as were the complaints, the Senate let the commission have its way; for it was clear that if the land question was to be settled at all, some such unceremonious vigor was necessary.

But this acquiescence had its limits. The Italian domain land was not solely in the hands of Roman citizens. Large tracts had been assigned to particular allied communities by decrees of the people or Senate, and other parts had been occupied with or without permission by Italians. The land commission at length attacked these possessions also.

The recapture of the portions simply occupied by non-Romans was doubtless in accord with formal law, and the same applied presumably to domain lands granted to the Italian communities; for the state did not thereby renounce its ownership, but made its grants to communities (just as to private persons) subject to revocation. But charges of bad faith by these allied or subject communities could not simply be disregarded like the complaints of private Roman citizens. The former might have no better legal claim than the latter, but in the case of the Latin possessions the real question was the political wisdom of giving fresh offense to communities so important from a military point of view and already so seriously estranged.

The decision lay in the hands of the middle party, which after the fall of Tiberius Gracchus had protected reform against the aristocracy; now it alone was able to put a limit on reform. The Latins pleaded personally with the most prominent man of this party, Scipio Aemilianus, to protect their rights, and he promised to do so. Mainly through his influence, in 129 B.C. a decree of the people took away from the commission and gave to the censors (and as their proxies, the consuls) the responsibility for deciding what was public and what was private land. This was in effect a mild way of suspending further land distribution. The consul Tuditanus, by no means Gracchan in his views and little inclined to sweat over the difficult task of land surveying, seized the opportunity of joining the army in Illyria and leaving his land duties undone. The commission continued to exist, but judicial decisions as to what constituted public land were lacking, and the commission was condemned to inactivity.

The reform party was outraged, even men like Publius Scaevola and Quintus Metellus expressing disapproval of Scipio's intervention. Other circles did not stop with disapproval. On a certain day Scipio had promised to make an address regarding relations with the Latins. On the morning of that day he was found dead in his bed. He was but fifty-six years old, in full health and vigor; he had spoken in public the day before, and that evening had retired earlier than usual to prepare the outline of his speech. That he was the victim of political assassination cannot be doubted. Shortly before, he himself had mentioned publicly the plots against him. What assassin's hand struck down the foremost statesman and general of the age was never discovered, and it ill becomes the historian either to repeat the reports handed down from contemporary gossip, or to make the childish attempt to deduce the truth from such materials. This only is clear, that the instigator of the deed must have belonged to the Gracchan party, and that the assassination of Scipio was the democratic reply to the aristocratic massacre at the temple of Fidelity.

There was no attempt to bring the murderer to justice. The popular party, correctly fearing that its leaders Gaius Gracchus, Flaccus, and Carbo would be dragged into the case whether guilty or not, opposed an inquiry with all its might; and the aristocracy, which lost in Scipio as much an antagonist as an ally, was not unwilling to let the matter drop. The general public and all men of moderate views were shocked—none more so than Quintus Metellus, who, though disapproving Scipio's interference with reform, turned away in horror from such confederates, and ordered his four sons to carry the body of his great antagonist to the funeral pyre. The funeral was hastily completed. With veiled head the last of the family of the conqueror of Zama was borne forth without anyone having been allowed to see his face, and the flames that licked at the remains of the illustrious man consumed with his body the traces of the crime.

The history of Rome records various men of greater genius than Scipio Aemilianus, but none equaling him in moral purity, in utter absence of political selfishness, and in generous love of country; and none, perhaps, was assigned by destiny a more tragic part. Conscious of the best of intentions and of no common abilities, he was doomed to see his country ruined before his eyes, while having to repress within himself every serious attempt to save it, because he clearly perceived that he would thereby only worsen the evil; doomed to the necessity of sanctioning outrages like the murder of Tiberius Gracchus, and at the same time of defending the victim's work against his murderers.

Yet he might claim that he had not lived in vain. To him, at least as much as to the author of the Sempronian law, the citizens of Rome owed the increase of nearly 80,000 new farm allotments. It was also he who stopped the land distribution when it had produced its optimum benefit. That it was time to call a halt was doubtless a matter of argument even among well-intentioned men; but the very fact that Gaius Gracchus did not seriously seek to distribute those additional public lands which might have been allotted under the law surely implies that Scipio chose substantially the right moment. Both measures were extorted from the factions, the first from the aristocracy, the second from the friends of reform, and for each its author paid with his life. It was Scipio's lot to return uninjured from many a battlefield that he might perish at home by an assassin's hand; but in his quiet chamber he died for Rome no less than if he had fallen before the walls of Carthage.

The land distribution was at an end, but the revolution went on. The revolutionary party, with the land commission constituting its leadership, had skirmished now and then with the government even in Scipio's lifetime. Carbo, in particular, one of the most talented orators of his time, had as tribune of the people in 131 B.C. given no little trouble. He had extended the practice of voting on legislative matters in the citizen assemblies, and had even proposed to permit the tribunes of the people to succeed themselves, the legal prohibition of which had thwarted

Tiberius Gracchus. The initial proposal had been frustrated by the resistance of Scipio, but some years later (apparently after his death) the law was reintroduced and passed, though with some limitations.

The principal object of the reform party, however, was to revive the land commission, whose work had been practically suspended. The leaders seriously discussed removing the obstacles interposed by the Italian allies by conferring citizenship on them, and the agitation largely assumed that course. To meet it the Senate, in 126 B.C., got the tribune Marcus Junius Pennus to propose that all noncitizens be dismissed from the capital; and despite resistance from the democrats, especially Gaius Gracchus, and the ferment caused in the Latin communities, the odious measure was carried. The following year Marcus Fulvius Flaccus as consul retorted by proposing to make it easier for the allied communities to acquire Roman citizenship, and to allow even those who had not acquired citizenship to appeal to the Roman comitia against penal judgments. But he stood almost alone, for Carbo had meanwhile changed his colors and become a zealous aristocrat, while Gaius Gracchus was absent as quaestor in Sardinia. Thus the project was frustrated by the resistance not only of the Senate, but also of the citizens, who were little inclined to extend their privileges to others. Flaccus left Rome to take supreme command against the Celts, thereby laying the groundwork for great new democratic schemes, while at the same time avoiding the difficulty of having to bear arms against the allies whom he had aroused.

As a result of the rejection of Flaccus' proposals, the thriving Campanian city of Fregellae, at that time perhaps the second city of Italy and the usual mouthpiece of all the Latin colonies in discussions with Rome, took up arms against Rome—the first instance in a hundred and fifty years of a serious insurrection against the Roman hegemony in Italy not instigated by foreign powers. On this occasion the fire was successfully extinguished before it had blazed in other allied communities. Not through superiority of the Roman arms but through the treachery of a Fregellan, the *praetor* [1] Lucius Opimius quickly became master of the revolted city, which lost its civic privileges and its walls, and was converted, like Capua, into a village. The colony of Fabrateria was founded on a part of its territory in 124 B.C., while the remaining land and the former city itself were distributed among the surrounding communities. This rapid and fearful punishment alarmed the allies; and endless impeachments for high treason pursued not only the Fregellans but also the leaders of the popular party in Rome, whom the aristocracy naturally regarded as accomplices of the revolt.

Meanwhile Gaius Gracchus reappeared at Rome. The aristocracy had first sought to detain the dreaded adversary in Sardinia, by failing to provide the usual replacement. Then, when he returned anyway, it had brought him to trial as one of the authors of the Fregellan revolt. But the citizenry acquitted him, and now he threw down the gauntlet. He became a candidate for the tribuneship, and was elected to that office for the year 123 B.C. at an unusually well-attended assembly. War was thus declared. The democratic party, always starved for leaders of ability, had from sheer necessity remained almost inactive for nine years; now, as the truce ended, it was headed by a man who, more honest than Carbo and more talented than Flaccus, was in every respect fitted to take the lead.

Gaius Gracchus (153-121 B.C.) was a man of greater stature than his older brother. Like the latter, he had no relish for vulgar pleasures and pursuits. He was a man of thorough culture and a brave soldier, who had served

■

---

1. Two *praetors* (of the total of six, at this period of the Republic) were charged with administering justice in the capital, while four others were assigned to four major provinces. See Glossary.

with distinction before Numantia under his brother-in-law Scipio, and afterward in Sardinia. But in talent, in character, and above all in depth of feeling, he was decidedly superior to Tiberius. The clarity and self-possession which the young man afterward displayed, under the pressure of all the varied labors required in carrying out his numerous laws, bespoke his genuine statesman's talent; and the passionate devotion with which his intimate friends clung to him, even unto death, testified to his lovable and noble nature. The personal suffering which he had undergone, and his enforced silence through nine long years, served only to heighten his purposeful energy, and the indignation locked in his heart only glowed with greater intensity against the party which had disorganized his country and murdered his brother. His passionate temperament made him the greatest orator that Rome ever had: even without it, he would probably be reckoned among the great statesmen of all time. The few remains of his recorded orations even in their present condition include several of heart-stirring power, and we can well understand how those who heard or even merely read them were carried away by the impetuous torrent of his words.

And yet, great master though he was of speech, he was himself at times so mastered by anger that the orator's flow became confused and faltering. In Gaius' nature there was no vein, as in his brother, of the kind of sentimental, shortsighted, and confused good nature that could seek to change the mind of a political opponent by entreaties or tears; he entered with full consciousness on a career of revolution and revenge. "To me too," his mother wrote to him, "nothing seems finer and more glorious than to retaliate upon an enemy, so far as it can be done without our country's ruin. But if this is not possible, then a thousand times rather than that our country should perish, may our enemies continue to remain what they are." Cornelia knew her son; his creed was just the reverse. Vengeance he would wreak on the wretched government at any price, though he himself and even the commonwealth were involved in the common ruin. The presentiment that fate would overtake him as surely as it overtook his brother only drove him to make haste, like a mortally wounded man who throws himself on the foe. The mother thought more nobly; but the son, with his deeply provoked, passionately excited, thoroughly Italian nature, has been more pitied than blamed by posterity, and posterity has been right in its judgment.

Tiberius Gracchus had brought a single administrative reform before the citizens. What Gaius Gracchus introduced, in a series of separate proposals, was nothing less than an entirely new constitution, the foundation-stone of which was the recent innovation that a tribune of the people should be free to succeed himself. This step enabled the popular chief to acquire a permanent and safe position. The next object was to attach the multitude of the capital steadfastly to him, for it was already plain that no reliance was to be placed on the country people who came to the city only from time to time. This purpose was served first of all by introducing the distribution of grain in the capital. The grain received by the state from the provincial tenths frequently had been given away at nominal prices to the citizens. Gracchus enacted that every citizen who personally presented himself in the capital should thenceforth receive monthly a definite quantity— apparently 1 ¼ bushels—from the public stores at a price not quite half of a low average figure; and for this purpose the public storehouses were enlarged by the construction of the new Sempronian granaries.

This distribution—which excluded the citizens living outside the capital, and thus could not fail to attract the whole mass of proletarian citizens to Rome—was designed to make the proletariat of the capital dependent upon the leaders of the popular party instead of upon the aristocracy, thus supplying the new master of the state at

one stroke with a bodyguard and a firm majority in the
comitia. For greater security in the latter, moreover, the
order of voting was changed: in future they were to vote
in an order determined by lot on each occasion, instead of
the five property-classes in each tribe giving their votes
one after another. But while these laws were designed
mainly to give the new chief complete command of the
capital and thereby of the state, the amplest control over
the comitial machinery, and the possibility if need be of
striking terror into the Senate and magistrates, at the
same time he set out energetically to correct the existing
social evils.

It is true that the Italian land question was in one sense
settled. The agrarian law of Tiberius, and even the land
commission, remained legally in force; the agrarian law
carried by Gaius Gracchus did nothing but restore to the
commission the jurisdiction which it had lost. That this
step was taken only as a matter of principle, and that the
distribution of land was resumed, if at all, only to a very
limited extent, is shown by the census, which gives exactly
the same number of citizens for the years 125 B.C. and
115 B.C. Gaius beyond doubt did not proceed further because the public lands held by Roman citizens were already largely distributed. The question of the lands held
by Latin allies could only be taken up in connection with
the very thorny problem of extending Roman citizenship.

On the other hand, he took an important step beyond
the agrarian law of Tiberius when he proposed the establishment of colonies in Italy at Tarentum and especially
at Capua. By that course he made the state land which
had been leased (and which was hitherto excluded from
distribution) liable also for parceling out—and parceling according to the colony system, rather than under
the previous method which excluded the founding of new
communities. Still more momentous was the measure by
which Gaius Gracchus first provided for colonies of citizens in the overseas territories. He despatched to the site

of Carthage some 6,000 colonists probably selected from Italian allies as well as from Roman citizens, and conferred on the new town (Junonia) the rights of a Roman citizen colony. The foundation of the colony was important, but still more important was the principle of overseas emigration thereby laid down, for it opened a permanent outlet for the Italian proletariat. At the same time, however, it abandoned the old principle that Italy alone did the governing, while the provinces were merely governed.

Beyond these measures, a further series of laws arose out of the general tendency to introduce milder and more humane principles in place of the antiquated severity of the existing constitution. For example, under the old laws there was no limit to the length of military service, except that no citizen was liable to ordinary service in the field before his eighteenth or after his forty-sixth year. When the occupation of Spain threatened to make service permanent, a new law seems to have granted the right of discharge to any one who had been in the field for six successive years, although this discharge did not protect him from being drafted again afterward. Later, perhaps about the middle of the second century B.C., the rule arose that twenty years in the infantry or ten years in the cavalry gave exemption from further military service. Gracchus renewed the rule (which seems often to have been infringed) that no citizen could be called into the army before his eighteenth year, and he apparently restricted the number of campaigns required for exemption from further service. The soldier's clothing, whose value had always been deducted from his pay, was also thereafter furnished by the state.

Further, there was a tendency in Gracchan legislation, if not to abolish capital punishment, at least to restrict it—a tendency which was felt to some extent even in the military jurisdiction. Since the beginnings of the republic the magistrate could not inflict a death sentence upon a citizen without consulting the community, except under martial law. Soon after the Gracchan period this right of appeal by the citizen appeared even in the camp, and the general's right to inflict capital punishment seems to have been restricted to allies and subjects. Moreover, the right of the community to inflict or rather confirm a sentence of death was further limited by the fact that Gracchus transferred jurisdiction over those crimes which most frequently resulted in capital sentences—poisoning and murder—from the public to permanent judicial commissions. These could not, like the tribunals of the people, be broken up by a tribune; there was no right of appeal to the community; and their sentences were as unlikely to be annulled by the community as those of the long-established civil *jurymen*.[2]

In the citizens' tribunals it had long been the rule that the accused could remain at liberty during his trial, and was allowed by surrendering his citizenship to save life and freedom, if not necessarily property, for even an exile could be fined. But summary arrest and complete execution of the sentence were legally possible, and were sometimes inflicted even upon persons of rank. For example, Lucius Hostilius Tubulus, praetor in 142 B.C. who was impeached for a heinous crime, was refused the privilege of exile, arrested, and executed. On the other hand, from the outset the judicial commissions seem to have been proscribed from touching the liberty or life of the citizen, but could at most only pronounce sentence of exile. Thus exile, which hitherto had been a mitigation of punishment for those found guilty, became for the first time a formal penalty. But this involuntary exile, like the

■

2. The term *juryman* is used in two senses: (1) a single arbitrator appointed to hear and settle disputes and suits between citizens; (2) a member of a jury (approximately 50) selected by lot from lists of eligible citizens to hear major cases before the permanent courts (quaestiones). See Glossary.

voluntary, left the banished person his property, to the extent not exhausted in paying fines and claims for compensation.

Lastly, Gaius Gracchus made no changes in the debt laws. However, respectable authorities assert that he held out to debtors the hope of reducing or wiping out their indebtedness—which, if it is correct, must also be considered a radical popular measure.

While Gracchus thus curried the support of the people both by the fact and the prospect of a material improvement in their position, he labored with equal energy for the ruin of the aristocracy. Perceiving clearly how insecure was any rule based solely on the proletariat, he applied himself to splitting the aristocracy and drawing a part of it over to his side. The materials for such a rupture already existed. The aristocracy of the rich, which had risen as one man against Tiberius Gracchus, consisted of two different bodies, comparable in some measure to England's peerage and city aristocracy. One group consisted of the tight little circle of governing senatorial families, who kept aloof from direct speculation and invested their immense capital partly in land, partly as sleeping partners in joint ventures. The core of the second group was composed of the speculators, who, as managers of these joint ventures or for their own account, conducted vast mercantile and financial enterprises throughout Rome's dominions.

This latter class, particularly since the middle of the third century B.C., had gradually moved alongside the senatorial aristocracy, though the legal exclusion of the senators from mercantile pursuits under a law proposed by Gaius Flaminius, a predecessor of the Gracchi, drew an outward line of demarcation between rich senators and those who were merely rich. In the present epoch the aristocracy of money began, under the name of the *equites,* to play a decisive part in political affairs. This name originally belonged only to the citizen-cavalryman in active service, but was gradually extended to all those who, as possessors of an estate of at least 400,000 sesterces, were liable for cavalry service. Thus it came to include the whole of upper Roman society, senatorial and nonsenatorial. But not long before the time of Gaius Gracchus a seat in the Senate had been ruled incompatible with service in the cavalry, thus eliminating the senators from those qualified to be equites. Accordingly, the equestrian order as a whole might be regarded the aristocracy of speculators as opposed to the aristocracy of the Senate. Nevertheless, younger members of senatorial families who had not entered the Senate continued to serve as equites and to bear the name. In fact, the citizen-cavalry as such—that is, the eighteen equestrian *centuries* [3]—was made up by the censors chiefly from the young senatorial aristocracy.

This order of the equites—substantially, the wealthy merchants—ran athwart the governing Senate in various ways. There was a natural antipathy between the genteel aristocrats and the men whose money had brought them rank. The ruling lords, especially the better class of them, stood as much aloof from business as the business man ignored political questions and intrigues. The two classes had already come into sharp conflict, particularly in the provinces; for while the provincials had far more reason than the Roman capitalists to complain of the partiality of Roman justice, yet the ruling lords of the Senate did not give the capitalists quite the absolute free hand, in exploiting the provinces, that the men of money would have desired. In spite of their common hatred of a foe like Tiberius Gracchus, there was a deep gulf between the nobility and the moneyed aristocracy. Gaius, more adroit than his brother, enlarged it until the old alliance

---

3. For voting purposes, Roman citizens were grouped into *centuries,* or hundreds. See Glossary.

was severed and the mercantile class brought over on his side.

The special distinctions of the man of the equestrian census from the rest of the multitude—the finger-ring of gold instead of iron or copper, and the preferred place at public festivals—may or may not have been conferred on the equites by Gaius Gracchus. However, they emerged at about this period, and the extension of these previously senatorial privileges to the equestrian order was quite in the style of Gracchus. His aim was to make the equites a privileged order intermediate between the senatorial aristocracy and the common multitude; and this aim was promoted more by such class-insignia, though trifling in themselves, and though many equites might not avail themselves of them, than by many a more important ordinance. The party of material interests by no means despised such honors, and yet was not to be gained through these alone. Gracchus perceived that the victory would doubtless go to the highest bidder, but that a massive bid was needed. Therefore, he offered control of the jury courts, and the revenues of Asia.

The Roman system of financial administration, under which indirect taxes as well as the rent from public land were gathered by middlemen, already gave the Roman capitalist class the most extensive advantages at the expense of the taxpayers. But direct taxation consisted either of fixed sums payable by the provincial communities—which of itself excluded the intervention of Roman capitalists—or, as in Sicily and Sardinia, of a ground-tenth levied in the provinces themselves, so that wealthy provincials and tributary communities commonly farmed the tenth of their districts as "tax land" and thereby kept at a distance the dangerous Roman middlemen.

Six years before, when the province of Asia had fallen to the Romans, the Senate had organized it substantially according to the first, or "fixed fee," system. Gaius Gracchus overturned this arrangement by a decree of the people. And he not only burdened the province, which hitherto had been almost free from taxation, with the most extensive indirect and direct taxes, particularly the ground-tenth; he also enacted that the tax-gathering for the province as a whole should be put up for auction in Rome—a rule which effectively excluded the provincials and called into existence an association of capitalists of colossal magnitude. A significant indication, moreover, of Gracchus' intention to make the capitalist order independent of the Senate was the enactment that the stipulated rent could no longer, wholly or partly, be remitted by the Senate at pleasure, but only under specific circumstances defined by law.

While the mercantile class was thus granted a gold mine, and the members of the new Asian tax partnership constituted a kind of "senate of merchants," a definite sphere of public action was also assigned to them in the jury courts. The jurisdiction of the citizens over criminal procedure, which was always very narrow among the Romans, was still further narrowed by Gracchus: most cases, whether civil or criminal in nature, were decided either by single jurymen or by permanent or extraordinary commissions. Both the former and the latter hitherto had been filled exclusively by senators; Gracchus transferred both functions of jurymen to the equestrian order, directing a new list of jurymen to be formed annually from all persons of equestrian rating, and excluding the senators themselves as well as, by an age limit, the young men of senatorial families. It is not improbable that the jurymen selected were chiefly the same men who led the great mercantile associations, particularly those farming the tax revenues of Asia and elsewhere, just because they had the closest personal interest in sitting in the courts; and if the lists of jurymen and the societies of tax gatherers thus coincided, one can all the more easily understand the significance of this new counter-senate.

The substantial result was that hitherto there had been but two authorities in the state—the government as the administering and controlling power, and the citizens as the legislative authority—with the courts divided between them. Now the moneyed aristocracy, united into a compact and privileged class on the solid basis of material interests, was also a judicial power, forming part of the state and taking its place on a footing of near equality with the ruling aristocracy. All the old antagonisms of merchant and nobleman could not fail to find practical expression in the jurymen's sentences. When the senator as provincial governor was called to a reckoning, his fate was no longer decided by his peers, but by great merchants and bankers. The feuds between Roman capitalists and Roman governors were thus transplanted from the provincial administration to the dangerous battleground of the courts. Not only was the aristocracy of the rich divided, but care was taken that their hostilities should always find fresh nourishment and easy expression.

With his weapons—the proletariat and the mercantile class—thus prepared, Gracchus set about his main work, the overthrow of the ruling aristocracy. The overthrow of the Senate meant first depriving it of its functions by legislative changes, and then ruining the existing aristocracy by measures of a more personal kind. Gracchus did both. The administrative function, in particular, had long been exclusively the Senate's; Gracchus took it away, partly by settling the most important administrative questions by popular legislation (or, in other words, practically through dictation by the tribunes), partly by restricting the Senate's role in current affairs, and partly by taking as much business as possible into his own hands. Some measures of this kind already have been mentioned. The new master of the state, without consulting the Senate, dealt with the state chest by imposing a permanent and oppressive burden on the public finances in the distribution of grain. He disposed of the public lands by sending out colonists not by decree of the Senate and people, but by decree of the people alone. He also interfered with provincial administration, overturning through a law of the people the financial constitution given by the Senate to the province of Asia and substituting an altogether different one for it.

A most important prerogative of the Senate—that of setting the functions of the two consuls—was not withdrawn, but was limited by requiring the Senate to fix these functions before the consuls concerned were elected. And with unrivaled activity Gaius gathered the most varied strands of government in his own hands. He himself watched over the distribution of grain, selected the jurymen, founded colonies in person despite the fact that his magistracy legally chained him to the city, regulated the highways and concluded building contracts, led the discussions of the Senate, and settled the consular elections. In short, he accustomed the people to the pre-eminence of one man, and overshadowed the lax and lame administration of the senatorial college by the vigor and versatility of his personal rule.

Gracchus interfered with the judicial prerogatives of the Senate even more than with its administration. We have already mentioned that he forbade the senators to sit as jurymen; the same course was adopted with regard to the Senate's practice of taking over the judicial function itself in exceptional cases. Under severe penalties he prohibited—apparently in his renewal of the law *de provocatione*—the appointment by senatorial decree of extraordinary commissions of high treason, such as that which after his brother's murder had sat in judgment on his adherents. The aggregate effect of these measures was that the Senate wholly lost the power of control, and retained only so much of the administrative function as the head of the state thought fit to leave to it.

But above and beyond these measures the governing aristocracy was also directly assailed. In an act of revenge, the law prohibiting extraordinary judicial commissions was given retroactive effect, thereby compelling Publius Popillius—the aristocrat who after the death of Nasica was the prime target of the democrats—to go into exile. (It is remarkable that this proposal was carried only by 18 to 17 votes in the assembly of the tribes, a sign of the aristocracy's influence with the multitude, at least in questions of a personal interest.) A similar but far less defensible decree—the proposal, directed against Marcus Octavius, that whoever had been deprived of his office by decree of the people should be forever prohibited from filling a public post—was recalled by Gaius at the request of his mother. He was thus spared the disgrace of openly mocking justice by a flagrant violation of the constitution, and of taking base vengeance on an honorable man who had not spoken any angry word against Tiberius Gracchus, and who had only acted in accordance with what he conceived to be his constitutional duty. But far more sweeping than these measures was the scheme of Gaius (which, it is true, was not carried through) to double the size of the Senate by adding 300 new members, who were to be elected from the equestrian order by the comitia. Such a wholesale creation of new peers would have reduced the Senate to abject dependence on the chief of state.

This was the political constitution which Gaius Gracchus projected and for the most part carried out during the two years of his tribunate (123-122 B.C.), apparently without encountering any resistance worth mentioning, and without requiring the use of force to attain his ends. The order in which these measures were carried is no longer recognizable from the confused accounts handed down to us, and various questions that arise must remain unanswered. But few elements of material importance seem to have escaped us. For on the principal mat-

ters we have quite trustworthy information; and Gaius,
unlike his brother, was not merely swept along the course
of events, but obviously had a well-considered and comprehensive plan which he implemented through a series of
special laws.

Now the Sempronian constitution itself shows clearly,
to all who are able and willing to see, that Gaius Gracchus
did not (as many well-intentioned people in ancient and
modern times have supposed) wish to place the Roman
republic on a new democratic basis. On the contrary, he
wished to abolish it and to introduce in its stead a *tyrannis*—in modern terms, an absolute (rather than a feudal
or theocratic) monarchy—in the form of a magistracy
made permanent by regular re-election and rendered absolute by unconditional control over the formally sovereign
comitia, an unlimited tribuneship of the people for life.
If Gracchus, as his words and especially his works plainly
testify, aimed at overthrowing the government of the
Senate, what other kind of government was possible but
the *tyrannis,* in a commonwealth which had outgrown
primary assemblies without creating a parliamentary system? Dreamers like his brother before him, and knaves
such as later times produced, might question this. But
Gaius Gracchus was a statesman; and though the formal
shape of his great work has not been handed down to us
and may be envisioned in various ways, yet he was beyond
doubt aware of what he was doing.

Just as the intention of usurping power cannot be mistaken, so will those who survey the entire circumstances
refuse to blame Gracchus. An absolute monarchy is a
great misfortune for any nation, but less of a misfortune
than an absolute oligarchy; and history cannot censure a
man who chooses the lesser suffering, least of all a man
so vehemently earnest and so far above vulgar selfishness
as Gaius Gracchus. Nevertheless, the fact may not be concealed that his whole legislation was pervaded with most
pernicious contradictions, on the one hand aiming at the

public good, while on the other hand ministering to the personal ambition and in fact the personal vengeance of the ruler.

Thus Gracchus earnestly worked to remedy social evils and to check the spread of pauperism, yet at the same time he intentionally created a street proletariat of the worst kind in the capital by his distributions of grain, which were designed to be, and became, the support of all the lazy and hungry rabble. Gracchus censured in the bitterest terms the Senate's venality, in particular laying bare with unsparing and just severity the scandalous buying and selling of the provinces of Asia Minor by Manius Aquilius; yet it was through the efforts of the same Gaius that the Roman citizens of the capital got themselves fed, in return for its cares of government, by the subjects of Rome. Gracchus warmly disapproved the disgraceful looting of the provinces: he not only instituted justly severe proceedings in particular cases, but also abolished the thoroughly corrupt senatorial courts, before which even Scipio Aemilianus had vainly staked his whole influence to punish the most flagrant criminals. Yet at the same time, by introducing courts composed of merchants, he delivered the provincials in chains to a party of vested interests, and thus to a despotism even more unscrupulous than that of the aristocracy; and he introduced into Asia a tax system compared with which even the taxation of Sicily after the Carthaginian model might be called mild and humane—just because on the one hand he needed the party of moneyed men, and on the other hand needed extensive new revenues to finance his distributions of grain and the other burdens. Gracchus beyond doubt desired a firm administration and even-handed dispensing of justice, as numerous thoroughly judicious ordinances testify. Yet his new system of administration rested on continuous individual usurpations only formally legalized, and he intentionally drew the courts—which every well-ordered state seeks to place at least aloof from politics, if not above it—into the midst of the whirlpool of revolution.

Admittedly much of the blame for these conflicting tendencies in Gaius Gracchus can be put on his position rather than on himself personally. At the very threshold of power he was confronted by the fatal dilemma, moral and political, that the same man had at the same time to act as a robber chieftain and as the first citizen of the state—a dilemma to which Pericles, Caesar, and Napoleon also had to make dangerous sacrifices. But the conduct of Gaius Gracchus cannot be explained entirely by this necessity. There also seethed in him the consuming passion for revenge, which foreseeing its own destruction hurls the firebrand into the house of the foe. He has himself told us what he thought of his jury law and similar measures intended to divide the aristocracy: he called them daggers which he had thrown into the Forum, that the men of rank might lacerate each other.

He was a political incendiary. Not only was the hundred years' revolution which dates from him the work of Gaius Gracchus, so far as it was any one man's work. He was above all the true founder of that terrible urban proletariat flattered and paid by the classes above it, which through its concentration in the capital (the natural result of the free distribution of grain) became at once utterly demoralized and aware of its power, and which—with its sometimes stupid and sometimes knavish demands, and its talk of the sovereignty of the people—lay like an incubus on the Roman commonwealth for five hundred years and only perished with it.

And yet, this greatest of political transgressors was in turn the savior of his country. There is scarcely a fundamental idea in Roman monarchy that is not traceable to Gaius Gracchus. From him proceeded the maxim (founded doubtless on the traditional laws of war, but new in the extension and practical application now given to it) that the land of the subject communities was the private property of the Roman state; and this maxim, which he employed primarily to support the state's right to tax that land at pleasure, as in the case of Asia, or to establish colonies, as in Africa, became afterwards a fundamental principle of law under the empire. He showed future demagogues and tyrants how to lean for support on material interests while breaking down the governing aristocracy, and how subsequently to legitimize the change of constitution by substituting strict and efficient administration for previous misgovernment.

To him, in particular, are traceable the first steps toward the reconciliation between Rome and the provinces which the establishment of monarchy could not but bring in its train. His attempt to rebuild a Carthage destroyed by Italian rivalry, and generally to open the way for Italian emigration toward the provinces, formed the first links in a long chain of momentous and beneficial actions. Right and wrong, fortune and misfortune, were so inextricably blended in this singular man and in his marvelous political construction that history may well—in this case, though in few others—reserve her judgment.

When Gracchus had substantially completed his new constitution for the state, he applied himself to a second and more difficult work, the question of the Italian allies. The views of the democratic leaders regarding it have already been described: they naturally sought the broadest extension of the Roman franchise, not merely to bring in the domains occupied by the Latins for distribution, but above all to strengthen their party by an enormous mass of new citizens, who might bring the comitial machine still more fully under their power by widening the body of privileged electors, and might abolish a distinction which with the fall of the republican constitution had lost most of its importance.

But here they encountered resistance from their own party, especially from that wing which ordinarily gave ready assent to anything, with or without understanding it. Since Roman citizenship seemed to those people like a partnership which gave them a share in sundry very tangible profits, they were not at all disposed to enlarge the number of the partners. The rejection of the Fulvian law in 125 B.C., and the insurrection of the Fregellans arising out of it, were significant indications both of the obstinate perseverance of that fraction of the citizens who ruled the comitia, and of the impatient urgency of the allies. Toward the end of his second tribunate (122 B.C.) Gracchus, probably spurred on by promises which he had given to the allies, made a second try. In concert with Marcus Flaccus—who, although a *consular,*[4] had again taken the tribuneship of the people, in order to carry the law which he had formerly proposed without success—he made a proposal to grant to the Latins the full franchise, and to the other Italian allies the former rights of the Latins.

The proposal, however, met united opposition from the Senate and the mob. The nature of this coalition and its style of conflict are clearly seen from an accidentally preserved fragment of the speech which the consul Gaius Fannius made to the citizens in opposing the proposal. "Do you then think," said the Optimate, "that if you confer the franchise on the Latins, you will be able to find a place in future—just as you are now standing there in front of me—in the assembly of citizens, or at the games and popular amusements? Do you not believe, on the contrary, that those people will occupy every spot?" Among the Romans of the fourth century B.C., who on a single day conferred the franchise on all the Sabines, such an orator might perhaps have been hissed. Those of the second found his reasoning uncommonly clear, and felt that the right to assign the Latin domains, which Gracchus offered as inducement, was far too low. The very fact that the Senate approved a proposal to eject all noncitizens

---

[4] A former consul, and hence an elder statesman. See Glossary.

from the city before the day of the decisive vote showed the fate in store for the plan. And when Livius Drusus, a colleague of Gracchus, interposed his veto against the law, the people received the veto in such a temper that Gracchus did not venture to proceed with the vote, or to prepare for Drusus the fate of Marcus Octavius.

This success apparently emboldened the Senate to attempt the overthrow of the victorious demagogue. The weapons of attack were substantially those which Gracchus himself had formerly used. His power rested both on the mercantile class and on the proletariat, but primarily on the latter, which in this conflict (neither side having any military force) played the part of an undisciplined army. It was clear that the Senate was not powerful enough to wrest either from the merchants or from the proletariat their new-found privileges: any attempt to assail the grain laws or the new jury arrangement would have led, in one form or another, to a street riot against which the Senate was utterly defenseless. But it was also clear that Gracchus himself and these merchants and proletarians were held together only by mutual advantage, and that the moneyed men were ready to accept their lucrative posts, and the populace its bread, as quickly from someone else as from Gaius Gracchus.

The institutions of Gracchus were immovably firm with a single exception—his own supremacy. The weakness of his personal position lay in the fact that there was no relation of genuine allegiance between the chief and his followers; and while the new constitution possessed all the other elements of vitality, it lacked one—the moral tie between ruler and ruled, without which every state rests upon feet of clay. The rejection of the proposal to give the Latins the franchise demonstrated with decisive clarity that the multitude had in fact never voted for Gracchus, but simply for itself. The aristocracy conceived the plan of giving battle to the author of the grain laws and land assignments on his own ground.

The Senate thus offered the proletariat not merely the same advantages as Gracchus had already given it, but still greater ones. Acting for the Senate, the tribune Marcus Livius Drusus proposed to relieve those who had received land under the law of Gracchus from payment of rent; to declare their allotments free and unrestricted property; and further, to provide for twelve Italian colonies of 3,000 colonists each, for which the people might choose suitable men as leaders. (Drusus himself declined—in contrast with the family complexion of the Gracchan commission—to be considered for this honorable duty.) Presumably the Latins were to bear the costs of the plan, for they occupied the only sizable public domain still remaining in Italy; and we find isolated enactments of Drusus—such as the regulation that a Latin soldier could be scourged only by the Latin officer set over him, and not by a Roman officer—which seem intended to indemnify the Latins for other losses.

The Senate's plan was not the most refined. The attempt to outbid the Gracchan opposition was too clear, the endeavor to create a bond between the nobles and the proletariat by exercising a joint tyranny over the Latins was too transparent. There was also the obvious question where—even granting that the whole domains assigned to the Latins were confiscated—enough public land was to be found for the formation of twelve new, populous, and compact colonies of citizens, since the Roman domains had been nearly all distributed. Lastly, Drusus' declaration that he would have nothing to do with the execution of his law was prudent to the point of folly.

But the clumsy snare was quite suited to the stupid quarry. Gracchus, on whose personal influence everything depended, was absent establishing the Carthaginian colony in Africa, and his lieutenant in the capital, Marcus Flaccus, played into the hands of the Senate by his vehement and maladroit conduct. The "people" accordingly ratified the Livian laws as readily as they had ratified the

Sempronian. Then, as usual, they repaid the latest bene-factor by inflicting a gentle blow on the earlier one, de-clining to re-elect Gracchus tribune when he ran for that office for the third time in 121 B.C. (On this occasion, however, there are alleged to have been unjust proceed-ings by the tribune presiding at the election, who had been offended by Gracchus.) Thus the foundation of Gracchus' despotism gave way beneath him. A second blow was in-flicted on him in the consular elections, which placed at the head of the state Lucius Opimius, who as praetor in 125 B.C. had conquered the Fregellans, and who was one of the most extreme and unscrupulous chiefs of the aristo-cratic party, a man firmly resolved to get rid of this dan-gerous antagonist at the first opportunity.

Such an opportunity soon occurred. On the tenth of De-cember, 122 B.C., Gracchus' term as tribune expired; on the first of January, 121 B.C., Opimius took up the *fasces* [5] as consul. The first attack, as was fair, was directed against the most useful but most unpopular measure of Gracchus, the re-establishment of Carthage. While the overseas colonies had hitherto been assailed only indi-rectly through the greater appeal of the Italian ones, it was now alleged that African hyenas had dug up the newly placed boundary stones of Carthage; and Roman priests, upon request, certified that such signs and portents were an express warning against rebuilding on a site ac-cursed of the gods. The Senate therefore felt compelled, as a matter of conscience, to propose a law prohibiting the founding of the colony of Junonia.

Gracchus, who with the other men nominated to estab-lish it was just then selecting the colonists, appeared on the day of voting at the Capitol to seek the rejection of the law. He wished to avoid violence, so as not to supply his opponents with the pretext they hoped for. But he was

5. The ceremonial axes which were the symbols of the consul's authority in the Roman state. See Glossary.

not able to prevent some of his faithful partisans, who re-
membered the fate of Tiberius and were well acquainted
with the plans of the aristocracy, from appearing in arms,
and in the immense excitement on both sides quarrels
could hardly be prevented. The consul Lucius Opimius offered the usual sacrifice on the porch of the Capitoline
temple. One of the attendants at the ceremony, Quintus
Antullius, with the holy entrails in his hand, haughtily ordered "bad citizens" to quit the porch, and seemed about
to lay hands on Gracchus himself. Thereupon a zealous
Gracchan drew his sword and cut the man down.

A fearful tumult arose, Gracchus vainly trying to address the people to disclaim responsibility for the sacri-
legious murder. He only furnished his antagonists with
an additional accusation, since, without being aware of it
in the confusion, he interrupted a tribune in the act of
speaking to the people—an offense for which an obsolete
statute prescribed the severest penalty.

The consul Lucius Opimius took steps to put down the
"insurrection for the overthrow of the republic," as the
aristocrats were fond of designating the day's events. He
himself passed the night in the temple of Castor in the
Forum; at early dawn the Capitol was filled with Cretan
archers, the senate house and Forum with men of the government party—the senators and those equites adhering
to them—who by order of the consul had all appeared in
arms, each attended by two armed slaves. None of the
aristocracy were absent; even the aged and venerable
Quintus Metellus, well disposed to reform, appeared with
shield and sword. An officer of ability and experience,
Decimus Brutus, was entrusted with the command of the
armed force as the Senate assembled in the senate house.
The bier with the corpse of Antullius was deposited in
front. The Senate, as if surprised, appeared *en masse* at
the door to view the dead body, and then retired to determine what should be done.

The leaders of the Gracchans had gone from the Capi-

tol to their houses. Marcus Flaccus had spent the night
preparing for war in the streets, while Gracchus apparently disdained to strive with destiny. Next morning,
when they learned of the preparations made by their enemies at the Capitol and the Forum, both proceeded to the
Aventine, the old stronghold of the popular party in the
struggles between patricians and plebeians. Gracchus went
silent and unarmed; Flaccus called the slaves to arms and
entrenched himself in the temple of Diana, while he sent
his younger son Quintus to the enemy's camp to arrange a
compromise if possible. The latter returned with the news
that the aristocracy demanded unconditional surrender,
and he also brought a Senate summons to Gracchus and
Flaccus to appear before it to answer for their violation
of the majesty of the tribunes. Gracchus wished to comply
with the summons, but Flaccus prevented him, although he
repeated his weak and mistaken attempt to move such opponents to compromise.

When instead of the two cited leaders young Quintus
Flaccus again appeared alone, the consul treated the failure to appear as the beginning of open insurrection. He
ordered the messenger arrested and gave the signal for
an attack on the Aventine, at the same time proclaiming
that the government would pay its weight in gold to who-
soever should bring in the head of Gracchus or Flaccus,
and offering amnesty to anyone who left the Aventine before the conflict began.

The ranks on the Aventine speedily thinned; the val-
iant nobility in union with the Cretans and slaves stormed
the almost undefended mount and killed all whom they
found, about 250 persons, mostly of humble rank. Marcus Flaccus fled with his eldest son to a place of concealment, but they were soon hunted out and put to death.
Gracchus had at the beginning of the conflict retired to
the temple of Minerva, and was about to pierce himself
with a sword when his friend Publius Laetorius seized his
arm and pleaded with him to preserve himself for better

times. Gracchus was induced to try to escape to the other
bank of the Tiber; but hastening down the hill, he fell and
sprained his foot. To gain time for him to escape, his two
attendants turned to face the pursuers and allowed themselves to be cut down, Marcus Pomponius at the Porta
Trigemina under the Aventine, Publius Laetorius at the
bridge over the Tiber where Horatius was said to have
once singly withstood the Etruscan army. Gracchus, attended only by his slave Euporus, reached the suburb on
the right bank of the Tiber. There, in the grove of Fur-
rina, the two dead bodies were found; it appears that the
slave had put to death first his master and then himself.

The heads of the two fallen leaders were handed over
to the government as required. The stipulated price, and
more, was paid to Lucius Septumuleius, a man of quality,
who brought in the head of Gracchus; but the murderers
of Flaccus, persons of humble rank, were sent away with
empty hands. The bodies of the dead were thrown into
the river, and the houses of the leaders were abandoned
to the pillage of the multitude.

Prosecutions against the partisans of Gracchus began
on a vast scale. As many as 3,000 of them are said to have
been strangled in prison, among them the eighteen-year-
old Quintus Flaccus, who had taken no part in the conflict, and who was universally lamented on account of his
youth and amiable disposition. In the open space beneath
the Capitol the altar of Camillus and other shrines
erected to internal peace were pulled down, and out of the
property of the killed or condemned traitors (which was
confiscated even to the portions of their wives) a new and
splendid temple of Concord with its basilica was erected
by the consul Lucius Opimius, in accordance with a decree
of the Senate.

It was indeed in keeping with the spirit of the age to remove the old memorials to civic peace, and to inaugurate
a new monument over the remains of the three grandsons
of the conqueror of Zama, all of whom—first Tiberius

Gracchus, then Scipio Aemilianus, and finally the youngest and greatest, Gaius Gracchus—had now been engulfed by the revolution. The memory of the Gracchi remained officially proscribed, and Cornelia was not even allowed to put on mourning for the death of her last son. But the passionate attachment which so many had felt toward the two noble brothers, especially toward Gaius, was touchingly displayed after their deaths in the almost religious veneration which the multitude, in spite of all police prohibition, continued to pay to their memory and to the spots where they had fallen.

III
RULE OF THE RESTORATION

The structure which Gaius Gracchus had reared became a ruin upon his death. His murder, like that of his brother, was primarily an act of vengeance, but it was at the same time a very real step toward restoring the old constitution, in that the monarch was removed just as the monarchy was about to be established. It was all the more so because, after the fall of Gaius and the sweeping and bloody prosecutions of Opimius, there was no one who by blood relationship to the fallen chief or by outstanding ability might feel even tempted to fill the vacant place. Gaius was childless, and Tiberius' son died before reaching manhood; thus the whole popular party was leaderless. The Gracchan constitution resembled a fortress whose walls and garrison were uninjured, but without a commander; and there was no one to fill the leader's place save the very government that had been overthrown.

So it happened. After Gaius' death the Senate spontaneously resumed its place—which was the more natural, because it had not been formally abolished by the tribune, but had been merely reduced to impotence by his exceptional proceedings. Yet we should greatly err if we regarded this restoration as nothing more than a return of the state-machine into the old track that had been trodden for centuries. Restoration is always revolution, but in this case it was rather the old governor than the old government that was restored. The oligarchy reappeared decked in the armor of the overthrown tyrant. As the Senate had beaten Gracchus with his own weapons, so it continued to govern substantially with the Gracchan constitution— though certainly with the idea of purging it in due course of the elements hostile to the aristocracy.

At first the reaction was directed mainly against individuals. Publius Popillius was recalled from banishment after the enactments against him had been canceled (121 B.C.), and a warfare of prosecution was waged against the adherents of Gracchus. The attempt of the popular party to have Lucius Opimius condemned for high treason

after his consulship was frustrated by the government.
The character of the restoration is significantly shown by
the progress of the aristocracy in soundness of sentiment.
The convert Gaius Carbo, once the ally of the Gracchi,
had but recently shown his zeal and usefulness by defending Opimius. But he remained the renegade: when the
same accusation was raised against him as against Opimius, the government was not unwilling to let him fall, and
Carbo, seeing himself lost between the two parties, died
by his own hand.

Thus the men of the reaction showed themselves true
aristocrats in personal questions. But they did not immediately attack the grain distribution, the taxation of the
province of Asia, or the Gracchan arrangement as to the
jurymen and courts. On the contrary, they not only spared
the mercantile class and the city proletariat, but continued to render homage to these groups (as formerly in introducing the Livian laws), cultivating the proletariat
even more than the Gracchi had done. This course was
not adopted merely because the Gracchan revolution
thrilled the minds of contemporaries and protected its
creations. The fostering and cherishing of the populace
was quite compatible with the interests of the aristocracy,
for nothing was sacrificed save the public welfare.

All those measures which Gaius Gracchus devised to
promote the general good—the best, but understandably
the least popular part of his program—were allowed by
the aristocracy to drop. The most speedily and successfully assailed was the noblest of his projects, the scheme
of introducing legal equality first between the Roman citizens and Italy, and thereafter between Italy and the provinces, and—since the distinction between the ruling and
consuming members of the state and the merely serving
and working members was thus done away with—at the
same time solving the social question by the most extensive and systematic emigration in history. With all the
determined and peevish obstinacy of dotage the restored

oligarchy clung to the hoary principle that Italy must remain the ruling land and Rome the ruling city in Italy.

Even in Gracchus' lifetime the claims of the Italian allies had been flatly rejected, and the great idea of overseas colonization had been attacked so seriously as to become the immediate cause of his downfall. After his death the government party easily set aside the scheme of restoring Carthage, although individual allotments already distributed were not disturbed. True, the aristocracy could not prevent the popular party from succeeding at another point: in the course of the conquests beyond the Alps which Marcus Flaccus had begun, the colony of Narbo (Narbonne) was founded in 118 B.C., the oldest city of Roman citizens outside Italy, which, probably protected by the mercantile interests, held its ground against repeated attacks by the government party and despite a Senate proposal to abolish it. But apart from this isolated and relatively unimportant exception, the government was uniformly successful in preventing further distribution of land outside Italy.

The Italian land question was settled in a similar spirit. The Italian colonies founded by Gaius, especially Capua, were canceled, and such of them as had already been planted were again broken up; only the unimportant one of Tarentum was allowed to continue, in the form of the new town of Neptunia, alongside the former Greek community. The domains already distributed by noncolonial assignment remained in the hands of the recipients, the restrictions imposed on them by Gracchus in the public interest—the ground rent and the prohibition of sale—having already been abolished by Marcus Drusus. On the other hand, the domains still possessed by right of occupation—which, except for the domain land enjoyed by the Latins, must have consisted mostly of estates left with their holders in accordance with the Gracchan maximum —were definitely reserved for their occupants, thus precluding the possibility of future distribution. It was pri-

marily from these lands, it seems, that the 36,000 new
farm allotments promised by Drusus were to have been
formed. But the aristocrats saved themselves the trouble
of inquiring where those hundreds of thousands of acres
of Italian public land were to be found, and quietly
shelved the Livian colonial law as having served its purpose. (The small colony of Scolacium is perhaps the only
one attributable to the colonial law of Drusus.) On the
other hand, under a law carried by the tribune Spurius
Thorius at the Senate's instigation, the allotment commission was abolished in 119 B.C., and the occupants of
public land were charged a fixed rent, whose proceeds
went to the benefit of the populace, apparently being
added to the fund for grain distribution. More sweeping
proposals, including perhaps an increase in the largesses of
grain, were averted by the judicious tribune Gaius Marius.

The final step was taken eight years afterward (111
B.C.), when by a new decree of the people the occupied
public land was made the rent-free private property of the
former occupants. The decree added that henceforth public land was not to be occupied at all, but was either to be
leased or was to lie open as public pasture; in the latter
case a very low maximum of ten head of large and fifty
head of small cattle was set, so that the small herdowner
would not be excluded. In these judicious regulations the
character of the occupation system was at last officially
recognized as baneful—but only after the state had been
denuded of practically all its lands. While the aristocracy
thus took care of itself by converting to private property
whatever occupied land was still in its hands, it also pacified the Italian allies, not by conferring on them the title
to the Italian public lands which they and more especially
their municipal aristocracy enjoyed, but merely by preserving unimpaired the rights to it guaranteed by their
charters. The popular party was in the unfortunate position that the most important material interests of the Italian allies ran diametrically counter to those of the prole-

tariat in the capital. In fact, the Italians entered into a kind of league with the Senate, which protected them from the extravagant designs of various popular demagogues.

While the reaction was thus careful to eradicate the germs of civic betterment in the Gracchan constitution, it remained powerless in the face of the darker forces that had been aroused by Gracchus. The city mob retained its recognized right to be fed, and the Senate acquiesced in the selection of jurymen from the mercantile order, repugnant though this yoke was to the better and prouder portion of the aristocracy. The fetters which the aristocracy wore did not beseem its dignity, but we do not find that it seriously sought to get rid of them. The law of Marcus Aemilius Scaurus in 122 B.C., which enforced the constitutional restriction on the voting of freedmen, was for long the only attempt (and that a very tame one) by the senators to restrain their mob tyrants. The proposal which the consul Quintus Caepio introduced in 106 B.C. for again entrusting trials to senatorial jurymen showed what the government wished, but it also showed how little it could do when the question was not one of squandering the public domains, but of carrying a measure against the desire of an entrenched order.

Not only was the government not emancipated from the inconvenient associates who shared its power, but these measures probably contributed further to disturb the uneasy agreement of the ruling aristocracy with the merchant class and with the proletariat. Both the latter were well aware that the Senate granted its concessions reluctantly and only from fear; neither group was permanently attached to the rule of the Senate by considerations of either gratitude or interest; both were ready to render similar services to any other master who offered more, or even as much; neither would hesitate, if opportunity arose, to thwart or undermine the Senate. Thus the restoration combined the sentiments of a legitimate aris-

tocracy with the governmental machinery of a tyrant. Its
rule not only rested on the same foundations as that of
Gracchus, but was less soundly consolidated. It was strong
when it joined hands with the populace to overthrow useful innovations, but it was utterly powerless when it had
to face the street mob or the entrenched merchants. It sat
on the throne with bad conscience and divided hopes, indignant at the institutions of the state which it ruled, and
yet incapable even of systematically assailing them, vacillating in all its conduct except where its own material advantage prompted a decision, a picture of faithlessness toward its own as well as the opposite party, of inward
inconsistency, of pitiful impotence, of the meanest selfishness—an unsurpassed ideal of misrule.

It could not be otherwise when the whole nation was
in a state of intellectual and moral decline, especially the
upper classes. The aristocracy before the period of the
Gracchi was not overly rich in talent, and the senate
benches were crowded by a pack of cowardly and dissolute nobles. Nevertheless there sat in it Scipio Aemilianus, Gaius Laelius, Quintus Metellus, Publius Crassus,
Publius Scaevola, and numerous other respectable and
able men, and a friendly observer might maintain that
the Senate showed a certain moderation in injustice and
a certain decorum in misgovernment.

On this aristocracy, overthrown and then reinstated,
lay the curse of restoration. For more than a century
they had governed without appreciable opposition; then
crisis revealed like a flash of lightning in a dark night
the abyss yawning beneath their feet. Was it any wonder that thereafter rancor always, and terror whenever
they dared, characterized the government of the nobility? Or that those who governed confronted the non-
governing multitude as a united and compact party, with
far more sternness and violence than before? Or that
family interests prevailed again, just as in the worst patrician days of old, so that the four sons and (probably)

the two nephews of Quintus Metellus (not to mention
sons-in-law and collateral relations)—with a single exception utterly insignificant men, some of whom, indeed,
were called to office because of their very simplicity—
within a fifteen-year period (123-109 B.C.) attained not
only the consulship but military triumphs as well? Or
that the more violent and cruel was the bearing of their
partisans toward the popular party, the more signally
were they honored, while every outrage and infamy were
pardoned in the genuine aristocrat? Or that rulers and
ruled resembled two parties at war, and in a warfare
which recognized no international law? It was unhappily
only too palpable that if the old aristocracy beat the
people with whips, this restored aristocracy chastised it
with scorpions. It returned to power, but it returned neither wiser nor better. Never before had the Roman ruling class been so utterly deficient in men of statesmanly
and military capacity.[1]

The administration, internal and external, was what
might be expected from such a government. The social
ruin of Italy spread with alarming rapidity. Since the
aristocracy had given itself legal permission to buy out
the small holders, and in its new arrogance allowed itself with growing frequency to drive them out without
pretense of purchase, the small farms disappeared like
raindrops in the sea. That the economic oligarchy at least
kept pace with the political is shown by the opinion of
Lucius Marcius Philippus, a man of moderate democratic
views, that about 100 B.C. there were hardly 2,000 well-
to-do families in the whole state. A practical corrobora-
tion was furnished by the Italian slave revolts which during the early years of the Cimbrian war broke out at
Nuceria, at Capua, and in the territory of Thurii. This

---

1. A paragraph omitted here describes Marcus Aemilius Scaurus, a leading "statesman" of his day, who, though "quite as accessible and bribable
as any other upright senator," could "discern with some cunning the moment when the matter began to be hazardous."

last conspiracy was so important that the urban praetor
had to march against it with a legion, and actually
overcame the insurrection not by force of arms but by
treachery.[2]

The provinces suffered still more. The legislation
which gave the mercantile class control over the magistrates compelled the latter to make common cause with
the former, and to purchase unlimited liberty of plundering without impeachment by unlimited indulgence toward the capitalists in the provinces. In addition to these
official and semiofficial robbers, pirates and freebooters
pillaged all the Mediterranean countries. In Asiatic waters especially the buccaneers carried their outrages so
far that even the Roman government was forced in
102 B.C. to dispatch to Cilicia a fleet, mainly composed
of vessels of the dependent mercantile cities, under the
praetor Marcus Antonius, who was invested with proconsular powers. This fleet captured a number of pirate
vessels and destroyed some strongholds, and the Romans
even settled themselves permanently in strong military
positions—the first step toward establishing the province of Cilicia, which thereafter appears among the Roman dominions. The purpose was commendable, but the
increase of piracy in Asiatic waters, and especially in
Cilicia, showed with what inadequate means the pirates
were combated from the new position.

Nowhere were the impotence and stupidity of the Roman provincial administration so conspicuously revealed
as in its handling of the slave insurrections, which seemed
to have revived simultaneously with the restoration of
the aristocracy. These uprisings, swelling from revolts
into wars—the one that emerged about 134 B.C. was perhaps the immediate cause of the Gracchan revolution—

2. In the original, Mommsen proceeds to describe briefly the leader of
the Thurian revolt, a debt-crazed Roman knight named Titus Vettius, and
notes the fear that led the Senate to halt certain gold-washing operations
lest too many slaves be concentrated in one place.

were renewed and repeated with dreary uniformity. Again, as thirty years before, a ferment pervaded the body of slaves throughout the empire. We have already mentioned the Italian conspiracies. The miners in the Attic silver mines rose in revolt, occupied the promontory of Sunium, and issuing thence pillaged freely in the surrounding country. Similar movements appeared at other places.[3] But the chief seat of these fearful commotions was once again Sicily, with its vast plantations and its hordes of slaves brought from Asia Minor. Anyone who still required proof of the quality of the internal government of the restored aristocracy might be referred to the origin and conduct of this second Sicilian slave war, which lasted for five years.

Wherever the eye might turn throughout the empire, the same causes and the same effects appeared. If the Sicilian slave war showed the government's incompetence even in its simplest task of keeping the slaves in check, simultaneous events in Africa highlighted the skill with which the Romans governed satellite states. At the same time the Sicilian slave war broke out, the astonished world beheld the spectacle of an insignificant dependent prince carrying out a fourteen years' usurpation and insurrection against the very republic which had shattered the kingdoms of Macedonia and Asia with one blow of its mighty hand.

The kingdom of Numidia was bordered on the one side by the Mauretanian kingdom of Tingis (the modern Morocco) and on the other by Cyrene and Egypt; it surrounded on the west, south, and east the narrow strip of coast that formed the Roman province of Africa. In addition to the old possessions of the Numidian chiefs, it embraced the great bulk of the African territory which Car-

3. A short section here omitted describes the Sicilian slave war of 104-99 B.C., in which the diligence of the slave leaders was more than matched by the incompetence of a succession of Roman commanders. The Roman victory was finally won in 99 B.C. by the consul Manius Aquillius.

thage had possessed during her heyday, including such
important cities as Hippo Regius (Bona) and Great
Leptis (Lebidah)—altogether the largest and best part
of the rich North African coast. Next to Egypt, Numidia
was unquestionably the most important Roman protectorate. After the death of Numidia's king Massinissa in
149 B.C., Scipio had so divided the powers of that prince
among his three sons Micipsa, Gulussa, and Mastanabal
that the firstborn obtained the palace and treasury, the
second the command of the army, and the third the administration of justice. Following the death of his two
brothers, the eldest, Micipsa, reigned alone, a feeble,
peaceful old man, more interested in the study of Greek
philosophy than in affairs of state. As his sons were not
yet grown, the reins of government were practically held
by his illegitimate nephew, Jugurtha.

Jugurtha was a worthy grandson of Massinissa. He
was a handsome man and a skilled and courageous rider
and hunter. His countrymen esteemed him as a clear and
sagacious administrator, and he had displayed his military ability as leader of the Numidian contingent before
Numantia under the eyes of Scipio. His position, and his
influence through his numerous friends and war comrades, made Micipsa decide to adopt him (120 B.C.),
and to make a will providing that his adopted son, Jugurtha, and his own two elder sons, Adherbal and Hiempsal, should jointly inherit and govern the kingdom just
as he himself had done with his two brothers. For greater
security, the Roman government guaranteed this arrangement.

Soon afterward, in 118 B.C., Micipsa died. But despite the provisions of the will, his legitimate sons—
the vehement Hiempsal still more than his weak elder
brother—soon came into violent collision with their
cousin, whom they regarded as an intruder. The idea of
a joint reign had to be abandoned. An attempt was made
to divide the heritage, but the quarrelsome trio could not

agree on their quotas of land and treasure, while the Roman government, which had the power to decide the matter, stood idly by as usual. A rupture took place, with Adherbal and Hiempsal characterizing their father's testament as spurious and disputing Jugurtha's claim, and Jugurtha coming forward as pretender to the whole kingdom. While the partition was still being discussed, Hiempsal was murdered by hired assassins; then a civil war broke out between Adherbal and Jugurtha. With his less numerous but better-disciplined and better-led troops Jugurtha seized the whole kingdom, cruelly persecuting the chiefs who adhered to his cousin. Adherbal escaped to the Roman province and proceeded to Rome to lodge his complaint.

Jugurtha had expected this, and was prepared for the threatened intervention. In the camp before Numantia he had learned more from Rome than military tactics. The Numidian prince, moving in Roman aristocratic circles, was at the same time initiated into the intrigues of Roman political cliques, and learned at first hand what might be expected from Roman nobles. Even then, sixteen years before Micipsa's death, he had entered into disloyal negotiations with influential Romans regarding the Numidian succession, and Scipio had found it necessary to admonish him that foreign princes should properly seek the friendship of the Roman state rather than that of individual Romans. Now, in the negotiations over the partition, the envoys of Jugurtha appeared in Rome armed with more than words, and the result showed that they had chosen the right means of persuasion. Adherbal's most zealous champions were convinced with incredible rapidity that Hiempsal had been put to death by his subjects on account of his cruelty, and that Adherbal was the aggressor in the war between him and Jugurtha.

Even the leading men in the Senate were shocked at the scandal, which Marcus Scaurus vainly sought to check.

The Senate silently passed over what had taken place. It ordained that the two surviving heirs should divide the kingdom equally between them, and that, in the interests of amity, the division should be supervised by a commission of the Senate. This was done: the ex-consul Lucius Opimius, well known for his services in crushing the Gracchan revolution, embraced the opportunity of reaping the rewards of his patriotism, and got himself placed at the head of the commission. Its decision turned out thoroughly in favor of Jugurtha, and not to the disadvantage of the commissioners. It is true that the capital, Cirta, with its port of Rusicade, was given to Adherbal. But by the same token there also fell to him the eastern part of the kingdom, consisting almost wholly of desert, while Jugurtha obtained the fertile and populous western half.

This was bad enough, but matters soon became worse. In order to defraud Adherbal of his portion, Jugurtha, under the pretext of self-defense, sought to provoke him to war. But when that weak man, rendered wise by experience, allowed Jugurtha's horsemen to ravage his territory unhindered and contented himself with lodging complaints at Rome, Jugurtha impatiently began the war without pretext. Adherbal was totally defeated near Rusicade, and threw himself into his adjacent capital of Cirta. While the siege was in progress, and Jugurtha's troops were skirmishing daily with the numerous Italians who were settled in Cirta and who took a more vigorous part in the defense of the city than the Africans themselves, the commission dispatched by the Senate on Adherbal's first complaint made its appearance. It was composed, of course, of inexperienced young men, such as the government then regularly employed in ordinary missions of state.

The envoys demanded that Jugurtha should allow them to enter the city, and that he should suspend hostilities and accept their mediation. Jugurtha summarily

rejected both demands, and the envoys hastened home—
like the boys they were—to report to the city fathers. The
Senate listened to the report, and allowed their countrymen in Cirta to fight on as long as they pleased. It was
not until a messenger of Adherbal's stole through the
enemy's entrenchments in the fifth month of the siege,
with a letter to the Senate full of the most urgent entreaties, that the latter roused itself and actually adopted
a resolution. It did not declare war, as the minority demanded, but sent a new embassy—an embassy, however,
headed by Marcus Scaurus, the great "conqueror" of the
Taurisci and the freedmen, the imposing hero of the aristocracy, whose mere appearance would surely bring the
refractory prince to heel. Jugurtha did indeed appear at
Utica as he was bidden, to discuss the matter with Scaurus. Endless debates were held, until the conference was
at last concluded without the slightest result having been
obtained. The embassy returned to Rome without declaring war, and the king returned to the siege of Cirta.
Adherbal, reduced to the last extremity, despaired of Roman support; and the Italians in Cirta, weary of the siege
and relying for their own safety on the terror of the Roman name, urged a surrender. The town capitulated.
Jugurtha condemned his adopted brother to death by torture, and ordered the entire adult male population of the
town, Italians as well as Africans, to be put to the sword.

A cry of indignation arose throughout Italy. The minority in the Senate and all citizens outside the Senate
unanimously condemned the government, which seemed to
regard the honor and interest of the nation as mere com-
modities for sale; and loudest of all was the outcry of the
mercantile class, which was most directly affected by the
sacrifice of the Roman and Italian merchants at Cirta.
Even now the majority of the Senate still struggled. They
appealed to the class interests of the aristocracy, setting
in motion all the contrivances of delay with a view to
preserving a little longer the peace that they loved. But

when Gaius Memmius, tribune-elect, an active and eloquent man, threatened publicly to call the worst offenders
to trial, the Senate permitted war to be declared against
Jugurtha.

The step seemed taken in earnest. The envoys of Jugurtha were summarily dismissed from Italy without a
hearing; the new consul Lucius Calpurnius Bestia, who
was distinguished at least among his fellow senators by
his judgment and activity, vigorously prepared for war;
Marcus Scaurus himself took a post as commander in the
African army. In a short time a Roman force was on
African ground, marching upward along the Bagradas
and advancing into the Numidian kingdom, where the
towns most remote from the seat of royal power, such as
Great Leptis, voluntarily sent in their submission. Boc-
chus, king of Mauretania, though the father-in-law of
Jugurtha, offered friendship and alliance to the Romans.
Jugurtha himself lost courage, and sent envoys to the
Roman headquarters to request an armistice.

The end of the contest seemed near, but it came even
more rapidly than was expected, and with an unforeseen
result. The treaty with Bocchus broke down because that
king, unfamiliar with Roman customs, had conceived that
he should be able to conclude a treaty so advantageous to
the Romans without bribery, and had therefore neglected
to furnish his envoys with the usual market price of Roman favors. Jugurtha knew better, and had not failed to
support his proposals for an armistice with an accompani-
ment of money. But he too was deceived: after the first
negotiations it turned out that not merely an armistice
but a final peace was purchasable at the Roman headquarters. The royal treasury was still rich with the savings of Massinissa, and the transaction was soon settled.
The treaty was concluded after a routine submission to
a council of war, which gave its consent after an irregular
and extremely summary discussion. Jugurtha ostensibly
submitted, but the merciful victor returned his kingdom

undiminished, in consideration of his paying a moderate fine and delivering up the Roman deserters and the war elephants. Most of the latter the king afterward repurchased by bargaining with individual Roman officers.

With this news a storm again broke in Rome. Everybody knew how the peace had been brought about; evidently even Scaurus was bribable, only at a higher than average price. The legality of the peace was seriously assailed in the Senate. Gaius Memmius declared that if the king had really surrendered unconditionally, he could not refuse to appear in Rome, and that he should therefore be summoned with a view to hearing from both sides how the thoroughly irregular negotiations for peace were carried on. The senators yielded to the inconvenient demand, but at the same time granted a safe-conduct to the king—inconsistent with his status, for he came not as an enemy, but as a suppliant.

Thereupon the king actually appeared at Rome and sought to be heard before the people, who were with difficulty restrained from tearing him to pieces as the murderer of the Italians at Cirta. But scarcely had Gaius Memmius addressed his first question to the king when one of his colleagues interposed his veto and enjoined the king to be silent. Here again African gold had been more powerful than the will of the sovereign people and their supreme representatives. Meanwhile the Senate debated the validity of the peace, with the new consul Spurius Postumius Albinus zealously seeking to cancel it in the expectation that the chief command in Africa would then devolve upon himself. This induced Massiva, a grandson of Massinissa living in Rome, to assert before the Senate his claim to the vacant Numidian kingdom. Thereupon Bomilcar, one of Jugurtha's confidants and doubtless acting on his instructions, had his master's rival assassinated, and when he was prosecuted for it, escaped from Rome with Jugurtha's aid.

This new outrage committed under the very nose of the

Roman government at least had the effect that the Senate now canceled the peace treaty and dismissed the king from the city. The war was resumed, and the consul Spurius Albinus was placed in command. But the African army was as disorganized as might be expected under such political and military superintendence. Not only had discipline ceased, and the looting of Numidian townships and even of Roman provincial territory become during the armistice the chief business of the Roman soldiery, but not a few officers had imitated their generals and made secret understandings with the enemy. Such an army was obviously powerless in the field, and if Jugurtha bribed the Roman general into inaction, as was afterward charged, he was but gilding the lily. Spurius Albinus therefore contented himself with doing nothing.

On the other hand, his brother, the equally foolhardy and incapable Aulus Postumius, who after Spurius' departure assumed the interim command, came up with the idea of seizing the treasures of the king by a bold midwinter *coup de main*. The gold was kept in the town of Suthul, which was difficult even to approach, and still more difficult to conquer. The army reached the town, but the siege was totally unsuccessful. Then the king, who had remained for a time with his troops in front of the town, went into the desert, and the Roman general sought to pursue him. This was precisely what Jugurtha wanted. In a nocturnal assault, favored both by the difficulties of the ground and Jugurtha's secret understandings with certain officers, the Numidians captured the Roman camp and drove the largely unarmed Romans before them in a complete and disgraceful rout. The terms of the capitulation —the marching off of the Roman army under the yoke, the immediate evacuation of all Numidia, and the reinstatement of the canceled treaty—were dictated by Jugurtha and accepted by the Romans early in the year 109 B.C.

This was too much to be borne. So exultant were the

Africans at the sudden and incredible prospect of an overthrow of alien domination that numerous tribes of the
desert flocked to the standards of the victorious king. But
public opinion in Italy vehemently rose against the corrupt and pernicious governing aristocracy, and broke out
in a storm of prosecutions, reflecting the special exasperation of the mercantile class, which swept away a succession of victims from the highest circles of the nobility.
On the proposal of the tribune Gaius Mamilius Lime-
tanus, and despite the timid attempts of the Senate to
avert the threatened punishment, an extraordinary jury
commission was appointed to investigate the alleged high
treason in connection with the Numidian succession settlement and the conduct of the war. It exiled the two former
commanders, Gaius Bestia and Spurius Albinus, and also
Lucius Opimius, the head of the first African commission
and the executioner of Gaius Gracchus, along with numerous less notable men of the government party.

That these prosecutions, however, were only a sop to
a section of public opinion, especially in mercantile circles,
and that there was little trace of popular indignation
against the contemptible government itself, is shown
clearly by the fact that no one ventured to attack the
guiltiest of the guilty—the prudent and powerful Marcus
Scaurus. On the contrary he was elected censor and, incredible as it may seem, was also chosen as one of the
presidents of the extraordinary commission. Still less was
there any attempt to interfere with the functions of the
government, and it was left solely to the Senate to end
the Numidian scandal in the gentlest manner possible for
the aristocracy. That it was time to do so was probably
becoming clear even to the most Bourbon of the aristocrats.

The Senate first canceled the second treaty of peace—
it somehow did not seem necessary to surrender to the
enemy the commander who had concluded it—and determined to renew the war, this time in all earnest. The su-

preme command in Africa was naturally entrusted to an
aristocrat, but to one of the few men of quality militarily
and morally equal to the task. Quintus Metellus was, like
the whole powerful family to which he belonged, a rigid
and unscrupulous aristocrat. As a magistrate, he doubtless reckoned it honorable to hire assassins for the good
of the state, and would presumably have ridiculed the
act of Fabricius toward Pyrrhus [4] as impractical knight-
errantry. But he was an inflexible administrator accessible
neither to fear nor to corruption, and he was also a judicious and experienced warrior.

In this last respect he was so free from prejudice that
he selected as his lieutenants not men of rank, but such
excellent officers as Publius Rutilius Rufus, esteemed in
military circles for his exemplary discipline and as the
author of an improved manual of drill, and the brave
Latin farmer's son Gaius Marius, who had risen from
the ranks. Attended by these and other able officers, Metellus presented himself to the African army in 109 B.C.
as consul and commander-in-chief. He found the army in
such disorder that the generals had not dared to lead it
into enemy territory; it was formidable only to the unhappy inhabitants of the Roman province. It was sternly
and speedily reorganized, and in the spring of 108 B.C.
Metellus led it over the Numidian frontier.

When Jugurtha saw the new face of things he gave
himself up for lost, and before beginning the struggle
made earnest proposals for an accommodation that would
ultimately have guaranteed nothing more than his life.
Metellus, however, was determined and perhaps even instructed not to end the war except with unconditional
surrender and the death of the daring prince—in fact the

---

4. Gaius Fabricius, a Roman envoy to King Pyrrhus of Epirus early in
the third century B.C., refused the king's bribe and also arranged for the
temporary release of some Roman prisoners on the solemn promise that
they would return. Over the years the incident came to symbolize honesty
carried to the point of a fault.

only outcome that could satisfy the Romans. Since his victory over Albinus, Jugurtha was regarded as the deliverer of Libya from the rule of the hated foreigner. Unscrupulous and cunning as he was, and unwieldy as was the Roman government, he might, if not crushed, at any time rekindle the war. Tranquillity could not be restored and the African army withdrawn until Jugurtha was in his grave. Officially Metellus gave evasive answers to the king's proposals; secretly he sought to persuade the envoys to deliver up their master, alive or dead. But the Roman general met his match in the field of assassination. Jugurtha saw through the plan, and prepared for desperate resistance.

Beyond the barren mountain range over which lay the route into the interior, a desert plain some eighteen miles wide extended as far as the river Muthul, which ran parallel to the mountains. This plain was bare of trees except in the immediate vicinity of the river, and was only intersected by a low ridge covered with brushwood. On this ridge Jugurtha awaited the Roman army. His troops were arranged in two masses: the first, consisting of a part of the infantry and the elephants, was disposed under Bomilcar at the point where the ridge abutted the river; the second, including the flower of the infantry and all the cavalry, was concealed in the brush higher up toward the mountain range. Upon leaving the mountains, the Romans saw the enemy in a position completely commanding their right flank; yet they had to leave the arid crests and reach the river over an open plain eighteen miles broad, under the eyes of the enemy's horse, and without light cavalry of their own. To solve this difficult problem Metellus dispatched a detachment under Rufus straight toward the river to pitch a camp, while the main body marched from the defiles of the mountains obliquely across the plain toward the ridge to dislodge the enemy there.

This march, however, threatened to destroy the army;

for while Numidian infantry occupied the mountain defiles as the Romans evacuated them, the main Roman col-
umn was assailed on all sides by swarms of enemy horsemen charging down from the ridge. Their constant onset
hindered the advance and threatened to turn the battle
into a series of confused and detached conflicts. At the
same time Bomilcar detained the corps under Rufus, to
prevent it from returning to help the main Roman army.

At last Metellus and Marius with a couple of thousand
soldiers succeeded in reaching the foot of the ridge; and
the Numidian infantry defending the heights, despite
their superior numbers and position, fled almost without
resistance when the legionaries charged rapidly up the
hill. The Numidian infantry facing Rufus held its ground
equally ill: it scattered at the first charge, and all its elephants were killed or captured. Late in the evening the
two Roman divisions, each victorious and each anxious as
to the other's fate, met between the two fields of battle.
The engagement attested alike Jugurtha's uncommon
military talent and the indestructible solidity of the Roman infantry, which alone had converted the strategic
defeat into a victory. Jugurtha sent most of his troops
home after the battle, and restricted himself to a skillful
guerilla warfare.

The two Roman columns, one led by Metellus and the
other by Marius—who, though of humble birth and rank,
occupied the highest staff position since the battle on the
Muthul—occupied the Numidian towns, putting to death
the adult male population of any place that did not open
its gates. But the largest of the eastern towns, Zama,
offered the Romans serious resistance, which Jugurtha
energetically supported. He even succeeded in surprising
the Roman camp, and the Romans were at last compelled
to abandon the siege and go into winter quarters. To provision his army more easily, Metellus transferred it to
the Roman province, leaving garrisons in the conquered

towns, and used the respite to institute fresh negotiations promising the king a tolerable peace.

Jugurtha readily responded. He agreed to pay 200,000 pounds of silver, and even delivered his elephants and 300 hostages, plus 3,000 Roman deserters, who were immediately put to death. At the same time, however, Bomilcar—who feared quite reasonably that upon the restoration of peace Jugurtha would surrender him to the Roman courts as the murderer of Massiva—was promised by Metellus rich rewards and judicial immunity if he would deliver the king dead or alive. But neither the official negotiation nor the intrigue was successful. When Metellus suggested that the king give himself up as a prisoner, the latter broke off negotiations. Bomilcar's confidential dealing with the Romans was unmasked, and he was arrested and executed.

These contemptible cabals admit of no apology, but the Romans had every reason to aim at securing the person of their antagonist. The war had reached the point where it could neither be carried further nor abandoned. The state of feeling in Numidia was shown by the revolt of Vaga, the most considerable of the occupied cities, where the whole Roman garrison was put to death except for the commandant Titus Turpilius Silanus, who was afterward (whether justly or not we cannot say) condemned by a Roman court-martial for dealing with the enemy. The town was surprised by Metellus on the second day of the revolt, and given over to the rigors of martial law. If such was the temper of the accessible and submissive dwellers on the banks of the Bagradas, what must have been the mood of the roving desert tribes? Jugurtha was the idol of the Africans, who readily overlooked a double fratricide by the liberator and avenger of their nation. When twenty years afterward a Numidian corps fighting for the Romans in Italy had to be sent back in all haste to Africa, because the son of Jugurtha appeared in the enemy ranks, we may infer how great was the influence which the king exercised over his people. How could a war be ended in a country whose geography and population allowed a leader who had won the sympathies of the nation to protract the struggle in endless guerilla conflicts, or even to let it die for a time in order to revive it afresh at the right moment?

When Metellus took the field in 107 B.C., Jugurtha nowhere held his ground. He appeared now at one point, now at another far distant, and it seemed as if one could as easily conquer the desert lions as these horsemen. A battle was fought, a victory was won, but it was difficult to say what the victory had gained, for the king had vanished into the distance. In the interior of modern Tunis, on the edge of the great desert, lay the fortified oasis Thala, where Jugurtha had retired with his children, his treasures, and his best troops to await better times. Metellus followed the king across a desert where the troops had to carry their water in skins for forty-five miles. Thala fell after a forty days' siege, but the Roman deserters destroyed the most valuable part of the booty, along with the building in which they ended their lives in a flaming pyre after the capture of the town. And more important, Jugurtha escaped with his children and his treasure.

Thus the virtual conquest of all Numidia seemed only to extend the war over a wider and wider area. In the south the free desert tribes heeded Jugurtha's call for a national war against the Romans. In the west King Bocchus of Mauretania, whose friendship the Romans had despised, seemed now disposed to make common cause with his son-in-law. He received him in his court and, uniting his own numberless swarms of horsemen with Jugurtha's followers, marched into the Cirta region where Metellus was in winter quarters. They began to negotiate, for it was clear that Bocchus held in the person of Jugurtha the real prize of the struggle. But whether his intentions were to sell his son-in-law dearly, or to take up the national war together with him, neither the Romans, nor Jugurtha, nor perhaps even the king himself knew; and he was in no hurry to abandon his ambiguous position.

At this point Metellus left the province, compelled by decree of the people to yield his command to his former lieutenant Marius, who was now consul. In 107 B.C. the latter assumed his new duties. For his high position he was indebted in some degree to a revolution. Relying both on the services he had rendered and on oracles which had been communicated to him, he had resolved to seek the consulship. If the aristocracy had supported the constitutional and quite proper candidacy of this able man, who was not at all inclined toward the opposition, nothing would have occurred but the enrollment of a new family in the consular list. Instead, this man of non-noble birth, who aspired to the highest public honor, was reviled by the whole governing crowd as a daring innovator and revolutionist—just as plebeian candidates had formerly been treated by the patricians, but now without any legal ground. Metellus sneered at the brave officer in sharp language: Marius was advised to delay his candidacy until Metellus' son, a beardless boy, could be his colleague, and he was allowed with the worst possible grace a leave of absence from military service that he might appear in Rome as a candidate for the consulship for 107 B.C.

There he amply requited his general for the insults he had suffered by criticizing before the gaping populace the conduct of the African war and the administration of Metellus in a disgracefully unfair and unmilitary manner. He did not disdain to serve up to the multitude (always whispering incredible inside stories about secret conspiracies among their noble masters) the silly tale that Metellus was purposely protracting the war in order to remain commander-in-chief. To the idlers of the street this

seemed quite obvious, while numerous persons unfriendly
to the government, and especially the justly indignant
mercantile order, desired nothing so much as an opportunity to goad the aristocracy at its most sensitive point.
Marius was not only elected to the consulship by an enormous majority, but, although the law of Gaius Gracchus
left with the Senate the assignment of consuls to their respective functions, in this case the arrangement which left
Metellus at his post was revoked by decree of the sovereign people, and the supreme command of the African
war was given to Marius.

Marius replaced Metellus in 107 B.C., and held the
command during the campaign of the following year. But
his confident promise to deliver Jugurtha bound hand and
foot was more easily given than fulfilled. He carried on
a desultory warfare with the desert tribes, reducing several previously unoccupied towns. He mounted an expedition to Capsa in the extreme southeast of the kingdom,
surpassing in difficulty even that against Thala. He took
the town by capitulation, and, in violation of the convention, ordered all the adult men to be slain—the only
means, no doubt, of preventing a renewal of revolt in that
remote city. He attacked a mountain stronghold on the
river Molochath where Jugurtha had conveyed his treas-
ure-chest, and just as he was about to abandon the siege
as hopeless, he gained possession of the virtually impregnable place through the exploit of some daring climbers.

Had Marius' object merely been to harden the army
by bold raids, or to procure booty for the soldiers, or even
to eclipse Metellus' desert march by an expedition going
still farther, his method of campaign might be justified.
But the main object which Metellus had steadfastly and
perseveringly kept in view—the capture of Jugurtha—
was in this way quite forgotten. Marius' expedition to
Capsa was as aimless a venture as that of Metellus to
Thala had been judicious, while the expedition to the
Molochath, which passed along the border of Maure-

tanian territory, was directly contrary to sound policy. King Bocchus, who could end the war favorably for the Romans or prolong it endlessly, now concluded a treaty with Jugurtha in which he promised active support to his son-in-law against Rome.

The Roman army, returning from the river Molochath, one evening found itself surrounded by immense masses of Mauretanian and Numidian cavalry, and was obliged to fight just as the divisions stood without forming in proper order and without any plan of battle. The Romans deemed themselves fortunate when their sadly thinned troops achieved safety for the night on two hills not far from each other. But the culpable negligence of the rejoicing Africans cost them the fruits of victory. They allowed themselves to be surprised in a deep sleep during the early dawn, and were dispersed by the Roman troops, which had been partly reorganized during the night. Thereafter the Roman army continued its retreat in better order and with greater caution; but it was again assailed simultaneously on all sides, and was in great danger until the cavalry officer Lucius Cornelius Sulla first dispersed the squadrons opposed to him and then, rapidly returning from their pursuit, threw himself upon Jugurtha and Bocchus where they personally led the onslaught against the Romans. Thus this attack also was successfully repelled, and Marius brought his army back to Cirta, its winter quarters.

We can understand why the Romans even now began to make the most zealous overtures to King Bocchus, whose friendship they had at first spurned, and who was now openly an enemy. There had been no formal declaration of war by Mauretania. King Bocchus was willing to resume his ambiguous role: without dissolving his agreement with Jugurtha or dismissing him, he began negotiations with the Roman general regarding an alliance with Rome. When agreement seemed to have been reached, the king requested that, for concluding the treaty and receiving the royal captive, Marius would send to him Lucius Sulla, who was known and acceptable to the king partly as a former envoy at the Mauretanian court, and partly because of the esteem of Mauretanian envoys to Rome whom Sulla had befriended.

Marius was in an awkward position. To decline the suggestion would probably lead to a breach of the negotiations; to accept it would throw his bravest and most aristocratic officer into the hands of an untrustworthy man who was patently playing a double game, and who seemed almost to have contrived the scheme to provide himself with hostages from both sides in the persons of Jugurtha and Sulla. But the desire to end the war outweighed all else, and Sulla agreed to undertake the perilous task. He boldly departed under the guidance of King Bocchus' son Volux, nor did he waver even when his guide led him through the midst of Jugurtha's camp. He rejected his attendants' cowardly proposals of flight, and marched beside the king's son uninjured through the enemy. The daring officer showed the same decisiveness in the discussions with Bocchus, who was at last compelled to make his choice.

Jugurtha was sacrificed. Under the pretext that all his requests were to be granted, he was lured into an ambush by his own father-in-law, his attendants were killed, and he himself was taken prisoner. The great traitor thus fell by the treachery of his closest kin. Sulla brought the crafty African in chains, together with his children, to the Roman headquarters.

The war which had lasted for seven years was at an end. The victory was primarily associated with the name of Marius. King Jugurtha in royal robes and in chains, along with his two sons, preceded the triumphal chariot when Marius entered Rome on the first of January, 104 B.C. By Marius' order the desert fox perished a few days later in the subterranean city prison, the old *Tullianum* at the Capitol—the "bath of ice," as the African called it when he crossed the threshold to be strangled or to perish from cold and hunger there.

But it could not be denied that Marius had the least important share in the final victory. The conquest of Numidia up to the desert's edge was the work of Metellus; the capture of Jugurtha was the work of Sulla; between the two Marius played a part scarcely in keeping with the dignity of an ambitious upstart. He reluctantly tolerated Metellus' assumption of the name of conqueror of Numidia, and he flew into a violent rage when King Bocchus consecrated a golden effigy at the Capitol representing the surrender of Jugurtha to Sulla. Yet in the eyes of unprejudiced judges the services of these two put the generalship of Marius very much in the shade—especially Sulla's brilliant expedition, which made his courage, his presence of mind, his acuteness, and his power over men apparent to the general himself and to the whole army. These military rivalries would have been trifling if they had not been mixed up with political conflicts, if the opposition had not supplanted the Senate's general by Marius, and if the government party had not, with deliberate intent to exasperate, praised Metellus and still more Sulla as military celebrities preferable to the nominal victor. The fatal consequences of these animosities will be seen in narrating the internal history.

Except for this, the Numidian insurrection passed without producing notable changes in political relations generally or even in those of the African province. Contrary to general policy in this period, Numidia was not converted into a Roman province, doubtless because it could not be held without an army to protect the frontier against the barbarians of the desert; and the Romans were certainly not disposed to maintain a standing army in Africa. They accordingly contented themselves with annexing the most westerly district of Numidia to the kingdom of Bocchus, and handing over the rest of Numidia to the last legitimate grandson of Massinissa, Jugurtha's half-brother Gauda, feeble in body and mind, who in 107 B.C. at the suggestion of Marius had asserted his claims before the Senate. At the same time the Gaetulian tribes of the interior were received as free allies among the independent nations that had treaties with Rome.

Of more importance than this regulation of the African protectorates were the political consequences of the Jugurthan war, though these have often been overestimated. To be sure, the evils of the government were revealed in all their nakedness. It was now judicially established, so to speak, that Rome's rulers regarded everything as venal—the treaty of peace and the right of intercession, the ramparts of the camp and the life of the soldier. Jugurtha merely spoke the truth when on leaving Rome he remarked that, if he had enough gold, he could buy the city itself.

The whole external and internal government of this period showed the same miserable baseness. The accidental fact that the war in Africa is more fully recounted to us than the other contemporary events distorts the perspective: nothing but what everybody had long known and what every diligent patriot had long been able to prove was revealed to contemporaries by these events. The fact, however, that they now had fresh, stronger, and more irrefutable proofs of the baseness of the restored senatorial government—a baseness surpassed only by its incompetence—might have been of importance if there had been an opposition and a public opinion to which the government must answer. But this war exposed the utter impotence of the opposition no less than it revealed the corruption of the government. It was impossible to govern worse than the restoration governed in the years 117-109 B.C.; it was impossible to be more defenseless and forlorn than was the Roman Senate in 109 B.C. Had there been a real opposition—that is, a party seeking a fundamental change in the constitution—

it would at least have made the attempt to overturn the restored Senate. No such attempt took place. The political question was converted into a personal one, the generals were changed, and one or two useless and unimportant people were banished.

Thus it was settled that the so-called popular party neither could nor would govern; that only two forms of government were possible in Rome, a tyranny or an oligarchy; that so long as there was nobody sufficiently prominent to grasp the reins of state, the worst mismanagement merely endangered individual oligarchs, but never the oligarchy; and that as soon as a vigorous pretender appeared, nothing was easier than to shake the rotten curule chairs. In this respect the appearance of Marius was significant, just because it was so utterly unwarranted. It would have been only natural if the citizens had stormed the senate house after the defeat of Albinus. But after Metellus had taken charge of the Numidian war, there was little further mismanagement and still less danger to the commonwealth; yet the first ambitious officer who turned up succeeded in doing what the elder Africanus had once threatened, and secured one of the principal military commands against the will of the governing body. Public opinion, powerless in the hands of the popular party, became irresistible in the hands of the future king of Rome.

This is not to say that Marius meant to play the pretender, at least when he asked the people for the supreme command in Africa. But whether or not he understood what he was doing, it was the beginning of the end of the restoration government when the comitial machine began to make generals, or, what amounted to the same thing, when every popular officer was legally able to nominate himself as general. Only one new element emerged in these preliminary crises—the introduction of military men and of military power into the political revolution. Whether the appearance of Marius presaged an immediate attempt to supersede the oligarchy by a tyranny, or whether it would pass away as a mere isolated encroachment on the prerogatives of the government, could not yet be determined; but it could be foreseen that if these beginnings should develop, their leader would not be a statesman like Gaius Gracchus but a commander of legions. The reorganization of the military system introduced by Marius in recruiting his African army, which did away with the property qualification formerly required and accepted the poorest citizen, if physically fit, for military service, may have been promulgated on purely military grounds, but it was none the less a momentous political event. The army was no longer composed of those who had something to lose, but became transformed into a host of people with nothing but their arms and what the general bestowed on them. The aristocracy ruled in 104 B.C. just as absolutely as in 134 B.C. But the portents of disaster had multiplied, and the sword had begun to appear on the political horizon alongside the crown.

The Jugurthan War had scarcely ended when Rome was seriously threatened by the wild tribes north of the Alps. The Cimbri and Teutones, allied with certain Swiss Celtic tribes (Helvetii), invaded eastern Gaul, defeated several Roman armies, and in 102 B.C. prepared for a major invasion of Italy. After a difficult and dangerous campaign they were finally destroyed by Marius (aided by Sulla and Catulus) in two great battles at Aquae Sextiae (modern Aix) and Vercellae in 102 and 101 B.C. Marius, again the military hero and savior of Rome, was elected consul (for the sixth time) for the year 100 B.C.

His consulship was turbulent. A demagogic tribune, Lucius Appuleius Saturninus, and a praetor, Servilius Glaucia, attempted to force through legislation which the Senate regarded as radical, including an agrarian law for the benefit of Marius' veterans. After much disorder and at least one political murder, a decree of martial law by the Senate (the so-called senatus consultum ultimum) *called on the consuls Marius and Valerius to defend the state by arms; and Saturninus and Glaucia were both killed in the ensuing street riot. Although details regarding this ominous year are scanty and untrustworthy, it clearly marked a further step in the progress of the revolution, and the first use of professional troops in civil dissension.*

IV

REVOLT OF THE ITALIAN SUBJECTS AND THE SULPICIAN REVOLUTION

Since the defeat of Pyrrhus, the Roman supremacy in Italy had existed for nearly two hundred years without having been shaken even in times of utmost peril. Instead of contending with the too-powerful capital, the Italian nation with the blood of its youth had helped its masters to subdue three continents. Its own position meanwhile had deteriorated. From a material viewpoint it had, indeed, little to complain about. Though the small and medium-sized Italian landholders suffered from the injudicious Roman grain laws, the larger landlords and still more the merchants and capitalists flourished, for the Italians enjoyed substantially the same protection and the same opportunities for milking the provinces as Roman citizens, and thus shared in the material advantages of Roman political ascendancy. In general, Italian economic and social conditions did not depend primarily on political distinctions: in Italian districts such as Umbria and Etruria the free farmer class had largely disappeared, while in others, such as the Abruzzi valleys, it still maintained a respectable footing or was almost untouched.

On the other hand, the political inferiority of Italy was daily displayed more harshly and openly. True, there was no formal breach of important rights. The communal freedom granted by treaty to the Italian communities was on the whole respected by the Roman government; and the attack which the Roman reform party had made on the Roman domains guaranteed to the better situated Italian communities had not only been earnestly opposed both by the strictly conservative and the middle party in Rome, but had soon been abandoned by the opposition.

But the rights which devolved upon Rome as the leading community—the conduct of military affairs, and the supervision of the whole administration—were exercised in a way that was almost as bad as if the allies had been subjects devoid of rights. The modifications of the fearfully severe martial law introduced in the second century B.C. seem to have been limited to Roman citizens. This is clearly true as regards executions under military law; and we may easily conceive the impression produced when (as happened in the Jugurthan war) Latin officers of repute were beheaded by sentence of the Roman council of war, while the lowest citizen-soldier had the right of appeal to the Roman civil courts. The proportions of Roman citizens and Italian allies called up for military service were not defined by treaty. However, in earlier times the two had furnished roughly equal numbers of soldiers; now, although the population ratio had probably changed in favor of the citizens, the demands on the allies had increased until two allies were levied for one citizen.

In like manner the civil superintendence, which the Roman government had always reserved to itself over the dependent Italian communities, was extended until the Italians lived at the whim of any one of the numberless Roman magistrates. In the important allied town of Teanum Sidicinum, for example, a consul had ordered the town's chief magistrate to be scourged in the marketplace because, when the consul's wife expressed a desire to bathe in the men's bath, the municipal officers had not cleared the bath quickly enough, and the place appeared to her not clean.[1] Similar outrages without doubt frequently occurred, nor could any real satisfaction for such deeds be obtained. As a result the variance which the wise Roman rulers of old had carefully fostered between the Latin allies and the other Italian communities tended to disappear. Allies and subjects now lived under a common oppression; the Latin could remind the Picentine that both were in like manner "subject to the fasces"; the overseers and slaves of former days were now united in hatred of the common despot.

While the status of the Italian allies was thus transformed from a tolerable dependence into an oppressive bondage, they were at the same time deprived of the

---

1. Several additional examples are recounted in the original.

hope of betterment. With the subjugation of Italy the Roman electorate had closed its ranks; granting the franchise to whole communities was stopped altogether, and its bestowal upon individuals was greatly restricted. A further step was now taken: in response to the agitation to extend the Roman franchise to all Italy in the Gracchan period, the very right of migration to Rome was attacked, and all noncitizens living in the capital were ejected by decree of the people and of the Senate—a measure as dangerous (because of the private interests that it injured) as it was odious. In short, the Italian allies had partly been brothers under Roman tutelage, protected rather than ruled, and not condemned to perpetual minority, and partly slaves who were tolerably treated and not utterly deprived of the hope of freedom. Now they were all subject in nearly equal degree and with equal hopelessness to the rods and axes of their Roman masters; and the best they might hope was, like privileged slaves, to transmit the kicks received from their masters downward to the poor provincials.

It is the nature of such differences that, restrained by the sense of national unity and by the memory of common dangers, they make their first appearance moderately. Then the breach gradually widens; and the relation between the rulers, whose might is their sole right, and the ruled, whose obedience reaches no further than their fears, at length expresses itself as naked force. Down to the revolt and razing of Fregellae in 125 B.C., which seemed officially to attest the altered character of the Roman rule, the ferment among the Italians did not have a genuine revolutionary character. The longing for equal rights had gradually risen from a silent wish to a strident demand, only to be the more flatly rejected the more strongly it was urged. It was soon apparent that a voluntary concession was not to be hoped for, and the determination to extort what had previously been respectfully requested began to appear. But the position of Rome at that time hardly permitted any realistic hope of success. Although the proportion of citizens to noncitizens in Italy cannot be accurately ascertained, the number of citizens was surely not much less than that of the Italian allies: against nearly 400,000 citizens capable of bearing arms there were perhaps 500,000-600,000 allies. So long as the citizens were united and there was no foreign enemy worth mentioning, the Italian allies, split into numberless isolated communities and connected with Rome by a thousand relations public and private, could never achieve a common front; and with moderate prudence the Roman government could control its troublesome and indignant subjects partly by the compact mass of the citizens, partly by the considerable resources of the provinces, and partly by setting one community against another.

Accordingly the Italians kept quiet until the revolution began to shake Rome; as soon as it had broken out, they began to take part in the maneuvers of the Roman factions. They made common cause first with the popular and then with the senatorial party, and gained equally little from either. They were driven to the conviction that while the best men of both parties acknowledged the justice of their claims, both groups of leaders were equally powerless to gain acceptance of those claims by the mass of their followers. They also observed that the most gifted, energetic, and celebrated statesmen of Rome, when they came forward as advocates of the Italians, were deserted by their adherents and overthrown. In thirty years of installing and deposing revolutionary and restoration governments, however their programs might vary, a short-sighted and narrow-minded spirit always sat at the helm.

Above all, the recent occurrences clearly showed how vain was the Italians' expectation that their claims would be attended to by Rome. As long as those demands were mixed up with those of the revolutionary party, and had been thwarted by the folly of the masses, the allies might comfort themselves with the belief that the oligarchy had been hostile to the proposers rather than to the proposals, and that it was still possible that the more intelligent Senate would accept a measure compatible with the interests of the oligarchy and salutary for the state. But the recent years, in which the Senate once more ruled almost absolutely, had shed a disagreeable light on the designs of the Roman oligarchy. Instead of the expected modifications, the Senate issued in 95 B.C. a consular law strictly prohibiting noncitizens from claiming the franchise, and threatening transgressors with trial and punishment—a law which repelled a large number of respectable persons from the ranks of Romans into those of Italians. In point of political folly this act completely parallels that famous act which led to the separation of North America from the mother-country; and it also became the immediate cause of a civil war.[2]

Amid the ferment which this law called forth throughout Italy, the star of hope once more seemed to rise in the person of Marcus Drusus. What had been deemed almost impossible—that a conservative should take up the ideas of the Gracchi, and become the champion of equal rights for the Italians—had occurred; a born aristocrat had resolved to reform the government and to emancipate the Italians at one and the same time, and to apply all his zeal and devotion to these generous plans. Whether he actually (as was reported) placed himself at the head of a secret league ramified through Italy, whose members were bound by oath to stand by each other for Drusus and the common cause, cannot be ascertained. But even if he avoided acts so dangerous and indefensible for a Roman official, it is certain that he did not stop with mere general promises, and that dangerous

2. The law was all the worse, Mommsen observes in the original, because it was sponsored by moderates.

connections were formed in his name, although perhaps
without his consent and against his will.

With joy the Italians heard that Drusus had carried
his first proposals in the Senate by a great majority; with
still greater joy they celebrated soon afterward his re-
covery from a severe illness. But as Drusus' program was
unveiled, a change took place: he could not venture to
bring forward his chief law; he had to postpone; he had
to delay; he had soon to retire. It was reported that the
Senate was vacillating, and threatening to fall away from
its leader; in rapid succession the tidings ran throughout
Italy that the law already passed had been annulled, that
the capitalists ruled more absolutely than ever, that Drusus himself had been struck down by an assassin, that he
was dead (autumn, 91 B.C.).

The last Italian hope for achieving citizenship by
agreement was buried with Drusus. A measure which so
energetic and conservative a man had been unable to
push through his own party under the most favorable circumstances was not to be gained at all by peaceful means.
The Italians could only submit patiently or repeat once
more, if possible with their united strength, the attempt
which had been crushed at Fregellae a generation before,
and thus by force of arms either destroy Rome and succeed to her heritage, or at least compel her to grant equality of rights. To take up the way of force was no doubt
a counsel of despair. As matters stood, a revolt of the
isolated Italian communities might appear still more
hopeless than the revolt of the American colonies against
the British empire; and with moderate prudence and energy the Roman government might crush this second insurrection like its predecessor.

But was it any less a counsel of despair to sit still and
let things take their course? When the Italians recalled
how the Romans had behaved in Italy without provoca-
tion, what could they expect now that the most consider-

able men in every Italian town were alleged to have had an understanding with Drusus directed against the party in power, and which might well be characterized as treasonable? All who had taken part in this secret league, and all who might be merely suspected of it, had no choice left save to take up arms or bow their necks for the axe of the executioner.

Moreover, the prospects were comparatively favorable for a general insurrection. We are not exactly informed how far the Romans had gone in dissolving the larger Italian confederacies; but it is not unlikely that the old Marsian, Paelignian, and perhaps even the Samnite and Lucanian leagues still existed, though without political significance and in some cases probably reduced to mere fellowships of festivals and sacrifices. An insurrection beginning now would still find a rallying point in these groups; but how soon would the Romans for this very reason abolish these also? Moreover, while the secret league allegedly headed by Drusus had lost in him its actual or expected chief, it continued to afford a nucleus for political organization of the revolt, whose military organization might be based on the armament and experienced soldiers in every allied town.

In Rome, on the other hand, no serious preparations had been made. To be sure, it was reported that all Italy was restless, and that the allied communities were maintaining a remarkable intercourse with each other. But instead of calling the citizens to arms the government contented itself with exhorting the magistrates and sending out spies to learn further details. The capital was so totally undefended that the resolute Marsian officer Quintus Pompaedius Silo, one of Drusus' most intimate friends, is said to have proposed leading a band of trusty associates into the city carrying swords beneath their cloaks, and seizing it by a *coup de main*. Preparations accordingly went forward for revolt. Treaties were concluded and arming went on silently but actively, until at last the insurrection broke out accidentally somewhat earlier than its leaders had intended.

The Roman praetor Gaius Servilius was informed by his spies that the town of Asculum in the Abruzzi was sending hostages to the neighboring communities. He proceeded thither with his legate Fonteius and a small escort, and delivered a violent and menacing harangue to the multitude, which was just then assembled in the theater for the celebration of the great games. The sight of the hated axes, and the sound of threats only too seriously meant, sparked the fuel of bitter hatred that had been accumulating for centuries. The Roman officials were torn to pieces in the theater; and immediately, as if intending by a fearful outrage to burn every bridge of conciliation, the gates were closed at the order of the local magistrates, and all Romans residing in the town were put to death and their property seized. The revolt ran through the peninsula like wildfire, until all central and southern Italy was in arms against Rome.[3]

The Etruscans and Umbrians stood by Rome, as they had already opposed Drusus. It is significant that these regions had been dominated by the aristocracy and the capitalist class from early times, while the middle class had totally disappeared, whereas in and near the Abruzzi region of southern Italy the farmer class had preserved its purity and vigor better than anywhere else. Accordingly, it was the farmers and the middle class in general who supported the revolt, while the municipal aristocracy adhered to the government of the capital. This also readily explains why there were isolated communities in the insurgent districts and minorities in the insurgent towns which remained loyal to Rome.[4] Early Roman policy had based its dominion over Italy on an aristocratic

■

3. In the original, Mommsen lists the principal revolted communities.
4. The original continues with examples of such loyal cities.

classification, skillfully adjusting the degrees of dependence to keep the less privileged communities in subjection by means of those with better rights, and the citizens within each community by means of the municipal aristocracy. Only now, under the wretched aristocratic government, was the solidity and strength of the structure built by the statesman of two and three centuries earlier put to the test; the edifice, though shaken, still held out against this storm. To say, however, that the more favored towns did not at the first shock abandon Rome is by no means to say that they would, as in the Hannibalic War, hold out after severe defeats without wavering in their allegiance. That fiery trial had yet to be endured.

The first blood was thus shed, and Italy was divided into two great military camps. It is true that the insurrection was still far from being an uprising of all the Italian allies; but it had already exceeded the reasonable hopes of the leaders themselves, and the insurgents might without arrogance think of offering the Roman government a fair accommodation. They sent envoys to Rome and bound themselves to lay down their arms in return for citizenship, but in vain. The public spirit that had been so long lacking at Rome seemed suddenly to return when the objective was to obstruct with stubborn narrowness a just demand that was now supported by impressive force. The immediate effect of the Italian insurrection was, as happened after the defeats in Africa and Gaul, the beginning of a series of prosecutions through which the capitalists took vengeance on those officials who were regarded (rightly or wrongly) as responsible for this mischief.

On the proposal of the tribune Quintus Varius, despite optimate resistance and tribunician interference, a special commission of high treason was appointed from the equestrian order (which supported the proposal with open violence) for the investigation of the "conspiracy" instigated by Drusus out of which the insurrection had sprung, and which now, with half of Italy in revolt, seemed palpably treasonable to the alarmed Romans. The commission's sentences thinned the ranks of the senators favoring mediation: among other notable men Drusus' intimate friend, the young and talented Gaius Cotta, was exiled, and the venerable Marcus Scaurus escaped the same fate with difficulty. Suspicion went so far against the partisans of Drusus that soon afterward the consul Lupus reported from the camp to the Senate regarding communications allegedly maintained between the optimates in his army and the enemy—a suspicion which, it is true, was soon shown to be unfounded by the arrest of Marsian spies. So far King Mithradates of Pontus might reasonably assert that the political hatreds aroused on the Roman side were more destructive to the state than the Social War [5] itself.

The outbreak of the insurrection and the terrorism of the commission of high treason produced at the outset at least a semblance of unity and vigor. Party feuds were silenced, and able officers of all shades—democrats like Gaius Marius, aristocrats like Lucius Sulla, friends of Drusus like Publius Sulpicius Rufus—placed themselves at the disposal of the government. The grain distributions were apparently slashed by a decree of the people to husband the financial resources of the state for war— a measure the more necessary since the hostile King Mithradates threatened at any moment to dry up one of the chief sources of Roman revenue by seizing the province of Asia. The courts, except for the commission of high treason, were suspended by decree of the Senate; and the only business attended to was the levying of soldiers and the manufacture of arms.

While Rome thus collected her energies for the impending war, the insurgents faced the more difficult task of political organization in the midst of the struggle. The

___

5. Or "War of the Allies," as this Italian revolt came to be called.

territory of the Paeligni, situated in the center of the Marsian, Samnite, Marrucinian, and Vestinian cantons, was in the heart of the insurgent districts. There, in the beautiful plain of the river Pescara, the town of Corfinium was selected as the Anti-Rome, or city of Italia, whose citizenship was conferred on the citizens of all the insurgent communities. A forum and a senate house were staked off on a suitable scale. A senate of five hundred members was charged with drafting a constitution and prosecuting the war. At its direction the citizens chose from the municipal senatorial ranks two consuls and twelve praetors, who, like the two consuls and six praetors of Rome, were invested with the supreme authority in war and peace. Latin, even then the prevailing language among the Marsians and Picentines, continued in official use, but the Samnite language of southern Italy was given equal status, and the two languages were used alternately on the silver pieces which the state began to coin after Roman models, thus breaking the two-century-old Roman monopoly of the coinage.[6]

Thus in the winter of 91-90 B.C. began the struggle—as one of the insurgent coins represents it—of the Sabellian ox against the Roman she-wolf. Both sides made zealous preparations: in Italia great stores of arms, provisions, and money were accumulated; in Rome the necessary supplies were drawn from the provinces and particularly from Sicily, and the long-neglected walls were repaired against any eventuality. The forces were in some measure equally balanced. The Romans replaced their Italian contingents partly by increased levies of citizens and of the largely Romanized inhabitants of the Celtic districts south of the Alps (10,000 of the latter served in the Campanian army alone), and partly by the Nu-

■

6. Mommsen further traces in the original how exact was the Italian copy of the Roman state, and how the Italians missed the opportunity to develop the modern institution of representative government.

midian and other overseas contingents. A war fleet was
assembled with the aid of the free cities of Greece and
Asia Minor. On each side, without reckoning garrisons,
as many as 100,000 soldiers were brought into the field,
and in ability, tactics, and armaments the Italians were
in no way inferior to the Romans.

The conduct of the war was difficult for both the insurgents and the Romans. The territory in revolt was extensive, but many fortresses adhering to Rome were scattered
through it. Thus the insurgents were compelled to combine a time-consuming siege warfare, which broke up their
forces, with the protection of an extended frontier. The
Romans could hardly do otherwise than combat the insurrection, which had no proper center, simultaneously in
all the insurgent districts. Militarily, the insurgent country
embraced two main districts: the northern, Latin-speaking
district, reaching from Picenum and the Abruzzi to the
border of Campania, where the chief Italian command
was held by the Marsian Quintus Silo, and the chief Roman command by Publius Rutilius Lupus, both as consuls;
and the southern district, including Campania, Samnium,
and the Sabellian-speaking communities, with forces under
the command of the insurgent consul Gaius Papius Mutilus against the Roman consul Lucius Julius Caesar. Co-
operating with these consular armies were six lieutenant-
commanders on the Italian side and five on the Roman,
with separate forces assigned to definite districts, leaving
the main armies to strike the decisive blow. The most
noted Roman officers—Gaius Marius, Quintus Catulus,
and the consulars Titus Didius and Publius Crassus, experienced in the Spanish war—offered themselves to the
consuls for these subordinate posts. The Italians had no
names so celebrated to oppose them, yet the result showed
that their leaders were fully equal to the Roman.

The initiative in this desultory war was largely with
the Romans, but was not decisively assumed by them. It
is surprising that the Romans did not concentrate their

troops to attack the insurgents with a superior force, and that the insurgents made no attempt to throw themselves upon the hostile capital. But we know too little of the circumstances to judge whether either side could have acted more effectively, or whether the remissness of the Roman government or the looseness of the insurgent federation contributed to lack of vigor in conducting the war. It is easy to see that such a pattern of war would lead to many victories and defeats, with final settlement long delayed; but it is no less plain that a detailed picture of such a war, with its simultaneous engagements by individual corps operating sometimes independently and sometimes in concert, cannot be prepared from the remarkably fragmentary accounts handed down to us.

Through the fog of history Mommsen nevertheless attempts in the original to piece together an account of the war's first year, which began with the Italians laying siege to loyal cities, and continued with varying successes in three main areas. In the south the Italians were sufficiently successful to cause the revolt to spread, with such important towns as Nola, Salernum, Stabiae, Pompeii, and Herculaneum declaring for the insurgents. These southern setbacks for the Romans were balanced by northern successes, which so turned the tables in that region that the Italians began the year as besiegers and ended it as besieged. In central Italy the fighting was inconclusive, with Marius restoring the seriously threatened Roman position.

Thus the first year ended, leaving in both political and military spheres sorrowful memories and dubious prospects. Both the Marsian and the Campanian armies of Rome had been weakened and discouraged by severe defeats. The northern army had been largely pinned down

to the protection of the capital; the communications of the
southern army at Neapolis were seriously threatened, as
the insurgents could easily break forth from Marsian or
Samnite territory and establish themselves between Rome
and Neapolis. It was accordingly deemed necessary to establish a chain of posts between Cumae and Rome. Politically the insurrection had gained ground on all sides; the
secession of Nola, the rapid capitulation of the large
Latin colony of Venusia, and the rumble of Umbro-Etrus-
can revolt were suspicious signs that the Roman system
of control was crumbling, and would not endure the final
trial. The government had already made the utmost demands on the citizenry; it had already, to man that chain
of posts along the coast, incorporated nearly 6,000 freedmen in the militia; and it had already required the severest
sacrifices from the allies that still remained faithful. The
bowstring could not be drawn tighter without risking disaster.

The morale of the citizens was abysmally low. After
the battle on the Tolenus, when the dead bodies of the
consul and numerous other notables were brought back to
the capital for burial, when the magistrates laid aside their
purple and insignia in token of public mourning, when the
government ordered the inhabitants of the capital to arm
en masse, many had given up all as lost. True, the worst
despondency was somewhat relieved after the victories
achieved by Lucius Caesar at Acerrae and by Pompeius
Strabo in Picenum: news of the former led the citizens in
the capital to lay aside the *saga,* or war dress, and resume
the usual togas, while news of the latter brought to an
end the public mourning. But it was clear that the Romans
had on the whole been worsted in the year's fighting, and
that both the Senate and the citizenry had lost that spirit
which had carried them to victory through all the crises of
the Hannibalic war. They still began war with the defiant
arrogance of old, but they knew not how to end it: rigid
obstinacy and tenacious persistence had been replaced by

a slack and cowardly disposition. After the first year of the war their outlook had so changed that they began to think of compromise. This was the wisest thing that could have been done—not because the Romans were compelled by force of arms to acquiesce, but because the perpetuation of Roman political dominance over the Italians was injurious to the commonwealth. It sometimes happens in public life that one error compensates another; in this case cowardice partly repaired the mischief that obstinacy had incurred.

The year 90 B.C. had begun with abrupt rejection of the insurgent offer of compromise, and with the opening of a campaign of prosecutions in which those passionate defenders of patriotic selfishness, the capitalists, took vengeance on all those suspected of counseling moderation. On the other hand the tribune Marcus Plautius Silvanus, who entered office on December 10 of that year, carried a law which took the treason commission out of the hands of the capitalist jurymen, and gave it to jurymen nominated by the free choice of the tribes without class qualification. The result was that the commission was converted from a scourge of the moderates into a scourge of the ultras, and exiled (among others) its own author Quintus Varius, who was blamed by the public voice for the worst excesses of the capitalist triumph—the poisoning of Quintus Metellus and the murder of Drusus.

More important than this candid political recantation was the change in policy toward the Italians. Exactly three hundred years had passed since Rome had been obliged to submit to a dictated peace; she was now worsted once more, and the peace she desired could be got only by yielding in some measure to her antagonists. With the communities which had risen in arms against Rome, the Romans could not bring themselves to make the required concessions; and even had they done so, the offer might well have been rejected. But if the bulk of the original demands were conceded to the communities that had re-

mained faithful, the semblance of voluntary concession
would be preserved, while the action might well prevent
the otherwise inevitable consolidation of the insurgents,
and thereby pave the way to victory.

Accordingly, the gates of Roman citizenship, so long
closed against all entreaties, now suddenly opened at the
knock of the sword. Even now, however, they were opened
reluctantly and annoyingly even for those admitted. A law
proposed by the consul Lucius Caesar conferred the Roman franchise on the citizens of all those allied communities not yet openly in arms against Rome; while a second
law, introduced by the tribunes Plautius Silvanus and
Gaius Papirius Carbo, designated a period of two months
during which an allied citizen might acquire the Roman
franchise by appearing personally before a Roman magistrate. But the voting rights of these new citizens were restricted as with freedmen: they could be enrolled in only
eight (the freedmen in only four) of the thirty-five tribes.
Whether the restriction was personal or hereditary cannot be determined with certainty.[7]

Considerable as were these concessions, if compared
with the rigid exclusiveness of the previous hundred and
fifty years, they were far from involving a capitulation to
the actual insurgents. On the contrary, they were intended
partly to retain the wavering communities, and partly to
encourage desertions from the ranks of the enemy. To
what extent these laws were applied cannot be accurately
stated, as we can specify only in general terms the extent
of the insurrection when they were issued. The main
point was that the Latin communities—including the
Latin colonies, except for the few that had passed over
to the insurgents—were thereby admitted to Roman citizenship. The law also applied to the loyal allied cities in
Etruria and southern Italy, such as Nuceria and Neapolis.

7. Mommsen describes in the original the somewhat different treatment
accorded to the Celtic communities south of the Alps.

To be sure, some especially privileged individual communities hesitated to accept the franchise (Neapolis, for example, with its treaty guaranteeing its citizens exemption from land service, its Greek constitution, and possibly domanial advantages besides). It was probably because of such scruples that this city, as well as Rhegium and perhaps other Greek communities in Italy, retained their constitutions and their official Greek language. At any rate, these laws extraordinarily enlarged the circle of Roman citizenship by bringing within it numerous important urban communities scattered from the Sicilian straits to the Po; and further, the country between the Po and the Alps, upon which the rights of the allies were conferred, was given the legal expectancy of eventual full citizenship.

Buoyed by these concessions, the Romans resumed the conflict against the insurgent districts with fresh courage. They had demolished as much of the existing structure as seemed necessary to keep the conflagration from spreading; thereafter, at least, it spread no farther. In Etruria and Umbria, where it was just breaking out, it was subdued rapidly, probably more by means of the Julian law than by success at arms. Copious and now trustworthy sources of aid were opened in the former Latin colonies and in the thickly peopled Po region; and with these, plus its citizens' own resources, Rome could proceed to quench the now isolated conflagration. The two former consular commanders returned to Rome, Caesar as censor elect, Marius because his conduct of the war was blamed as vacillating and slow (at sixty-six, he was declared to be in his dotage). This objection was probably groundless; Marius showed at least his bodily strength by appearing daily in the circus, and as commander-in-chief he seems on the whole to have displayed his old ability in the last campaign. But he had not achieved the brilliant success which alone could have rehabilitated him after his political failure, and thus the celebrated champion was to his chagrin

unceremoniously put upon the shelf. His place in the Marsian army was taken by the consul for the new year, Lucius Porcius Cato, who had fought with distinction in
Etruria, and that of Caesar in the Campanian army by
his lieutenant, Lucius Sulla, to whom were due some of
the major successes of the previous campaign. Gnaeus
Pompeius Strabo retained, now as consul, the Picenian
command he had held so successfully.

Thus began the second campaign in 89 B.C. The insurgents opened it before the winter was over by boldly
attempting to send a Marsian army of 15,000 men to
Etruria, to aid the insurrection brewing in northern Italy.
But Strabo intercepted and so totally defeated it that only
a few got back to their homes. When the season allowed
the Roman armies to take the offensive, Cato entered
Marsian territory and successfully encountered the enemy
there, but he fell during an attack on the enemy's camp
near the Fucine Lake, so that the command of operations
in central Italy devolved upon Strabo. The latter employed himself partly in pressing the siege of Asculum,
and partly in subduing the Marsian, Sabellian, and Apulian districts. To relieve hard-pressed Asculum, his native town, the insurgent commander Iudacilius appeared
with a Picentine army and attacked the besiegers, while
at the same time the garrison sallied out and threw itself
on the Roman lines. It is said that 75,000 Romans fought
on this day with 60,000 Italians. Victory remained with
the Romans, but Iudacilius succeeded in throwing himself
and part of his relieving army into the town. The siege
continued, protracted by the strength of the place and the
desperate defense of the inhabitants, who recalled only
too well the terrible declaration of war within its walls.
When Iudacilius at length saw the day of capitulation approach, he ordered the leading Roman sympathizers put
to death by torture, and then died by his own hand. So
the gates were opened, and Roman executions replaced
Italian; all officers and respectable citizens were executed,

the rest were driven forth to beggary, and all property was confiscated.[8]

The Roman southern army under Lucius Sulla also took the offensive and penetrated into southern Campania, which was occupied by the enemy. Stabiae was taken and sacked by Sulla in person (April 30, 89 B.C.), and Herculaneum by Titus Didius, who himself apparently fell in the assault on the town. Pompeii resisted longer. The Samnite general Lucius Cluentius came to its relief, but was repulsed by Sulla; and when, with Celtic reinforcements, he renewed his attempt, he was so totally defeated (owing chiefly to the wavering of these untrustworthy auxiliaries) that his camp was taken and he himself was cut down with most of his troops in their flight toward Nola. The grateful Roman army conferred on its general the grass wreath—the homely decoration accorded to a soldier who had saved a division of his comrades. Without pausing to besiege Nola or the other Samnite-occupied Campanian towns, Sulla at once advanced into the interior, which was the heart of the insurrection. The advanced season alone put an end to the campaign there.[9]

The state of affairs had undergone a complete change. Powerful, victorious, aggressive at the start of the campaign, the insurgents emerged from it humbled, beaten, and hopeless. All northern Italy was pacified. In central Italy the Romans held both coasts and almost all of the Abruzzi; Apulia as far as Venusia, and Campania as far as Nola, were in their hands; and the occupation of the Hirpinian territory severed the communications between the only two regions still in open resistance, the Samnite and the Lucano-Bruttian. The insurrection resembled an

■

8. How the fall of Asculum was followed by the subjugation of the nearby districts, including the insurgent capital of Italia, is told in a brief passage here omitted.
9. After several victories, including the capture of the Samnite capital Bovianum, which Mommsen describes in the original.

immense conflagration dying out; ashes, ruins, and smoldering brands were everywhere; here and there flames still blazed up; but the fire was no longer dangerous. It is regrettable that the causes of this sudden change cannot be clearly discerned from the superficial accounts available to us. While the dextrous leadership of Strabo and Sulla, and especially the more energetic concentration and offensive use of the Roman forces doubtless contributed materially to that result, political causes may also have speeded the singularly rapid fall of the insurgents. The law of Silvanus and Carbo may have succeeded in carrying defection and treason into the ranks of the enemy; and misfortune, as so often happens, may have thrown an apple of discord among the loose insurgent federation.

We see only (and this fact implies the breaking up of Italia, which must have been attended by violent convulsions) that the Samnites—perhaps under the leadership of the Marsian Quintus Silo, who had been the soul of the insurrection and who had gone as a fugitive to Samnium after the Marsian capitulation—now formed another organization confined to their own territory: after "Italia" was vanquished, they continued the struggle as "Safini" or Samnites. Aesernia was converted into the last fortress that sheltered Samnite freedom; an army reportedly consisting of 30,000 infantry and 1,000 cavalry was strengthened by the freeing of 20,000 slaves; and five generals were placed at its head, with Silo the first and Mutilus next. With astonishment the Romans beheld the Samnite wars reviving after a lapse of two centuries, and saw that resolute nation of farmers making a fresh attempt to force the recognition of their country's independence. But this resolution of despair could not change the main course of events. Although mountain warfare in Samnium and Lucania might take time and sacrifices, the insurrection was substantially at an end.

Meantime, however, a fresh complication appeared; it

had become imperative to declare war against Mithradates, king of Pontus, and to send one consul and a consular army to Asia Minor in the following year (88 B.C.). Had this Asiatic war broken out a year earlier, the simultaneous revolt of half of Italy would have constituted an immense peril to the Roman state. Now that Rome's incredible good fortune had once more been evinced in the rapid collapse of the Italian insurrection, this new Asiatic war was not really dangerous—the less so because Mithradates arrogantly refused the Italian bid for direct assistance. Still, it was highly inconvenient. The day was past when the Romans without hesitution carried on an Italian and a foreign war simultaneously; the formation of a new army seemed scarcely practicable, and the treasury was utterly exhausted. But the government resorted to what expedients it could. The sale of building sites on and near the citadel in Rome, which had remained unoccupied since ancient times, furnished the requisite pecuniary means in the form of 9,000 pounds of gold. No new army was formed, but Sulla's forces in Campania were earmarked for departure as soon as affairs in southern Italy permitted—which would be soon, to judge from the progress of the northern army under Strabo. So the campaign of 88 B.C. began amidst favorable prospects for Rome,[10] when the turn of events in the capital unexpectedly gave fresh life to the well-nigh extinguished insurrection.

Rome was in a fearful ferment. The attack of Drusus on the equestrian courts and his downfall at the hands of the equestrian party, followed by the two-edged Varian prosecutions, had sown the bitterest discord between aristocrats and capitalists as well as between moderates and ultras. Events had completely justified the party of concession; what it had proposed to grant, Rome had been compelled largely to concede; but the concession, like the

10. In the original, Mommsen goes on to describe the Roman clean-up campaigns of this year.

earlier refusal, bore the stamp of obstinate and short-
sighted envy. Instead of granting equal rights to all Italian communities, Rome continued the old inferiority in another form. A great number of Italian communities had
received Roman citizenship, but with the offensive stigma
that the new citizens were placed on nearly the same footing as freedmen occupied alongside of the freeborn. The
Romans had irritated rather than pacified the communities between the Po and the Alps by the concession of
Latin rights. They had withheld the franchise from a considerable portion of the Italians, namely, the insurgent
communities which had again submitted. And finally, instead of legally re-establishing the former treaties annulled by the insurrection, they had at most merely renewed them, subject to revocation at pleasure.

The discrimination in voting rights was the more offensive for its political absurdity: the government's hypocritical care for the unstained purity of the electorate appeared ridiculous to every unprejudiced person. But all
these restrictions were dangerous, inviting every demagogue to advance his schemes by taking up the demands of
the new citizens and the Italians excluded from the franchise. While the clearer-headed aristocrats accordingly
found these partial and grudging concessions as inadequate as those discriminated against, they sorely missed
from their ranks the numerous excellent men exiled by
the Varian commission, whom it was the more difficult to
recall because they had been condemned by a verdict not
of the people but of the special jury commission; for while
they would not hesitate to cancel one decree of the people by means of a second, the canceling of a jury verdict by
the people appeared a very dangerous precedent.

Thus neither the ultras not the moderates were content
with the outcome of the Italian crisis. But still deeper indignation swelled the heart of old Marius, who had left
for the Italian war with fresh hopes and had returned reluctantly, conscious of having rendered new services in re-

turn for new mortifications, with the bitter feeling of being despised rather than dreaded by his enemies, and with that gnawing spirit of vengeance in his heart that feeds on its own poison. Politically he was excluded like the new citizens: incapable and awkward though he might be, his name was still a formidable weapon in the hand of a demagogue.

These political convulsions were combined with the rapid decay of military discipline. The seeds sown by enrolling the proletariat in the army sprouted with alarming rapidity during the demoralizing insurrectionary war, which compelled Rome to call up every man capable of bearing arms, and which above all carried political partisanship directly into the general's headquarters and the soldier's tent. The effects soon appeared in the slackening of all the bonds of discipline. During the siege of Pompeii the commander of the Sullan besieging corps, the consular Aulus Postumius Albinus, was killed with stones and bludgeons by his own soldiers, who thought themselves betrayed by their general to the enemy; and even Sulla, the commander-in-chief, contented himself with exhorting the troops to wipe out the memory of that occurrence by brave conduct in battle. The authors of that deed were the marines, long the least respectable of the troops, but a division of legionaries raised chiefly from the city populace soon followed their example. Instigated by Gaius Titius, one of the heroes of the market-place, it laid hands on the consul Cato, who only by accident escaped death; Titius was arrested, but not punished. When Cato soon afterward perished in combat, his own officers, and particularly the younger Gaius Marius, were charged (we cannot tell whether justly or unjustly) with causing his death.

Perhaps still worse, this political and military crisis was compounded by an economic crisis among the Roman capitalists as a result of the Social War and the Asiatic troubles. The debtors, unable to raise even the interest

due and yet inexorably pressed by their creditors, on the
one hand requested from the proper judicial authority, the
urban praetor Asellio, a respite to enable them to dispose
of their possessions; while on the other they searched
among the obsolete usury laws and, according to the ancient rule, sued their creditors for fourfold the amount
of interest paid contrary to law. Asellio bent the actually
existing law into conformity with the letter, and processed
the desired actions for interest in the usual way; whereupon the offended creditors assembled in the Forum
under the leadership of the tribune Lucius Cassius, and
attacked and killed the praetor before the temple of
Concord in his priestly robes just as he was presenting a
sacrifice—an outrage which was not even made a subject
of investigation. On the other hand, it was said in debtor
circles that the suffering multitude could only be relieved
by "new account-books"—that is, by canceling the claims
of all creditors against all debtors.

Thus matters once again stood just as they had during
the earlier class warfare. Once again the capitalists in
league with the standpat aristocracy made war against the
oppressed multitude and the middle class which sought to
moderate the law's severity; once again Rome stood on
the brink of that abyss into which the despairing debtor
drags his creditor along with him. But since those former
days the simple organization of a great agricultural city
had been succeeded by the social antagonisms of a world
capital, and by that demoralization which prince and beggar share alike; now all the incongruities existed on a
broader, sharper, fearfully grander scale. The Italian war
brought all the disparate political and social elements
among the citizens into collision, and laid the foundation
for a new revolution.

An accident led to its outbreak. In 88 B.C. the tribune
Publius Sulpicius Rufus proposed that every senator who
owed more than 2,000 *denarii* should forfeit his seat in the
Senate; that citizens sentenced by nonfree jury courts be

free to return home; and that the new citizens, and freedmen as well, be allowed to vote in all the tribes. It was
at least surprising to hear these proposals from the mouth
of such a man. Born in 124 B.C., he owed his political importance not so much to his noble birth, important connections, and hereditary wealth as to an oratorical talent
equaled by none of his contemporaries. His powerful
voice, his lively gestures sometimes bordering on the theatrical, and his luxuriant flow of words arrested, even if
they did not convince, his hearers. A strong Senate partisan from the outset, his first public appearance was in the
impeachment of Norbanus, who was mortally hated by the
government party. Among the conservatives he shared
the sentiments of Crassus and Drusus. We do not know
why he solicited the tribuneship for 88 B.C., thereby renouncing his patrician nobility; but his persecution (along
with all the moderates) by the conservatives does not
seem to have made him a revolutionist, and he certainly
did not seek to overthrow the constitution in the manner
of Gaius Gracchus. It would rather seem that, as the only
moderate of note who had come unscathed through the
Varian prosecutions, he felt called upon to complete Drusus' work by setting aside the remaining discriminations
against the new citizens—for which purpose he needed the
tribunate.[11]

It was easy to foresee that his opposition would not be
slight; that the equally narrow-minded aristocrats and
capitalists would display the same stupid jealousy after
the end of the insurrection as before its outbreak; that
the great majority of all parties would secretly or openly
characterize the partial concessions made in time of peril
as unnecessary softness, and would passionately resist
every attempt to extend them. The fate of Drusus had

11. In a brief further passage omitted here, Mommsen further attests to
Sulpicius' moderate designs, and discusses his personal and political motives for advancing them.

shown what came of relying solely on the majority of the
Senate to carry conservative reforms; it was quite understandable that Drusus' successor should attempt to carry
out similar designs under a cloak of demagoguery. Sulpicius accordingly disdained to win over the Senate by
using the bait of the jury courts, and found stouter support in the freedmen and above all in an armed retinue—
consisting, by unfriendly reports, of 3,000 hired men and
an "opposition-senate" of 600 young men of good families—which accompanied him in the streets and in the
Forum.

His proposals accordingly met with determined resistance from most of the Senate, which first, to gain time,
induced the consuls Lucius Cornelius Sulla and Quintus
Pompeius Rufus to decree extraordinary religious observ-
ances during which popular assemblies were suspended.
Sulpicius replied by a violent tumult in which among others
young Quintus Pompeius, son of one consul and son-in-
law of the other, met his death and the lives of both consuls themselves were seriously threatened (Sulla is said to
have escaped only because Marius opened his house to
him). The conservatives were obliged to yield. Sulla
agreed to countermand the announced solemnities, and the
Sulpician proposals passed without further trouble.

But this was far from an end to the matter. Though the
aristocracy in the capital might give up the fight, there was
for the first time another power in Italy which could not
be overlooked—the two strong and victorious armies of
the proconsul Strabo and the consul Sulla. The political
position of Strabo might be ambiguous; but Sulla, though
he had submitted to open violence for the moment, was
on the best terms with the Senate majority. Moreover he
had, immediately after countermanding the solemnities,
departed for Campania to join his army. To terrify the
unarmed consul by bludgeon-men, or threaten the defenseless capital by the swords of the legions, amounted to the
same thing in the end; and Sulpicius assumed that his op-

ponent would now meet violence with violence, returning at the head of his legions to overthrow the conservative demagogue along with his laws. Perhaps he was mistaken. Sulla was just as keen for the war against Mithradates as he was probably repelled by the political odors of the capital. Considering his unrivaled spirit of indifference and political nonchalance, it is quite likely that, let alone, he would have embarked for Asia immediately upon capturing the long-besieged city of Nola.

But whatever Sulla's intentions, Sulpicius sought to parry the expected blow by the scheme of taking the supreme command from him. For this purpose he joined with Marius, whose name was still sufficiently popular to make a proposal to give him the chief Asiatic command seem plausible to the multitude, and whose military position and ability might be useful in the event of a rupture with Sulla. Sulpicius probably overlooked neither the danger involved in placing that vengeful and ambitious old man at the head of the Campanian army, nor the scandalous irregularity of giving an extraordinary supreme command to a private citizen by decree of the people. But Marius' proven incompetence as a statesman was a guarantee of sorts that he would not seriously endanger the constitution; and above all, Sulpicius' personal position (if he had estimated Sulla's designs correctly) was so perilous that he could hardly heed such considerations. That the worn-out hero Marius readily took the bid of anyone who would hire him was a matter of course; for years he had longed for the command in an Asiatic war, and also perhaps for a chance to settle accounts once and for all with the majority of the Senate. Accordingly, on the proposal of Sulpicius, Marius was by decree of the people invested with extraordinary supreme power, command of the Campanian army, and direction of the war against Mithradates; and two tribunes were sent to the camp at Nola to take over the army from Sulla.

Sulla was not the man to obey such orders. If anyone

had a right to the chief command in the Asiatic war, it was he. A few years before he had commanded with great success in the same theater; he had contributed more than any other man to subduing the Italian insurrection; and as consul in the year when the Asiatic war broke out, he had been given the command in the customary way with the full consent of his friend and colleague, who was also related to him by marriage. It was expecting much to suppose that he would, bowing to a decree of the populace, give up his command to an old military and political antagonist who might involve the army in all manner of violent and preposterous proceedings. Sulla was neither easygoing enough to comply with such an order, nor dependent enough to be compelled. His army, as a result of Marius' alterations of the military system, in addition to the moral laxity and the military strictness of its discipline in the hands of Sulla, was little better than a band of mercenaries devoted to their leader and contemptuous of political affairs. Sulla himself was a hard, cool, clear-headed man, in whose eyes the sovereign citizenry was a rabble, Marius a bankrupt swindler, legality an empty phrase, and Rome herself an ungarrisoned and defenseless city that could be captured far more easily than Nola.

On these views he acted. He assembled his soldiers (six legions, or about 35,000 men) and announced the summons that had arrived from Rome, not forgetting to hint that the new commander-in-chief would doubtless lead to Asia Minor not the present army, but another formed of fresh troops. The superior officers, still more citizens than soldiers, kept aloof, and only one of them followed the general toward the capital. But the soldiers, anticipating in Asia an easy war and endless booty, were furious; in a moment the two tribunes were torn to pieces, and from all sides the general was implored to lead a march on Rome. Without delay the consul started, formed a junction with his like-minded colleague along the way, and arrived by quick marches—little troubling himself about the deputies who hastened from the city to detain him—beneath the walls of the capital. Suddenly Rome beheld Sulla's columns take their station at the bridge over the Tiber and at the Colline and Esquiline gates; then two legions in battle array, their standards at their head, passed the sacred *pomerium* which they were forbidden by law to enter. Many a worse quarrel had been settled within those walls without a Roman army breaking the sacred peace of the city; now that step was taken primarily over the miserable question of what officer should command in Asia.

The legions advanced as far as the height of the Esquiline, where the showers of missiles and stones from the roofs made the soldiers waver. But Sulla himself brandished a blazing torch, and with threats of firing the houses the legions cleared their way to the Esquiline market place. There the force hastily collected by Marius and Sulpicius repelled the first invading columns by superior numbers. But reinforcements came up from the gates; another division of Sullans prepared to flank the defenders by the street of the Subura: and the latter were obliged to retire. At the temple of Tellus, where the Esquiline begins to slope towards the great Forum, Marius once more attempted a stand; he exhorted the Senate and all the citizens to block the path of the legions. But he himself had transformed them from citizens to mercenaries, and his own work turned against him; they obeyed not their government, but their general. Even when the slaves were called to arms with the promise of freedom, no more than three appeared. Nothing remained for the leaders but to flee through the still unoccupied gates, and within a few hours Sulla was absolute master of Rome. That night the watchfires of the legions blazed in the great market place of the capital.

The first military intervention in civil quarrels made it clear that the political strife had reached the point where only naked force was decisive, and also that the bludgeon was of no avail against the sword. The conservative party drew the sword, and accordingly in due time experienced the truth of the Gospel's ominous words regarding those who first employ it. For the moment it triumphed completely, and could consolidate the victory at its pleasure. As a matter of course the Sulpician laws were repealed, and their author and his twelve most notable adherents were proscribed for arrest and execution as enemies of their country. Sulpicius was seized and put to death at Laurentum, and his head was by Sulla's orders exposed in the Forum at the very spot where but a few days before he had stood in the full vigor of youth and eloquence. The rest of the proscribed, even including old Marius, were pursued by their would-be assassins.

After hair-raising adventures by land and sea, Marius was finally captured in the salt-marshes near Minturnae and turned over to that town's officials for execution. But the executioner, a German slave, "trembled before the eyes of his old conqueror and the axe fell from his hands, when the general in his powerful voice haughtily demanded whether he dared to kill Gaius Marius." The town officials, "ashamed that the savior of Rome should meet greater respect from slaves he had sent into bondage than from fellow citizens to whom he had brought freedom," gave him a ship in which to escape. After further astonishing adventures in Numidia, Marius and the other political fugitives found temporary refuge together on a small island off the Tunisian coast.

To remove existing evils and prevent future revolutions, Sulla proposed a new series of laws. Nothing seems to have been done for the hard-pressed debtors except that the rules as to maximum interest were enforced. Directions were also given for establishing a number of colonies, and the Senate, which had been greatly thinned by the battles and prosecutions of the Social War, was filled up by admitting 300 new senators (naturally selected in the interests of the aristocracy). And last, elective and legislative arrangements were materially altered. The old Servian voting system, under which those with estates of 100,000 sesterces and up possessed almost half of the votes, replaced the arrangements that had been introduced in 241 B.C. to reduce the dominance of the upper classes. Thus in electing the consuls, praetors, and censors, the nonwealthy were practically excluded from exercising the suffrage. The right of tribunes of the people to introduce legislation was restricted by requiring that every proposal be submitted first to the Senate; only after Senate approval could it come before the people.

These enactments called forth by the Sulpician attempt at revolution bear an altogether peculiar character. Sulla ventured without consulting the citizens or jurymen to condemn to death twelve distinguished men, including magistrates actually in office and the most famous general of his time, and publicly to defend these proscriptions—a violation of the laws of appeal which was severely censured even by such extreme conservatives as Quintus Scaevola. He ventured to overthrow a 150-year-old elective arrangement in favor of one long obsolete and proscribed. He ventured practically to withdraw the right of legislation from its two primary sources, the magistrates and the comitia, and to transfer it to a group that had never possessed any privilege other than that of being asked for advice. Never had any democrat dispensed justice so tyrannically, or remodeled the constitution with such reckless audacity, as this conservative reformer.

But a look at substance instead of form leads to very different conclusions. Revolutions have nowhere been crushed, least of all in Rome, without demanding a certain number of victims, who under forms more or less tinged with justice atone for the crime of being vanquished. Anyone who recalls the prosecutions by the victorious party after the fall of the Gracchi and Saturninus will be inclined to praise Sulla for his candor and comparative moderation, first in that he accepted war as war and placed the enemies whom he defeated beyond the pale of the law, and second in that he limited the number of victims by allowing no outbreak of fury against lesser persons.

A similar moderation appears in his political changes. His legislative innovation—the most important and apparently the most comprehensive—merely brought the letter of the constitution into harmony with its spirit. The ability of any consul, praetor, or tribune to propose any measure to the citizens, and bring it to a vote without debate, was irrational from the first and had daily become more so. It was tolerated only because in practice the Senate had exercised the right of prior deliberation and had regularly crushed any proposal, if put to premature vote, by means of the political or religious veto. The revolution had swept away these safeguards; and as a result the system had now developed to that absurd point where any petulant knave might overthrow the state with the law's blessing. Under such circumstances what was more natural, more necessary, more truly conservative than to recognize formally the power which the Senate had hitherto exercised by a circuitous process?

Much the same might be said for the return to the old voting system. The earlier constitution was based on it, and even the reform of 241 B.C. had merely restricted the privileges of men of wealth. But since then a financial revolution had occurred, which might well justify a raising of the property requirement. The new timocracy [12] thus changed the letter of the constitution only to remain faithful to its spirit, while at the same time it at least mildly attempted to check the disgraceful purchase of votes. And lastly, the regulations in favor of debtors and the resump-

---

12. In Aristotle, a state where political position depends on wealth.

tion of colonization gave express proof that Sulla, though disapproving the impetuous proposals of Sulpicius, was, like Sulpicius and Drusus (and all the more far-seeing aristocrats), favorable to economic reform—a conclusion supported by the circumstance that he proposed these measures after the victory and entirely of his own free will.

Combining with such considerations the fact that Sulla disturbed neither the equestrian courts nor the grain distribution, the opinion seems warranted that the Sullan arrangements of 88 B.C. substantially followed the outlines of the Gracchan constitution. On the one hand, he altered as times required the traditional rules that endangered the existing government; while on the other he sought to remedy the existing social evils, so far as either could be done without touching ills that lay still deeper. Contempt for constitutional formalism, together with clear perceptions, praiseworthy intentions, and a vivid appreciation of the intrinsic value of existing arrangements marks his legislation throughout. But it also bears a certain frivolous and superficial character; a great amount of good nature was required to believe that fixing a maximum rate of interest would remedy the confused relations of debtors and creditors, or that the right of prior discussion by the Senate would prove more resistant to future demagoguery than the right of veto and religion had once been.

In fact, new clouds had already begun to overcast the clear sky of the conservatives. The Asian problem was becoming more threatening daily. The state had already suffered grave injury from the delay of the army's departure for Asia, which on no account could be postponed longer. Sulla hoped to leave guarantees against a new assault on the oligarchy in Italy, partly in the consuls to be elected under the new system, and especially in the armies engaged in suppressing the remnants of the Italian insurrection. The consular choice, however, did not go to Sulla's candidates, but to Lucius Cornelius Cinna, one of the most determined oppositionists, and Gnaeus Octavius, a dyed-in-the-wool aristocrat. It may be presumed that the capitalist party by this choice retaliated on the author of the law regulating interest. Sulla accepted this unpleasant outcome with the declaration that he was glad to see the citizens exercising their constitutional right of choice, and contented himself with requiring both consuls to swear that they would faithfully observe the existing constitution.

Of the armies, the northern one would become crucial once the bulk of the Campanian army departed for Asia. Sulla got the command of the former entrusted by decree of the people to his devoted colleague Quintus Rufus, and secured the recall of the former general Gnaeus Strabo in such a way as to spare his feelings—the more important because Strabo belonged to the equestrian party, and his hands-off attitude during the Sulpician troubles had caused the aristocracy no small anxiety. Rufus took over in Strabo's stead, but within a few days he was killed by the soldiers, and Strabo resumed the command he had hardly abdicated. He was popularly regarded as the instigator of the murder; it is certain that he was a man capable of such a deed, that he reaped the fruits of the crime, and that he punished the known perpetrators only with words.

The death of Rufus and the return of Strabo represented a new and serious danger, but Sulla did nothing to deprive the latter of his command. Soon afterward, when his consulship expired, he found himself urged by his successor Cinna to depart at once for Asia, where his presence was certainly urgently needed, while at the same time proceedings were begun against him by one of the new tribunes. The dullest eye could see that a new attack on him and his party was in preparation. Sulla's only alternatives were either to break openly with Cinna (and perhaps with Strabo) and once more march on Rome, or depart for another continent and let Italy stew in its own juice. Sulla decided—whether more from patriotism or indifference will never be ascertained—on the latter. He handed command of the corps in Samnium to the trustworthy and experienced Quintus Metellus Pius, who received in Sulla's stead the proconsular command over lower Italy; gave the conduct of the siege of Nola to the propraetor Appius Claudius; and early in 87 B.C. embarked with his legions for the East.

The Asiatic threat came from Mithradates VI, a dependent king who had expanded his original kingdom of Pontus around the eastern coast of the Black Sea, and southward into Cappadocia. Mommsen describes Mithradates as "an Oriental ruler of the ordinary stamp, coarse, full of the most sensual appetites, superstitious, cruel, perfidious, and unscrupulous, but so vigorous in organization, and so powerful in physical endowments, that his defiant laying about him and his unshaken courage in resistance frequently look like talent, and sometimes even like genius."

Knowing something of the power of Rome, Mithradates throughout his land-grabbing took pains to avoid an open break, but a rupture occurred late in 89 B.C. through the machinations of a greedy Roman official, Manius Aquillius. (Later, as Mithradates' captive, his avarice was sated by molten gold poured down his throat.) Once the die was cast, Mithradates energetically prosecuted the war. The wholesale massacre of Roman business men in the Greek cities of Asia Minor was the act of a man determined to fight to the end. He strengthened his Armenian alliance, sought support from Greece, Crete, and Egypt, filled the Mediterranean with privateers, recruited a foreign legion (largely from Roman and Italian political refugees), and reportedly raised an army of 250,000 foot-soldiers and 40,000 horse. During 88 B.C. his troops overran practically all Asia Minor, and penetrated into Greece. Thus Sulla's first objective was to free Greece.

Once landed, the comparatively small Sullan army of 30,000 easily defeated Mithradates' general Archelaus and restored the bulk of the Greek mainland to Roman control. Archelaus held out in Athens, supplied by sea through the port of the Piraeus. A long siege was necessary, in which Sulla was severely handicapped by lack of a fleet. But Athens was finally stormed in March,

86 B.C., and soon afterward the Asiatic army in Greece was nearly annihilated.

In the meantime the new revolutionary Senate in Rome had ordered Sulla superseded in his command, and had sent Lucius Flaccus with two legions to Greece. Flaccus found Sulla's troops stoutly attached to their victorious commander, and therefore continued to Asia Minor with only the forces he had brought from Italy. Shortly afterward he met death in an insurrection of the soldiers fomented by his own lieutenant, Gaius Fimbria, who then took over the command.

By the spring of 85 B.C., Mithradates' general position had sharply deteriorated. His senseless cruelties and his subversion of the existing social order (freeing of slaves, general remission of debts, etc.) caused such cities as Smyrna, Ephesus, and Sardis to defect to the Romans. Sulla, now supported by a growing fleet recruited and organized by his able adjutant Lucius Lucullus, had invaded Asia Minor in the wake of Fimbria after clearing all Greece of enemy forces. The king therefore sued for peace, and Sulla, aware how endlessly the war could be protracted, and himself anxious to return to Italy, was willing to make terms which largely restored the former situation. The second Roman army, under the command of Fimbria, was easily taken over by encouraging the Fimbrian soldiers to defect to the Sullans. So successful was this solicitation that Fimbria, in despair, fell upon his sword.

Sulla wintered his victorious army in the rich cities of western Asia Minor. He laid a heavy indemnity on the communities that had supported Mithradates, and executed the more prominent partisans of the king. But he lacked time and means to make a thorough reorganization, and when he quit the province for Italy in 84 B.C., he left it ravaged by war and a prey to tax gatherers, moneylenders, and pirates.

Early in 83 B.C. he landed at Brundisium, with an

army of veterans at his back who had no loyalty save to loot and to their commander. "His arrival," remarks Mommsen, "was preceded by a report addressed to the Senate describing his campaigns in Greece and Asia, the writer of which appeared to know nothing of his deposition from command. It was the mute herald of the impending restoration."

Sulla had much to restore. He had left the government in the hands of two hopelessly antagonistic consuls, the die-hard conservative Gnaeus Octavius and the rabble-rousing adventurer Lucius Cornelius Cinna. Scarcely had he turned his back in 87 B.C. than the revolution he had suppressed by force broke out with new vigor. Cinna re-offered the Sulpician law, and was driven out of the city after a street battle in which thousands of his partisans were killed. He successfully appealed to the soldiers at Capua, and with this force as a nucleus was able to raise money and recruits among the newly-enfranchised Italian allies. Marius, bitterly bent on revenge, returned from exile on Cinna's invitation. By cutting off Rome's food supply, they forced a surrender of the city. The stubborn Gnaeus Octavius, "true to his oft-expressed principle that he would rather die than concede one iota to his outlawed opponents, refused even now to flee. In his consular robes he awaited the assassin, who was not slow to appear."

A reign of terror, instigated by Marius, immediately began. Measured by the number of its victims, it was less bloody than some previous political massacres, but the prominence and high public estimation of the men slain, and the cold brutality with which it was carried out, made it a horror for decades to come. At least five former consuls and countless other conservative notables were murdered under Marius' personal supervision. "His revenge was not satisfied by the deaths of his victims: he forbade burial of the bodies; gave orders that the heads of slain senators be hung from the rostra in the Forum;

ordered particular corpses to be dragged through the streets; . . . and publicly embraced the man who brought him, as he sat at table, the head of the former consul Marcus Antonius, whom he had with difficulty been restrained from seeking out in his hiding-place and slaying with his own hand." Even after Marius died of a fever in January, 86 B.C., "loaded with the execration of all parties and the hatred of the whole nation," the murders continued, until Quintus Sertorius wiped out the Marian executionary bands.

For fours years, 87-84 B.C., Cinna "governed" as consul—"not [Mommsen remarks] according to a possibly erroneous plan, but according to no political plan at all." The Sullan laws were repealed, Sulla's estates were laid waste, and only with difficulty did his wife and children escape to his Macedonian headquarters. But the revolutionary government's most energetic single action during its four years' tenure of power was the raising of 100,000 troops to oppose Sulla's return.

Against this force Sulla could place in the scale only his five legions—probably scarcely 40,000 men, even including some contingents levied in Macedonia and Greece. True, this army during seven years' warfare had been weaned from politics, and attached to its general (who pardoned debauchery, brutality, even mutiny in his soldiers, required nothing but bravery and loyalty toward their general, and promised them the most extravagant rewards from victory) with that kind of soldierly enthusiasm which is the more powerful because the noblest and meanest passions often combine to produce it. Sulla's soldiers voluntarily swore to stand firmly by each other, and voluntarily brought their savings to the general as a contribution to the war's cost. But despite the weight of this solid and select body of troops, Sulla saw that a united and resolute Italy could not be subdued with five legions. To settle accounts with the popular party and their incapable autocrats would not have been difficult; but united with that party was the whole mass of those who desired no oligarchic restoration, and above all the whole body of new citizens—both those whom the Julian law had deterred from taking part in the insurrection, and those whose revolt had brought Rome to the brink of ruin.

Surveying this situation, Sulla was far removed from the blind exasperation which characterized most of his party. While the state was in flames, his friends being murdered, his houses destroyed, and his family driven into exile, he had remained at his post till the Roman frontier was secured. He now treated Italian affairs with the same patriotic and judicious moderation, doing whatever he could to pacify the middle party and the new citizens, and to prevent the civil struggle from assuming the far more dangerous form of a fresh war between the Romans and their Italian allies.

The first letter which Sulla addressed to the Senate had expressly disclaimed a reign of terror. In harmony with its terms, he now offered unconditional pardon to all who would break with the revolutionary government, and caused his soldiers man by man to swear that they would treat the Italians as friends and fellow citizens. So binding were Sulla's declarations guaranteeing the new citizens their political gains that the democratic leader Carbo demanded hostages from every civic community in Italy. (The proposal broke down under general indignation and the opposition of the Senate.) The chief difficulty of Sulla's position was that, in view of the faithlessness and perfidy which prevailed, the new citizens had every reason to doubt whether he could make his party keep its word after victory.

In the spring of 83 B.C. Sulla landed his legions at Brundisium. On receiving the news, the Senate declared the commonwealth in danger, and granted the consuls

unlimited powers; but these incapable leaders were surprised by a landing that might have been foreseen for
years. The government's army was still at Ariminum, the
ports were not garrisoned, and (incredibly) there was
not a man in arms along the whole southeastern coast.
The consequences were soon apparent. Brundisium itself,
a considerable community of new citizens, opened its
gates to Sulla; all Messapia and Apulia followed its example; and the army marched through the area as
through a friendly country, uniformly maintaining the
strictest discipline.

From all sides the scattered conservative remnant
flocked to the camp. Quintus Metellus came from Liguria
(where he had gone after escaping from Africa) to resume as Sulla's colleague the proconsular command withdrawn from him by the revolution, and Marcus Crassus
appeared from Africa with a small band of armed men.[1]
More important, deserters began to appear from the
democratic camp—for instance, the refined and respected
Lucius Philippus, one of the few consulars who had come
to terms with the revolutionary government. He was
graciously received by Sulla, and given the honorable and
easy task of occupying the province of Sardinia. Quintus
Lucretius Ofella and other officers were likewise received
and at once employed. Even Publius Cethegus, one of the
senators banished by Sulla, obtained pardon and a position in the army.

Still more important was the gain of the Picenum district, substantially due to Strabo's young son Gnaeus
Pompeius [hereafter called Pompey]. The latter, like
his father originally no conservative, had even served in
Cinna's army. But his father's service against the revolution was not forgotten, and he found himself threatened
with an indictment requiring him to give up the booty

■

---

1. Many of the aristocratic newcomers, Mommsen observes in the original,
were of far less use.

allegedly embezzled by his father after the capture of Asculum. The personal protection of the consul Carbo, plus the eloquence of the consular Lucius Philippus and the young Quintus Hortensius, averted financial ruin; but his dissatisfaction remained. On the news of Sulla's landing he went to Picenum, where he had extensive possessions and the best municipal connections, and set up the standard of the Optimate party in Auximum. The district, mostly inhabited by old citizens, joined him; the young men, many of whom had served with him under his father, readily followed the courageous leader who at twenty-two was as much soldier as general, and who at the head of his cavalry vigorously assailed the enemy.

The Picenian corps soon grew to three legions. Three separate forces were dispatched from the capital against him, but the young general, dexterously using the dissensions that arose among them, had the skill to evade them or to beat them in detail and join Sulla's main army. Sulla saluted him as *Imperator* [2] and showed him honors withheld from his other noble supporters—presumably thereby also rebuking them indirectly for their lack of energy.

Thus reinforced both morally and materially, Sulla and Metellus marched through the still insurgent Samnite districts towards Campania. The enemy force advanced toward the same district, and it seemed as if the issue would there be decided. The army of the consul Gaius Norbanus was already at Capua, where a new colony of citizens had just been installed with great ceremony, and the second consular army was likewise advancing along the Appian road. Before it arrived, however, Sulla was in front of Norbanus. A last attempt at mediation by Sulla led only to the arrest of his envoys. With fresh indignation his veteran troops assailed the enemy, and their first charge down from Mount Tifata broke the enemy ranks drawn up in the plain. Norbanus took the

2. In this case, an officer of equal rank. See Glossary.

remnant of his force into Capua and the new colony of
Neapolis, and allowed himself to be blockaded there.

By this victory Sulla's troops replaced their apprehension about their weak numbers with a full conviction of
their superiority. Instead of besieging the remains of the
defeated army, Sulla invested the towns where they took
shelter and advanced along the Appian highway against
Teanum, where the consul Scipio was posted. To him
also, before beginning battle, Sulla made fresh and apparently sincere proposals for peace. The weak Scipio
entered into them; an armistice was concluded; the two
generals, both members of the same noble *gens,* both men
of culture and refinement and for many years colleagues
in the Senate, met in personal conference; they discussed
several questions; they made such progress that Scipio
dispatched a messenger to Capua to procure his colleague's opinion.

The Sullans, well supplied with money by their general, had no trouble in persuading the anxious recruits
over their cups that it was better to have them as comrades than foes. In vain Sertorius warned his general to
stop this dangerous intercourse. The agreement which
had seemed so near was not effected, and Scipio denounced the armistice. But Sulla maintained that the
agreement had been already concluded; whereupon Scipio's soldiers, under the pretext that their general had
wrongfully denounced the armistice, passed over *en
masse* to the ranks of the enemy. The scene ended with
universal embracing before the commanding officers of
the revolutionary army. Sulla ordered the consul to resign his office—which he did—and offered to have him
and his staff escorted to any point they desired. Scipio,
however, was hardly at liberty when he resumed his office
and began to collect fresh troops. Sulla and Metellus
took up winter-quarters in Campania and, after the failure of a second attempt to come to terms with Norbanus,
maintained the blockade of Capua during the winter.

Sulla's achievements in the first campaign secured the submission of Apulia, Picenum, and Campania, the dissolution of one consular army, and the vanquishing and blockading of the other. The Italian communities, compelled to choose between oppressors, in numerous cases entered into negotiations with him, and caused the political rights which they had won from the opposition party to be guaranteed by the general in formal separate treaties. It was Sulla's hope, as well as his boast, that he would overthrow the revolutionary government in the next campaign and again march into Rome.

But despair gave the revolution fresh energies. The consuls were two of its most vigorous leaders, Carbo and Gaius Marius the younger. (The fact that the latter, at age 20, could not legally hold the consulship was as little heeded as any other constitutional point.) Quintus Sertorius, who continued to prove an inconvenient critic, was ordered to raise new troops in Etruria and then to proceed to his province of Hither Spain. To replenish the treasury the Senate was obliged to decree the melting of the gold and silver vessels of the temples—a considerable quantity, as may be seen from the fact that after several months' warfare there still remained nearly 14,000 pounds of gold and 6,000 pounds of silver.

In the large area of Italy which still voluntarily or under compulsion adhered to the revolution, warlike preparations went forward with vigor. Newly formed divisions of some strength came from Etruria, where the communities of new citizens were very numerous, and from the region of the Po. The veterans of Marius in great numbers answered the call of his son. But preparations for the struggle proceeded with greatest eagerness in insurgent Samnium and some Lucanian districts. It was certainly not from devotion to the revolutionary government that numerous Oscan contingents reinforced its armies; but it was well understood there that an oligarchy restored by Sulla would not acquiesce, like the lax Cinnan government, in the existing *de facto* independence of these lands. Therefore the age-old rivalry of Sabellian against Latin flamed afresh in the struggle against Sulla,[3] and the campaign of 82 B.C. was begun on both sides with greater resources and increased hatred. The revolution in particular threw away the scabbard, outlawing (at Carbo's suggestion) all senators who went over to Sulla's camp. Sulla was silent. He probably thought that they were pronouncing sentence on themselves.

The army of the Optimates was divided, Metellus undertaking, with the support of the Picenian insurrection, to advance to Upper Italy, while Sulla marched from Campania against the capital. Carbo opposed the former, Marius choosing to encounter the main enemy army in Latium. Advancing along the Via Latina, Sulla met the Marian army not far from Signia. They retired before him as far as the so-called "Port of Sacer," between Signia and the chief stronghold of the Marians, the strong Praeneste. There Marius drew up his force, about 40,000 strong, for battle. He was the true son of his father in savage fury and personal bravery, but his troops were not the trained veterans with which the latter had fought his battles, and still less could the inexperienced young man compare with the old master. His troops soon gave way, the defeat being hastened by a division which switched sides even during the battle. More than half the Marians were killed or captured, and the remnant, unable to keep the field or gain the other bank of the Tiber, was compelled to seek shelter in the nearby fortresses.

With the capital, which the democrats had neglected to provision, thus irrecoverably lost, Marius ordered the commanding praetor Lucius Brutus Damasippus to evacuate it, but before doing so to put to death all the outstanding Optimates who still survived. This injunction

3. In a brief section here omitted, Mommsen notes the national character of the war for Samnium.

of the son, which even outdid the bestialities of his father, was carried into effect. Damasippus convoked the Senate under a pretext, and the marked men were struck down partly during the sitting and partly on their flight from the senate house. Notwithstanding the previous massacre there were still several victims of note, among them the two best legal orators of the day, the former *aedile* [4] Publius Antistius, who was also young Pompey's father-in-law, and the former praetor Gaius Carbo, son of the well-known friend and subsequent opponent of the Gracchi. The slain also included the consular Lucius Domitius and even the venerable pontifex maximus, Quintus Scaevola, who had escaped the dagger of Fimbria only to bleed to death during these last throes of the revolution in the vestibule of the temple of Vesta entrusted to his guardianship. With speechless horror the multitude saw the corpses of these last victims dragged through the streets and thrown into the river.

The broken bands of Marius threw themselves into the strong neighboring cities of Norba and Praeneste, Marius entering the latter with the treasure and most of the fugitives. Sulla left an able officer, Quintus Ofella, before Praeneste just as he had done in the previous year before Capua, with instructions not to waste his strength in besieging the town, but by blockade to starve it into surrender. Sulla himself advanced from different sides upon the capital, which he found abandoned by the enemy, and occupied it without resistance. Barely taking time to ease the minds of the people by an address and to make the most necessary arrangements, he immediately set out for Etruria, that together with Metellus he might rid Northern Italy of the enemy.

Metellus had meanwhile encountered and defeated Carbo's lieutenant Carrinas at the river Aesis, which

4. Lesser officials whose various duties included policing the capital, judging minor disputes, supervising public festivals, and the like. See Glossary.

separated the district of Picenum from the Gallic province, but had been obliged to forego any further advance when Carbo came up in person with his superior
army. Carbo, however, became anxious about his communications upon learning of events near Rome. He retreated to the Flaminian road intending to set up headquarters at Ariminum, from whence he might hold the
passes of the Apennines on the one hand and the valley
of the Po on the other. In this retreat different divisions
fell into the hands of the enemy, and Carbo's rearguard
was broken in a brilliant cavalry engagement by Pompey; nevertheless Carbo on the whole attained his object. The consular Norbanus took the command in the
valley of the Po, while Carbo himself proceeded to
Etruria.

The march of Sulla with his victorious legions to
Etruria again altered the situation, as three Sullan armies
from Gaul, Umbria, and Rome established communications with each other. Metellus with the fleet went past
Ariminum to Ravenna, and at Faventia cut communications between Ariminum and the valley of the Po. Pompey and his contemporary and rival Crassus penetrated
from Picenum by mountain paths into Umbria and gained
the Flaminian road at Spoletium, where they defeated
Carbo's legate Carrinas and shut him up in the town. (He
succeeded, however, in escaping from it on a rainy night
and making his way, though not without loss, to the army
of Carbo.) Sulla himself marched from Rome into
Etruria with his army in two divisions, one of which advancing along the coast defeated the corps opposed to it
at Saturnia; the second, led by Sulla in person, fell in
with the army of Carbo in the valley of the Clanis, and
sustained a successful conflict with his Spanish cavalry.
But the pitched battle fought between Carbo and Sulla
in the region of Clusium, though not properly decisive,
was in favor of Carbo to the extent that Sulla's victorious
advance was checked.

In the vicinity of Rome events also appeared to take a favorable turn for the revolutionary party. For while the Optimates were concentrating all their energies on Etruria, the popular party put forth the utmost efforts to break the blockade of Praeneste. Even the governor of Sicily, Marcus Perpenna, set out for that purpose, though it does not appear that he reached Praeneste. Nor was the very considerable corps under Marcius, detached by Carbo, any more successful: assailed and defeated by enemy troops from Spoletium, demoralized by disorder, want of supplies, and mutiny, one portion went back to Carbo, another to Ariminum, and the rest dispersed.

But help in earnest came from Southern Italy. There the Samnites under Pontius of Telesia, and the Lucanians under their experienced general Marcus Lamponius, set out for Praeneste, nor was it possible to prevent their departure. They were joined in Campania by part of the democratic garrison of Capua, which swelled their troops to a reported 70,000 men. Thereupon Sulla, leaving behind a corps against Carbo, returned to Latium and took up a well-chosen position in the defiles in front of Praeneste, where he barred the route of the relieving army. In vain the garrison attempted to break through the lines of Ofella; in vain the relieving army attempted to dislodge Sulla. Both remained immovable in their strong positions, even after Damasippus at Carbo's orders had reinforced the relieving army with two legions.

While the war thus stood still in Etruria and in Latium, matters came to a decision in the valley of the Po, where the general of the democracy, Gaius Norbanus, had hitherto maintained the upper hand. He had attacked Metellus' lieutenant Marcus Lucullus with superior forces and shut him up in Placentia, and had at length turned against Metellus in person. He encountered the latter at Faventia, and immediately attacked late in the afternoon with his troops fatigued by their march. The consequence was the complete defeat and total break-

ing up of his corps, of which only about 1,000 men returned to Etruria. On the news of this battle Lucullus
sallied forth and defeated the division left behind to oppose him. The Lucanian troops of Albinovanus deserted
in a body, their leader making up for his hesitation by inviting the chief officers of the revolutionary army to banquet with him and causing them to be put to death. In
general, everyone who could now concluded his peace.
Ariminum with all its stores and treasures fell into the
hands of Metellus, Norbanus embarked for Rhodes, the
whole region between the Alps and Apennines acknowledged the government of the Optimates, and the troops
hitherto employed there were freed to attack Etruria, the
last province where their antagonists still kept the field.

When Carbo received this news in his camp at Clusium,
he lost his nerve. Although he still had a considerable
body of troops under his command, he fled from his
headquarters secretly and embarked for Africa. Part of
his abandoned troops followed their general's example
and went home, part of them were destroyed by Pompey, and Carrinas led the remainder to Latium to join
the army at Praeneste. There no change had meanwhile
taken place, and the final decision drew near. The troops
of Carrinas were not numerous enough to shake Sulla's
position, and the vanguard of the oligarchic army was approaching under Pompey. In a few days the net would
draw tight around the army of the democrats and the
Samnites.

Its leaders then determined to abandon the relief of
Praeneste and throw themselves on Rome, only a good
day's march distant. By so doing they were militarily
ruined, for their line of retreat would fall into Sulla's
hands; and even if they got possession of Rome, they
would inevitably be crushed within a city ill-suited for defense, and wedged between the far superior armies of
Metellus and Sulla. Safety, however, was not an object.
Revenge alone dictated their march, the last outbreak

of fury in the passionate revolutionists and especially in the despairing Sabellians. Pontius of Telesia was in earnest when he proclaimed to his followers that, in order to get rid of the wolves which had robbed Italy of freedom, the forest which harbored them must be destroyed.

Never was Rome in more fearful peril than on the first of November, 82 B.C., when Pontius, Lamponius, Carrinas, and Damasippus advanced along the Latin road and encamped about a mile from the Colline gate. It was threatened with a day like July 20, 389 B.C., or June 15, A.D. 455—the days of the Celts and the Vandals. The time was gone by when a *coup de main* against Rome was a foolish enterprise, and the assailants could have no want of connections in the capital. The volunteers who sallied from the city, mostly youths of quality, were scattered like chaff. The only hope of safety rested on Sulla. The latter, on learning of the departure of the Samnite army for Rome, had likewise set out in all haste for the capital. The appearance of his foremost horsemen under Balbus during the morning revived the sinking courage of the citizens. About midday he appeared in person with his main force, and immediately drew up his ranks for battle at the temple of the Erycine Aphrodite before the Colline gate.

His lieutenants begged him not to send his exhausted troops into action at once; but Sulla took into consideration what the night might bring on Rome, and, late as it was in the afternoon, ordered the attack. The battle was obstinately contested and bloody. Sulla's left wing, which he led in person, gave way as far as the city wall, so that it became necessary to close the city gates. Stragglers even brought accounts to Ofella that the battle was lost, but on the right wing Marcus Crassus overthrew the enemy and pursued him as far as Antemnae. This somewhat relieved the left wing, and an hour after sunset it in turn began to advance. The fight continued throughout the night and even into the following morning; and it was only the defection of a division of 3,000 men, who turned their arms against their former comrades, that put an end to the struggle and saved Rome.

The army of the insurgents, for which there was no retreat, was completely extirpated. The prisoners taken in the battle—between 3,000 and 4,000 in number, including the generals Damasippus, Carrinas, and the severely wounded Pontius—were brought by Sulla's orders on the third day after the battle to the Villa Publica in the Campus Martius, and there were massacred to the last man, so that the clatter of arms and the groans of the dying were distinctly heard in the neighboring temple of Bellona, where Sulla was holding a meeting of the Senate. It was a ghastly execution and ought not to be excused; but it is not right to forget that those very men who perished there had fallen like a band of robbers on the capital and its citizens, and, had they found time, would have destroyed them as far as fire and sword can destroy a city.

With this battle the war was effectively at an end. The garrison of Praeneste surrendered, when it learned the issue of the battle at Rome from the heads of Carrinas and other officers thrown over the walls. The leaders, the consul Gaius Marius and the son of Pontius, fell on each other's swords after failing in an attempt to escape. The multitude cherished the hope that the victor would even now have mercy upon them, but the time for mercy was past. The more unconditionally had Sulla up to the last moment granted full pardon to those who came over to him, the more inexorable he showed himself toward the leaders and communities that had held out to the end. Of the Praenestine prisoners, 12,000 in number, most of the Romans and some individual Praenestines as well as the women and children were released. But the Roman senators, the great majority of the Praenestines, and all of the Samnites were disarmed and cut to pieces, and the rich city was given up to pillage.

After such an occurrence it was natural that the cities of new citizens which had not yet capitulated should continue their resistance with the utmost obstinacy. In the Latin town of Norba, for instance, when Aemilius Lepidus got into it by treachery, the citizens killed each other and set fire to their own homes in order to deprive their executioners of vengeance and of booty. In Lower Italy Neapolis had already been taken by assault, and Capua seems to have voluntarily surrendered; but Nola was not evacuated by the Samnites until 80 B.C. On his flight from Nola the last surviving leader of the Italians, the consul of the insurgents in the hopeful year of 90 B.C., Gaius Papius Mutilus, disowned by his wife to whom he had stolen in disguise and with whom he had hoped to find asylum, fell on his sword in Teanum before the door of his own house. As for the Samnites, the dictator declared that Rome would have no rest so long as Samnium existed, and that the Samnite name must therefore be extirpated from the earth. He verified these words in terrible fashion on the prisoners taken before Rome and in Praeneste, and he appears to have undertaken a raid for the purpose of laying waste the country, to have captured Aesernia, and to have converted that hitherto flourishing and populous region into the desert which it has since remained.

A longer resistance was offered by Populonium in Etruria and above all by the impregnable Volaterrae. The latter, garrisoned by an army of four legions gathered out of the remnants of the beaten party, stood a two years' siege conducted first by Sulla in person and then by the former praetor Gaius Carbo, the brother of the democratic consul, till at length in 79 B.C., three years after the battle at the Colline Gate, the garrison capitulated on condition of free departure. But in this terrible time neither military law nor discipline could be trusted. The entering army raised a cry of treason and stoned its too humane general, and a troop of horse sent by the Roman government cut down the garrison as it withdrew according to the terms of the capitulation. The victorious Sullan army was distributed throughout Italy, and all the insecure townships were furnished with strong garrisons. Under the iron hand of the Sullan officers the last palpitations of the revolutionary and national opposition slowly subsided.

There was still work to be done in the provinces. Sardinia had been speedily wrested by Lucius Philippus from the democratic governor Quintus Antonius (82 B.C.), and Transalpine Gaul offered little or no resistance; but in Sicily, Spain, and Africa the cause of the popular party still seemed by no means lost. Sicily was held for them by the trustworthy Marcus Perpenna. Quintus Sertorius had the skill to win the support of the provincials in Hither Spain, and to form from among the Roman settlers a not inconsiderable army, which soon closed the passes of the Pyrenees. In this he gave fresh proof that he was at home wherever he was stationed, and amid all the incapables of the revolution he was the only really capable man.

In Africa the governor Hadrianus, who followed the path of revolution too zealously and began to free the slaves, had been attacked in his official residence and burnt with his attendants (82 B.C.) during a tumult instigated by the Roman merchants of Utica. Nevertheless the province adhered to the revolutionary government, and Cinna's son-in-law, the young and able Gnaeus Domitius Ahenobarbus, was invested with the supreme command there. Propaganda had even been spread among the Numidian and Mauretanian protectorates. Their legitimate rulers, Hiempsal II son of Gauda, and Bogud son of Bocchus, apparently sided with Sulla. But with the aid of the Cinnans the former had been dethroned by the democratic pretender Hiarbas, and similar feuds agitated the Mauretanian kingdom. The consul Carbo, fleeing from Italy, tarried on the island of Cossyra (Pantellaria) between Africa and Sicily, apparently at a loss whether he should flee to Egypt or attempt to renew the struggle in one of the faithful provinces.

Sulla dispatched Gaius Annius as governor of Further Spain and Gaius Valerius Flaccus as governor of the Ebro province. They were spared the difficult task of forcing the passes of the Pyrenees, because the general sent thither by Sertorius had been killed by one of his own officers and his troops had thereafter melted away. Sertorius, much too weak to maintain an equal struggle, hastily collected the nearest divisions and embarked at New Carthage—for what destination he knew not himself, perhaps for the coast of Africa or for the Canary Islands; it mattered little, provided only Sulla's arm could not reach him. Spain then willingly submitted to the Sullan magistrates (about 81 B.C.), and Flaccus fought successfully with the Celts and with the Spanish Celtiberians.

Pompey was sent as propraetor to Sicily, and, when he appeared on the coast with 120 sail and six legions, the island was evacuated by Perpenna without resistance. From there Pompey sent a squadron to Cossyra, and captured the Marian officers sojourning there. Marcus Brutus and the others were immediately executed; but Pompey ordered that the consul Carbo should be brought before him at Lilybaeum in order that he might personally hand him over to the executioner—disregarding the protection accorded to him during past perils by that very man.

Having been ordered to go on to Africa, Pompey with his superior army defeated the not inconsiderable forces collected by Ahenobarbus and Hiarbas, and, declining for the moment to be saluted as imperator, at once gave the signal for assault on the hostile camp. He thus became master of the enemy in one day, Ahenobarbus being among the fallen. With the aid of King Bogud, Hiarbas was seized and slain at Bulla, and Hiempsal was reinstated in his hereditary kingdom. A general campaign against the inhabitants of the desert, among whom a number of Gaetulian tribes recognized as free by Marius were made subject to Hiempsal, removed the tarnish from the Roman name, and in forty days after Pompey's landing all was at an end in Africa. The Senate instructed him to break up his army—an implied hint that he was not to be allowed a triumph, which according to precedent an extraordinary magistrate could not claim. The general murmured secretly, the soldiers loudly; and it seemed for a moment as if the African army would revolt against the Senate and Sulla would have to take the field against his son-in-law. But Sulla yielded, and allowed the young man to boast of being the only Roman who had become a triumphator before he was a senator (March 12, 79 B.C.). In fact, Sulla "the Fortunate" (not perhaps without a touch of irony) saluted the youth on his return from these easy exploits as "the Great."

In the East also, after the embarkation of Sulla in the spring of 83 B.C., there had been no peace. The restoration of the old state of affairs and the subjugation of individual towns in Asia as in Italy cost various bloody struggles. Against the free city of Mytilene in particular Lucius Lucullus was finally obliged to bring up troops, after having exhausted all gentler measures; and even a military victory did not put an end to the obstinate resistance of the citizens.

Meanwhile the Roman governor of Asia, Lucius Murena, had again fallen athwart King Mithradates. Since signing the peace the latter had busied himself in strengthening his rule, which was shaken even in the northern provinces. After pacifying the Colchians by appointing his able son Mithradates as their governor, he had then done away with that son, and was now preparing for an

expedition into his Bosporan kingdom. The assurances of
Archelaus (who had been obliged to seek an asylum with
Murena) that these preparations were directed against
Rome induced Murena, under the pretext that Mithradates still kept possession of Cappadocian frontier districts, to move his troops toward the Cappadocian Co-
mana and thus to violate the Pontic frontier.

Mithradates contented himself with complaining to
Murena and, when this was in vain, to the Roman government. In fact, commissioners from Sulla made their appearance to dissuade the governor, but he did not submit.
On the contrary he crossed the Halys and entered on undeniably Pontic territory, whereupon Mithradates resolved to repel force by force. His general Gordius had
to detain the Roman army till the king came up with far
superior forces and compelled battle. Murena was vanquished with great loss and driven back over the Roman
frontier to Phrygia, and the Roman garrisons were expelled from all Cappadocia. Murena still had the effron-
tery to call himself the victor and to assume the title of
imperator as a result of these exploits. But the sharp
lesson and a second admonition from Sulla persuaded him
to push the matter no further, and the peace between
Rome and Mithradates was renewed. This foolish feud,
while it lasted, had postponed the reduction of Mytilene.
It was only after a long siege by land and by sea, in which
the Bithynian fleet rendered good service, that Murena's
successor succeeded in taking the city by storm in 79 B.C.

Thus ended ten years' revolution and insurrection in
the West and in the East. The state once more had unity
of government and peace within and without, and after
the terrible convulsions of the last years even this relief
was welcome. Whether it was to furnish more than a
mere relief, whether the remarkable man who had succeeded in the difficult task of vanquishing the public foe,
and in the more difficult work of subduing the revolution,
would be able to accomplish the most difficult task of

all—re-establishing the social and political order shaken
to its very foundations—was soon to be decided.

About the time the first pitched battle was fought between Romans and Romans, on the night of July 6, 83
B.C., a venerable temple that had been erected by the
kings, dedicated by the youthful republic, and spared by
the storms of five hundred years—the temple of the Roman Jupiter on the Capitol—went up in flames. It was
no augury, but rather a symbol of the status of the Roman constitution. It, too, lay in ruins and needed reconstruction. The revolution was no doubt vanquished, but
victory was far from implying a routine restoration of the
old government. The mass of the aristocracy certainly
felt that now, after the death of the two revolutionary
consuls, it would be enough to arrange for the ordinary
supplemental election and leave it to the Senate to take
any further steps for rewarding the victorious army,
punishing the most guilty revolutionists, and possibly also
for preventing similar outbreaks.

But Sulla, in whose hands the victory had for the moment concentrated all power, formed a more correct
judgment of the situation. The aristocracy of Rome in
its best days had not risen above an adherence—partly
noble and partly narrow—to traditional forms: how
could the clumsy government of old be in a position to
carry out thoroughly and energetically a comprehensive
reform of the state? At the present moment, after crisis
had swept away almost all the Senate's leading men, the
vigor and intelligence requisite for such an enterprise
were more lacking than ever. How useless was aristocratic
blood alone, and how low was Sulla's regard for it, is
shown by the fact that, except for his relation-by-mar-
riage Quintus Metellus, his chosen lieutenants were all
from the middle party or deserters from the democratic

camp—e.g., Lucius Flaccus, Lucius Philippus, Quintus Ofella, and Gnaeus Pompey.

Sulla was as keen on re-establishing the old constitution as the most vehement aristocrat. But he understood (though perhaps not fully, for how in that case could he have put his hand to the work at all?) better than his party the enormous difficulties of this work of restoration. Comprehensive concessions, so far as concession did not affect the essence of oligarchy, and the establishment of an energetic system of repression and prevention, he regarded as unavoidable; but he saw clearly that the existing Senate would refuse or mutilate every concession, ruin every systematic reconstruction. Since Sulla had done what he felt necessary after the Sulpician revolution without much thought of their advice, he was determined under far more critical circumstances to restore the oligarchy, not with the aid of but in spite of the oligarchs.

However, Sulla was not now consul as he had been then, but possessed merely proconsular—i.e., military—power. He needed an authority that was at once extraordinary and as constitutional as possible, in order to impose his reforms on friends and foes. Therefore, in a letter to the Senate he announced that it seemed essential to place the guidance of the state in the hands of one man with unlimited powers, and that he deemed himself called to this difficult task. This proposal, though disagreeable to many, was in effect a command. At the Senate's direction Lucius Valerius Flaccus, as interim holder of the supreme power, proposed to the citizens that Sulla should receive blanket approval of all his past acts as consul and proconsul; that for the future he should be empowered without appeal to adjudicate on the life and property of the citizens, to deal at his pleasure with the public land, to alter the boundaries of Rome, of Italy, and of the state, to dissolve or establish urban communities in Italy, to dispose of the provinces and dependent states, to confer the supreme command, to nominate proconsuls and propraetors, and to regulate the state for the future by means of new laws; that he alone should judge when he had fulfilled his task and might deem it time to resign this extraordinary magistracy; and that during its continuance it should depend on his pleasure whether the ordinary supreme magistracy should exist side by side with his own or should remain in abeyance.

As a matter of course the proposal was adopted without opposition in November of 82 B.C., and the new master of the state, who as proconsul had avoided entering the capital, appeared for the first time within the walls of Rome. His new office derived its name from the dictatorship, which had been practically abolished since the Hannibalic war. But since he was preceded by twice as many lictors as the dictator of earlier times, this new "dictatorship for the making of laws and the regulation of the commonwealth" (as its official title ran) was in fact quite different from the earlier magistracy, which had been limited as to duration and powers, had not excluded appeal to the citizens, and had not annulled the ordinary magistracy. It much more resembled that of the *decemviri legibus scribendis*,[5] who likewise came forward as an extraordinary government with unlimited fulness of powers superseding the ordinary magistracy, and practically at least administered their office as one which was unlimited in point of time. Or one might say that this new office, with its absolute power based on a decree of the people and restrained by no set term or colleague, was merely the old monarchy, which in fact rested only on the agreement of the citizens to obey one of their number as absolute lord.

■

5. Ten extraordinary officials chosen in the middle of the fifth century B.C. to act in place of the consuls, for the purpose of drafting a code of laws which would regularize the consuls' powers. They produced the first legal code of the Roman republic, the law of the Twelve Tables.

It was urged even by contemporaries, in vindication of
Sulla, that a king is better than a bad constitution; and as
the former title of dictatorship implied a limited reassumption, so this new dictatorship involved a complete
reassumption of the regal power. Thus Sulla's course
paralleled that which Gaius Gracchus had followed with
so wholly different a design. Once more the conservatives
had to borrow from their opponents. The protector of
the oligarchic constitution had to come forward as a
tyrant in order to avert the ever-threatening tyranny.
There was not a little of defeat in this last victory of the
oligarchy.

Sulla had neither sought nor desired this difficult and
dreadful labor of restoration. But since his only choice
was to leave it to utterly incapable hands or to undertake
it himself, he set forth with remorseless energy. First of
all came a settlement with the guilty. Sulla was personally
inclined to pardon. Sanguine in temperament, he could
indeed show violent rage, and well might they beware
who saw his eye gleam and his cheeks color. But the vin-
dictiveness which characterized Marius in his embittered
old age was altogether foreign to Sulla's disposition. Not
only had he borne himself with comparatively great moderation after the revolution of 88 B.C.; even the second
revolution, whose fearful outrages had affected him so
personally and severely, had not disturbed his equilib-
rium. As the executioner was dragging the bodies of his
friends through the streets of the capital, he had sought
in the East to save the life of the blood-stained Fimbria;
and when the latter died by his own hand, he had given
orders for his decent burial. On landing in Italy he had
earnestly offered to forgive and forget, and no one who
came to make peace had been rejected. Even after his
first successes he had negotiated in this spirit with Lucius
Scipio. It was the revolutionary party which not only had
broken off these negotiations, but had at the last moment

before their downfall resumed the massacres more fearfully than ever, and had in fact conspired with their country's inveterate foes for the destruction of Rome.

The cup was now full. Immediately after assuming the regency, Sulla outlawed all the civil and military officials who had actively aided the revolution after the convention with Scipio (which according to Sulla's assertion was validly concluded), and such other citizens as had markedly aided its cause. Whoever killed one of these outlaws was not only exempt from punishment, but also was paid 12,000 *denarii* for the execution. Anyone who befriended an outlaw, even the nearest relative, was liable to the severest punishment. The property of those outlawed was forfeited to the state, and their children and grandchildren were excluded from a political career, though if of senatorial rank they were bound to assume their share of senatorial burdens. These last enactments also applied to the estates and the descendants of those who had died for the revolution—penalties never before inflicted on those who had borne arms against their fatherland. Most terrible of all was the vagueness of the proposed categories, which brought immediate remonstrance in the Senate, and which Sulla himself sought to remedy by directing the names of the proscribed to be publicly posted and fixing June 1, 81 B.C., as the date for closing the proscription lists.

Much as this bloody roll, swelling daily until it amounted to 4,700 names, excited the just horror of the multitude, at least it checked the caprice of the executioners. Sulla's hatred was directed solely against the authors of the hideous massacres of 87 and 82 B.C. By his command the tomb of Gaius Marius was broken open, his ashes were scattered in the Anio, the monuments of his victories over Africans and Germans were overthrown, and, as death had snatched him and his son from Sulla's vengeance, his adopted nephew Marcus Marius Gratidianus (twice praetor and a great favorite with the popu-

lace) was executed amid the cruelest tortures at the tomb
of Catulus, the most deservedly regretted of the Marian
victims.

Death had already swept away many of Sulla's most
notable opponents. Among the leaders there survived
only Gaius Norbanus, who killed himself at Rhodes while
the town magistrates were deliberating on his surrender;
Lucius Scipio, for whom insignificance and probably also
noble birth procured permission to end his days in peace
at his retreat in Massilia; and Quintus Sertorius, who
was wandering about as an exile on the coast of Mauretania. But still the heads of slaughtered senators were
piled up at one of the entrances into the Forum, where
the dictator had ordered them publicly exposed; and
among men of the second and third rank death reaped
a fearful harvest. In addition to those placed on the list
for their services in or on behalf of the revolutionary
army—sometimes on account of money advanced to or
relations of hospitality formed with one of its officers—
retaliation fell specially on those capitalists ("the hoard-
ers") who had sat in judgment on senators and speculated
in Marian confiscations. Altogether, about 1,600 of the
equites were inscribed on the proscription list. In like
manner the professional accusers, the worst scourge of
the nobility, who made it their trade to bring senators
before the equestrian courts, now had to suffer for it:
"How comes it to pass," an advocate asked, "that they
have left the courts to us, when they were putting the
accusers and judges to death?"

For many months the most savage and disgraceful
passions raged without restraint throughout Italy. In
the capital a Celtic band was primarily charged with the
executions, and Sullan soldiers and officers traveled the
districts of Italy for the same purpose. But every volunteer was also welcome, and the rabble high and low
pressed forward both to earn the rewards of murder and
to gratify their own vengeful or covetous designs under

the cloak of political prosecution. It sometimes happened
that the assassination preceded rather than followed the
placing of the name on the execution list. One example
shows the way in which these executions took place. At
Larinum, a town of new citizens favorable to Marian
views, one Statius Albius Oppianicus had fled to Sulla's
headquarters to avoid a charge of murder. He returned
after the victory as the regent's commissioner, deposed
the town magistrates in favor of himself and his friends,
and outlawed and killed the person who had threatened
to accuse him, along with his nearest relatives and friends.
Countless persons—including not a few stout friends of
the oligarchy—fell as the victims of private hostility or
of their own riches. The fearful confusion, and the culpable indulgence which Sulla displayed here as always toward those close to him, prevented punishment of even
ordinary crimes perpetrated amid the disorder.

Confiscated property was dealt with similarly. For
political reasons Sulla sought to induce the respectable
citizens to buy it, and many pressed forward, none more
zealously than the young Marcus Crassus. Under the circumstances extensive depreciation was unavoidable and
was indeed to some extent the inevitable result of the
Roman practice of selling confiscated property for a
round sum payable in cash. Nor did the regent forget
himself; his wife Metella and others close to him, even
including freedmen and boon companions, were sometimes allowed to purchase without competition and sometimes had the purchase money wholly or partially remitted. One of his freedmen, for instance, is said to have
purchased a property worth 6,000,000 sesterces for
2,000, and one of his subalterns is said to have acquired
by such speculations an estate of 10,000,000 sesterces.
Indignation was so great that even during Sulla's regency
an advocate asked whether the nobility had waged civil
war solely to enrich their freedmen and slaves. But in
spite of this depreciation the proceeds of the confiscated

estates totaled 350,000,000 sesterces—which gives some idea of the enormous extent of the confiscations falling chiefly on the wealthiest portion of the citizenry.

It was altogether a fearful punishment. There was no longer legal appeal or pardon; mute terror lay on the land like a leaden weight; and free speech was silenced alike in the capital and in the country town. The oligarchic reign of terror bore a different stamp from that of the revolution. While Marius had glutted his personal vengeance in the blood of his enemies, Sulla seemed to regard terrorism in the abstract, so to speak, as a thing necessary in introducing the new despotism, and to organize and prosecute his massacres almost with indifference. But the Sullan reign of terror was the more horrible for its conservative sponsorship and its lack of passion. The commonwealth seemed all the more irretrievably lost, when the frenzy and the crime on both sides were equally balanced.

In regulating the relations of Italy with the capital, Sulla—although in general he treated as null all state acts done during the revolution except the transaction of current business—firmly adhered to the principle laid down by the revolutionary government that every citizen of an Italian community was thereby a Roman citizen as well. The distinctions between citizens and allies, between old citizens with more rights and new citizens with fewer, were abolished for good. In the case of the freedmen alone the unrestricted right of suffrage was again withdrawn, and for them the old state of things was restored. To the aristocratic ultras these might seem great concessions. Sulla perceived that it was necessary to wrest these mighty levers out of the hands of the revolutionary chiefs, and that the rule of the oligarchy was not materially endangered by increasing the number of citizens.

But this concession in principle was combined with a most rigid inquisition, conducted by special commissioners with the co-operation of the garrisons distributed throughout Italy, with regard to particular communities. Several towns were rewarded: for instance, Brundisium, the first community to join Sulla, obtained the customs exemption so important for a seaport. More were punished, the less guilty being required to pay fines, pull down their walls, and raze their citadels. Those guilty of the most obstinate resistance had a part or all of their territory confiscated—as according to law it might well have been, whether they were regarded as citizen-communities which had borne arms against their fatherland, or as allied states which had waged war with Rome contrary to their treaties of perpetual peace. In this case all the dispossessed citizens were deprived both of their municipal and of the Roman franchise, receiving instead the lowest Latin rights. Sulla thus avoided furnishing the opposition with a nucleus of Italian subject-communities with inferior rights, for the homeless dispossessed were necessarily soon lost in the mass of the proletariat.[6]

These arrangements gave the regent control both of those Roman public lands which had been handed over to the former allied communities, and the confiscated territories of the guilty communities. Sulla employed them for settling the soldiers of the victorious army. Most of these new settlements were established in Etruria, but some were set up in Latium and Campania, where Praeneste and Pompeii among other places became Sullan colonies. To repeople Samnium was, as we have said, no part of the regent's design. A great part of these assignments took place according to the Gracchan plan, so that the settlers were attached to an already existing urban community. The extent of this settlement is shown by the number of land-allotments, which is set at 120,000. Some portions of land were used otherwise, such as the lands bestowed on the temple of Diana at Mount Tifata; others,

■

6. In the original, Mommsen goes on to describe several communities whose lands were thus confiscated.

such as the Volaterran domain and a part of the Arretine, remained undistributed; and still others, according to the old abuse legally forbidden but now revived, were seized by Sulla's favorites.

Sulla aimed at various objects in this colonization. First, he redeemed the pledge given to his soldiers. Secondly, in so doing he adopted the idea of the reform party and the moderate conservatives which he himself had implemented as early as 88 B.C.—namely, augmenting the number of the small agricultural proprietors in Italy by breaking up the larger holdings. How seriously he wished this is shown by the renewed prohibition against combining allotments. Above all, he saw these settled soldiers as standing garrisons who would protect his new constitution along with their own property. For this reason, where the whole territory was not confiscated, as at Pompeii, the colonists were not amalgamated into the city community, but the old citizens and the colonists were constituted as separate bodies of citizens within the same enclosing wall.

In other respects these colonial foundations were based like the older ones on a decree of the people, but only in the sense that the regent acted according to a specific clause in the Valerian law. In reality they originated from the ruler's extensive powers, and thus recalled the freedom with which the kings of old disposed of the state property. But to the extent that the Sullan colonies retained the contrast between the soldier and the citizen, which in other colonies did not exist, the Sullan colonies formed a kind of standing army of the Senate, and might be designated as military colonies in contrast to the older ones.

Along with this creation of an army for the Senate was the measure by which the regent selected from the slaves of the proscribed more than 10,000 of the youngest and most vigorous men, and formed them into a body. These new Cornelians, whose freedom was linked to the legality of Sulla's constitution, were designed as a sort of body-

guard to help the oligarchy control the city populace, on
which in the absence of a garrison everything depended.

These extraordinary supports by which the regent
shored up the oligarchy, weak and fragile though they
might appear even to their author, were yet the only possible buttresses short of expedients (such as the formation of a standing army) which would have put an end to
the oligarchy far sooner than the attacks of demagogues.
The permanent foundation of the oligarchy's governing
power was of course the Senate, whose strength was so
increased and concentrated that it might defy its un-
organized opponents at every point of attack.

Forty years of compromise were at an end. The Gracchan constitution which had survived the first Sullan reform of 88 B.C. was completely set aside. Since the time
of Gaius Gracchus the government had conceded the
right of support to the proletariat of the capital, and
bought it off by regular distributions of grain to the citizens domiciled there; Sulla abolished these largesses.
Gaius Gracchus had organized and consolidated the capitalist order by selling in Rome the tax rights of the province of Asia; Sulla abolished the system of middlemen,
and converted the former contributions of the Asiatics
into fixed taxes, which were imposed on the several districts according to assessment rolls. Gaius Gracchus had
yielded the capitalist class an indirect share in government
by giving it control of the jury courts, which on occasion proved itself stronger than the official administration and government; Sulla abolished the equestrian and
restored the senatorial courts. The Gracchan period had
granted the equites a special place at the popular festivals, such as the senators had long possessed; Sulla rele-
gated the equites to the plebeian benches. Thus the equestrian order shaped by Gaius Gracchus was deprived of
its political existence by Sulla. The Senate was to exercise the supreme legislative, administrative, and judicial
power unconditionally, indivisibly, and permanently, and

was to be distinguished by outward tokens as not only a privileged but as the only privileged order.

For this purpose the Senate needed first to have its ranks filled and to be placed on a footing of independence. The number of senators had been fearfully reduced by the recent crises. Sulla doubtless allowed those exiled by the equestrian courts to return, such as the consular Publius Rutilius Rufus (who made no use of the permission) and Gaius Cotta the friend of Drusus. But this made only slight amends for the gaps created in the Senate's ranks by the revolutionary and reactionary reigns of terror. Accordingly the Senate was extraordinarily reinforced by about 300 new senators, nominated by the popular assembly from the equestrian census, and selected, one may be sure, chiefly from the young men of senatorial houses and from Sullan officers and others brought into prominence by the last revolution. For the future also the mode of admission to the Senate was regulated anew and placed on an essentially different basis.

The original continues with a discussion in detail of Sulla's other constitutional changes:

1. *The political mobility of candidates for office was sharply reduced by requiring that candidates for the consulship serve first as quaestor, aedile, and praetor, with a gap of five years after the quaestorship, and two years after the other offices. Re-election to the same office was prohibited except after a lapse of ten years.*

2. *The tribunes, while still retaining their old veto power, were severely restricted in its exercise; they were in addition forbidden to propose legislation to the citizens' assemblies without previous Senate consent; and after the tribuneship, they were barred from seeking higher office. This fettering of the tribunician power was the most important single measure for insuring the permanent preponderance of the Senate.*

3. *The civil and military authority was completely separated by requiring the consuls and praetors to serve two years, the first of which was to be spent in purely civil administration in Rome and Italy, and the second (as proconsul or propraetor) in a foreign military command.*

4. *The once important office of censor was reduced to comparative impotence.*

5. *The courts were expanded and completely reformed, with the regularization of criminal jurisdiction as distinct from civil suits to recover damages or redress injuries.*

Such was the constitution which Lucius Cornelius Sulla gave to the commonwealth of Rome. The Senate and the equestrian order, the citizens and proletariat, Italians and provincials, accepted it as dictated, if not without grumbling, at any rate without rebelling. Not so the Sullan officers. The Roman army had totally changed its character. The Marian reform had certainly rendered it more ready for action and more useful militarily than when it shrank from combat before the walls of Numantia. But it had at the same time been converted from a citizen-army into a band of mercenaries with no fidelity to the state; it was a body faithful to its commander only if he had the personal skill to gain its attachment. The civil war had given fearful witness to this total change in the spirit of the army: six commanding generals—Albinus, Cato, Rufus, Flaccus, Cinna, and Gaius Carbo—had fallen at the hands of their own soldiers.

Sulla alone had been able to keep control of the dangerous crew, and only by indulging their wild desires as no Roman general had ever done before. If he thus earns the blame of destroying the old military discipline, the censure, while not entirely groundless, is still unjust. He was indeed the first Roman magistrate who could discharge his military and political task only by coming forward as a military adventurer. But he had not sought the military dictatorship for the purpose of abasing the state before the soldiery; his object had been rather the opposite one of compelling everything in the state, especially the army and its officers, to submit once more to the civil authority. When this became evident, opposition appeared among his own staff. The oligarchy might play the tyrant in respect to other citizens. But it seemed intolerable that the very generals whose good swords had earned the place of the overthrown senators should now be summoned to obey this same Senate.

The two officers in whom Sulla had placed most confidence resisted the new order of things. When Pompey, whom Sulla had entrusted with the conquest of Sicily and Africa and had selected for his son-in-law, received orders from the Senate to dismiss his army after accomplishing his task, he was so far from complying as to fall little short of open insurrection. Quintus Ofella, whose firm perseverance in front of Praeneste brought success in the last and most severe campaign, openly violated the new ordinances by becoming a candidate for the consulship before holding the inferior offices. With Pompey Sulla effected at least a compromise, if not a cordial reconciliation. He knew his man sufficiently not to fear him. He did not resent the impertinent Pompey's remark to his face that more people worshiped the rising than the setting sun, and he gave the vain youth the empty marks of honor which he craved.

If in this instance he appeared lenient, he showed in the case of Ofella that he did not mean to let his marshals take advantage of him. When Ofella appeared unconstitutionally as a candidate, Sulla had him cut down in the market place, and then explained to the assembled citizens that he had ordered the deed, and gave his reason for doing it. Thus the opposition of his staff to the new order was silenced for the moment, but its continued ex-

istence furnished the practical commentary on Sulla's remark that what he did on this occasion could not be done
a second time.

One thing, perhaps the most difficult of all, still remained to bring the emergency situation into accord with
the forms of the new or old laws. It was facilitated by
the fact that Sulla never lost sight of the ultimate goal.
Although the Valerian law gave each of his edicts the
force of law, he had used the extraordinary prerogative
only in the case of transient measures, especially the proscriptions, where participation would simply have compromised the Senate and the citizens needlessly. Normally he had himself observed those regulations which
he prescribed for the future. That the people were consulted, we read in the law as to the quaestors which is still
partly extant; and the same is attested of other laws, for
example, those regarding the confiscation of public lands.
In like manner the Senate was consulted on the more important administrative acts, such as the sending forth and
recall of the African army and the conferring of the
charters of towns. In the same spirit Sulla caused consuls
to be elected even for 81 B.C., by which at least the odious custom of dating by the regency was avoided. Nevertheless the power still lay exclusively with the regent, and
the election was directed so as to fall on secondary personages.

In the following year, however, Sulla revived the full
constitution, and administered the state as consul together with his comrade-in-arms Quintus Metellus, retaining the regency but allowing it to lie dormant. He saw
well how dangerous it was for his own institutions to perpetuate the military dictatorship. When the new state of
things seemed likely to hold its ground, and the largest
and most important portion of the new arrangements had
been completed (although various matters, particularly
in colonization, still remained to be done), he allowed
completely free elections in 79 B.C., declined re-election

to the consulship as incompatible with his own ordinances, and at the beginning of the year resigned the regency soon after the new consuls Publius Servilius and Appius Claudius had entered office.

Even callous hearts were impressed when the man who had dealt at his pleasure with the lives and property of millions, at whose nod so many heads had fallen, who had mortal enemies dwelling in every street of Rome and in every town of Italy, and who without an ally of equal standing or even, strictly speaking, a political party had brought to an end his work of reorganizing the state, a work offending a thousand interests and opinions—when this man appeared in the market place, voluntarily renounced his plenitude of power, discharged his armed attendants, dismissed his lictors, and bade the dense throng of citizens speak if anyone desired from him a reckoning. All were silent. Sulla descended from the rostra, and, attended only by his friends, returned home on foot through the midst of the very populace which eight years before had razed his house to the ground.

Posterity has not properly evaluated either Sulla the man or his work of reorganization, as indeed it is apt to misjudge those who swim against the current of their times. In fact, Sulla is one of the most remarkable—we may say unique—characters in history. Physically and mentally of easy temperament, blue-eyed, fair, of a complexion singularly light but blushing with every passion (though otherwise a handsome man with piercing eyes), he seemed unlikely to be of more moment to the state than his ancestors, who since the days of his great-great-grandfather Publius Cornelius Rufinus (consul 290 and 277 B.C.), one of the most distinguished generals and conspicuous men of the times of Pyrrhus, had remained in second-rate positions.

He desired nothing from life but serene enjoyment. Reared in the cultivated luxury which was at that time common even in the less wealthy senatorial families of

Rome, he speedily and adroitly possessed himself of all
the fullness of sensuous and intellectual enjoyments which
the combination of Hellenic polish and Roman wealth
could secure. He was equally welcome as a pleasant companion in the aristocratic salon and as a good comrade-
in-arms. His acquaintances high and low found in him a
sympathetic friend and a ready helper in time of need,
who gave his gold with far more pleasure to his embarrassed comrade than to his wealthy creditor. Passionate
was his homage to the winecup, still more passionate to
women: even in his later years he was no longer the regent when he took his place at table after the business of
the day was finished.

A vein of irony, one might even say of buffoonery, pervaded his whole nature. Even when regent he gave orders, while conducting the public sale of the property of
the proscribed, that a donation from the spoil should be
given to the author of a wretched panegyric which was
handed to him, on condition that the writer should promise never to sing his praises again. When he justified before the citizens the execution of Ofella, he did so by
relating to the people the fable of the countryman and
the lice. He delighted to choose his companions among
actors, and was fond of sitting at wine not only with
Quintus Roscius—the Roman Talma—but also with far
inferior players. Indeed, he was himself not a bad singer,
and even wrote farces for performance within his own
circle.

Yet amid these jovial Bacchanalia he lost neither
bodily nor mental vigor. In the rural leisure of his last
years he still zealously followed the chase, and the fact
that he brought the writings of Aristotle from conquered
Athens to Rome attests his interest in more serious reading. The typical Roman character rather repelled him.
Sulla had nothing of the blunt hauteur which the grandees
of Rome were fond of showing in the presence of the
Greeks, or the pomposity of narrow-minded great men.

On the contrary, he freely indulged his humor, appeared (doubtless to the scandal of many of his countrymen) in Greek towns in the Greek dress, and induced his aristocratic companions to drive their chariots personally at the games. He retained none of those half-patriotic, half-selfish hopes which in countries of free constitution lure young men of talent into the political arena, and which he too like all others probably felt at one time. In such a life as his, oscillating between passionate intoxication and more than sober awakening, illusions are speedily dissipated. Wishing and striving probably appeared to him folly in a world which was absolutely governed by chance, and in which, if men were to strive after anything at all, this chance could be the only aim of their efforts.

He followed the general tendency of the age in addicting himself at once to skepticism and superstition. His whimsical credulity was not the plebeian superstition of a Marius, who got a priest to prophesy to him for money and determined his actions accordingly; still less was it the fanatic's sullen belief in destiny. It was that faith in the absurd, which necessarily appears in every man who has simply ceased to believe in a connected order of things —the superstition of the fortunate player, who deems himself privileged by fate to throw the right number on each and every occasion. In practical questions Sulla understood very well how to satisfy ironically the demands of religion. When he emptied the treasuries of the Greek temples, he declared that the man whose chest was replenished by the gods themselves could never fail. When the Delphic priests reported to him that they were afraid to send the requested treasures, because the harp of the god emitted a clear sound when they touched it, he replied that they might now send them all the more readily since the god evidently approved his design.

Nevertheless he fondly flattered himself that he was the chosen favorite of the gods, especially Aphrodite, to whom he assigned a pre-eminence down to his last years.

In his conversations as well in his autobiography he often prided himself on the intercourse which the immortals held with him in dreams and omens. Having more right than most men to be proud of his achievements, he was proud rather of his uniquely faithful fortune. He was fond of saying that improvised enterprises always turned out better with him than those systematically planned; and one of his strangest whims—that of regularly stating the number of those who had fallen on his side in battle as *nil*—was nothing but the childishness of a child of fortune. It was but the reflection of his natural disposition, when, having reached the culminating point of his career and seeing all his contemporaries at a dizzy depth beneath him, he assumed the designation of the Fortunate—Sulla Felix—as a formal surname, and bestowed corresponding appellations on his children.

Nothing lay further from Sulla than steadfast ambition. Unlike the average aristocrat of his time, he had too much sense to regard the inscription of his name in the roll of the consuls as the goal of his life. He was too indifferent, and not enough of an ideologue, to be disposed voluntarily to engage in the reform of the rotten structure of the state. He remained where birth and culture placed him, in the circle of genteel society, and passed through the usual routine of offices. He had no occasion to exert himself, and left such drudgery to the political working-bees, of whom there was in truth no lack. Thus in 107 B.C. on the allotment of the quaestorial places, accident brought him to Africa to the headquarters of Gaius Marius. The untried man-of-fashion from the capital was not very well received by the rough, boorish general and his experienced staff. Provoked by this reception Sulla, fearless and skilful as he was, rapidly mastered the profession of arms, and in his daring expedition to Mauretania first displayed that peculiar combination of audacity and cunning which led his contemporaries to say of him that he was half-lion and half-fox, and that the fox in him was more dangerous than the lion.

To the young, highborn, brilliant officer, who was confessedly the real means of ending the vexatious Numidian war, the most splendid career now lay open. He took part also in the Cimbrian war, and manifested his singular talent for organization in the management of the difficult task of providing supplies. Yet even now the pleasures of life in the capital had far more attraction for him than war or even politics. During the praetorship which he held in 93 B.C., after having failed in a previous candidacy, it once more chanced that in his province, the least important of all, there occurred the first victory over King Mithradates and the first treaty with the mighty Arsacids, as well as their first humiliation. The Social War followed. It was primarily Sulla who decided its first act (the Italian insurrection) in favor of Rome, and thus won for himself the consulship by his sword. It was also he who as consul suppressed the Sulpician revolt with energetic rapidity.

Fortune seemed to make it her special mission to eclipse the old hero Marius by means of this younger officer. The capture of Jugurtha and the defeat of Mithradates, both of which Marius had striven for in vain, were accomplished in subordinate positions by Sulla. In the Social War, in which Marius lost his renown as a general and was deposed, Sulla established his military repute and rose to the consulship. The revolution of 88 B.C., which was also above all a personal conflict between the two generals, ended with the outlawry and flight of Marius. Almost without desiring it, Sulla had become the most famous general of his time and the shield of the oligarchy. New and more formidable crises ensued—the Mithradatic war, the Cinnan revolution—yet the star of Sulla continued always in the ascendant. Like the captain who seeks not to quench the flames of his burning ship but continues to fire on the enemy, Sulla ignored the revolution raging in Italy and persevered in Asia till the public foe was subdued. Then, having done with that foe, he crushed anarchy and saved the capital from the firebrands of the desperate Samnites and revolutionists.

The moment of his return home was for Sulla an over-powering one in joy and in pain: he himself relates in his memoirs that during his first night in Rome he was not able to close an eye, and we may well believe it. But still his task was not at an end, for his star was destined to rise still higher. Absolute autocrat as any king, and yet constantly standing on the ground of formal right, he bridled the ultra-reactionary party, annihilated the Gracchan constitution which for forty years had hamstrung the oligarchy, and compelled first the capitalists and the urban proletariat, and ultimately the arrogant militarists nurtured in the bosom of his own staff, to yield once more to the law which he strengthened afresh. He established the oligarchy on a more independent footing than ever, placed the executive power in its hands, committed to it the legislation, the courts, and the supreme military and financial power, and furnished it with a sort of bodyguard in the liberated slaves and a sort of army in the military colonists. Lastly, when the work was finished, the creator bowed to his own creation, and the absolute autocrat became of his own volition once again a simple senator.

In all this long military and political career Sulla never lost a battle, was never compelled to retrace a step, and, led astray neither by friends nor foes, brought his work to the goal which he had himself proposed. He had reason, indeed, to thank his star. The capricious goddess of fortune seemed in his case to have exchanged caprice for steadfastness, and to have taken pleasure in loading her favorite with successes and honors whether he desired them or not. But history must be more just toward him than he was toward himself, and grant him a higher rank than mere favorite of fortune.

We do not mean that the Sullan constitution was a work of political genius, such as those of Gracchus and Caesar. There does not occur in it (as is implied in its very nature as a restoration) a single new idea in statesmanship. All its most essential features—admission to the Senate by the holding of the quaestorship, the abolition of the censor's right to eject a senator from the Senate, the initiative of the Senate in legislation, the conversion of the tribunician office into an instrument of the Senate for fettering the *imperium,* the prolonging of the supreme office to two years, the transference of military command from the popularly elected magistrate to the senatorial proconsul or propraetor, and even the new criminal and municipal arrangements—were not created by Sulla, but were institutions which had previously grown out of the oligarchic government, and which he merely regulated and fixed. And even the proscriptions, confiscations, and other horrors attending his restoration, when compared with the doings of Nasica, Popillius, Opimius, Caepio, etc.—are they anything more than the customary oligarchic mode of getting rid of opponents?

On the Roman oligarchy of this period no judgment can be passed save one of inexorable and remorseless condemnation. Like everything else connected with it, the Sullan constitution is completely involved in that condemnation. To accord praise which the genius of a bad man bribes us into bestowing is to sin against the sacred character of history; but we may be allowed to bear in mind that Sulla was far less answerable for the Sullan restoration than the body of the Roman aristocracy, a centuries-old ruling clique which was yearly becoming more enervated and embittered, and that any hollowness and iniquity in that restoration is ultimately traceable to the aristocracy. Sulla reorganized the state not as the master of a house who puts his shattered estate in order according to his own lights, but as a temporary overseer who faithfully follows instructions. It is fallacious in such a case to transfer the ultimate responsibility from the master to the manager.

We estimate the importance of Sulla much too highly, or rather we dismiss too lightly those terrible proscriptions, ejections, and restorations—for which there never could be and never was any reparation—when we regard them as the work of a bloodthirsty tyrant placed by chance at the head of the state. These and the terrorism of the restoration were the deeds of the aristocracy, and Sulla was nothing more in the matter than, to use the poet's expression, the executioner's axe playing the unconscious instrument of the conscious thought. Sulla carried out his part with rare, in fact superhuman, perfection. Within the limits laid down for him, his work was not only grand but even useful. Never has any aristocracy in process of such extensive and continuing decay found a guardian so willing and able as Sulla to wield for it the sword of the general and the pen of the legislator without regard for personal power. There is no doubt a difference between the case of an officer who refuses the sceptre from public spirit and that of one who throws it away from a cloyed appetite. But in total absence of political selfishness (though in this one respect only) Sulla deserves to be ranked with Washington.

But the whole country, and not merely the aristocracy, was more indebted to him than posterity was willing to confess. Sulla definitely concluded the Italian revolution, insofar as it was based on the disabilities of individual less privileged districts as compared with others of broader rights. Thus, by compelling his party to recognize the equality of all Italians before the law, he became the real and ultimate author of the political unity of Italy —a gain not too dearly purchased by years of disorder and streams of blood. But Sulla did still more. For over half a century the power of Rome had been declining, and anarchy had been her normal condition. The government of the Senate under the Gracchan constitution was anarchy, and the government of Cinna and Carbo was a still worse example of a leaderless state (most clearly reflected in that equally confused and unnatural league with the Samnites), the most uncertain, intolerable, and mischievous of all conceivable political conditions—in fact, the beginning of the end. It is not too much to say that the long-undermined Roman commonwealth must necessarily have fallen to pieces, had not Sulla saved it by his intervention in Asia and Italy.

It is true that the Sullan constitution was as short-lived as that of Cromwell, and it was not difficult to see that his structure was far from solid. But it is arrant thoughtlessness to forget that without Sulla the very site of the building would probably have been swept away by the waves; and even the blame for its flimsiness does not fall primarily on Sulla. The statesman builds only what can be built in the sphere assigned to him. Sulla did whatever a conservative could do to save the old constitution. He himself had a foreboding that while he might erect a fortress, he could not create a garrison, and that the utter worthlessness of the oligarchs would defeat any attempt to save the oligarchy. His constitution resembled a temporary dike thrown into the raging breakers, and it was no reproach to the builder if some ten years later the waves swallowed up the artificial structure which was not even defended by those whom it sheltered. The statesman has no need to cite praiseworthy isolated reforms (for example, of the Asiatic revenue system and of criminal justice) to avoid summarily dismissing Sulla's ephemeral restoration. He will admire it as a judiciously planned reorganization of the Roman commonwealth carried out under infinite difficulties, and he will place the deliverer of Rome and the father of Italian unity almost on a par with Cromwell.

However, it is not the statesman alone who may sit in judgment on the dead. The conscience of mankind will rightly never reconcile itself to what Sulla did or suffered others to do. Sulla not only established his despotic power by unscrupulous violence; in doing so he also called things by their right name with brutal frankness. Thus he has irreparably offended the great mass of the weak-hearted who are more revolted at the name than at the thing. But the cool and dispassionate character of his crimes makes him appear morally more revolting than the criminal who acts from passion. Outlawries, rewards to executioners, confiscations of goods, summary procedure against insubordinate officers—such things had occurred a hundred times without seriously offending the rudimentary political morality of ancient times. But it was unprecedented that the names of the outlaws should be publicly posted and their heads publicly exposed; that a set sum should be fixed for the bandits who slew them, and the sums duly entered in the public account books; that the confiscated property should be sold under the hammer in the public market like the spoil of an enemy; that the general should order a disobedient officer to be cut down on the spot, and acknowledge the deed before all the people. This public mockery of humanity was also a political error, contributing no little to envenom later revolutionary crises; and on that account a dark shadow even today deservedly darkens the memory of the author of the proscriptions.

Sulla may also be justly blamed that, while in all important matters he acted with remorseless vigor, in lesser and especially in personal questions he very frequently yielded to his sanguine temperament and dealt according to his likes or dislikes. Where he felt real hatred, as for example against the Marians, he let it rage unrestrained even against the innocent; and he himself boasted that no one had better repaid friends and foes. He did not disdain to use his unlimited power to accumulate a colossal fortune. The first absolute monarch of the Roman state, he verified the maxim of absolutism—that the laws do not bind the prince—forthwith in the case of those laws which he himself issued regarding adultery and extravagance.

But his lenience toward his own party and his own circle was more pernicious for the state than his indulgence toward himself. The laxness of military discipline, though partly enjoined by his political necessities, may be reckoned in this category; but far more pernicious was his indulgence toward his political adherents. The extent of his occasional forbearance is hardly credible. For instance, Lucius Murena was not only released from punishment for defeats which he sustained through arrant perversity and insubordination, but he was even allowed a triumph. Gnaeus Pompey, who had behaved still worse, was still more extravagantly honored by Sulla. The extent and the enormity of the proscriptions and confiscations probably arose not so much from Sulla's own wish as from this spirit of indifference, which in his position indeed was hardly more pardonable. That Sulla with his intrinsically energetic and yet withal indifferent temperament should conduct himself sometimes with incredible indulgence, sometimes with inexorable severity, may readily be conceived. The oft-repeated saying that before his regency he was a good-natured, mild man, but when regent a bloodthirsty tyrant, carries in it its own refutation. If as regent he displayed the reverse of his earlier gentleness, it must rather be said that he punished with the same careless nonchalance with which he pardoned. This half-ironical frivolity pervades his whole political life. It is always as if the victor, just as it pleased him to credit his victory to good fortune, regarded the victory itself as worthless; as if he had some premonition of the vanity and transience of his own work; as if after the manner of a steward he preferred making repairs to pulling down and rebuilding, and allowed himself in the end to be content with a sorry plastering to conceal the flaws.

But whatever he was, this Don Juan of politics was a man of one mold. His whole life attests the stability of his nature, for Sulla remained unchangeably the same in the most diverse situations. The same temper which made him seek once more the idleness of the capital, after his brilliant successes in Africa, also made him find rest and refreshment in his Cumaean villa after possessing complete and absolute power. His saying that public affairs were a burden which he threw off as soon as he could was no mere phrase. After his resignation he remained himself entirely, without peevishness or affectation, glad to be rid of public affairs and yet interfering now and then when opportunity offered. Hunting, fishing, and the composition of his memoirs occupied his leisure hours, though as a diversion he arranged, at the request of the discordant citizens, the internal affairs of the neighboring colony of Puteoli as confidently and speedily as he had formerly arranged those of the capital. His last action on his sickbed related to the collection of a contribution for rebuilding the Capitoline temple, whose completion he was never to witness.

Little more than a year after retirement, in his sixtieth year and still vigorous in body and mind, he was overtaken by death: after a brief illness (he was writing at his autobiography only two days before his death) the rupture of a blood vessel carried him off in 78 B.C. His faithful fortune did not desert him even in death. He could have no wish to be sucked once more into the political vortex, and be obliged to lead his old warriors against a new revolution. Yet such was the state of affairs in Spain and in Italy that he could hardly have avoided this task had his life been prolonged. Even now, when it was suggested that he should have a public funeral in the capital, numerous voices silent during his lifetime were raised against showing this last honor to the dead tyrant. But his memory was still too fresh and the dread of his old soldiers too vivid, so it was resolved that the body should be conveyed to the capital for the last rites.

Italy never witnessed a grander funeral. In every place

through which the deceased was borne in regal attire, with his well-known standards and fasces before him, the inhabitants and above all his old soldiers joined the mourning train. It seemed as if the whole army would once more meet round the dead hero who in his lifetime had often led it and always victoriously. When the endless procession reached the capital, where the courts kept holiday and all business was suspended, two thousand golden chaplets awaited the dead—the last honorary gifts of the faithful legions, of the cities, and of his more intimate friends.

Sulla, faithful to the usage of the Cornelian house, had ordered that his body should be buried without being burnt. Others were more mindful of what past days had done and future days might do: by command of the Senate, the corpse of the man who had disturbed the bones of Marius was committed to the flames. Headed by all the magistrates and the whole Senate, by the priests and priestesses in their official robes and the band of noble youths in equestrian armor, the procession arrived at the great market place. At this spot, filled by his achievements and almost by the sound of his dreaded words, the funeral oration was delivered over the deceased; thence the bier was borne on the shoulders of senators to the Campus Martius, where the funeral pyre was erected. While the flames yet blazed, the equites and the soldiers held their race of honor round the corpse. Then the ashes of the regent were deposited in the Campus Martius beside the tombs of the ancient kings, and the Roman women mourned him for a whole year.

When Sulla died in 78 B.C., the oligarchy which he had restored ruled with absolute sway over the Roman state. However, since it had been established by force, it still needed force to maintain its ground against numerous secret and open foes. It was not opposed by any single party with clear objectives and acknowledged leaders, but by a mass of diverse elements lumped together under the general name of the popular party, though in reality opposing the restoration on various grounds and with very different objects.

There were the jurists who neither engaged in nor understood politics, but who detested Sulla's high-handed dealing with the lives and property of citizens. Even during Sulla's lifetime, when all other opposition was silent, the strict jurists had resisted the regent. The Cornelian laws, for example, which deprived various Italian communities of the Roman franchise, were treated in judicial decisions as null and void; and in like manner the courts held that, where a citizen had been made a prisoner of war and sold into slavery during the revolution, his franchise was not forfeited. There was also the remnant of the old liberal minority in the Senate, which in former times had labored to effect a compromise with the reform party and the Italians, and which was now similarly inclined to soften the rigid oligarchic constitution of Sulla by concessions to the Populares. There were, moreover, the strict Populares, the honest, credulous, narrow-minded radicals, who staked property and life on the current party slogans only to discover with painful surprise after the victory that they had been fighting for a phrase instead of a reality. Their special aim was to re-establish the power of the tribunes, which Sulla had sharply limited rather than abolished, and which exercised over the multitude a still more mysterious charm because the institution was in fact an empty phantom. More than a thousand years later, the mere name of tribune of the people revolutionized Rome.

Most important of all, there were numerous powerful groups whom the Sullan restoration had left unsatisfied, or whose political or private interests it had directly injured. Among those ranked the dense and prosperous population of the region between the Po and the Alps, which naturally regarded the bestowal of Latin rights in 89 B.C. as merely an instalment of the full Roman franchise, and so afforded a ready soil for agitation. There were also the freedmen, influential in numbers and wealth, and especially dangerous through their concentration in the capital, who could not bear being reduced by the restoration to their earlier and practically useless suffrage. In the same position stood the great capitalists, who maintained a cautious silence, but preserved as usual their tenacity of resentment and their equal tenacity of power. The proletariat of the capital, which equated free bread to true freedom, was likewise discontented, and still deeper exasperation prevailed among the citizen-communities affected by the Sullan confiscations.[1]

Finally, the agitation extended to the entire families and freedmen of those democratic chiefs who had lost their lives, or who wandered along the Mauretanian coasts or lived at the court and in the army of Mithradates in all the misery of exile. According to the close family ties governing the political feeling of that age, it was a point of honor that those left behind should try to procure for exiled relatives the privilege of returning to their native land, and, in the case of the dead, at least a removal of the stigma attaching to their memory and to their children, and a restitution to the latter of their paternal estate. More especially the children of the proscribed, whom the regent had reduced to political pariahs, thereby received from the state a virtual summons to rebel against it.

To the opposition might also be added the whole body

---

1. The original continues by listing several such communities.

of ruined men, all the rabble high and low whose means
had been spent in refined or vulgar debauchery; the aristocratic lords whose only mark of quality was their debts;
the Sullan troopers whom the regent could make into
landholders but not into farmers, and who, after squandering their first inheritance from the vanquished, longed
to succeed to a second. All these awaited only the un-
folding of the banner which invited them to fight against
the existing order, whatever else might be inscribed
on it.

For similar reasons all ambitious men of talent attached themselves to the opposition. There were some to
whom the closed circle of the Optimates denied admission or opportunity for rapid advancement, and who
therefore attempted to break through the laws of oligarchic exclusiveness and seniority by means of popular
favor. There were also the more dangerous men, whose
ambitions went beyond merely fiddling with history within
the confines of political intrigues. On the lawyer's platform in particular—the only field of legal opposition left
open by Sulla—even during the regent's lifetime such as-
pirants waged lively war against the restoration with the
weapons of formal jurisprudence and combative oratory.
For instance, the adroit speaker Marcus Tullius Cicero
(born January 3, 106 B.C.), son of a landholder of
Arpinum, speedily made himself a name by the mingled
caution and boldness of his opposition to the dictator.
Such efforts were of little importance if the opponent desired only to procure for himself a curule chair, where
he might sit contentedly for the rest of his life. But if
this chair should not satisfy a popular man, then some successor to Gaius Gracchus would inevitably launch a life-
or-death struggle. For the present however, no leader appeared motivated by such daring ambition.[2]

---

2. Mommsen continues here in the original to describe the domination of
political life by the political clubs.

Among the older generation of Optimates the civil wars had left not a single man of repute except the shrewd and eloquent Lucius Philippus (consul in 91 B.C.), who, formerly of popular leanings, then leader of the capitalist party against the Senate, closely associated with the Marians, and lastly passing over to the victorious oligarchy in sufficient time to earn thanks and commendation, had managed to escape between the parties. Among the next generation the most notable aristocrats were Quintus Metellus Pius (consul in 80 B.C.), Sulla's comrade in dangers and victories; Quintus Lutatius Catulus, consul in the year of Sulla's death and son of the victor of Vercellae; and two younger officers, the brothers Lucius and Marcus Lucullus, the former of whom had fought with distinction under Sulla in Asia, the latter in Italy. But even those four men rose little above the average caliber of the Optimates of this age. Catulus was like his father a man of refinement and honesty, but his talents were limited and he was certainly no soldier. Metellus was of estimable character and an able and experienced officer; and it was because of his recognized ability (rather than his close relations as kinsman and colleague of the regent) that he was sent in 79 B.C. to Spain, where the Lusitanians and the Roman emigrants under Quintus Sertorius were bestirring themselves afresh. The two Luculli were also capable officers—particularly the elder, who combined very respectable military talents with thorough literary culture and leanings to authorship, and appeared honorable also as a man. But as statesmen, even these better aristocrats were not much less shortsighted than the average senators of the time.[3]

Of the men who were neither ardent partisans nor open opponents of the Sullan constitution, the eyes of the mul-

■

3. It was the gradual decline of moral standards—Mommsen continues in the original—that led such men to waste "the best part of their lives in more or less ingenious idleness."

titude sought out young Gnaeus Pompey (born September 29, 106 B.C.), who at Sulla's death was twenty-eight years old. The fact was a misfortune for the admired as well as for the admirers, but it was natural. Sound in body and mind; a capable athlete who even as a superior officer vied with his soldiers in leaping, running, and lifting; a vigorous and skilled rider and fencer; a bold leader of volunteer bands—the young Pompey had become imperator and triumphator while still too young to qualify for any magistracy or for the Senate, and had acquired an esteem second only to Sulla himself. Indeed, he had obtained from the indulgent regent—half in recognition, half in irony—the surname of the Great.

Unhappily, his mental endowments by no means corresponded with these unprecedented successes. He was neither bad nor incapable; he was a thoroughly ordinary man, created by nature to be a good sergeant, who was called upon by circumstances to be a general and a statesman. An intelligent, brave, experienced, thoroughly excellent soldier, he was even in military matters without trace of any higher gifts. It was characteristic of him as a general, as well as in other respects, to set forth with a caution bordering on timidity, and, if possible, to give the decisive blow only when he had established an immense superiority over his opponent. His culture was the average culture of the time; although entirely a soldier, he did not neglect when he went to Rhodes to admire dutifully and to reward the rhetoricians there. His integrity was that of a rich man who manages his property with discretion. He did not disdain to make money in the usual senatorial way, but he was too cold and too rich to incur special risks, or draw down on himself conspicuous disgrace.

It was the vice so common among his contemporaries, rather than any virtue of his own, that gave him the reputation—doubtless comparatively well warranted—of integrity and disinterestedness. His "honest countenance" became almost proverbial, and even after his death he was esteemed as a worthy and moral man. He was in fact a good neighbor, who did not join in the revolting schemes by which the grandees of that age extended the bounds of their domains through forced sales or still worse measures at the expense of their humbler neighbors.

In domestic life he displayed affection for his wife and children; and, to his credit, he was the first to depart from the barbarous custom of putting to death the captive kings and generals of the enemy, after they had been exhibited in triumph. But this did not prevent him from separating from his beloved wife at Sulla's command, because she belonged to an outlawed family, or from ordering with great composure that men who had stood by him in his hour of need should be executed before his eyes at the nod of that same master. He was not cruel, though he was reproached with being so; but—perhaps worse—he was cold and unimpassioned in good as in evil. In the tumult of battle he faced the enemy fearlessly; in civil life he was a shy man, whose cheek flushed on the slightest occasion. He spoke in public not without embarrassment, and generally was angular, stiff, and awkward in discourse. With all his haughty obstinacy he was (as most persons are who make a display of their independence) a pliant tool in the hands of men who knew how to manage him, especially his freedmen and hangers-on, by whom he had no fear of being controlled.

For nothing was he less qualified than for a statesman. Uncertain as to his aims, unskilful in his choice of means, shortsighted and helpless in great matters and small, he sought to conceal his indecision under a solemn silence, and, when he thought to play a subtle game, to deceive himself in the belief that he was deceiving others. By his military position and his territorial connections he acquired almost inadvertently a considerable personal following, through which great deeds might have been accomplished. But Pompey was incapable of leading a party, and, if it still kept together, it did so through sheer force of circumstance. In this as in other things he reminds us of Marius; but Marius, with his boorish roughness and sensuous passion, was still less intolerable than this most tiresome and most starched of all artificial great men.[4]

Marcus Crassus cannot, any more than Pompey, be reckoned an unconditional adherent of the oligarchy. He was a person highly characteristic of his time. A few years older than Pompey, he too belonged to the circle of the high Roman aristocracy, had obtained the usual education befitting his rank, and had fought with distinction under Sulla in the Italian war. Far inferior to many of his peers in mental gifts, literary culture, and military talent, he outstripped them by his boundless activity and by the perseverance with which he strove to possess everything and to become all-important. Above all, he threw himself into speculation. Purchases of estates during the revolution formed the foundation of his wealth, but he disdained no branch of gain. He engaged in building in the capital on a great scale; he entered into partnership with his freedmen in the most varied undertakings; he acted as banker both in and out of Rome, in person or through agents; he advanced money to his colleagues in the Senate, and undertook when necessary to execute commissions or to bribe the tribunals on their account.

He was far from nice in the matter of making profit. During the Sullan proscriptions a forgery in the lists had been proved against him, for which reason Sulla made no further use of him in affairs of state. He did not refuse to accept an inheritance, though the will which contained his name was a blatant forgery. He made no objection when his bailiffs by force or by fraud dislodged the petty

4. Mommsen's personal contempt for Pompey is amplified in a further passage of the original, which charges Pompey with being a frightened man whose "deeply agitated life passed joylessly away in a perpetual inner contradiction."

holders from lands which adjoined his own. However, he avoided open collisions with criminal justice, and lived like a genuine moneyed man in homely and simple style.

Through such means Crassus rose in the course of a few years from a man of ordinary senatorial fortune to be the master of wealth which not long before his death, after defraying enormous extraordinary expenses, still amounted to 170,000,000 sesterces. He had become the richest of Romans, and thus a great political power. If, according to his expression, no one might call himself rich who could not maintain an army from his revenues, a man who could do so was hardly any longer a mere citizen.

In reality Crassus aimed at a higher object than the possession of the best-filled money chest in Rome. He grudged no pains to extend his connections. He knew how to salute by name every citizen of the capital. No suppliant was refused his assistance in court. Nature had done little for him as an orator, for his speech was dry, his delivery monotonous, and his hearing poor. But his tenacity of purpose, which no fatigue deterred and no enjoyment distracted, overcame such obstacles. He was never unprepared, and never extemporized. Hence he became a pleader always ready and always in demand, for whom few causes were too bad, and who knew how to influence the judges by his connections as well as by his oratory, and also on occasion by his gold.

Half the Senate was in debt to him. His habit of advancing interest-free "loans" revocable at pleasure made a number of influential men dependent on him, the more so because like a genuine man of business he made no political distinctions, maintained connections everywhere, and readily lent to every one who was able to pay or be otherwise useful. The most daring party leaders, who attacked recklessly in all directions, were careful not to quarrel with Crassus. He was the bull of the herd, whom it was wise not to provoke.

That a man so disposed and so situated could not strive after humble aims is clear; and, in a very different way from Pompey, Crassus knew like a banker the objects and the means of political speculation. From the beginnings of Rome, money had been a political power; this age was such that everything seemed as accessible to gold as to iron. If in a time of revolution a capitalist aristocracy might think of overthrowing the oligarchy, then a man like Crassus might raise his eyes above the consulship and the embroidered mantle of the triumphators. For the moment he was a Sullan and a friend of the Senate, but he was too much of a financier to bind himself to a single party or to pursue anything save his personal advantage.

Why should Crassus, the wealthiest and best-connected man in Rome, and a speculator on the grandest scale, not speculate also on the crown? Alone, perhaps, he could not attain this object. But he had carried out many great transactions in partnership, and it was not impossible that a suitable partner might present himself. It is characteristic of the age that a mediocre orator and officer, a politician who mistook activity for energy and covetousness for ambition, one who at bottom had nothing but a colossal fortune and a trader's talent for forming connections—that such a man, relying on the omnipotence of cliques and intrigues, could stand on a level with the first generals and statesmen of his day, and contend with them for the highest prize which allures political ambition.

In the opposition proper, both among the liberal conservatives and among the Populares, the storms of revolution had wrought fearful havoc. Among the former, the only surviving man of note was Drusus' friend and ally Gaius Cotta, banished in 91 B.C. and then brought back by Sulla's victory to his native land. He was a shrewd man and a capable advocate, but neither the weight of his party nor his personal standing enabled him

to play more than a respectable secondary part. Among
the rising youth in the democratic party twenty-four-
year-old Gaius Julius Caesar (probably born July 12,
102 B.C.) drew toward him the eyes of friend and foe.
His relationship with Marius and Cinna (his father's
sister had been the wife of Marius, he himself had married Cinna's daughter); his courageous refusal—unlike
Pompey—to divorce his young wife Cornelia at the dictator's bidding; his bold persistence in the priesthood
given him by Marius but revoked by Sulla; his wander-
ings under the threat of proscription, which was averted
with difficulty by the intercession of his relatives; his
bravery in the conflicts before Mytilene and in Cilicia, a
bravery which no one had expected from the tenderly
reared and almost effeminate boy; even the warnings of
Sulla regarding the "boy in the petticoat," in whom more
than a Marius lay concealed—all these were precisely so
many recommendations in the eyes of the democratic
party. But Caesar could only arouse hopes for the future.
The men whose age and public position would have called
them to seize the reins of the party and the state were all
dead or in exile.

Thus the democratic leadership, in the absence of any
strong claimant, was open to any one who might pose as
the champion of oppressed popular freedom. Thus it fell
to Marcus Aemilius Lepidus, a Sullan who from dubious
motives deserted to the camp of the democracy. Once a
zealous Optimate and a large purchaser of proscribed
estates at auction, as governor of Sicily he had so scandal-
ously plundered the province that he threw himself into
the opposition to evade the threat of impeachment.

It was a gain of doubtful value. No doubt the opposition thus acquired a well-known name, a man of quality,
and a vehement orator in the Forum; but Lepidus was an
insignificant and indiscreet man who did not deserve to
lead either in council or in the field. Nevertheless the opposition welcomed him, and the new leader succeeded not

only in deterring his accusers from prosecuting him, but also in carrying his election to the consulship for 78 B.C. (In this he was helped not only by the treasures from Sicily, but also by the foolish endeavor of Pompey to show Sulla and the pure Sullans what he could do.) Now that the opposition had found a new leader in Lepidus, who had become the supreme magistrate of the state, the speedy outbreak of a new revolution in the capital might clearly be foreseen.

But even before the democrats moved in the capital, the democratic emigrants had again bestirred themselves in Spain. The soul of this movement was Quintus Sertorius. This excellent man, a native of Nursia in the Sabine land, was of a soft and tender nature—as shown by his almost enthusiastic love for his mother, Raia—and at the same time of the most chivalrous bravery, as was proved by the honorable scars which he brought home from the Cimbrian, Spanish, and Italian wars. Although untrained as an orator, he excited the admiration of learned advocates by the natural flow and the striking self-possession of his address. His remarkable talent as military leader and statesman shone by contrast, especially during the revolutionary war which the democrats so wretchedly and stupidly mismanaged. He was admittedly the only democratic officer who knew how to prepare and to conduct war, and the only democratic leader who opposed with statesmanlike energy the senseless and furious excesses of his party. His Spanish soldiers called him the new Hannibal, and not merely because he had, like that hero, lost an eye in battle. In reality he reminds us of the great Phoenician by his equally cunning and courageous strategy, by his adroitness in attracting foreign nations to his interest and making them serviceable to his ends, by his prudence in success and misfortune, by his ingenious quickness in turning his victories to good account and averting the consequences of his defeats.

It is doubtful whether any Roman statesman up to his

time can be compared to Sertorius in versatile talent.
After Sulla's generals had compelled him to quit Spain,
he had led a restless life of adventure along the Spanish
and African coasts, sometimes in league and sometimes
at war with the Cilician pirates who haunted these seas,
and with the chieftains of the roving tribes of Libya. The
victorious Roman restoration had pursued him even
there. When he was besieging Tingis (Tangiers), a corps
under Pacciaecus from Roman Africa had come to the
help of the prince of the town; but Pacciaecus was totally
defeated, and Tingis was taken by Sertorius. On hearing
of such achievements the Lusitanians, who despite their
pretended submission maintained an effective independence, and annually fought with the Roman governors of
Further Spain, sent envoys to Sertorius in Africa inviting him to join them and offering him the command of
their militia.

Sertorius, who twenty years earlier had served under
Titus Didius in Spain and knew the resources of the land,
decided to accept the invitation; he embarked for Spain
about 80 B.C., leaving behind a small detachment on the
Mauretanian coast. The straits separating Spain and Africa were occupied by a Roman squadron commanded by
Cotta. To steal through it was impossible, so Sertorius
fought his way through and succeeded in reaching the
Lusitanians. No more than twenty Lusitanian communities placed themselves under his orders, and he could
muster only 2,600 "Romans," a considerable part of
whom were deserters from the army of Pacciaecus or
Africans armed after the Roman style. Sertorius saw that
everything depended on organizing his loose guerilla
bands around a strong nucleus of troops possessing Roman organization and discipline. To this end he reinforced the band which he had brought with him by levying 4,000 infantry and 700 cavalry, and with this one
legion and swarms of Spanish volunteers advanced
against the Romans.

The Roman command in Further Spain was held by Lucius Fufidius, who through his absolute devotion to Sulla—well tried amid the proscriptions—had risen from subaltern to propraetor. He was totally defeated on the Baetis, leaving 2,000 Romans covering the field of battle. Messengers hastily summoned the governor of the adjoining Ebro province, Marcus Domitius Calvinus, to check the further advance of the Sertorians, and the experienced Quintus Metellus also soon appeared (79 B.C.), sent by Sulla to relieve the incapable Fufidius in southern Spain. But they did not succeed in quelling the revolt. In the Ebro province not only was the army of Calvinus destroyed and he himself slain by Sertorius' lieutenant Lucius Hirtuleius, but Lucius Manlius, the governor of Transalpine Gaul, who had crossed the Pyrenees with three legions to help his colleague, was totally defeated by the same brave leader. With difficulty Manlius escaped with a few men to Ilerda (Lerida) and thence to his province, losing his whole baggage on the march through a sudden attack of the Aquitanian tribes.

In Further Spain Metellus penetrated into the Lusitanian territory; but Sertorius succeeded during the siege of Longobriga (not far from the mouth of the Tagus) in luring a division under Aquinus into an ambush, and thereby compelling Metellus himself to raise the siege and to evacuate Lusitania. Sertorius followed him, defeated on the Anas (Guadiana) the corps of Thorius, and inflicted vast damage by guerilla warfare on the army of the commander-in-chief himself. Metellus, a methodical and somewhat clumsy tactician, was in despair at this opponent who obstinately declined a decisive battle, but cut off his supplies and communications and constantly hovered round him on all sides.

These extraordinary successes of Sertorius in the two Spanish provinces were the more significant in that they were not merely military in nature. The emigrants as such were not formidable, nor were isolated successes of

the Lusitanians under this or that foreign leader of much
moment. But with great political and patriotic sagacity
Sertorius acted, whenever he could, not as a hired leader
of a Lusitanian revolt against Rome, but as Roman general and governor of Spain, in which capacity he had in
fact been sent by the former rulers. He began to form
the principal emigrants into a senate which increased to
300 members, and which conducted its affairs and nominated its magistrates in the Roman fashion. He regarded
his army as Roman, and filled the officers' posts without
exception with Romans. He faced the Spaniards as a governor levying troops and other support from them by
virtue of his office; but he was a governor who, instead of
exercising the usual despotism, sought to attach the provincials to Rome and to himself personally.

His chivalrous character made it easy for him to adopt
Spanish habits, and he excited in the Spanish nobility the
most ardent enthusiasm for the wonderful foreigner
whose spirit was so like their own. According to the warlike custom which existed in Spain as among the Celts
and the Germans, thousands of the noblest Spaniards
swore to stand faithfully by their Roman general unto
death; and in them Sertorius found more trustworthy
followers than in his own countrymen and party comrades. He did not disdain to make use of the superstition
of the ruder Spanish tribes, and to have his plans of war
brought to him as commands of Diana by the white fawn
of the goddess.

At all times he exercised a just and gentle rule. His
troops, at least so far as his eye and his arm reached, had
to maintain the strictest discipline. Gentle as he usually
was in punishing, he showed himself inexorable when any
outrage was perpetrated by his soldiers on friendly soil.
He also sought to better permanently the condition of
the provincials. He reduced taxes, and directed the soldiers to construct winter barracks for themselves, so that
the oppressive burden of quartering the troops was re-

moved, and with it a source of unspeakable mischief and annoyance. For the children of Spaniards of quality an academy was erected at Osca (Huesca), in which they received the higher instruction usual in Rome, learning to speak Latin and Greek and to wear the toga. This remarkable measure, by no means merely designed to take gently from the allies the hostages that in Spain were inevitable, was a continuation of and an advance on the great project of Gaius Gracchus and the democratic party for gradually Romanizing the provinces. It was the first attempt to accomplish this Romanization not by extirpating the old inhabitants and filling their places with Italian emigrants, but by Romanizing the provincials themselves.

The Optimates in Rome sneered at the wretched emigrant, the runaway from the Italian army, the last of the robber band of Carbo. The sorry taunt recoiled upon its authors. Including the Spanish general levy, some 120,-000 infantry, 2,000 archers and slingers, and 6,000 cavalry had been brought into the field against Sertorius. Facing this enormously superior force Sertorius had not only held his ground in a series of successful conflicts and victories, but had also brought the greater part of Spain under his power. In the Further province Metellus was confined to the districts immediately occupied by his troops, and all the tribes who could had taken the side of Sertorius. In the Hither province, after the victories of Hirtuleius, a Roman army no longer existed. Emissaries of Sertorius roamed throughout Gaul, as there, too, the tribes began to stir, and bands gathering together began to make the Alpine passes insecure.

Lastly, the sea belonged quite as much to the insurgents as to the legitimate government, since the insurgents' pirate allies were almost as powerful in the Spanish waters as the Roman ships of war. At the promontory of Diana (now Denia, between Valencia and Alicante) Sertorius established a fixed station for the corsairs, where they could lie in wait for Roman ships conveying supplies to

the Roman maritime towns and the army, carry away or
deliver goods for the insurgents, and provide a means of
communication with Italy and Asia Minor. The constant
readiness of these men to spread the conflagration excited a high degree of apprehension, especially when so
much combustible matter was accumulated throughout the
Roman empire.

*Unfortunately, the democratic standard in Rome was
in no such capable hands. The consul Lepidus, sent out
by an incredibly myopic Senate to quell a revolt in Etruria, promptly turned his army against Rome. He was defeated beneath the city's walls by his co-consul, the Optimate Quintus Catulus. The remnant of Lepidus' army
finally made its way to Spain led by the former praetor
Marcus Perpenna.*

While the oligarchy was thus victorious over Lepidus,
it found itself compelled by the dangerous turn of the
Sertorian war to make concessions which violated the letter as well as the spirit of the Sullan constitution. It was
absolutely necessary to send a strong army and an able
general to Spain. Pompey showed plainly that he desired,
or rather demanded, this commission. The pretension was
bold. It was bad enough that the oligarchy had again allowed this secret opponent an extraordinary command,
under pressure of the Lepidan revolution. But it was far
worse to disregard all the rules instituted by Sulla for the
magisterial hierarchy, and to give a man who had filled
no civil office one of the most important provincial governorships, under circumstances which made observance
of the normal one-year term out of the question.

Thus the oligarchy, quite apart from the respect due
their general Metellus, had good reason to oppose earnestly this new attempt of the ambitious youth to perpetuate his exceptional position. But this was not easy. In
the first place, they had not a single man fitted for the

difficult post of general in Spain. Neither of the consuls of the year showed any desire to measure himself against Sertorius; what Lucius Philippus said in a full meeting of the Senate was all too true—that among all the senators of note, not one was able and willing to command in a serious war.

Yet they might have got over this (after the manner of oligarchs when they have no capable candidate) by filling the place with some sort of makeshift, if Pompey had merely desired the command and had not demanded it with the backing of an army. He had already lent a deaf ear to Catulus' demands that he dismiss his army. It was at least doubtful whether those of the Senate would find a better reception, and the consequences of a breach no one could calculate. The aristocracy itself might well be outweighed, if the sword of a well-known general were thrown into the opposite scale. So the majority resolved on concession. Not from the people (who constitutionally should have been consulted when a private man was to be invested with the supreme magisterial power) but from the Senate, Pompey received proconsular authority and the chief command in Hither Spain. Forty days after he had received it, he crossed the Alps in the summer of 77 B.C.

The new general first found employment in Gaul, where no formal insurrection had broken out, but where serious disturbances had occurred at several places. As a punishment he deprived the cantons of the Volcae-Arecomici and the Helvii of their independence, and placed them under Massilia. He also laid out a new road over the Cottian Alps, and so shortened communications between Gaul and the valley of the Po. Since this work consumed the best season of the year, it was not till late in autumn that Pompey crossed the Pyrenees.

Meanwhile, Sertorius had not been idle. He had dispatched Hirtuleius into the Further province to keep Metellus in check, and had himself tried to follow up his

complete victory in the Hither province and prepare to
receive Pompey. Those isolated Celtiberian towns still
loyal to Rome were attacked and reduced one by one, until at last the strong town of Contrebia (southeast of
Saragossa) had fallen. In vain the hard-pressed towns
sent message after message to Pompey; he would not be
induced by any entreaties to depart from his customary
slow advance. With the exception of the maritime towns
defended by the Roman fleet, and the districts of the
Indigetes and Laletani in the northeast corner of Spain
(where Pompey had established himself after crossing
the Pyrenees, and had made his raw troops bivouac
throughout the winter to inure them to hardships), all of
Hither Spain had acknowledged the rule of Sertorius,
while the upper and middle Ebro district continued the
mainstay of his power. Even the apprehension which the
fresh Roman force and its celebrated general excited in
the insurgent army had a salutary effect. Marcus Perpenna, who hitherto had claimed an independent command over the force which he had brought from Liguria,
was compelled by his soldiers on the news of Pompey's
arrival to place himself under his abler colleague.

For the campaign of 76 B.C. Sertorius again employed
the corps of Hirtuleius against Metellus, while Perpenna
with a strong army took up his position on the lower Ebro
to prevent Pompey from crossing the river, if he should
march (as was expected) in a southerly direction to effect
a junction with Metellus, and along the coast for the sake
of procuring supplies. The corps of Gaius Herennius was
assigned to support Perpenna. Farther inland, on the upper Ebro, Sertorius in person sought to subdue several
districts friendly to Rome, while holding himself ready to
aid either Perpenna or Hirtuleius as circumstances demanded. It was still his intention to avoid any pitched battle, and to annoy the enemy by petty conflicts and supply
interruptions.

Pompey, however, forced the Ebro against Perpenna

and took up a position on the river Pallantias near Saguntum, from which the Sertorians maintained their communications with Italy and the east. The time had come
for Sertorius to appear in person, and throw his superior
numbers and genius into the scale against the superior
soldiers of his opponent.

For a considerable time the struggle centered around
the town of Lauro (on the Jucar, south of Valencia),
which had declared for Pompey and was therefore besieged by Sertorius. Pompey exerted himself to the utmost
to relieve it. But after several of his divisions had been
assailed separately and cut to pieces, the great warrior
found himself—just when he thought he had surrounded
the Sertorians, and had invited the besieged to observe
the capture of the besieging army—suddenly outmaneu-
vered. To avoid being himself surrounded, he had to witness from his camp the capture and burning of the allied
town and the carrying off of its inhabitants to Lusitania—
an event which induced several wavering communities in
central and eastern Spain to switch to Sertorius.

Meanwhile, Metellus fought with better fortune. In a
sharp engagement at Italica (not far from Seville),
which Hirtuleius had imprudently risked, and in which
both generals fought hand to hand and Hirtuleius was
wounded, Metellus compelled him to evacuate the Roman
territory proper and throw himself into Lusitania. This
victory permitted Metellus to unite with Pompey. The
two generals took up their winter quarters in 76-75 B.C.
in the Pyrenees, resolving in the next campaign to attack
the enemy jointly in his position near Valentia. But while
Metellus was still approaching, Pompey offered battle to
the main enemy army, hoping to wipe out the stain of
Lauro and gain the expected laurels alone. Sertorius joy-
fully embraced the opportunity of fighting Pompey before Metellus arrived.

The armies met on the river Sucro (Jucar). After a
sharp conflict Pompey was beaten on the right wing and

was himself carried from the field severely wounded. Afranius conquered on the left and took the camp of the Sertorians, but during its pillage he was suddenly assailed by Sertorius and also compelled to give way. Had Sertorius been able to renew the battle the next day, the army of Pompey might have been annihilated. But meanwhile Metellus had come up, had overthrown the corps of Perpenna ranged against him, and had taken his camp. It was not possible to resume the battle against the united armies.

The successes of Metellus, the junction of the hostile forces, and the sudden stagnation after the victory diffused terror among the Sertorians. As not unfrequently happened with Spanish armies, most of the Sertorian soldiers dispersed. But the despondency passed as quickly as it had come. The white fawn, which represented in the eyes of the multitude the military plans of the general, was soon more popular than ever. In a short time a new army confronted the Romans in the level country to the south of Saguntum (Murviedro), which firmly adhered to Rome, while Sertorian privateers intercepted Roman supplies by sea, and scarcity made itself felt in the Roman camp. Another battle took place in the plains of the river Turia (Guadalaviar), and the struggle was long undecided. Pompey with the cavalry was defeated by Sertorius, and Pompey's brother-in-law and quaestor, the brave Lucius Memmius, was slain. On the other hand Metellus vanquished Perpenna and victoriously repelled the attack of the enemy's main army, receiving himself a wound in the conflict.

Once more the Sertorian army dispersed. Valentia, which Gaius Herennius held for Sertorius, was taken and razed to the ground. The Romans probably cherished a momentary hope that they were done with their tough antagonist. The Sertorian army had disappeared, and the Roman troops, penetrating far into the interior, trapped the general himself in the fortress of Clunia on the upper Douro. But while they vainly besieged this rocky stronghold, the insurgent communities assembled their forces elsewhere. Sertorius himself stole out of the fortress, and even before the end of the year was once more a general at the head of an army.

Again the Roman generals had to take up winter quarters with the cheerless prospect of an inevitable renewal of their Sisyphean toils. It was not even possible to winter in the region of Valentia, so important on account of the communication with Italy and the East, but so fearfully devastated by friend and foe. After leading his troops first into the territory of the Vascones (Biscay), Pompey himself spent the winter in the territory of the Vaccaei (around Valladolid), and Metellus even in Gaul.

The Sertorian war was thus five years old, and still without prospect of termination. The Roman state suffered from it beyond description. The flower of the Italian youth perished amid the exhausting fatigues of these campaigns. The public treasury was not only deprived of the Spanish revenues, but in paying and maintaining the Spanish armies had to lay out very considerable sums which the government hardly knew how to raise. Spain was devastated and impoverished, and the flourishing Roman civilization there received a severe shock. This was to be expected in an insurrectionary war waged with so much bitterness, and which all too often occasioned the destruction of whole communities.

Even the towns which adhered to Rome bore countless hardships. Those situated on the coast had to be provisioned by the Roman fleet, while the situation of the faithful communities in the interior was almost desperate. Gaul suffered hardly less, partly from requisitions of infantry and cavalry, of grain and money, and partly from the oppressive burden of winter quarters, which became intolerable as a result of the bad harvest of 74 B.C. Almost all the local treasuries were compelled to borrow from the Roman bankers, burdening themselves with a crushing load of debt.

Both generals and soldiers carried on the war with reluctance. The generals faced an opponent far superior in talent, a tough and protracted resistance, and a warfare whose perils were grave and whose successes were both difficult and far from brilliant. It was even asserted that Pompey was scheming to get himself recalled from Spain and entrusted with a more desirable command. The soldiers, too, found little satisfaction in a campaign in which they got only hard blows and worthless booty, and in which their very pay was doled out to them with extreme irregularity. Pompey reported to the Senate, at the end of 75 B.C., that pay was two years in arrears, and that the army was threatening to break up.

The Roman government might certainly have obviated many of these evils if it could have carried on the Spanish war with less slackness, to say nothing of better will. In the main, however, it was neither the government's fault nor the fault of its generals that a genius so superior as that of Sertorius was able to carry on this petty warfare year after year, despite his numerical and military inferiority, on terrain so favorable to insurrectionary and piratical warfare. With its end so uncertain, the Sertorian insurrection showed every prospect of becoming intermingled with other contemporary revolts—which added to its dangerous character, at a time when the Romans were contending on every sea with the pirates, in Italy with the revolted slaves, in Macedonia with the tribes on the lower Danube, and in the East with Mithradates, who was partly induced by the success of the Spanish insurrection to try once more the fortune of arms.

That Sertorius formed connections with the Italian and Macedonian enemies of Rome cannot be distinctly affirmed, although he certainly was in constant intercourse with the Marians in Italy. With the pirates, on the other hand, he had previously formed an avowed league; and he had also long maintained relations with Mithradates through the Roman emigrants staying at his court. He now concluded a formal treaty of alliance with the Pontic king, ceding to him the Roman protectorates in Asia Minor but not the Roman province of Asia. He promised, moreover, to send him an officer qualified to lead Mithradates' troops, plus a number of soldiers, while the king in turn bound himself to transmit to Sertorius forty ships and 3,000 talents. The wise politicians in Rome were already recalling the time when Italy found itself threatened by Philip from the east and Hannibal from the west. They predicted that the new Hannibal, like his predecessor, could first subdue Spain; that he could then lead his Spanish armies into Italy sooner than Pompey; and finally that he could, like the Phoenician before him, summon the Etruscans and Samnites to arms against Rome.

This comparison was more ingenious than accurate. Sertorius was far from being strong enough to renew the gigantic enterprise of Hannibal. He was lost if he left Spain, where all his successes were bound up with the peculiarities of the country and the people; and even there he was more and more compelled to renounce the offensive. His admirable skill as a leader could not change the nature of his troops. The Spanish militia retained its character of being as untrustworthy as the wave or the wind, now collecting in masses to the number of 150,000, now melting way to a mere handful. The Roman emigrants likewise remained insubordinate, arrogant, and stubborn. Those types of armed forces which require keeping a corps together for a considerable time, such as cavalry, were of course very inadequately represented in his army. The war gradually swept off his ablest officers and the flower of his veterans; and even the most trustworthy communities, weary of being harassed by the Romans and maltreated by the Sertorian officers, began to show signs of impatience and wavering allegiance.

What is remarkable is that Sertorius, in this respect
also like Hannibal, never deceived himself as to the hopelessness of his position. He passed up no opportunity for
compromise, and would have been ready at any moment
to give up his command on the assurance of being allowed
to live peacefully in his native land. But political ortho-
doxy knows nothing of compromise and conciliation. Sertorius might not recede or step aside, but was compelled
inevitably to advance along the path he had entered, however narrow and giddy it might become.

The representations which Pompey addressed to
Rome, and which derived emphasis from the behavior of
Mithradates in the east, were successful. The Senate sent
him the necessary supplies of money as well as two fresh
legions. Thus reinforced, the two generals went to work
again in the spring of 74 B.C. and once more crossed the
Ebro. Eastern Spain was wrested from the Sertorians
through battles on the Jucar and Guadalaviar, after
which the struggle centered on the upper and middle Ebro
around Sertorius' chief strongholds of Calagurris, Osca,
and Ilerda. As in the earlier campaigns, here too Metellus
gained the most important successes. His old opponent
Hirtuleius, who again confronted him, was completely
defeated and killed along with his brother—an irrepa-
rable loss for the Sertorians. Sertorius, receiving the unfortunate news just as he was about to assail the enemy
opposed to him, cut down the messenger on the spot lest
the tidings discourage his troops. But the news could not
be long concealed, and one insurgent town after another
surrendered.[5]

When the two Roman generals went into winter quarters—Pompey to Gaul, Metellus to his own province—
they were able to look back on considerable results. A
great portion of the insurgents had submitted or had been

■

5. Several such towns are listed in the original.

subdued by arms. The campaign of the following year (73 B.C.) ran a similar course, with Pompey especially restricting the field of the insurrection slowly but steadily.

The defeats of the insurgents were soon reflected in the feeling in their camp. The military successes of Sertorius became like those of Hannibal, necessarily less and less important. People began to question his military talent; he was no longer, it was alleged, what he had been; he spent the days in feasting or over his cups; he squandered money as well as time. The number of the deserters, both individuals and communities, began to increase. Soon projects formed by the Roman emigrants against the life of the general were reported to him. They sounded credible enough, especially as various officers of the insurgent army, Perpenna in particular, had submitted reluctantly to the supremacy of Sertorius, and the Roman governors had long promised amnesty and a high reward to any one who should kill him.

Sertorius, on hearing such allegations, replaced his Roman guards with select Spaniards. Against the suspects themselves he proceeded with fearful but necessary severity, in some cases condemning various of the accused to death without the advice of his council. Whereupon the malcontents whispered that he was now more dangerous to his friends than to his foes.

A second conspiracy was soon discovered among his own staff, and whoever was denounced had to take flight or die. But all were not betrayed, and the remaining conspirators, especially Perpenna, found in the circumstances a new incentive for haste. In the headquarters at Osca, on Perpenna's instigation, a brilliant victory was reported to the general as having been achieved by his troops. At the festive banquet arranged by Perpenna, Sertorius appeared as usual with his Spanish retinue. Contrary to former custom in the Sertorian headquarters, the feast soon became a revel. Strong words passed at table, and it seemed as if some of the guests sought opportunity for an altercation.

Sertorius threw himself back on his couch, and seemed anxious to ignore the disturbance. A winecup was dashed on the floor as Perpenna gave the signal. Marcus Antonius, at Sertorius' table, dealt the first blow. When Sertorius turned and attempted to rise, the assassin leaped upon him and held him down while the other guests at table, all in the conspiracy, threw themselves on the struggling pair and stabbed the defenseless general while his arms were pinioned. With him died his faithful attendants.

Thus ended, in 72 B.C., one of the greatest if not the very greatest man that Rome had hitherto produced, a man who under more fortunate circumstances might perhaps have become the regenerator of his country, done to death by the treason of the wretched band of emigrants whom he was condemned to lead against his native land. History loves not the Coriolani, nor has she made any exception even with this most magnanimous, most gifted, most deserving to be regretted of them all.

The murderers thought to succeed to the heritage of the murdered. After Sertorius' death Perpenna, as the highest among the Roman officers of the Spanish army, laid claim to the chief command. The army submitted, but with mistrust and reluctance. However men had murmured against Sertorius in his lifetime, death reinstated the hero in his rights, and vehement was the indignation of the soldiers when, on the publication of his testament, the name of Perpenna was read forth among the heirs. A part of the soldiers, especially the Lusitanians, dispersed. The remainder had a presentiment that with the death of Sertorius their spirit and their fortune had departed.

Accordingly, at the first encounter with Pompey the miserably led and despondent ranks of the insurgents were utterly broken, and Perpenna, among other officers, was taken prisoner. The wretch sought to purchase his life by delivering up Sertorius' correspondence, which would have compromised numerous prominent men in Italy. Pompey, however, ordered the papers to be burnt unread, and handed him over to the executioner along with the other insurgent chiefs. The emigrants who had escaped dispersed, most of them fleeing into the Mauretanian deserts or joining the pirates.[6]

Sulla's good fortune seemed to cling to his creation after he had been laid in the grave, and to protect it better than its incapable and negligent guardians. The Italian opposition had broken down from the haste and incompetence of its leader, that of the emigrants from dissension within their own ranks. These defeats, although largely the result of the opposition's perverseness and discord, were nonetheless victories for the oligarchy. The curule chairs were rendered once more secure.

The Sertorian war was not the only threat to the oligarchy, for barbarian pressure was increasing along the Danube; Mediterranean piracy threatened to halt seaborne commerce; the Italian slaves were in open revolt; and relations with the East were deteriorating rapidly. A series of campaigns managed to secure temporarily the Danubian frontier, but it proved extremely difficult to clear the sea of the pirates, now organized into a soldier-state peopled by "the ruined men of all nations, the hunted refugees of all vanquished parties, everyone that was wretched and daring." Though Publius Servilius in a three-year campaign destroyed numerous pirate vessels and strongholds along the rugged Asian coast, piracy continued almost unabated by transferring its headquarters temporarily to other spots.

■

6. The original continues here by describing the clean-up in Spain after the Roman victory.

*In the same period came the greatest of the Roman
slave revolts, led by the gladiator Spartacus. A Roman
captive being trained to fight in the public games, he escaped in 73 B.C. to become leader of an outlaw band. By
successful encounters first with local militia and then with
regular Roman troops, the little band acquired arms and
recruits until it swelled to 40,000 men, and spread its rav-
ages from the Po to the Sicilian strait. A two-year campaign led by both consuls was needed to defeat the Sparta-
cists, who still perished primarily because of dissension in
their own ranks.*

*In Asia Minor, the second Mithradatic war began (like
the first) not because of intent, but because of each side's
suspicion of the other's preparations. Mithradates made
the first overt move in 74 B.C., and the Senate responded
by naming as commander one of Rome's unsung military
geniuses, the consul Lucius Lucullus. Lucullus managed to
trap Mithradates' gigantic army beneath the walls of the
city of Cyzicus, which the king was besieging; and he is
said to have lost 200,000 soldiers to famine, disease, and
Roman arms before fleeing with the remains of his army
by sea. Lucullus promptly regained control of the sea with
a hastily organized fleet, and by land carried the offensive
into Mithradates' own kingdom of Pontus. The decisive
battle occurred in 72 B.C. at the city of Cabira, where a
Roman cavalry success led to the pell-mell flight of the
whole Pontic army. While scattered cities held out for
two years, Lucullus effectively occupied the whole kingdom, Mithradates becoming a near-captive of his son-in-
law, King Tigranes of Armenia.*

*Lucullus next resolved to chastise Tigranes, despite
senatorial opposition and the weakness of his own forces
—barely 30,000 men, only half of whom could be spared
for an Armenian invasion. In 69 B.C. Lucullus crossed the
Euphrates and marched straight for Tigranes' capital of
Tigranocerta, which he besieged. Tigranes soon arrived
with a vast army from the interior to lift the siege; and*

though he had been warned to avoid battle with the Romans, he ignored the warning when he saw that the Roman force ready for battle (the siege of the city continued) numbered scarcely 10,000 men. But a sudden Roman attack on the rear of the Armenian cavalry threw it against its own still unformed infantry, which fled without striking a blow. Mommsen regards Lucullus' victory before Tigranocerta as "one of the most brilliant" in Roman military history.

Lucullus' two daring campaigns would have yielded a victorious peace but for the reappearance of Mithradates, who took over command of the war from his fainthearted son-in-law. To nourish the struggle, Mithradates sought with marked success to transform it into a national Asiatic war against the western invader. Militarily, he altered his tactics by using his infantry only defensively, while harassing the Romans with a huge and active cavalry.

Deep in hostile country, Lucullus could only seek to force a military decision by striking deeper still. In midsummer of 68 B.C. he set out for the last great Armenian city, Artaxata. But when the long-suffering Roman soldiers (many had seen eighteen years' service) found themselves amid snow and ice while still far from their goal, they mutinied and forced a retreat. Lucullus managed it with his usual skill, and on the way back captured the stronghold of Nisibis as a safe winter haven. But his absence threw the whole weight of the Asiatic offensive on the Roman occupation troops left behind, and the Roman corps in Pontus was surrounded and totally destroyed.

With this defeat came word from Rome that release of the Roman veterans in the East had been decreed, and that the consul Manius Glabrio had been given Lucullus' command. Though Glabrio showed no desire to take charge at this difficult juncture, in the ensuing confusion over who was to command and what troops were willing to fight, Mithradates reoccupied his whole kingdom; and by the spring of 66 B.C. the Romans, despite Lucullus' brilliant achievements, were exactly where they had been eight years before.

Let us review the events of the decade of the Sullan restoration. None of the external or internal developments during that period—neither the insurrection of Lepidus, nor the enterprises of the Spanish emigrants, nor the wars in Thrace and Macedonia and in Asia Minor, nor the risings of the pirates and the slaves—necessarily constituted of itself a grave danger to the state; yet in all these struggles the nation had well-nigh fought for its very existence.

The reason was that every task was left undone so long as it might still be done with ease. Neglect of the simplest precautions produced the most dreadful mischiefs and misfortunes, and transformed dependent classes and impotent kings into antagonists on a footing of equality. To be sure, the insurrections of the popular opposition and of the slaves were subdued. But such victories neither solidified the government at home nor strengthened it abroad. It was no credit to Rome that in an eight-year struggle, marked by more defeats than victories, the government's two most celebrated generals had failed to master the insurgent chief Sertorius and his Spanish guerillas, and that only the dagger of his friends decided the Sertorian war in favor of the legitimate government. As for the slaves, it was far less an honor to have conquered them than a disgrace to have fought them on equal terms for years.

Little more than a century had elapsed since the Hannibalic war, and it must have brought a blush to the cheek of every honorable Roman when he reflected on the nation's fearfully rapid decline since that great age. Then the Italian slaves stood like a wall against the veterans of Hannibal; now the Italian militia scattered like chaff before the bludgeons of runaway serfs. Then every plain captain acted if need be like a general, and fought often unsuccessfully, but always honorably; now it was difficult to find even a tolerably efficient leader among all the officers of rank. Then the government preferred to take the last farmer from the plow rather than forego the acquisition of Spain and Greece; now it was on the verge of abandoning both these long-since-conquered regions merely to defend itself against runaway slaves at home. Spartacus as well as Hannibal had traversed Italy with an army from the Po to the Sicilian straits, beaten both consuls, and threatened Rome with blockade. The enterprise which took the greatest general of antiquity to conduct it, against the Rome of former days, could now be undertaken by a daring bandit captain. Was there any wonder that such victories over rebels and robber chiefs produced no national upsurge?

The foreign wars had produced still less satisfactory results. It is true that the outcome of the Thraco-Macedonian war was not unfavorable, although far from corresponding to the cost. On the other hand, in the wars in Asia Minor and with the pirates the government had exhibited utter failure. The former ended with the loss of all conquests made in eight bloody campaigns, the latter with the total driving of the Romans from "their own sea." Once Rome, fully conscious of her irresistible power by land, had transferred her superiority also to the other element; now the mighty state was powerless at sea and apparently on the point of also losing its hegemony in Asia.

All the material benefits which a state exists to confer —security of frontiers, undisturbed peaceful intercourse, legal protection, and regulated administration—began to vanish for all the nations united in the Roman state. The gods of blessing seemed all to have mounted to Olympus, leaving the miserable earth at the mercy of official or volunteer plunderers and tormentors. Nor was this decay felt merely by those possessing political rights and public spirit. The slave revolts and the brigandage and piracy brought the sense of it home to the remotest valley and the humblest hut of Italy, and constituted a personal calamity for every one who pursued trade and commerce or bought a bushel of wheat.

If the authors of this dreadful and unparalleled misery are sought, it is not difficult to share the blame among many. The slaveowners whose hearts were in their moneybags, the insubordinate soldiers, the cowardly, incapable, or foolhardy generals, the demagogues running after shadows, all bore their share of the blame. Or, to speak more accurately, who did not share it? It was instinctively felt that this misery, this disgrace, this disorder were too colossal to be the work of any one man. As the greatness of the Roman commonwealth was the work not of prominent individuals, but rather of a soundly organized body of citizens, so the decay of this mighty structure was not the work of some destructive genius but rather the result of a general disorganization. The great majority of the citizens were good for nothing, and every rotten stone helped to bring about the ruin of the whole structure. The whole nation suffered for what was the whole nation's fault.

It was unfair to hold the government, as the ultimate organ of the state, responsible for all the state's curable and incurable diseases; but it was certainly true that the government deserved a liberal share of the general culpability. In the Asiatic war, for example, where no individual of the ruling group conspicuously failed, and where Lucullus, from a military viewpoint, acted with ability and even glory, it was all the more clear that the blame for the failure lay in the system and in the government as such —primarily, in that particular war, in the initial abandonment of Cappadocia and Syria, and in the awkward relations of an able general with a governing group incapable of energetic decision.

Likewise in combating piracy the Senate's sound idea

of a general clean-up was first spoiled in the execution and then totally dropped, in order to revert to the old foolish system of sending legions against the coursers of the sea. The expeditions of Servilius and Marcius to Cilicia, and of Metellus to Crete, were undertaken on this system; and in accordance with it Triarius had the island of Delos surrounded by a wall for protection against the pirates. Such attempts to secure the dominion of the seas remind us of that Persian great-king who ordered the sea to be scourged with rods to make it obey him.

Doubtless, therefore, the nation had good reason for blaming its failure primarily on the restoration government. A similar misrule had always accompanied the reestablishment of the oligarchy, after the fall of the Gracchi as after that of Marius and Saturninus. Yet never before had it shown at the same time such violence and such laxity, never before had it been so corrupt and so pernicious. When a government cannot govern it ceases to be legitimate, and whoever has the power has also the right to overthrow it.

It is no doubt unhappily true that an incapable government may long trample underfoot a nation's welfare and honor, before men are found who are able and willing to wield against that government its own formidable weapons, and to forge the justifiable revolution out of the moral revolt of the good and the distress of the many. But a game played with the fortunes of nations, however long and merry and undisturbed it may be, is ever a treacherous game, which in its own time entraps the players; and no one blames the axe when it is laid to the root of the tree that bears such fruit. For the Roman oligarchy that hour had now come. The Asiatic war and the pirate campaigns provided the immediate cause of the overthrow of the Sullan restoration and the establishment of a revolutionary military dictatorship.

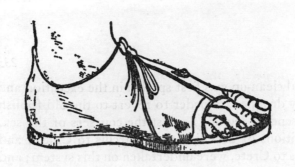

VII

THE FALL OF THE

OLIGARCHY AND THE

RULE OF POMPEY

Despite all perils, the Sullan constitution still stood unshaken. The assault on it by Lepidus and Sertorius had been repulsed with little loss. True, the government had neglected to finish the half-completed building in the energetic spirit of its creator. Characteristically, it neither parceled out the lands which Sulla had earmarked for distribution, nor abandoned its claim to them, but left the former owners in a provisional possession, and indeed even allowed individuals to take over various undistributed tracts according to the old occupation system which had been abolished by the Gracchan reforms.

Whatever Sullan enactments were inconvenient for the Optimates were ignored or canceled.[1] But though these violations of the Sullan ordinances by the government helped to shake the entire structure, there was no revival of the Sempronian laws.

Many men sought to re-establish the Gracchan constitution, or to achieve piecemeal what Lepidus and Sertorius had sought through revolution. Under pressure from Lepidus the government had already consented soon after Sulla's death to a limited revival of the grain distribution, doing what it could to satisfy the populace on this vital question. When despite those distributions the high price of grain (occasioned chiefly by piracy) produced such a scarcity in Rome as to lead to street rioting in 75 B.C., extraordinary purchases of Sicilian grain by the government relieved the most severe distress; and a grain law introduced by the consuls for 73 B.C. regulated the purchases of Sicilian grain and furnished the government, although at the expense of the provincials, with better means of preventing similar evils.

But in less material questions—restoring the power of the tribunes, and setting aside the senatorial tribunals— the government offered more decided resistance. The dispute over the tribuneship was begun as early as 76 B.C.,

■

1. The original enumerates several examples.

immediately after the defeat of Lepidus, by the tribune of the people Lucius Sicinius, perhaps a descendant of the man of the same name who had first held this office over four hundred years earlier; but it failed before the resistance of the active consul Gaius Curio. In 74 B.C. Lucius Quinctius resumed the agitation, but was persuaded to stop by the authority of the consul Lucius Lucullus. The matter was raised the following year with greater zeal by Gaius Licinius Macer, who—characteristic of the period—carried his literary studies into public life, and (just as he had read in the Annals) counseled the citizens to disobey the conscription laws.

There were also well-founded complaints regarding the administration of justice by the senatorial jurymen. A man of any influence could hardly be convicted. Not only did accused senators find understandable sympathy among their colleagues, who often had been or were likely to be accused; the jurymen's votes were also frequently for sale. Several senators had been convicted of this crime. Men pointed with the finger at others equally guilty, and the most respected Optimates, such as Quintus Catulus, granted in open session that the complaints were quite well-founded. Individual glaring cases compelled the Senate on several occasions, as in 74 B.C., to discuss means for checking the venality of juries, but only of course till the first outcry had subsided and the matter could be allowed to slip out of sight.

This wretched administration of justice resulted especially in a system of plundering and torturing the provincials which made previous outrages seem tolerable and moderate. Robbery had been somewhat legitimized by custom, so that the commission on extortions might be regarded as an institution for taxing the senators returning from the provinces for the benefit of their colleagues at home. But when an esteemed Sicilian was condemned to death by the Roman governor *in absentia* and without a hearing, because he had been unwilling to become the governor's accomplice in a crime; when even Roman citizens, if they were not equites or senators, were no longer safe in the provinces from the rods and axes of the Roman provincial magistrate; when the oldest right in Roman democracy, security of life and person, began to be trodden underfoot by the ruling oligarchy—then even the public in the Forum began to listen to the complaints regarding its magistrates in the provinces, and the unjust judges who shared the moral responsibility for such misdeeds.

The opposition of course did not fail to assail its opponents in the tribunals, almost the only ground left to it. The young Gaius Caesar, who also (so far as his age allowed) agitated zealously for the re-establishment of the tribunician power, in 77 B.C. brought to trial one of the most respected partisans of Sulla, the consular Gnaeus Dolabella, and in the following year another Sullan officer, Gaius Antonius. Marcus Cicero in 70 B.C. called to account Gaius Verres, one of the most wretched of Sulla's creatures and one of the worst scourges of the provincials. Again and again the dark picture of the proscriptions, the fearful sufferings of the provincials, and the disgraceful state of Roman criminal justice were unfolded before the assembled multitude with all the pomp and bitterness of Italian rhetoric and sarcasm, and the departed conqueror as well as his living instruments were unrelentingly exposed to wrath and scorn. The re-establishment of the tribunician power (with which the freedom, might and prosperity of the republic seemed somehow magically bound up), the reintroduction of the "stern" equestrian tribunals, and the renewal of the censorship for cleansing the supreme governing board of its corrupt and pernicious elements, were daily and loudly demanded by the orators of the popular party.

But all this got nowhere. There was scandal and outcry enough, but exposing the government up to and beyond its just deserts yielded no real result. In the absence of military interference the material power still lay with the citizens of the capital; and the "people" that thronged its streets and made magistrates and laws were in fact no better than the governing Senate. The government doubtless had to come to terms with the multitude, where its own immediate interest was at stake: this was the reason for reviving the Sempronian grain law. But it was inconceivable that this populace would have earnestly supported an idea or even a judicious reform.

What Demosthenes said of his Athenians was justly applicable to the Romans of this period—the people were zealous for action so long as they stood round the platform and listened to proposals of reforms; but when they went home, no one thought further of what he had heard in the market place. However the democratic agitators might stir the fire, it was purposeless in the absence of inflammable material. The government knew this, and made no concessions on important questions of principle. At the utmost it consented (about 72 B.C.) to grant amnesty to a portion of those who had become exiles with Lepidus.

What concessions were made came less from democratic pressure than from the mediating attempts of the moderate aristocracy. But of the two laws which the single surviving leader of this section, Gaius Cotta, carried in his consulate of 75 B.C., that concerning the tribunals was set aside again the very next year; and the second, which repealed the Sullan enactment disqualifying for other offices those who had held the tribunate (but retained the other limitations) excited like all half-measures the displeasure of both parties. The conservative reform party lost its most notable head in the death of Cotta (about 73 B.C.), and thereafter was steadily compressed between the extremes, which were becoming daily more marked. But of these extremes the government party, wretched and remiss as it was, naturally held the advantage against the equally wretched and incapable opposition.

But this favorable situation changed when differences sharpened between the government on one hand and its more ambitious supporters on the other. First among these stood Pompey. He was doubtless a Sullan; but we have already shown how little he was at home among his own party, how his lineage, his history, and his hopes separated him from the nobility whom he was officially regarded as protecting. The breach had been widened irreparably during the general's Spanish campaigns. Only under pressure had the reluctant government associated him with their true representative, Quintus Metellus; and he in turn accused the Senate, probably not without cause, of having by careless or malicious neglect brought about the defeats of the Spanish armies and endangered the expedition. Now he returned victorious over his open and secret foes at the head of a veteran army wholly devoted to him, desiring assignments of land for his soldiers and a triumph and the consulship for himself.

The latter demands collided with the law. Pompey, though several times invested in an extraordinary way with supreme official authority, had not yet held any ordinary magistracy and was still not even a member of the Senate; and only those who had held the lesser magistracies could become consul, only those who had been invested with the ordinary supreme power could triumph. The Senate was legally entitled, if he sought to become consul, to bid him begin with the quaestorship; and if he requested a triumph, it might remind him of the great Scipio, who under like circumstances had renounced his triumph over conquered Spain. Pompey was also dependent constitutionally on the good will of the Senate to obtain the lands promised to his soldiers.

However, even if the Senate (as in its feebleness was very conceivable) should grant Pompey the triumph, the consulate, and the assignments of land, in return for his executioner's service against the democratic chiefs, the best the 36-year-old general might hope for would be burial in senatorial indolence among the long series of peaceful senatorial Imperators. What his heart really longed for—command in the Mithradatic war—he could never expect the Senate voluntarily to bestow. In obvious self-interest the oligarchy could not permit him to swell his African and European trophies with those of a third continent; the laurels to be plucked copiously and easily in the East were reserved for pure aristocrats.

But if the celebrated general did not find support among the oligarchy, there remained (since neither the time nor Pompey's temperament was suited for setting up a purely personal rule) no alternative save to make common cause with the democratic party. No personal interest bound him to the Sullan constitution. He could pursue his personal objects as well (if not better) with a more democratic one. On the other hand, he found all that he needed in the democratic party. Its adroit leaders were ready and able to relieve the somewhat wooden hero of the cares of political leadership, and yet were much too insignificant to be able or even willing to vie with the celebrated general for the titular leadership and especially for the supreme military control. Even Gaius Caesar, by far the most important of them, was simply a young man who had gained a name far more by his daring exploits and fashionable debts than by his fiery eloquence, and who could not but feel greatly honored when the world-renowned Imperator allowed him to be his political adjutant. That popularity to which men like Pompey, with pretensions greater than their abilities, usually attach more value than they are willing to confess would surely fall in fullest measure to the young general who brought victory to the almost forlorn cause of the democracy. The rewards sought for himself and his soldiers would then follow of themselves.

In general it seemed that if the oligarchy were overthrown, the complete lack of any democratic chiefs of
consequence would enable Pompey himself to determine
his future position. It could also hardly be doubted that
adding the victorious general, whose army still stood compact and unbroken in Italy, to the opposition party must
necessarily overturn the existing order of things. Government and opposition were equally powerless; so soon as
the latter could back up its words with the sword of a
victorious general, the government would surely be overcome, perhaps even without a struggle.

Pompey and the democrats thus found themselves impelled into coalition. Personal dislikes were probably not
lacking on either side. The victorious general could hardly
love the street orators, nor could these hail with pleasure
the executioner of Carbo and Brutus as their chief; but
political necessity outweighed all moral scruples for the
moment.

The democrats and Pompey, however, were not the
sole parties to the league. Marcus Crassus was in a similar situation with Pompey. Although also a Sullan, his
politics were quite as personal as those of Pompey, and
by no means those of the ruling oligarchy. He, too, was
now in Italy at the head of a large and victorious army,
with which he had just suppressed the rising of the slaves.
Having to choose whether he would enter the coalition or
ally himself with the oligarchy against it, he chose the
latter as doubtless the safer course. With his colossal
wealth and his influence on the political clubs of the capital he was in any case a valuable ally. But under the existing circumstances it was an incalculable gain when the only
army which could have defended the Senate against the
troops of Pompey also joined the attackers. And the
democrats, who were probably somewhat uneasy at their
alliance with the too powerful general, were not displeased at the appearance of Marcus Crassus as a counterpoise and perhaps a future rival.

Thus, in the summer of 71 B.C., the first coalition took place between the popular party and the two Sullan generals. The generals adopted the democratic party program, and immediately were promised in return the consulships for the coming year. Pompey was also to have a triumph and the desired allotments of land for his soldiers, while Crassus as the conqueror of Spartacus would at least be granted the honor of a solemn entrance into the capital.

To oppose this coalition of the two Italian armies, the great capitalists, and the popular party the Senate had nothing save perhaps the second Spanish army under Quintus Metellus. But Sulla had truly predicted that what he did could not be done a second time. Metellus, by no means inclined to involve himself in a civil war, had discharged his soldiers immediately after crossing the Alps. So nothing was left for the oligarchy but to submit to the inevitable. The Senate granted the dispensations necessary for the consulship and triumph, and Pompey and Crassus were elected consuls for 70 B.C. without opposition, while their armies encamped before the city on pretext of awaiting their triumph. Even before taking office, Pompey gave his public and formal adherence to the democratic program at an assembly of the people held by the tribune Marcus Lollius Palicanus. The change of the constitution was thus in principle decided.

Now the Sullan institutions were attacked in earnest. First of all the tribuneship regained its earlier authority. Pompey himself as consul introduced the law which gave back to the tribunes their time-honored prerogatives, and in particular the initiative of legislation. It was a singular gift indeed from the hand of a man who had done more than anyone living to despoil the community of its ancient freedoms.

With regard to jurymen, Sulla's regulation that the roll of the senators was to serve as the list of jurymen was doubtless abolished. However, this by no means led to a simple restoration of the Gracchan equestrian courts. The new Aurelian law stipulated that the jury rolls were to consist of one-third senators and two-thirds men of the equestrian census, and that half of the latter must have filled the office of district president. This last was a further concession to the democrats, since according to it at least a third of the criminal jurymen were indirectly derived from the elections of the tribes. The reason why senators were not totally excluded is probably due partly to Crassus' relations with the Senate, but also to the support of the coalition by the senatorial middle party—as indicated by the introduction of the new law by the praetor Lucius Cotta, the brother of the deceased moderate leader.

Equally important was the abolition of Sulla's arrangements for the taxation of Asia. The governor of Asia at that time, Lucius Lucullus, was directed to re-establish the system of farming the revenue introduced by Gaius Gracchus. Thus this important source of money and power was restored to the great capitalists.

Lastly, the censorship was revived. The elections for it which the new consuls fixed soon after taking office fell, in obvious mockery of the Senate, on the two consuls for 72 B.C., Gnaeus Lentulus Clodianus and Lucius Gellius, who had been stripped of their commands by the Senate because of their wretched management of the war against Spartacus. It may readily be conceived that these men used all the powers of their important office to annoy the Senate and curry favor with the new holders of power. The unparalleled number of 64 senators, at least an eighth of the Senate, were deleted from the rolls, including Gaius Antonius, formerly impeached without success by Gaius Caesar, Publius Lentulus Sura, the consul in 71 B.C., and probably a further number of the more obnoxious creatures of Sulla.

Thus in 70 B.C. affairs had reverted in the main to the situation that prevailed before the Sullan restoration.

Again the populace of the capital was fed by the state, in other words by the provinces. Again the tribunician authority gave every demagogue legal license to thwart the administration of the state. Again the moneyed nobility, as farmers of the revenue and possessors of judicial control over the governors, raised their heads alongside the government as powerful as ever. Again the Senate trembled before the verdict of equestrian jurymen and before the censorial censure.

The system of Sulla, based on the monopoly of power by the nobility to the complete exclusion of the mercantile aristocracy and of the populace, was thus completely overthrown. Leaving out some subordinate enactments, which were not abolished till later, only two groups of Sulla's general ordinances survived. One was the concessions he found it necessary to make to the opposition, such as the recognition of the Roman franchise of all the Italians. The other comprised those nonpartisan enactments with which even judicious democrats found no fault, such as the restriction of the freedmen, the regulation of the spheres of the magistrates, and the reform of the criminal law.

The coalition was more agreed regarding these questions of principle than with respect to the personal questions which such a political revolution raised. As might be expected, the democrats were not content with the general recognition of their program. They now demanded a restoration in *their* sense—revival of the commemoration of their dead, punishment of the murderers, recall of the proscribed from exile, removal of the political disqualification that lay on their children, restoration of the estates confiscated by Sulla, and indemnification at the expense of the heirs and assistants of the dictator. These would certainly be the logical consequences of a pure democratic victory, but the victory of the coalition of 71 B.C. was very far from being such. The democrats gave it their name and their program, but it was the officers who had joined the movement, and above all Pompey, who gave it power and completion. These could never yield their consent to a reaction which would not only have shaken the existing state of things to its foundations, but would ultimately have turned against themselves. Men still had a lively recollection of whose blood Pompey had shed, and how Crassus had laid the foundation of his enormous fortune.

It was therefore natural, but at the same time symbolic of the democratic weakness, that the coalition of 71 B.C. took not the slightest step towards giving the democrats revenge or even rehabilitation. The supplementary collection of all money still owed for confiscated estates bought by auction, or even remitted to the purchasers by Sulla (for which the censor Lentulus provided in a special law) can hardly be regarded as an exception. For while not a few Sullans were thereby severely affected in their personal interests, yet the measure itself was essentially a confirmation of the Sullan confiscations.

The work of Sulla was thus destroyed; but what was to be the future order of things was a question raised rather than decided by that destruction. The coalition, kept together solely by the common object of setting aside the restoration, dissolved effectively if not formally when that object was attained. The question of who was to have the predominant power seemed on the verge of an equally speedy and violent solution. The armies of Pompey and Crassus still lay before the city's gates. The former had indeed promised to disband his soldiers after his triumph on the last day of December, 71 B.C. However, he had at first omitted to do so, in order to complete the revolution under the pressure which his army applied on the city and the Senate—a course which the army of Crassus had also followed. This reason existed no longer, but still the dissolution of the armies was postponed. It looked as if one of the two generals allied with the democracy would seize the military dictatorship and place oligarchs and democrats in the same chains.

This one could only be Pompey. From the first Crassus had played a subordinate part in the coalition. He had been obliged to propose himself, and even owed his consular election mainly to the proud intercession of Pompey. Far the stronger, Pompey was obviously master of the situation. If he availed himself of it, it seemed as if he must surely become what the popular instinct even now considered him—the absolute ruler of the mightiest state in the civilized world. Already the whole fawning multitude crowded around the future monarch. Already his weaker opponents played their last gambit by seeking a new coalition. Crassus, full of old and recent jealousy towards the younger rival who had so thoroughly outstripped him, made overtures to the Senate and attempted by unprecedented largesses to attach to himself the multitude—as if the oligarchy which Crassus himself had helped to break down, and the ever ungrateful multitude, could have stood off the veterans of the Spanish army. For a moment it appeared that the forces of Pompey and Crassus might come to blows before the gates of the capital.

But the democrats averted this catastrophe by their sagacity and their pliancy. For their party no less than for the Senate and Crassus, it was all-important that Pompey should not seize the dictatorship. With a truer discernment of their own weakness, and of the character of their powerful opponent, the democratic leaders tried the method of conciliation. Pompey lacked no qualification for the crown save the first of all—kingly courage. We have already described the man with his effort to be at once a loyal republican and master of Rome, with his vacillation and indecision, with his pliancy that concealed itself under the boast of independence. This was the first great trial to which destiny subjected him, and he failed to stand it.

The pretext under which Pompey refused to dismiss his army was that he distrusted Crassus, and therefore could not take the initiative in disbanding the soldiers. The democrats induced Crassus to make gracious advances in the matter, and to offer the hand of peace to his colleague before the eyes of all. In public and in private they entreated Pompey to add to his double merit of having vanquished the enemy and reconciled the parties a third and yet greater service of preserving internal peace and banishing the fearful threat of civil war. Whatever could tell on a vain, unskillful, vacillating man—all the flattering arts of diplomacy, all the theatrical apparatus of patriotic enthusiasm—was put in motion to obtain the desired result. And what was most important, the well-timed offer of Crassus left Pompey no alternative but to come forward openly as tyrant or to retire.

Thus at length he yielded, and consented to disband his troops. The command in the Mithradatic war, which he had doubtless hoped to obtain when he had allowed himself to be chosen consul for 70 B.C., he could not now desire, since Lucullus seemed to have practically ended that war. He thought it beneath his dignity to accept the consular province assigned him by the Senate under the Sempronian law, and Crassus followed his example. Accordingly, when Pompey resigned his consulship on the last day of 70 B.C., he retired wholly from public affairs, at least officially, and declared that he wished thenceforth to lead a life of quiet leisure as a simple citizen. He had assumed a position in which he was obliged to grasp at the crown; being unwilling to do so, he had no part left but the empty one of a candidate for a throne resigning his pretensions.

The retirement of the man to whom the first place belonged reproduced a political situation similar to that of the Gracchan and Marian epochs. Sulla had strengthened the senatorial government, but had not created it. By the same token, after the bulwarks erected by Sulla had fallen the Senate nevertheless continued, in the main, to rule, although the constitution with which it governed (virtually the restored Gracchan constitution) was pervaded by a spirit hostile to the oligarchy. The democrats had reestablished the Gracchan system, but without a new Gracchus it was a body without a head; and recent events had shown anew that neither Pompey nor Crassus could permanently be such a head. Thus the democratic opposition, for want of a leader who could take the helm, had to content itself with hampering and annoying the government at every step.

Between the oligarchy and the democracy, however, there now appeared the capitalist party, which in the recent crisis had made common cause with the latter, but which the oligarchs now zealously sought to draw over as a counterpoise to the democracy. Courted on both sides, the moneyed lords did not neglect to profit from their advantageous position. By decree of the people in 67 B.C. they regained the last of their former privileges, the fourteen benches reserved for the equestrian order in the theater. On the whole, they again drew closer to the Senate without breaking abruptly with the democrats. The relations of the Senate to Crassus and his followers point in this direction. However, the closer feeling between the Senate and the capitalist interests seems to have been brought about chiefly by the Senate's withdrawal of the administration of the province of Asia from Lucius Lucullus, the ablest of the senatorial officers. The change was made at the instance of the tax farmers whom he had so sorely annoyed.

But while the factions in Rome indulged in their customary quarrels without reaching any decision, events in the East followed the fatal course already described; and these events produced a new crisis in the politics of the capital. Both by land and sea the war had taken a most unfavorable turn. At the beginning of 67 B.C. the Pontic army of the Romans was destroyed, and their Armenian army was falling apart during its retreat. All their conquests were lost, the sea was wholly in the power of the pirates, and the price of grain in Italy had thereby so much increased that there was fear of actual famine. To be sure, these calamities were partly the fault of the generals, especially the utter incapacity of the admiral Marcus Antonius and the temerity of the otherwise able Lucius Lucullus. The popular opposition had also by its revolutionary agitations materially contributed to the breakup of the Armenian army. But of course the government was held solely responsible for all the mischief which had arisen, and the indignant hungry multitude desired nothing so much as an opportunity to settle accounts with the Senate.

It was a decisive crisis. The oligarchy, though degraded and disarmed, was not yet overthrown, for the management of public affairs remained in the hands of the Senate. But it would fall if its opponents should take over that management, especially the superintendence of military affairs; and this was now possible. If proposals for a different and better management of the war were submitted to the populace in its present mood, the Senate was obviously not in a position to prevent their passing; and interference by the citizens in these crucial questions amounted practically to deposing the Senate and transferring the conduct of the state to the opposition.

Once more the configuration of events put the decision into the hands of Pompey. For over two years the famous general had lived as a private citizen in the capital. His voice was seldom heard in the senate house or in the Forum. In the former he was unwelcome and without decisive influence; in the latter he was inept in the stormy proceedings of the factions. But when he did show himself, it was with his full retinue of hangers-on, high and low, and the very solemnity of his reserve impressed the multitude. If he, still surrounded with the full luster of his extraordinary successes, should now offer to go to the East, the citizens would doubtless readily invest him with all the mililtary and political power he might ask.

For the oligarchy, which saw in the political-military dictatorship their certain ruin, and in Pompey himself their most hated foe, this was an overwhelming prospect. But the democratic group too could take little comfort in the situation. However desirable in itself might be the ending of the government of the Senate, for it to take place in this way made it less a triumph for their faction than a personal victory for their overpowerful ally. The latter might easily become much more dangerous to the democratic group than the Senate had been. The danger fortunately avoided a few years before, when the Spanish army was disbanded and Pompey had retired, would recur in increased measure if Pompey should now be placed at the head of the armies of the East.

On this occasion, however, Pompey acted, or at least allowed others to act, on his behalf. In 67 B.C. two laws were proposed, one of which, besides decreeing the long-demanded discharge of the soldiers of the Asiatic army who had served their terms, also replaced its commander-in-chief Lucius Lucullus with one of the consuls of the current year, Gaius Piso or Manius Glabrio. The second revived and extended the plan proposed by the Senate seven years earlier for clearing the sea of pirates. A single general was to be named by the Senate from the ex-consuls to command the whole Mediterranean from the Pillars of Hercules to the coasts of Pontus and Syria, and to exercise by land, concurrently with the respective Roman governors, supreme command over the coasts for fifty miles inland. His tenure of office was three years.

This extraordinary commander was granted a staff such as Rome had never seen—twenty-five lieutenants of senatorial rank, all invested with praetorian insignia and powers, and two sub-treasurers with quaestorian prerogatives, all to be appointed by the commander-in-chief. He was allowed to raise as many as 120,000 infantry, 5,000 cavalry, and 500 warships, and for this purpose to dispose absolutely of the means of the provinces and protectorates. Moreover, the existing fleet and a considerable number of troops were handed over to him at once. The state treasure of the capital, the provinces, and the dependent communities were placed absolutely at his command; and despite the severe financial distress, a sum of 144,000,000 sesterces was to be paid to him at once from the state chest.

It is clear that this law, especially its clauses relating to the expedition against the pirates, virtually set aside the government of the Senate. The ordinary supreme magistrates chosen by the citizens were the proper generals of the commonwealth, and, strictly speaking, the extraordinary magistrates needed confirmation by the citizens to act as generals. But the community had no constitutional power to appoint to particular commands: and it was only on the motion of the Senate, or of a magistrate entitled to hold office as general, that the voters had now and then interfered and conferred such special functions. Ever since there had been a free Roman state the Senate had held the decisive voice, and its prerogative had been fully recognized. Demagogic politicians had no doubt previously assailed this power. But even in the most important of the past cases—the transference of the African command to Gaius Marius in 107 B.C.—a magistrate constitutionally entitled to hold the office of general had been entrusted by a resolution of the citizens with a definite expedition.

Now, however, the voters were investing a private citizen not only with the extraordinary authority of the supreme magistracy, but also with a definite sphere of office. That the Senate might choose this man from the ranks of the consulars was a mitigation in form only; the choice left to it was really no choice, since in the presence of the excited populace the Senate could entrust the chief command of the seas and coasts to no one save Pompey.

But more dangerous still was the practical abolition of senatorial control by the creation of an office with almost unlimited military and financial powers. While the office of general was formerly restricted to a term of one year, to a definite province, and to military and financial resources strictly measured out, the new extraordinary office had from the outset a duration of three years, which of course did not exclude a further prolongation. It held sway over the greater portion of all the provinces and even Italy, which formerly was free from military control. The soldiers, ships, and treasures of the state were placed almost without restriction at its disposal. Even the fundamental principle of the constitutional law of the Roman republic—that the highest military and civil authority could not be conferred without the consent of the electorate—was infringed in favor of the new commander-in-chief. Since the law conferred in advance praetorian rank and praetorian prerogatives on the twenty-five adjutants whom the extraordinary general was to appoint, the highest office of republican Rome became subordinate to a newly created office which the future might name, but which even now was in effect a monarchy. Such a law laid the train for a total revolution in the existing order of things.[2]

The democracy, discontented as its leaders might be in secret, could not very well come forward publicly against the projected law. They could not in any case have hindered its passage; and opposition would have produced an open break with Pompey, thereby compelling him either to make approaches to the oligarchy or pursue his per-

■

2. In the original, Mommsen seeks to explain Pompey's apparent decisiveness in this question by noting that the measure had a certain sort of legality; that Pompey could not prudently risk the dilatory support of the Senate; and that the proponents of the new law "probably took the decision to a considerable extent out of the hands of their shortsighted and resourceless patron."

sonal policy in the face of both parties. The democrats had to accept their alliance, hollow as it was, and to take the opportunity of at least overthrowing the Senate and passing from opposition to government, while leaving the ultimate issue to the future and to the well-known weakness of Pompey's character. Accordingly their leaders—the praetor Lucius Quinctius, who seven years before had exerted himself for the restoration of the tribunician power, and the former quaestor Gaius Caesar—supported the proposed law, known as the Gabinian law from the tribune who brought it forward.

The privileged classes were furious—including the mercantile aristocracy, which felt its exclusive position endangered by so far-reaching a revolution, and which once more recognized its true patron in the Senate. When the tribune Gabinius appeared in the senate house after introducing his proposals, the senators were almost on the point of strangling him with their own hands, disregarding how ruinous for them this method of argument must in the end have proved. The tribune escaped to the Forum and summoned the multitude to storm the senate house, but the sitting was terminated before the ultimate violence occurred. The consul Piso, champion of the oligarchy, who accidentally fell into the hands of the multitude, would certainly have become a victim of the popular rage had not Gabinius come up and, in order that his sure triumph might not be endangered by unseasonable acts of outrage, liberated the consul.

Meanwhile the exasperation of the people remained undiminished, and constantly found fresh nourishment from the high price of grain and from numerous more or less absurd rumors. It was said, for example, that Lucius Lucullus had invested in Rome the money entrusted to him for carrying on the Asiatic war, and had attempted with its aid to bribe the praetor Quinctius into withdrawing from the cause of the people. It was whispered that the Senate intended the "second Romulus," as they called

Pompey, to meet the fate of the first, who according to legend had been torn to pieces by the senators.

When the day of voting arrived, the multitude stood densely packed in the Forum, and all the buildings from whence the rostra could be seen were covered to the roofs with spectators. All Gabinius' colleagues had promised their veto to the Senate, but in the presence of the surging masses all were silent save Lucius Trebellius, who had sworn to himself and to the Senate to die rather than yield. When he exercised his veto, Gabinius interrupted the voting on his law and proposed that Trebellius be dealt with as Octavius had formerly been by Tiberius Gracchus, that is, immediately removed from office. The vote was taken and the reading of the tablets began. When the first seventeen tribes had declared for the proposal and the next affirmative vote would give it the majority, Trebellius, forgetting his oath, pusillanimously withdrew his veto. In vain did the tribune Otho then endeavor to preserve legal precedent by urging that two generals be elected instead of one. In vain the aged Quintus Catulus, the most respected man in the Senate, exerted his last energies for the amendment that the lieutenant-generals be chosen by the people rather than appointed by the commander-in-chief. Otho could not even secure a hearing amid the noise of the multitude; and while the well-calculated forbearance of Gabinius procured a respectful hearing for Catulus, his plea was nonetheless disregarded. Gabinius' proposals were not only passed unaltered, but supplementary requests made by Pompey were instantly and completely agreed to in detail.

With great expectations men saw Pompey and Glabrio depart for their respective destinations. The price of grain had fallen to normal immediately after the passage of the Gabinian proposals—an evidence of the hopes attached to the grand expedition and its glorious leader. As we shall see, these hopes were not merely fulfilled but surpassed. In three months the clearing of the seas was completed. Since the Hannibalic war the Roman government had displayed no such energy. Compared to the lax and incapable administration of the oligarchy, the democratic-military opposition had most brilliantly earned its title to the reins of the state. The unpatriotic and clumsy attempts of the consul Piso to put paltry obstacles in the way of Pompey's arrangements for suppressing piracy in Narbonese Gaul only increased the exasperation of the citizens against the oligarchy and their enthusiasm for Pompey. In fact, it was only the personal intervention of the latter that prevented the assembly of the people from summarily removing the consul from office.

Meanwhile the confusion on the Asiatic continent had become still worse. Glabrio, who was to take up Lucullus' command against Mithradates and Tigranes, had not proceeded much beyond the coast of Asia Minor; and while he had aroused the soldiers against Lucullus by various proclamations, he had forced Lucullus to retain the supreme command by refusing himself to take it over. Against Mithradates, of course, nothing was done, and the Pontic cavalry ravaged Bithynia and Cappadocia with impunity. Pompey had been led by the war against the pirates to transport his own army to Asia Minor, and nothing seemed more natural than to give him the supreme command in the Pontic-Armenian war which he himself had long desired. But the democratic faction did not, as may readily be conceived, share the wishes of its general, and carefully avoided taking any initiative in the matter. Quite probably its leaders had induced Gabinius not to give the command of both the Mithradatic and pirate wars to Pompey, but to entrust the former to Glabrio. On no account could they wish to increase and perpetuate the position of the already too-powerful general. Pompey himself exhibited his customary passive attitude. Perhaps he would have returned home after fulfilling his mission against the pirates, but for an incident unexpected by all parties.

One Gaius Manilius, an utterly worthless and insignificant man, had as tribune lost favor both with the oligarchy and with the popular party by his legislative inepitude. In the hope of sheltering himself under the wing of the powerful general, by procuring for him what everyone knew he eagerly desired but had not the boldness to demand, Manilius proposed (1) that the citizens recall Glabrio from Bithynia and Pontus, and Marcus Rex from Cilicia, and (2) that their offices, as well as the conduct of the war in the East, also be entrusted to Pompey, apparently without any time limit and with the fullest authority to negotiate alliances and treaties of peace.

The serious proposal of so important a measure by such a man clearly showed the disorganization of the Roman governmental machinery; the initiative of any demagogue, however insignificant, combined with the prejudices of the incapable multitude, was to decide the most difficult questions of government policy. The Manilian proposal was acceptable to none of the political groups, yet it encountered little serious resistance. The democratic leaders did not dare oppose it for the same reasons which had forced them to acquiesce to the Gabinian law. They kept their displeasure and their fears to themselves and spoke publicly in favor of Pompey. The moderate aristocrats declared themselves for the Manilian proposal because after the Gabinian law resistance seemed vain; and far-seeing men already perceived that the Senate's true interest was to draw Pompey over to their side in anticipation of the break which might be expected between him and the democrats. Lastly, the trimmers blessed the day when they too seemed to have an opinion and could come forward decidedly without losing favor in any quarter. (It is significant that Marcus Cicero first appeared on the political platform in support of the Manilian proposal.) Only the strict Optimates, with Quintus Catulus at their head, showed their colors and spoke against the proposition, which, of course, was converted into law by a majority bordering on unanimity.

Pompey thus added to his earlier extensive powers the administration of the most important provinces of Asia Minor, so that there scarcely remained a spot within the Roman world that was not under his control, and the conduct of a war which (like the expedition of Alexander) had a definite beginning but no foreseeable end. Never since Rome stood had such power been united in the hands of a single man.

The Gabinio-Manilian proposals ended the struggle between the Senate and the popular leaders which the Sempronian laws had begun sixty-seven years before. As the Sempronian laws first transformed the revolutionary party into a political opposition, the Gabinio-Manilian laws first converted it from an opposition into a government. As it had been a great moment when the first breach of the existing constitution was made by disregarding the veto of Octavius, so it was a moment no less significant when the last bulwark of senatorial rule fell with the withdrawal of the veto of Trebellius. This was so generally felt that even the indolent souls of the senators were convulsively roused by this death-struggle. But the war over the constitution terminated in a far different and more pitiful fashion than it had begun. A truly noble youth had begun the revolution; it was concluded by intriguers and demagogues of the lowest type. The Optimates had begun the struggle with a tenacious defense of even forlorn positions; they ended by resort to violence, grandiloquent weakness, and pitiful perjury.

What had once been a daring dream was now attained: the Senate had ceased to govern. But when the few old men who had seen the first storms of revolution and heard the words of the Gracchi compared that time with the present, they found that everything had changed—countrymen and citizens, life and manners, the law of the state and the discipline of the camp. Well might those painfully smile who compared the ideals of the Gracchan period with their realization.

But such reflections belonged to the past. For the present and perhaps also for the future the fall of the aristocracy was an accomplished fact. The oligarchs resembled a broken army whose scattered bands might serve to reinforce another body of troops, but could no longer stay in the field or risk a combat on their own account. But as the old struggle came to an end, a new one was simultaneously beginning—the struggle between the two forces hitherto leagued for the overthrow of the aristocratic constitution, the popular opposition and the growing military power.

The exceptional position of Pompey under the Gabinian law, and still more under the Manilian, was incompatible with a republican organization. As even then his opponents urged with good reason, he had been appointed not general but regent of the empire; not unjustly was he designated "king of kings" by a Greek familiar with eastern affairs. If he should return from the East victorious and with increased glory, with well-filled chests, and with troops ready for battle and devoted to his cause, who could call a halt were he to stretch forth his hand to seize the crown? Would the aged consular Quintus Catulus summon forth the senators against the first general of his time and his veteran legions? Could the aedile-elect Gaius Caesar call forth the multitude, whose eyes he had just feasted on his three hundred and twenty pairs of gladiators with their silvered equipage?

Soon, exclaimed Catulus, it would be necessary once more to flee to the rocks of the Capitol in order to save liberty. It was not the prophet's fault that the storm came not from the East, as he expected, but that fate fulfilled his words more literally than he had himself anticipated by sending the destroying tempest a few years later from Gaul.

How strong was Mommsen's prejudice against Pompey is vividly illustrated by the history of the next few years, which saw a rapid series of spectacular achievements by that general. By careful military preparations, plus a judicious policy of moderation toward his piratical opponents once armed resistance was broken, he completely cleared the western Mediterranean in forty days. Then, transferring his forces to eastern waters, he finished the cleanup in forty-nine days more. In these two short campaigns he substantially freed the Roman world of an incubus that had oppressed it for generations.

In the following spring (66 B.C.), Pompey led his army of some 50,000 regulars in the Third Mithradatic War. After lengthy tactical maneuvering he managed to lead the king's army into a night ambush where it was almost totally destroyed. Mithradates again sought help from his son-in-law, King Tigranes of Armenia, and again in vain; with a price on his head he was forced to flee to the hinterland of his Pontic kingdom stretching around the eastern rim of the Black Sea. Pompey pursued, accepting on the way the voluntary submission of Tigranes and the ancient Armenian capital of Artaxata.

"At the beginning of 66," Mommsen summarizes, "there was not a Roman soldier beyond the bounds of the old Roman possessions; at its close King Mithradates was an exile wandering in the ravines of the Caucasus, and King Tigranes sat upon his throne not as King of Kings, but as a Roman vassal." Achievements like these are hardly consistent with Mommsen's general picture of Pompey as a sluggish, incompetent "sergeant-nature."

Pompey pursued the fleeing Mithradates as far as present-day Tiflis, then turned toward the Black Sea and bent his efforts toward subduing a long list of barbarian and semicivilized peoples. Mithradates himself sought once more to organize an army and mount a campaign against the Romans from a base on the northern side of the Black Sea; but at last his officers, his troops, and his subjects deserted him. He died in 63 B.C., in his 68th year, a suicide to avoid falling into the hands of his mutinous son, Pharnaces. So great a victory was his death regarded by the Romans that the messengers who brought the news to Pompey wore crowns of laurel.

Well before Mithradates' death, however, Pompey had turned southward to regulate the confused affairs of Syria. After its incapable king had been deposed, it too, like Pontus and Bithynia, became an outright Roman province. Around the edge of the new provinces the Romans forged a ring of dependencies; and everywhere they sought to strengthen Graeco-Roman civilization against the Oriental feudalism of the countryside. This general settlement of affairs in the East was Pompey's creative work. But it was yet to be ratified and made permanent by the government in Rome. It is today impossible to settle the precise limits of Pompey's legal authority to act for the government, but it is certain that he expected his acts to be approved without argument. His failure on his return to Rome to secure this blanket approval was an important factor in driving him into the arms of Caesar, with fateful consequences for the history of the next fifteen years.

Pompey's triumphal march through the streets of Rome on September 28-29, 61 B.C., may perhaps have been, as Mommsen uncharitably dubs it, an "insipid extravagance." But for all that, Pompey in five years of invariably successful marches, battles, punitive expeditions, and reorganizations had achieved no less than the establishment of the Roman imperial system in the East.

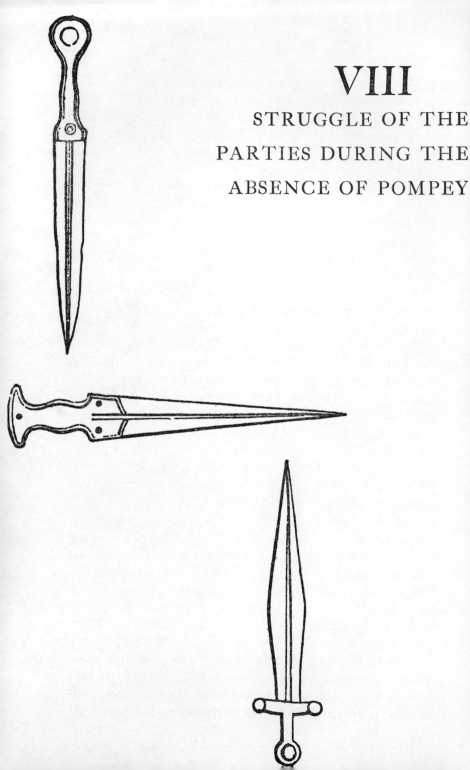

VIII
STRUGGLE OF THE
PARTIES DURING THE
ABSENCE OF POMPEY

With the passage of the Gabinian law the parties in the capital changed places. As soon as Pompey took his command in the field, what was regarded as his party similarly took command in the capital. To be sure, the nobility still stood in compact array, and the comitial machinery continued to elect consuls who (as the democrats put it) were already chosen in their cradles; for not even the holders of power could break down the influence of the old families. But unfortunately the consulate, at the very moment when the "new men" were virtually excluded from it, began itself to pale before the newly risen star of the military.

The aristocracy felt this, and without quite confessing it they gave themselves up for lost. Except for Quintus Catulus, who with honorable firmness persevered at his difficult post as champion of a vanquished party down to his death in 60 B.C., there was no top-ranking Optimate who sustained the interests of the aristocracy with courage and steadfastness. Their most talented and famous men, such as Quintus Metellus Pius and Lucius Lucullus, practically abdicated and sought dignified retirement in their villas, in the attempt to forget the Forum and the senate house amid their gardens and libraries, their aviaries and fishponds. This was of course still more true among the younger aristocrats, who were either wholly absorbed in luxury and literature or turned towards the rising sun.

Among the younger men there was a single exception. Marcus Porcius Cato, born in 95 B.C., was a man of the best intentions and of rare devotion, and yet one of the most quixotic and cheerless phenomena in an age so replete with political caricatures. Honorable and steadfast, earnest in purpose and in action, full of attachment to his country and to its hereditary constitution, but dull in intellect and sensuously as well as morally destitute of passion, he might well have made a tolerable state comptroller. But unfortunately he fell early under the power of formalism, swayed partly by the Stoic catchwords whose abstract baldness and spiritless isolation made them fashionable among the gentility of that day, and partly by the example of his great-grandfather whom he deemed it his mission to reproduce. He began to walk about the sinful capital as a model citizen and mirror of virtue, to scold at the times like the old Cato, to travel on foot instead of riding, to accept no interest on loans, to decline badges of distinction as a soldier, and to herald the restoration of the good old days by going without a shirt, after the precedent of King Romulus. His ancestor was a gray-haired farmer whom hatred and anger made an orator, who wielded in equally masterful style the plow or the sword, and whose narrow but original and sound common sense ordinarily hit the nail on the head. This young caricature was an unimpassioned pedant from whose lips dropped scholastic wisdom, who was everywhere seen sitting book in hand, a philosopher who understood neither the art of war nor any other art, a cloud-walker amid moral abstractions.

Yet he attained to moral and thereby even to political importance. In an utterly wretched and cowardly age his courage and negative virtues told powerfully on the multitude. He even formed a school, and there were individuals (true, only a few) who in their turn copied and caricatured afresh this living model of a philosopher. From the same cause also stemmed his political influence. As the only prominent conservative who possessed at least integrity and courage, if not talent and insight, he was always ready to throw himself into the breach whether it was necessary to do so or not. Thus he soon became the recognized champion of the Optimate party, to which neither his age nor his rank nor his intellect entitled him. Where sheer perseverance of a single man was efficacious he achieved some admitted successes; and in questions of detail, especially of a financial character, he often judiciously interfered, as he was never absent from a meeting of the Senate. His quaestorship in fact formed an epoch, for as long as he lived he checked the details of the budget, maintaining of course a constant warfare with the farmers of the taxes.

For the rest, he simply lacked every ingredient of a statesman. He was incapable of even comprehending a political aim and of surveying political relations. His whole tactics consisted in setting his face against everyone who deviated or seemed to him to deviate from the traditional moral and political catechism of the aristocracy, and thus of course he played into the hands of his opponents as often as he helped his own party. The Don Quixote of the aristocracy, he proved by his character and his actions that, although an aristocracy still existed, there was not the ghost of an aristocratic policy.

To battle with such an aristocracy brought little honor, but the democratic attacks of course did not cease on that account. The popular demagogues threw themselves on the broken ranks of the nobility like a pack of scavengers, and the surface of the political pond was ruffled into high waves of foam. The multitude joined in with greater alacrity since Gaius Caesar especially kept them in good humor by the extravagant magnificence of his games (65 B.C.)—in which all the equipment, even the cages of the wild beasts, appeared of massive silver—and generally by a liberality which was all the more princely for being based solely on reckless borrowing.

The attacks on the nobility were of the most varied kind. The abuses of aristocratic rule afforded copious materials, and magistrates and advocates who were liberal or assumed a liberal cloak, like Gaius Cornelius, Aulus Gabinius, and Marcus Cicero, continued systematically to unveil the most scandalous Optimate misdeeds and to propose laws against them. The Senate was directed to give audience to foreign envoys on set days, in order to prevent the usual postponement. Debts contracted by foreign ambassadors in Rome were declared nonactionable, as this was the only means of seriously checking the corruptions which formed the order of the day in the Senate. The right of the Senate to set aside the laws in particular cases was restricted, as was the abuse whereby every Roman of rank with private business in the provinces got himself appointed a Roman envoy by the Senate. The penalties against vote-buying and unlawful electioneering were strengthened, the latter having especially increased by the efforts of ousted senators to recover their seats through re-election. What had hitherto been taken for granted was now laid down as law, that the praetors were bound to administer justice in conformity with the rules set forth by them upon entering office.

Above all, however, efforts were made to complete the democratic restoration and to reinstate the major Gracchan ideas in suitable contemporary form. The election of the priests by the comitia, which Gnaeus Domitius had introduced and Sulla had again abolished, was re-established by a law of the tribune of the people Titus Labienus in 63 B.C. The democrats were fond of pointing out that the Sempronian grain laws were far from fully restored, while glossing over the fact that under the changed circumstances—the straitened condition of the public finances and the great increase in the number of Roman citizens—full restoration was quite impracticable.

In the country between the Po and the Alps, the agitation for political equality with the Italians was zealously fostered. As early as 68 B.C. Gaius Caesar traveled from place to place among the Transpadanes for this purpose. In 65 B.C. Marcus Crassus as censor arranged to place the inhabitants directly on the roll of citizens, an effort frustrated only by the resistance of his colleague. The attempt seems to have been repeated regularly in the following censorships. As formerly Gracchus and Flaccus had been the patrons of the Latins, so the present democratic leaders presented themselves as protectors of the Transpadanes, and Gaius Piso (consul in 67 B.C.) came to re-

gret that he had ventured to outrage one of these followers of Caesar and Crassus.

On the other hand, these same leaders were quite indisposed to advocate political equality for freedmen. The
tribune of the people Gaius Manilius, who in a thinly attended assembly procured the renewal of the Sulpician
law as to the suffrage of freedmen, was immediately dis-
avowed by the democratic leaders, and with their consent
the law was canceled by the Senate the day after its passage. In the same spirit, all strangers who possessed neither Roman nor Latin citizenship were ejected from the
capital by decree of the people in 65 B.C. Thus the intrinsic inconsistency of the Gracchan policy, at once seeking
to help the excluded obtain admission into the circle of
the privileged while maintaining the distinctive rights of
the privileged, was handed down to the successors of the
Gracchi. Caesar and his friends on the one hand held forth
to the Transpadanes the prospect of the franchise; on the
other they assented to the discrimination against the
freedmen, and to the protection of the Italians in Italy
against the industry and trading skill of the Hellenes and
Orientals.[1]

The democratic leaders were still more vehement in all
personal questions. To be sure, prudence enjoined them
not to urge the restoration of the estates confiscated by
Sulla, that they might not split with their own allies over
a question of material interests, which will almost always
defeat a purely political movement. The recall of the emigrants was too closely connected with this question of
property to appear advisable. On the other hand, great
efforts were made to restore political rights to the children of the proscribed, and the heads of the senatorial
party were incessantly subjected to personal attack. Thus
Gaius Memmius initiated a process against Marcus Lucul-

■

1. The popular party also (Mommsen continues in the original) re-established the right of the people to set aside judicial decisions.

lus in 66 B.C.; his more famous brother was allowed to wait three years for his well-deserved triumph; and Quintus Metellus, the conqueror of Crete, and Quintus Rex were similarly insulted.

It produced a still greater sensation when the young democratic leader Gaius Caesar not only presumed to compete in 63 B.C. for the supreme pontificate with the two most distinguished aristocrats, Quintus Catulus and Publius Servilius, but carried the day among the citizens. The heirs of Sulla, especially his son Faustus, found themselves constantly threatened with an action for the refunding of the public moneys which, it was alleged, had been embezzled by the regent. There was even talk of resuming the democratic impeachments on the basis of the Varian law.

The individuals who had taken part in the Sullan executions were, as may readily be conceived, prosecuted with the utmost zeal. When in 65 B.C. the quaestor Marcus Cato, in his pedantic integrity, himself demanded back from them as state property the rewards which they had received for murder, it is hardly surprising that the next year Gaius Caesar, as president of the commission regarding murder, summarily treated as null and void the Sullan ordinance which declared that a proscribed person might be killed with impunity, and caused the most noted of Sulla's executioners, Lucius Catilina, Lucius Bellienus, and Lucius Luscius, to be brought before his jurymen and partially condemned.

Lastly, the long-proscribed democratic heroes and martyrs were once again publicly praised and their memory celebrated. Gaius Marius, at whose name all hearts had once throbbed, was not only the man to whom Italy owed her deliverance from the northern barbarians: he was at the same time the uncle of the present leader of the democrats. Loudly had the multitude rejoiced when Gaius Caesar in 68 B.C. ventured illegally to show the honored features of the hero in the Forum at the interment of his widow. Three years later the emblems of victory, which Marius had caused to be erected in the Capitol and Sulla had ordered to be thrown down, one morning unexpectedly glittered afresh in gold and marble at the old spot. The veterans of the African and Cimbrian wars crowded around the statue of their beloved general with tears in their eyes, and in presence of the rejoicing masses the Senate did not dare seize the trophies which the same bold hand had renewed in defiance of the laws.

But all these doings, however noisy, were of trifling political importance. The oligarchy was vanquished and the democracy had attained the helm. It was to be expected that underlings of various grades should hasten to give additional kicks to the prostrate foe, that the democrats should have their basis in law and their worship of principles, that their doctrinaires should not rest till all the popular prerogatives were restored, and should occasionally make themselves ridiculous, as legitimists are wont to do. But taken as a whole, the agitation was aimless. Indeed, it betrays the perplexity of its authors in seeking an object for their activity, for it concentrated almost wholly on subordinate matters or on things already largely settled.

It could not be otherwise. In their struggle with the aristocracy the democrats had conquered, but they had not conquered alone. They still awaited the fiery trial of reckoning not with their former foe, but with their too-powerful ally, who was substantially responsible for their victory, and into whose hands they had placed unparalleled military and political power because they dared not refuse him. The general of the seas and of the East was still busy appointing and deposing kings. How long it would take him, or when he would declare the war ended, no one could say but himself; for the time of his return— in short, the day of reckoning—was left in his hands like everything else. Meanwhile the parties in Rome sat and waited. The Optimates looked forward to the arrival of the dreaded general with comparative calm. They could

only gain by the rupture they saw approaching between
Pompey and the popular party. The democrats on the
contrary waited with painful anxiety, and sought to use
the interval allowed to them by Pompey's absence to lay
a countermine against the impending explosion.

This policy again coincided with that of Crassus, who
had no course left for countering his envied and hated rival but to ally himself more closely than before with the
democrats. During the first coalition a special bond had
joined Caesar and Crassus as the two weaker parties, and
a common interest and a common danger strengthened the
link between the richest and the most insolvent of the Romans. While the democrats publicly described Pompey as
the head and pride of their party, and seemed to direct all
their arrows against the aristocracy, preparations were
secretly made against him.

These attempts of the democrats to escape from the
impending military dictatorship have far greater historical significance than their noisy agitation against the nobility, for the most part employed only as a mask. It is
true that they were carried on behind a curtain of secrecy
which our sources allow us to pierce only occasionally, for
both that age and the succeeding one had reasons for
throwing a veil over the matter. But in general both the
course and the object of these efforts are completely clear.
The military power could only be effectually checkmated
by another military power. The purpose of the democrats
was to seize the reins of government after the example of
Marius and Cinna; then to entrust one of their leaders
with the conquest of Egypt or the governorship of Spain
or some similar ordinary or extraordinary office; and thus
to find in him and his military force a counterpoise to
Pompey and his army.

For this they required a revolution directed immediately against the nominal government, but in reality
against Pompey as the designated monarch. To effect this
revolution, there was perpetual conspiracy in Rome from

the passing of the Gabinio-Manilian laws down to the return of Pompey. The capital lived in anxious suspense. The depressed temper of the capitalists, the suspensions of payments, and the frequent bankruptcies were heralds of the fermenting revolution, which seemed as though it must also produce a totally new political configuration. The project of the democrats, which pointed beyond the Senate at Pompey, implied a community of interest between that general and the Senate. But in attempting to offset Pompey's dictatorship with another more agreeable, the democrats in effect accepted the general principal of military government, and sought to drive out Satan by Beelzebub. Thus a question of principle became in their hands a question of persons.

The first step towards the proposed revolution was to be the overthrow of the existing government by an insurrection primarily instigated in Rome by democratic conspirators. The moral condition of both the lowest and the highest ranks of society in the capital presented the materials for this purpose in lamentable abundance. We need not describe again here the character of the free and the servile proletariat of the capital. It was already said that only a poor man was qualified to represent the poor, an idea which suggested that the mass of the poor might constitute itself an independent power alongside the oligarchy of the rich, and perhaps play the tyrant instead of allowing itself to be tyrannized.

But equivalent ideas were not wanting even in the circles of the young men of rank. The fashionable life of the capital shattered not merely the fortunes of men, but also their vigor of body and mind. That elegant world of fragrant ringlets, of fashionable mustachios and ruffles— merry as were its doings in the dance and with the harp, and early and late at the winecup—yet concealed in its bosom an alarming abyss of moral and economic ruin, of well- or ill-concealed despair, of frantic or knavish resolves. These circles sighed openly for a return of the days of Cinna, with its proscriptions and confiscations and its wiping out of debts. There were people enough, including not a few of respected lineage and unusual abilities, who only waited the signal to fall like a gang of robbers on civil society and recoup by pillage the fortunes which they had squandered. Where a band gathers, leaders are not wanting; and in this case men were soon found who were fitted to be captains of banditti.

The late praetor Lucius Catilina [2] and the quaestor Gnaeus Piso were distinguished among their peers not merely by their genteel birth and superior rank. They had completely burned their bridges behind them, and impressed their accomplices by their dissoluteness quite as much as by their talents. Catiline especially was one of the most wicked men of that wicked age. His villainies belong to the records of crime, not history; but his very appearance—the pale countenance, the wild glance, the gait by turns sluggish and hurried—betrayed his dismal past. He possessed in high degree the qualities required in the leader of such a band: the faculty of enjoying all pleasures and of bearing all privations, courage, military talent, knowledge of men, the energy of a felon, and that horrible mastery of vice which knows how to seduce the weak and train the fallen to crime.

To form from such elements a conspiracy to overthrow the existing order of things was not difficult for men who possessed money and political influence. Catiline, Piso, and their fellows entered readily into any plan which promised proscriptions and the cancellation of debts. Catiline also had a special grudge against the aristocracy, because it had opposed the candidacy of such an infamous and dangerous man for the consulship. As one of Sulla's executioners he had hunted the proscribed at the head of a band of Celts, and had killed among others his own aged father-in-law with his own hand; now he readily con-

■

2. More generally known to history as Catiline, and hereafter so called.

tracted to perform similar services for the opposite party. A secret league was formed, said to number over 400 individuals. It included associates in all the districts and urban communities of Italy, in addition to the numerous recruits who would, as a matter of course, flock unbidden from the ranks of the dissolute youth to any insurrection which promised a wiping out of debts.

In December of 66 B.C.—so we are told—the leaders of the league thought that they had found the fitting occasion for striking a blow. The two consuls elected for 65 B.C., Publius Cornelius Sulla and Publius Autronius Paetus, had just been convicted of electoral bribery, and thus according to law had forfeited their right to hold office. Both thereupon joined the league. The conspirators resolved to procure the consulship for them by force, and thereby to seize possession of the supreme power.

On the day when the new consuls should enter office—January 1, 65 B.C.—the senate house was to be assailed by armed men, the new consuls and other victims were to be put to death, and Sulla and Paetus were to be proclaimed as consuls after the canceling of the judicial sentence which excluded them. Crassus was then to be invested with the dictatorship and Caesar with the mastership of the horse, doubtless with a view to raising an imposing military force while Pompey was still far away in the Caucasus. Captains and common soldiers were hired and instructed, and Catiline waited on the appointed day near the senate house for the signal, which was to be given him by Caesar on a hint from Crassus. But he waited in vain; Crassus was absent from the decisive sitting of the Senate, and on this occasion the projected insurrection failed.

A still more comprehensive plan was then devised for February 5th, but this also was frustrated because Catiline gave the signal too early, before all the bandits had arrived. Thereupon the secret came out. The government did not venture to proceed openly against the conspiracy, but it assigned a guard to the threatened consuls, and it opposed the conspiratorial band with another band paid by the government. To remove Piso, it was proposed that he be sent as quaestor with praetorian powers to Hither Spain; and Crassus consented, in the hope of securing through him the resources of that important province for the insurrection. Proposals going further were prevented by the tribunes.

So runs the account that has come down to us, obviously the version current in government circles. Its credibility in detail must, in the absence of any means of checking it, be considered moot. As for the main question—the participation of Caesar and Crassus—the testimony of their political opponents certainly cannot be regarded as sufficient evidence. But their known actions during this period correspond with striking exactness to the secret moves which this report ascribes to them. The attempt of Crassus, who was censor in this year, to enroll the Transpadanes on the list of citizens was itself a revolutionary enterprise. It is still more remarkable that Crassus also made preparations to enroll Egypt and Cyprus in the list of Roman provinces, and that Caesar about the same time had a proposal submitted to the people to send him to Egypt, in order to reinstate the king whom the Alexandrians had expelled.

These machinations suspiciously coincide with the charges raised by their antagonists. The truth cannot be established with certainty. However, it is highly probable that Crassus and Caesar mounted a plan to establish a military dictatorship during Pompey's absence; that Egypt was selected as the basis of this democratic military power; that the attempted insurrection of 65 B.C. had been contrived to achieve these goals; and that Catiline and Piso were mere tools in the hands of Crassus and Caesar.

For the moment the conspiracy came to a standstill. The elections for 64 B.C. took place without Crassus and

Caesar renewing their attempt to get possession of the consulship, perhaps for the reason that a relative of the democratic leader, Lucius Caesar, a weak man occasionally used by his kinsman as a tool, was on this occasion a candidate. But the news from Asia urged them to make haste. The affairs of Asia Minor and Armenia were already completely settled. The democratic strategists might proclaim that ending the Mithradatic war demanded the capture of the king, that it was therefore necessary to continue the pursuit round the Black Sea, and that above all things Pompey should keep aloof from Syria. But the general, not concerning himself about such talk, had left Armenia in the spring of 64 B.C. and marched towards Syria. If Egypt was to be used as a democratic springboard there was no time to be lost. Otherwise, Pompey might easily arrive in Egypt before Caesar.

The conspiracy of 66 B.C., far from being broken up by the government's timid measures of repression, was again astir when the consular elections for 63 B.C. approached. The persons involved were presumably about the same, and the plan was but little altered. The leaders of the movement again kept in the background. On this occasion they had set up as candidates for the consulship Catiline himself and Gaius Antonius, the younger son of the orator and a brother of the general who had earned such a bad name in Crete. Antonius was originally a Sullan like Catiline, and like the latter had been brought to trial some years before by the democratic party and ejected from the Senate. Otherwise he was an indolent, insignificant, utterly bankrupt man with none of the qualifications of a leader, who willingly lent himself as a tool to the democrats for the prize of the consulship and the advantages attached to it.

Through these consuls the heads of the conspiracy intended to seize the government, arrest the children of Pompey as hostages, and take up arms in Italy and in the provinces against Pompey. On the first news of the rising in the capital, the governor Gnaeus Piso was to raise the banner of insurrection in Hither Spain. Sea communication with him was impossible, since Pompey commanded the seas. For this purpose the conspirators counted on their old friends the Transpadanes—among whom there was great agitation, and who of course would have received the franchise at once—and on various Celtic tribes. The threads of the plot reached as far as Mauretania, where one of the conspirators, the Roman speculator Publius Sittius, compelled by financial embarrassments to keep out of Italy, had armed a troop of desperadoes; with these he wandered about as a leader of freelances in western Africa, where he had old commercial connections.

The party put all its energies into the election struggle. Crassus and Caesar staked their money—whether their own or borrowed—and their connections to procure the consulship for Catiline and Antonius. The comrades of Catiline strained every nerve to elect the man who promised them not only the magistracies and priesthoods, the palaces and country estates of their opponents, but above all deliverance from their debts—and who, they knew, would keep his word. The aristocracy was in great perplexity, chiefly because it was not able even to offer opposition candidates. That such a candidate risked his head was obvious. The times were past when a post of danger tempted the citizen, and now even ambition was hushed in the presence of fear. Accordingly the nobility contented themselves with making a feeble attempt to check electioneering intrigues by issuing a new law respecting the purchase of votes (which, however, was thwarted by the veto of a tribune of the people) and with turning over their votes to a candidate who, if not acceptable, was at least inoffensive.

This candidate was Marcus Cicero, a notorious political trimmer accustomed to flirt at times with the democrats, at times with Pompey, at times (from a somewhat greater distance) with the aristocracy, and to lend his services as an advocate to every influential man under impeachment without distinction of person or party. (He numbered even Catiline among his clients.) He belonged properly to no party or—what was much the same—to the party of material interests, which was dominant in the courts and was pleased with the eloquent pleader and the courtly and witty companion. He had connections enough in the capital and the country towns to have a chance alongside of the candidates proposed by the democracy; and as the nobility (although with reluctance) and the Pompeians voted for him, he was elected by a great majority.

The two democratic candidates received almost the same number of votes; but a few more fell to Antonius, whose family was more prominent than that of his fellow-candidate. This accident frustrated the election of Catiline and saved Rome from a second Cinna. A little before this Piso had (it was said at the instigation of Pompey) been put to death in Spain by his native escort. With Antonius alone as consul nothing could be done. Cicero weaned him away from the conspiracy even before they entered on their offices, by renouncing his legal privilege of having the consular provinces determined by lot, and handing over to his debt-ridden colleague the lucrative governorship of Macedonia. The essential preliminary moves of the conspiracy were thus again thwarted.

Meanwhile, developments in Asia grew daily more perilous for the democrats. The reorganization of Syria proceeded rapidly, and already invitations had come to Pompey from Egypt to occupy that country for Rome. The democratic leaders could not but fear that they would hear next of Pompey in person on the banks of the Nile. This very apprehension probably explains the attempt of Caesar to get himself sent by the people to Egypt for the purpose of aiding the king against his rebellious subjects. It failed apparently through the disinclination of great and small to undertake anything whatever against the interest of Pompey. His return home, and the probable catastrophe which it involved for the democrats, were always drawing nearer. But as often as the string of the bow had been broken, there still must be a fresh attempt to bend it. The city was in sullen ferment, and frequent conferences among the top conspirators indicated that some new step was contemplated.

Their intent became manifest when the new tribunes took office on December 10, 64 B.C. One of them, Publius Servilius Rullus, immediately proposed an agrarian law designed to give the democratic leaders a position similar to that of Pompey under the Gabinio-Manilian laws. The nominal object was the founding of colonies in Italy. The land for these, however, was not to be gained by dispossession. On the contrary, all existing private rights were guaranteed, and even the illegal occupations of the most recent times were converted into full ownership. Only the leased Campanian domain was to be parceled out and colonized, with the government acquiring the rest of the land by ordinary purchase.[3]

To execute this measure, decemvirs with special powers were to be nominated for a five-year term of office, to be assisted by 200 subalterns from the equestrian order. However, the decemvirs were to be chosen only from those candidates who presented themselves personally, and (as in the elections of priests), only seventeen of the thirty-five tribes, chosen by lot, were to take part in the election. It needed no great acuteness to see that the object was to create a power like that of Pompey, only with a somewhat less military and more democratic hue. The jurisdiction was needed to convert Egypt into a military base against Pompey. The clause forbidding the choice of

---

3. The money for the land purchases was to come from a variety of sources listed in the original, the most important being the sale of overseas public land, war booty, special taxes on subject communities, and the revenues from newly annexed provinces.

an absent person excluded Pompey, and the reduction of the number of tribes entitled to vote was designed to make the election easier to control.

But this attempt completely missed fire. The multitude, preferring to have their grain handed out to them under the shade of Roman porticoes rather than to cultivate it for themselves in the sweat of their brow, received the proposal itself with complete indifference. They also soon came to feel that Pompey would never acquiesce in a move so offensive to him, and that a party whose alarm impelled it to such wild schemes must be in trouble. Under the circumstances it was not difficult for the government to frustrate the proposal. The new consul Cicero saw another opportunity of exhibiting his talent for giving a final kick to the beaten party, and even before the waiting tribunes could exercise their veto the author withdrew his proposal. The democracy had gained nothing but the unpleasant lesson that the great multitude still adhered to Pompey, out of love or fear, and that every proposal which seemed to be directed against him was certain to fail.

Wearied by all this vain agitation and scheming, Catiline determined to push the matter to a decision, and during the summer took steps to open the civil war. Faesulae, a very strong Etrurian town which swarmed with the impoverished and the desperate, and which fifteen years earlier had been the center of the Lepidan revolt, was selected as the insurrectionary headquarters. Thither were despatched the consignments of money, much of which was furnished by ladies of quality in the capital who were implicated in the conspiracy. There arms and soldiers were collected under the temporary command of the old Sullan captain Gaius Manlius, as brave and conscience-free a man as ever any soldier of fortune. Similar though less extensive preparations were made at other points in Italy. The Transpadanes were so excited that they seemed only waiting for the signal to strike. In the Bruttian country, on the east coast of Italy, in Capua, and wherever else great bodies of slaves were accumulated, a second slave insurrection like that of Spartacus seemed imminent.

Even in the capital something was brewing, it seemed to those who saw the haughty bearing of the debtors summoned to appear before the urban praetor. The capitalists were unspeakably anxious, and it was necessary to prohibit the export of gold and silver and to set a watch over the principal ports. The plan of the conspirators was simply this: during the consular election for 62 B.C., for which Catiline had again announced himself, the consul conducting the election as well as the inconvenient rival candidates were to be murdered, in order to carry the election for Catiline at any price. In case of necessity, armed bands from Faesulae and the other rallying points were to be brought in against the capital.

Cicero, always quickly and completely informed by his male and female agents of the transactions of the conspirators, on the day fixed for the election denounced the conspiracy in the full Senate and in presence of its principal leaders. Catiline did not condescend to deny it. He answered haughtily that if the election for consul should fall on him, the great headless party would certainly no longer want a leader against the small party led by wretched heads. But as unmistakable evidence of the plot was not before them, the timid Senate did nothing more than postpone the election, and approve the exceptional measures which the magistrates might deem suitable. Thus the election battle approached, in this case a real battle, for Cicero had formed an armed bodyguard of younger men, mainly from the mercantile order. This armed force covered and dominated the Campus Martius, and the conspirators were not successful either in killing the consul conducting the election or in carrying the election for their candidate.[4]

■

4. Recent study has shown Mommsen's detailed chronology of the Catilinarian conspiracy to be at fault, and his erroneous dates have been omitted in the preceding paragraph.

Meanwhile, preparations for civil war continued. On October 27th Gaius Manlius planted at Faesulae one of the Marian eagles from the Cimbrian war, round which the army of the insurrection was to flock, and summoned the robbers from the mountains as well as the country people to join him. His proclamations, following the old traditions of the popular party, demanded liberation from burdensome debt and a modification of the insolvency procedure, which still involved forfeiting the debtor's freedom if the debt exceeded his estate. It seemed as though the rabble of the capital, posing as the legitimate successor of the old plebcian farmers and fighting its battles under the glorious eagles of the Cimbrian war, wished to dishonor not only the present but also the past of Rome.

The rising, however, remained isolated. At the other centers the conspiracy did not go beyond collecting arms and holding secret conferences, since resolute leaders were everywhere lacking. This was fortunate for the government, for its own irresolution and the clumsiness of its rusty machinery had prevented it from making any military preparations whatever against the long-threatened civil war. Only now was the general levy called out, and superior officers ordered to the several regions of Italy that each might suppress the insurrection in his own district. At the same time the gladiatorial slaves were ejected from the capital, and street patrols were ordered because of the fear of incendiarism.

Catiline was in a painful position. His plan called for a simultaneous rising in the capital and in Etruria at the time of the consular elections. The failure of the former and the outbreak of the latter endangered his person as well as his whole undertaking. Now that his partisans at Faesulae had risen in arms against the government, he could no longer remain in the capital; yet everything depended on his inducing the conspirators of the capital to strike even before he left Rome—for he knew his helpmates too well to rely on them in such a matter. The more considerable of the conspirators—the former consul Publius Lentulus Sura and the two former praetors Publius Autronius and Lucius Cassius—were incapable men: Lentulus was an ordinary aristocrat of big words and great pretensions, but slow in conception and irresolute in action; Autronius was distinguished for nothing but his powerful screaming voice; while as for Lucius Cassius, no one could comprehend how such a fat, stupid man had fallen among the conspirators.

But Catiline did not dare place his abler partisans, such as the young senator Gaius Cethegus and the equites Lucius Statilius and Publius Gabinius Capito, at the head of the movement. Even among the conspirators the traditional hierarchy of rank was observed, the anarchists themselves believing that they could not carry the day unless a consular or at least a praetorian were at their head. Therefore, however urgently the army of the insurrection might need its general, and however perilous it was for the latter to tarry in the capital after the outbreak of the revolt, Catiline nevertheless resolved to remain for a time in Rome. Accustomed to impose on his cowardly opponents by audacious insolence, he showed himself publicly in the Forum and in the senate house, replying to threats that they should beware of pushing him too far, and that if they should set the house on fire he would be compelled to extinguish the conflagration in ruins. In reality neither private persons nor officials ventured to lay hands on the dangerous man. It was almost a matter of indifference when a young nobleman brought him to trial on a charge of violence, for the larger question would have been decided long before the case could be tried.

However, the projects of Catiline failed, chiefly because the government's agents had made their way into the circle of the conspirators and accurately reported every detail of the plot. For instance, when the conspirators appeared before Praeneste, which they had hoped to surprise by a *coup de main,* they found the inhabitants warned and armed. With everything miscarrying in like fashion, even Catiline found it advisable to fix his departure a few days hence. But at a last conference of the conspirators, held at Catiline's urgent behest on the night of November 6-7, it was resolved to assassinate the consul Cicero as the principal leader of the governmental opposition. In order to obviate any treachery, it was resolved to execute the plan at once. Accordingly, early on the morning of November 7th the selected murderers knocked at the house of the consul, but were repulsed by the reinforced guard. On this occasion too the government's spies had foiled the conspirators.

The next day Cicero convoked the Senate. Even now Catiline ventured to appear and defend himself against the indignant attacks of the consul, who unveiled before his face the events of the last few days; but men no longer listened to him, and he sat amid empty benches. He left the sitting and proceeded, as doubtless he had planned to do anyway, to Etruria. Here he proclaimed himself consul and assumed a waiting attitude, in order to advance against the capital as soon as the insurrection broke out there. The government outlawed Catiline and Manlius, as well as their comrades who did not lay down their arms by a certain day. New levies were called out, with the army to oppose Catiline being placed under the consul Gaius Antonius, who was notoriously implicated in the conspiracy, and whose character made it wholly fortuitous whether he would lead his troops against Catiline or over to him. The government's plans seemed directly calculated to convert this Antonius into a second Lepidus.

No stronger steps were taken against the leaders of the conspiracy who had remained in Rome, although everyone pointed the finger at them, and the insurrection in the capital was far from being abandoned by the conspirators. On the contrary, it had been set by Catiline himself before his departure. A tribune was to give the signal by calling an assembly of the people. The following night Cethegus was to dispatch the consul Cicero; Gabinius and Statilius were to set the city on fire simultaneously at twelve places; and communication was to be established as soon as possible with the army of Catiline, which meantime would be advancing. Had Lentulus, who headed the conspirators after Catiline's departure, listened to the urgent pleas of Cethegus and struck rapidly, the conspiracy might even then have been successful. But the conspirators were just as incapable and as cowardly as their opponents, and weeks elapsed without a decision.

At length the countermine brought about a decision. Lentulus in his tedious fashion, which sought to cover his negligence in immediate and necessary matters by projecting large and distant plans, had entered into negotiations with the deputies of a Celtic canton, the Allobroges, who were then in Rome. He had attempted to implicate these representatives of a thoroughly disorganized and bankrupt commonwealth in the conspiracy, and had given them messages and letters to his confidants. The Allobroges left Rome, but were arrested close to the gates on the night of December 2-3 by the Roman authorities, and their papers were taken from them. The Allobrogian deputies had obviously lent themselves as spies to the Roman government, and had carried on the negotiations only with a view to securing the desired proofs implicating the ringleaders of the conspiracy.

The next morning Cicero with the utmost secrecy ordered the arrest of the most dangerous leaders of the plot. Lentulus, Cethegus, Gabinius, and Statilius were taken, though some others escaped seizure by flight. The guilt of both the arrested and the fugitives was completely evident. Immediately after the arrest the intercepted letters, whose seals and handwriting the prisoners could not deny, were laid before the Senate, and the captives and witnesses were heard. Further confirmatory facts, deposits of arms in the houses of the conspirators, and threatening expressions which they had employed were presently forthcoming. The existence of the conspiracy was fully established, and at Cicero's suggestion the most important documents were immediately published as news-sheets.

The indignation against the anarchist conspiracy was general. The oligarchy would gladly have used the revelations to settle accounts with the popular party in general and Caesar in particular, but it was too thoroughly broken to prepare for him the fate it had once prepared for the two Gracchi and Saturninus. The multitude of the capital was especially shocked by the incendiary schemes of the conspirators. The merchants and business interests naturally saw this war of debtors against creditors as a struggle for their very existence, and in tumultuous excitement their youth crowded round the senate house brandishing their swords against the open and secret partisans of Catiline. Though its ultimate authors were still at liberty, the conspiracy was paralyzed by the capture or flight of the whole staff entrusted with its execution; and the band assembled at Faesulae could accomplish little unless supported by an insurrection in the capital.

In a tolerably well-ordered commonwealth the matter would now have been at an end, and the military and the courts would have done the rest. But in Rome matters had reached a point where the government could not even keep a couple of prominent noblemen in safe custody. The slaves and freedmen of Lentulus and the other captives were stirring, and it was alleged that plans were afoot to liberate them by force from the private houses in which they were detained. Thanks to the anarchist doings of recent years, there was no lack of ringleaders in Rome who contracted at fixed rates for riots and deeds of violence; Catiline knew what had occurred, and was near enough to attempt a *coup de main* with his bands. How much of these rumors was true we cannot tell, but there was ground for apprehension when the government had neither troops nor even a respectable police force at its command, and was therefore left at the mercy of any gang of bandits.

Under these circumstances, it was suggested that any attempts at liberation might be precluded by immediate execution of the prisoners. Constitutionally, this was not possible. According to the ancient and sacred right of appeal, a sentence of death could be pronounced against a Roman citizen only by the whole citizenry; and since the courts established by the citizenry had themselves become antiquated, a capital sentence was no longer pronounced at all.

Cicero would gladly have rejected the hazardous suggestion. Unimportant as the legal question itself might be to the advocate, he knew well how useful it is for an advocate to be called liberal, and he had no desire to alienate the democratic party forever by shedding this blood. But those around him, especially his genteel wife, urged him to crown his services to his country by this bold step. The consul, anxiously endeavoring like all cowards to avoid the appearance of cowardice while trembling before the formidable responsibility, in his distress convoked the Senate and left it to decide on life or death for the four prisoners.

This of course had no meaning, for the Senate was constitutionally even less entitled to act than the consul: but when was cowardice ever consistent? Caesar made every effort to save the prisoners, and his speech, full of covert threats of future vengeance, made the deepest impression. Although all the consulars and the great majority of the Senate had already declared for the execution, most of them, led by Cicero, seemed again inclined to stay within the limits of the law. But when Cato in pettifogging fashion cast suspicion on the waverers as being accomplices of the plot, and pointed to the preparations for liberating the prisoners by a street riot, he succeeded in raising a fresh alarm which produced a majority for immediate execution.

Implementing the decree naturally devolved on the consul who had called it forth. Late on the evening of December 5 the prisoners were brought from their previous quarters, and conducted across the still-crowded market place to the prison in which condemned criminals were kept. It was a subterranean vault twelve feet deep at the foot of the Capitol, which had formerly served as a well-house. Lentulus was conducted by the consul himself, the others by praetors, all attended by strong guards; but the anticipated attempt at rescue did not take place. No one knew whether the prisoners were being conveyed to a secure place of custody or to the scene of execution. At the door of the prison they were handed over to the executioners, and were strangled in the subterranean vault by torchlight.

The consul had waited before the door till the executions were accomplished. Then his well-known voice proclaimed to the multitude waiting in silence in the Forum, "They are dead." Far into the night the crowds moved through the streets and exultantly hailed the consul, to whom they believed that they owed the security of their houses and their property. The Senate ordered public festivals of gratitude, and the first men of the nobility, Marcus Cato and Quintus Catulus, saluted the author of the sentence of death with the title (now heard for the first time) of "father of his fatherland."

But it was a dreadful deed, and all the more dreadful because it appeared great and praiseworthy to a whole people. Never perhaps has a commonwealth more lamentably declared itself bankrupt than did Rome through this resolution, adopted in cold blood by the majority of the government and approved by public opinion. A few political prisoners, who were no doubt guilty under law, but who had not forfeited life, were put to death in all haste because the prisons were insecure and there were insufficient police. With the humor seldom lacking in a historical tragedy, this act of the most brutal tyranny was carried out by the most unstable and timid of all Roman statesmen, and the "first democratic consul" was selected to destroy the palladium of the ancient freedom of the Roman commonwealth.

After the conspiracy in the capital had thus been nipped in the bud, there remained the task of putting down the insurrection in Etruria. The army of about 2,000 men which Catiline found on his arrival had increased nearly five-fold by the numerous recruits who already formed two tolerably full legions, though only about a fourth of these were sufficiently armed. Catiline had withdrawn his force into the mountains and avoided battle with the troops of Antonius, in order to complete the organization of his bands while awaiting the outbreak of the insurrection in Rome.

The news of its failure broke up the insurgent army, and most of the less-compromised returned home. The desperate remnant attempted to cut its way through the Apennine passes into Gaul; but when the little band arrived at the foot of the mountains near Pistoria it found itself caught between two armies. In front of it was the corps of Quintus Metellus, which had come up from Ravenna and Ariminum to occupy the northern slope of the Apennines; behind it was the army of Antonius, who had at length yielded to the urgings of his officers and agreed to a winter campaign. Wedged in on both sides, with his supplies running out, Catiline had no course left but to throw himself on his nearest foe, Antonius.

In a narrow valley enclosed by rocky mountains the conflict took place between the insurgents and the troops of Antonius. The latter, in order to avoid being the personal executioner of his former allies, had under a pretext entrusted the command for this day to a brave officer who had grown gray under arms, Marcus Petreius. The supe-

rior strength of the government army was of little account, owing to the nature of the battlefield. Both Catiline and Petreius placed their most trusted men in the
foremost ranks, and quarter was neither asked nor given.
The conflict lasted long, and many brave men fell on both
sides. Catiline, who before the battle began had sent back
his horse and those of all his officers, showed on this day
that nature had destined him for no ordinary things, and
that he knew both how to command as a general and how
to fight as a soldier.

At length Petreius with his guard broke the center of
the enemy and attacked the two wings from within. This
decided the victory. The corpses of the Catilinarians
(3,000 were counted) covered the ground where they had
fought. The officers and the general himself had near the
end thrown themselves on the enemy, and thus found the
death they sought. Antonius was rewarded by the Senate
with the title of Imperator, and new thanksgiving festivals showed that the government and the governed were
beginning to become accustomed to civil war.

The anarchist plot had thus been suppressed in the capital as in Italy with bloody violence. The only further re-
minders of it were the criminal processes which thinned
the ranks of the beaten party, and the large accessions to
the robber bands of Italy. One of these, for instance,
made up of the remains of the armies of Spartacus and
Catiline, was destroyed two years later in 60 B.C. by a
military force in the territory of Thurii.

But it is important to keep in mind that the blow fell
not merely on the anarchists who had conspired to fire
the capital and had fought at Pistoria, but on the whole
democratic party. That this party, and in particular Crassus and Caesar, had a hand in this conspiracy as well as in
the plot of 66 B.C. may be regarded as historically if not
judicially established. To be sure, the mere fact that Catulus and other Optimates accused the democratic leaders of
complicity, and that Caesar, as senator, spoke and voted

against the brutal judicial murder contemplated by the oligarchy, could only be regarded as proof by a partisan sophist. But other facts are more weighty. According to precise and irrefutable testimony, Crassus and Caesar were major supporters of Catiline's candidacy for the consulship. And when Caesar brought the executioners of Sulla before the commission for murder in 64 B.C. he allowed the most guilty and infamous of all, Catiline, to be acquitted.

It is true that Cicero, in his revelations of December 3rd, did not name Caesar and Crassus among the conspirators. But it is notorious that the informers denounced not merely those against whom the subsequent investigation was directed, but also many "innocent" persons whom Cicero thought it politic to erase from the list. In later years, when he had no reason to disguise the truth, he expressly named Caesar among the accomplices.[5] A further indirect but significant indication lies in the fact that of the four persons arrested on December 3rd, the two least dangerous, Statilius and Gabinius, were handed over to be guarded by Caesar and Crassus. It was obviously intended that the latter should either, if they permitted an escape, be compromised before the public as accessories, or, if they did not, be compromised in the eyes of their fellow-conspirators as renegades.

The following scene in the Senate shows how matters stood. Immediately after the arrest of Lentulus and his comrades, a messenger dispatched by the conspirators to Catiline was seized by agents of the government, and, after having been assured that he would not be prosecuted, was induced to make a comprehensive confession before a full meeting of the Senate. But when he came to the critical points and in particular named Crassus as hav-

---

5. Ed. note: this is most doubtful. While there is some credible contemporary evidence that Cicero so accused Crassus, the only support for a Ciceronian accusation of Caesar is a statement of very low credibility made by Plutarch 150 years later.

ing commissioned him, he was interrupted by the senators; and on the suggestion of Cicero it was resolved not only to cancel the whole statement without further inquiry, but also to imprison its author, notwithstanding the amnesty assured to him, until he should have both retracted the statement and confessed who had instigated him to give such false testimony!

Here it is abundantly clear that the man who called Crassus the bull of the herd had a very accurate knowledge of the state of affairs, and also that the majority of the Senate with Cicero at their head were tacitly agreed that revelations should not be permitted to go beyond a certain limit. The public was not so nice, and the young men who had taken up arms to ward off the incendiaries were exasperated against Caesar more than anyone else. When he left the Senate on December 5th they pointed their swords at his breast, and he narrowly escaped with his life on the same spot where the fatal blow fell on him seventeen years afterwards; he did not enter the senate house again for a considerable time.

Any one who studies the conspiracy impartially will not be able to resist the suspicion that Catiline was backed by more powerful men, who relied on the lack of a legally complete chain of evidence and on the lukewarmness and cowardice of the half-informed Senate, which greedily clutched at any pretext for inaction. These men knew how to hinder the authorities from serious interference with the conspiracy, how to procure free departure for the insurgent chief, and even how to manage the declaration of war and the sending of troops against the insurrection so that it was almost equivalent to a reinforcing army. While the course of the events thus testifies that the ramifications of the plot reached far higher than Lentulus and Catiline, it is also worth noticing that when Caesar had got to the head of the state much later, he was very close to the only surviving Catilinarian, Publius Sittius the leader of the Mauretanian free bands, and that he modified the debt laws quite as the proclamations of Manlius had demanded.

All these pieces of evidence speak clearly enough. But even if they did not, the desperate position of the democrats in the face of the military power—which since the Gabinio-Manilian laws had assumed an ever more threatening visage—renders it almost certain that they (as is usual in such cases) found their last resort in secret plots and in alliance with anarchy. The circumstances were very similar to those of the Cinnan times. While Pompey occupied in the East a position nearly the same as Sulla once did, Crassus and Caesar sought to raise against him in Italy a power like that which Marius and Cinna had possessed, with the view toward employing it better than the latter had done.

The road to this result lay once more through terrorism and anarchy, and Catiline was certainly the right man to blaze that trail. Naturally the more reputable democratic leaders kept as far in the background as possible, and left to their unclean associates the dirty work whose political results they hoped later to appropriate. Still more naturally, when the plot had failed, the higher-ups made every effort to conceal their part in it. And when the former conspirator, Caesar, later became the target of political plots, the veil was for that very reason drawn only the more closely over those darker years in the life of the great man, and special apologies were written for him with that very object.

For five years Pompey had stood at the head of his armies and fleets in the East, for five years the democratic party at home had conspired to overthrow him. The result was discouraging. With unspeakable exertions it had not only accomplished nothing, but had suffered enormous moral as well as material loss. Even the coalition of 71 B.C. was scandalous to pure democrats, although their party at that time had only allied itself with two distinguished men of the opposition and bound them to its program. But now the democratic party had made common cause with a band of murderers and bankrupts, almost all of whom were likewise deserters from the camp of the aristocracy, and had at least temporarily accepted their program. The capitalist party, one of the chief elements of the coalition of 71 B.C., was thus estranged and driven into the arms of the Optimates or anyone else who could protect it against anarchy.

Even the multitude of the capital, who had no objection to a street-riot but still found it inconvenient to have their houses set on fire over their heads, became somewhat alarmed. It is remarkable that in this very year (63 B.C.) the full re-establishment of the Sempronian grain laws took place, proposed in the Senate by Cato. The league of the democratic leaders with anarchy had obviously created a breach between the former and the citizens of the city; and the oligarchy sought, not without some temporary success, to enlarge this chasm and draw over the masses to their side. Lastly, Pompey had been partly warned and partly exasperated by all these cabals. After all that had occurred, and after the democrats had virtually torn asunder the ties which connected them with Pompey, they could hardly with propriety make the request—which in 70 B.C. had had a certain amount of reason to it—that he should not destroy with the sword the democratic power which he had raised, and which had raised him.

Thus the democratic party was disgraced and weakened, but above all it was exposed to ridicule through the merciless illumination of its perplexity and debility. Where the humiliation of the overthrown government and similar unimportant matters were concerned, it was great and potent; but every one of its attempts at a real political success had failed. Its relation to Pompey was as false as it was pitiful. While loading him with praise and demonstrations of homage, it was concocting against him one intrigue after another, and one after another, like so many soap bubbles, they burst of themselves. The general of the East and of the seas, far from spending himself against them, appeared not even to notice them, and to win his victories in the political arena as Hercules triumphed over the Pygmies, without being aware of it.

The attempt to kindle civil war had failed miserably. Although the anarchist section had at least displayed some energy, the democrats, while knowing how to hire conspirators, had not known how to lead them or to save them or to die with them. Even the old languid oligarchy, strengthened partly by the masses passing over to it from the popular party, and still more by the unmistakable community of interests between itself and Pompey, had been enabled to suppress the attempted revolution and thereby achieve a last victory over the democrats. Meanwhile king Mithradates was dead, Asia Minor and Syria were regulated, and Pompey's return to Italy might be expected at any moment. The decision was not far off— but it is scarcely possible any longer to speak of a decision between the general who returned stronger and more famous than ever, and the popular party humbled beyond parallel and utterly powerless. Crassus prepared to embark his family and his gold and seek an asylum somewhere in the East, and even so elastic and energetic a nature as Caesar seemed on the point of giving up the game as lost. In the year 63 B.C. he was a candidate for the office of pontifex maximus. When he left his home on the morning of the election, he declared that if he should lose, he would never again cross the threshold of his house.

When Pompey again turned his eyes homeward, for the second time he found the diadem at his feet. The Roman commonwealth had long been tending towards such a catastrophe. It was obvious to every unbiased observer, and had been remarked a thousand times, that monarchy was inevitable if the rule of the aristocracy should come to an end. The Senate had now been overthrown by the civil democratic opposition and the military power. The only remaining questions were the persons, names, and forms for the new order, and these were already clearly enough indicated in the partly democratic and partly military elements of the revolution.

The events of the preceding five years had set the final seal on this impending transformation of the commonwealth. In the newly erected Asiatic provinces, which gave regal honors to their organizer as the successor of Alexander the Great, and received his favorite freedmen like princes, Pompey had laid the foundations of his rule, and found the treasures, the army, and the halo of glory which the future prince of the Roman state required. Moreover, the anarchist conspiracy in the capital and the civil war connected with it had made it glaringly clear to every one who studied political or even purely economic affairs that a government without authority or military power, such as that of the Senate, exposed the state to the equally ludicrous and formidable tyranny of political sharpers, and that a constitutional change to connect the military power more closely with the government was indispensable if social order was to be maintained. So the ruler had arisen in the East as the throne had been erected in Italy. To all appearances the year 62 B.C. was destined to be the last of the republic and the first of the monarchy.

True, this goal was not to be reached without a struggle. The 500-year-old constitution under which the insignificant town on the Tiber had risen to unprecedented greatness and glory had sunk its roots into the soil to a depth beyond human ken, and no one could calculate what convulsions might attend the attempt to overthrow it. Several rivals had been outrun by Pompey in the race towards the great goal, but they were not entirely out of the running. It was not inconceivable that all these elements might combine to overthrow the new holder of power, and that Pompey might find Quintus Catulus and Marcus Cato united in opposition to him with Marcus Crassus, Gaius Caesar, and Titus Labienus.

But the inevitable struggle could not have been undertaken under circumstances more favorable for Pompey. It was highly probable that, with the memory of the Catilinarian revolt still fresh, any rule which promised order and security at the cost of freedom would win over the whole middle party—including not only the merchants who concerned themselves only with their material interests, but also a great part of the disorganized and politically hopeless aristocracy, which had to content itself with hoping for riches, rank, and influence through a timely compromise with the prince. Perhaps even a portion of the democrats, so sorely smitten by recent blows, might submit in the hope of realizing part of their demands from the military chief they had raised to power.

In any case, of what importance were the parties in Italy in the presence of Pompey and his victorious army? Twenty years earlier Sulla, after concluding an armistice with Mithradates, had with five legions been able to effect a restoration against the course of history and in the face of the whole liberal party, from moderate aristocrats through liberal merchants down to anarchists, which had been arming for years. Pompey's task was far less difficult. He returned after having fully carried out his various missions by land and sea. He might expect no serious opposition save that of the extreme parties, each of which by itself could do nothing, and which even if leagued together were no more than a coalition of fundamentally hostile factions. Completely unarmed, they were leaderless, without organization in Italy, without support in the provinces, and, above all, without a military force or a general. Their ranks included hardly a soldier of note (to say nothing of an officer) who could have ventured to call out the citizens to oppose Pompey.

It was also noteworthy that the volcano of revolution, which had now been blazing for seventy years and feeding on its own flame, was visibly burning itself out. It was very doubtful whether an attempt to arm the Italians for a political struggle would succeed as it had in the days of Cinna and Carbo. If Pompey exerted himself, how could he fail to effect the revolution which seemed the inevitable next step in the development of the Roman commonwealth?

Pompey, who had seized the right moment when he undertook his mission to the East, seemed willing to go forward. In the autumn of 63 B.C. Quintus Metellus Nepos arrived from Pompey's camp and came forward as a candidate for the tribuneship. His express purpose was to use that position to procure for Pompey (by special decree of the people) the immediate command of the war against Catiline, and subsequently the consulship for 61 B.C. The excitement in Rome was great, for it was assumed that Nepos was acting under Pompey's direct or indirect orders. The desire of Pompey to appear in Italy at the head of his Asiatic legions, and to administer simultaneously the supreme military and civil power, was regarded as a further step on the way to the throne, and the mission of Nepos a semiofficial proclamation of the monarchy.

Everything turned on the attitude of the two great political parties towards these overtures, on which their future position and the future of the nation depended. However, the reception which Nepos met was in its turn determined by the existing relations of the parties to Pompey, which were of a very peculiar kind. Pompey had gone to the East as general of the popular party. He had reason enough to be displeased with Caesar and his ad-

herents, but no open rupture had taken place. It is probable that Pompey, who was far away and preoccupied
with other things, and who was also quite destitute of
political insight, by no means understood at that time the
extent and mutual connection of the democratic intrigues
aimed at him. Perhaps he even took a haughty and short-
sighted pride in ignoring these underground cabals.

There was moreover the fact, which had much weight
with a character of the type of Pompey, that the democrats never lost sight of outward respect for the great
man. In 63 B.C. they had granted him, by special decree
of the people, unprecedented honors and decorations
which were quite unsolicited (as he preferred it). But
even if all this had not been the case, Pompey's own well-
understood interest was to continue at least outwardly his
adherence to the popular party. Democracy and monarchy are so closely related that Pompey, in aspiring to
the crown, could scarely do other than continue to call
himself the popular champion.

While personal and political reasons thus combined to
keep Pompey close to the democratic leaders, despite all
that had taken place, nothing was done to bridge the gulf
which had separated him from his Sullan partisans since
he deserted to the democratic camp. His personal quarrel
with Metellus and Lucullus transferred itself to their extensive and influential followings. The paltry opposition
of the Senate—all the more exasperating to a character
of so paltry a mold—had dogged his whole career as a
general. He felt keenly that the Senate had not taken the
smallest step to honor the extraordinary man according
to his deserts, that is, by extraordinary means. Lastly, it
should not be forgotten that the aristocracy was then in-
toxicated by its recent victory and the democrats deeply
humbled, and that the aristocracy was led by the pedanti-
cally stiff and half-witless Cato against that supple democratic master of intrigue, Caesar.

Such were the parties amid which the emissary of Pompey appeared. The aristocracy not only regarded the proposals announced on behalf of Pompey as a declaration of war against the constitution, but treated them openly as such, and took not the slightest pains to conceal their alarm and indignation. With the express design of combating these proposals, Cato had himself elected as tribune of the people along with Nepos, and abruptly repelled the repeated attempts of Pompey to approach him personally. Thus Nepos naturally felt no obligation to spare the aristocracy, but attached himself the more readily to the democrats. These, pliant as ever, submitted to the inevitable and chose freely to concede the command in Italy as well as the consulship rather than let the concession be wrung from them by force.

A cordial understanding soon blossomed. In December of 63 B.C. Nepos publicly accepted the democratic view of the executions recently decreed by the Senate as unconstitutional judicial murders. That his lord and master saw them in the same light is implied by his significant silence regarding the voluminous vindication which Cicero had sent to him. On the other hand, Caesar's first act as praetor was to call Quintus Catulus to account for alleged embezzlement in the rebuilding of the Capitoline temple, and to transfer the completion of the temple to Pompey.

This was a masterstroke. Catulus had already been building at the temple for fifteen years, and seemed quite disposed to continue until he died. An attack on this abuse of a public commission—an abuse covered only by the reputation of the noble commissioner—was entirely justified and highly popular. But to show Pompey the prospect of replacing the name of Catulus with his own, on this proudest spot of the first city of the globe, was to offer him the thing which delighted him most and did no harm to the democrats—abundant but empty honor. At the same time the aristocracy, which could not possibly allow its best man to fall, was brought into the most disagreeable collision with Pompey.

Meanwhile Nepos had brought his proposals concerning Pompey before the citizenry. On the day of the voting Cato and his friend and colleague, Quintus Minucius, interposed their veto. When Nepos disregarded this and continued the reading, Cato and Minucius threw themselves on their colleague and forced him to stop. An armed band liberated him and drove the aristocratic section from the Forum, but Cato and Minucius returned with armed bands of their own and ultimately maintained the field of battle for the government.

Encouraged by this victory of their bands over those of their antagonist, the Senate suspended the tribune Nepos as well as the praetor Caesar, who had vigorously supported him in proposing the law. Their deposition from office by the Senate was prevented by Cato, undoubtedly more because it was unconstitutional than because it was injudicious. Caesar disregarded the decree, and continued his official functions till the Senate used violence against him. At this news the multitude appeared before his house and placed itself at his disposal. He alone was to decide whether the struggle in the streets should begin, or whether at least the proposals of Nepos should be taken up and the military command in Italy procured for Pompey. As this was not in Caesar's interest he induced the crowds to disperse, whereupon the Senate rescinded his suspension. Nepos himself had set out for Asia immediately after his suspension to report the results of his mission to Pompey.

Pompey had every reason to be content with the way things were going. The road to the throne now involved civil war, and he owed it to Cato's incorrigible perversity that he could begin this war with good reason. After the illegal condemnation of the adherents of Catiline, after the unparalleled acts of violence against the tribune Nepos, Pompey might wage war both as champion of the party of order against the Catilinarians, and as defender of the two palladia of Roman public freedom—the right of appeal and the inviolability of the tribunate of the people.

It seemed almost impossible that Pompey should neglect this second opportunity, and with open eyes put himself again into the painful position which resulted from the dismissal of his army in 70 B.C., and from which only the Gabinian law had released him. But the closer came the crown, as much as his whole soul longed after it, when action had to be taken his heart and his hand once more failed him. This man, ordinary in every respect except his pretensions, would doubtless gladly have placed himself beyond the law if he could only have done so legally. His very lingering in Asia betrayed his misgivings. He could easily have arrived in January of 62 B.C. with his fleet and army at the port of Brundisium, and received Nepos there. His tarrying the whole winter in Asia had the immediate injurious result that the aristocracy, which of course pressed the campaign against Catiline as best it could, had meanwhile got rid of his bands, and thus removed the most feasible pretext for bringing the Asiatic legions into Italy.

For a man like Pompey, who for lack of faith in himself and in his star timidly clung in public life to formal right, and for whom the pretext was nearly as important as the motive, this circumstance was of serious weight. He probably said to himself that his army was not wholly lost even if he dismissed it, and that if necessary he could still raise a force sooner than any other party chief. He noted that the democrats were waiting submissively for his instructions, and that he could deal with the refractory Senate even without soldiers. Other such considerations doubtless suggested themselves, in which there was just enough truth to make them seem plausible to one who wished to deceive himself.

Once more the peculiar temperament of Pompey turned the scale. He was one of those men who might be capable of a crime, but not of insubordination; in both a good and

a bad sense, he was every inch a soldier. Outstanding men
respect the law as a moral necessity, ordinary men as a
traditional everyday rule. For this very reason military
discipline, where law most often dons the guise of habit,
fetters all but the most self-reliant men with a magic spell.
It has often been observed that the soldier, even where
determined to refuse obedience, involuntarily resumes his
place in the ranks when obedience is demanded. It was this
feeling that made Lafayette and Dumouriez hesitate at
the last moment before the breach of faith and break
down. To this Pompey also succumbed.

In the autumn of 62 B.C. Pompey embarked for Italy.
While everyone in the capital was preparing to receive
the new monarch, news came that he had broken up his
legions upon landing and was en route to the capital with
a small escort. Fortune never did more for mortal man
than it did for Pompey, if it is a piece of good fortune to
be presented with a crown without trouble. But on those
who lack courage the gods lavish every favor and every
gift in vain.

The parties breathed freely. For the second time Pompey had abdicated, and his already vanquished competitors might again start the race—in which the strangest
entry was Pompey himself. In January of 61 B.C. he came
to Rome. His position was awkward, and vacillated so
much between the parties that people gave him the nickname of Gnaeus Cicero. He had in fact lost favor with
all. The anarchists saw in him an adversary, the democrats an inconvenient friend, Marcus Crassus a rival, the
wealthy class an untrustworthy protector, the aristocracy
a declared foe. He was still the most powerful man in the
state, with his military adherents scattered throughout
Italy, his influence in the provinces, particularly in the
East, his military fame, and his enormous riches. But instead of the enthusiastic reception on which he had
counted, he was more than coolly met, and still cooler was
the treatment given to the demands which he presented.

He requested for himself, as already announced by Nepos, a second consulship, and he of course demanded also a confirmation of his arrangements made in the East and a fulfillment of his promise to furnish his soldiers with land. These demands raised a systematic opposition in the Senate, sparked by the personal exasperation of Lucullus and Metellus Creticus, the old resentment of Crassus, and the conscientious folly of Cato. The second consulship was immediately and bluntly refused. The very first request which the returning general addressed to the Senate, that the election of the consuls for 61 B.C. be put off till after his entry into the capital, had been rejected, and there was still less likelihood of obtaining the necessary senatorial dispensation from Sulla's law forbidding re-election. As to his arrangements in the eastern provinces, Pompey naturally asked their confirmation as a whole. Lucullus carried a proposal that every ordinance should be separately discussed and voted upon, which opened the door for endless annoyances and a multitude of defeats in detail. The promise of land for the soldiers of the Asiatic army was ratified in general by the Senate, but also extended to the Cretan legions of Metellus; and still worse, it was not executed because the treasury was empty, and the Senate was not disposed to meddle with the public domains for this purpose.

Pompey, in despair of mastering the persistent and spiteful opposition of the Senate, turned to the citizens. But he understood still less how to conduct his movements on this field. The democratic leaders, though they did not openly oppose him, had no reason to make his interests their own, and so kept aloof. Pompey's own instruments —such as Marcus Pupius Piso and Lucius Afranius, who were elected consuls respectively in 61 and 60 B.C. by his influence and partly by his money—showed themselves unskillful and useless. When at length the assignment of land for the Asiatic veterans was submitted to the citizens by the tribune Lucius Flavius as a general agrarian law,

the proposal, not supported by the democrats and openly
opposed by the aristocracy, was defeated.

The exalted general now sued almost humbly for the
favor of the masses, for it was at his instigation that the
Italian tolls were abolished in 60 B.C. under a law proposed by the praetor Metellus Nepos. But he played the
demagogue without skill or success, his reputation suffering while he did not attain his objectives. He had completely run himself into a noose. One of his opponents
summed up his political position by saying that he had
endeavored "to conserve by silence his embroidered triumphal mantle." In fact there was nothing left for him
to do but to fret.

Then a new combination offered itself. The leader of
the democratic party had actively employed the political
calm which had followed Pompey's retirement. When
Pompey returned from Asia, Caesar had been little more
than another Catiline—a personal bankrupt and chief of
a political party that had dwindled almost into a club of
conspirators. But since then he had, after administering
the praetorship (62 B.C.), been made governor of Further Spain, and thereby had been able partly to rid himself of debt, and partly to lay the foundation for his military repute. His old friend and ally Crassus had been
induced, in the hope of finding support against Pompey,
to relieve him even before he left of his most oppressive
obligations.

He had made full use of his brief sojourn in Spain. Returning in 60 B.C. as Imperator with filled chests and
well-founded claims to a triumph, he came forward as a
candidate for the consulship; and when the Senate refused him permission to announce himself as a candidate
in absentia, he abandoned without hesitation the honor of
the triumph. For years the democrats had striven to raise
one of their partisans to the supreme magistracy, through
which they might attain a military power of their own.
It had long been clear that the political struggle could

only be settled by military force. But the history of the coalition between the democrats and the military chiefs, which ended the rule of the Senate, showed with inexorable clarity that such an alliance ultimately subordinated the civil to the military elements, and that if the popular party would really rule, it must make generals of its own leaders instead of allying itself with generals alien or even hostile to it. The attempts to carry the election of Catiline as consul, and to create a military base in Spain or Egypt, had failed. Now a possibility arose of procuring for their most important leader the consulship and the consular province in the usual constitutional way, and of rendering themselves independent of their dubious and dangerous ally Pompey by the establishment of a power base, so to speak, in their own democratic household.

But the more the popular party sought to travel this path, which offered not merely the most favorable but also the only prospect of real success, the more surely it might count on resolute political resistance. Everything depended on who were its opponents in this matter. By itself, the aristocracy was not formidable; but it had just been shown in the Catilinarian affair that it could still exert influence where it was supported by the commercial interests and by the adherents of Pompey. Several times it had frustrated Catiline's candidacy for the consulship, and it would certainly attempt the same against Caesar. And even if Caesar were chosen in spite of it, his election alone did not suffice. He needed several undisturbed years outside of Italy to create a firm military base, and the nobility would leave no stone unturned to thwart his plans during this period of preparation.

Thus the idea naturally occurred whether the aristocracy might not again be isolated as in 71-70 B.C., and an alliance based on mutual advantage established between the democrats with their ally Crassus on the one side and Pompey and the great capitalists on the other. For Pompey such a coalition was certainly political suicide.

His weight in the state rested on the fact that he was the
only party leader who also commanded legions, which
even if dissolved were still in a sense at his disposal. The
democratic plan was precisely intended to deprive him of
this preponderance, and to place their own chief by his
side as a military rival. Never could he consent to this,
and least of all personally help to a post of supreme command a man like Caesar, who had already given him
enough trouble as a mere political agitator, and who had
also just furnished brilliant proofs of his military capacity in Spain.

But on the other hand, the caviling opposition of the
Senate and the indifference of the multitude to his wishes
had made Pompey's position, especially with reference to
his old soldiers, so painful and so humiliating that his well-
known character might welcome such a coalition, if it
could release him from that disagreeable situation. As for
the commercial party, it was to be found on whatever side
the power lay. As a matter of course it would not hang
back if it saw Pompey and the popular party combining
anew in earnest. It happened, moreover, that just at that
time Cato's severity—otherwise very laudable—toward
the tax farmers had put the great capitalists once more
at swords' points with the Senate.

So the second coalition was formed in the summer of
60 B.C. Caesar was assured of the consulship for the
following year and, in due course, a governorship. Pompey was promised the ratification of his Asiatic arrangements and an assignment of lands for his soldiers. Caesar
likewise promised the equites to procure for them, by
means of the citizens, what the Senate had refused. Crassus was at least allowed to join the league, although without obtaining definite promises for an agreement which
he could not refuse.

Exactly the same elements—indeed, the same persons
—concluded the league with one another in the summer
of 60 B.C. as in the autumn of 71 B.C., but how com-

pletely changed was the position of the parties! Before, the democrats were nothing but a political party, while their allies were victorious generals at the head of armies. Now, the democratic chief was himself an Imperator crowned with victory and full of magnificent military schemes, while his allies were retired generals without forces. Then the democrats won victories of principle, and in return for those victories conceded the highest state offices to their two confederates. Now they hard-headedly grasped the supreme civil and military power for themselves, making concessions to their allies only on subordinate points. (Significantly, not even Pompey's demand for a second consulship was granted.) Then the democrats sacrificed themselves to their allies; now the latter were forced to trust in them.

Most completely changed of all, however, was the character of the democratic party itself. No doubt it had always contained at its very core a monarchic element. But the constitutional ideal which floated in more or less clear outline before its best intellects was always that of a civil commonwealth, a Periclean state, in which the power of the prince rested on the fact that he represented the citizens in the noblest and most accomplished manner, and the best and noblest of the citizenry recognized him as the man whom they thoroughly trusted. Caesar too began with some such views, but simply as ideals which might influence realities rather than be directly realized. Neither the simple civil power, as Gaius Gracchus possessed it, nor the arming of the democratic party, as Cinna had inadequately attempted, was able to maintain a permanent superiority in the Roman commonwealth. The military machine fighting not for a party but for a general, the rude force of the *condottieri,* after having first appeared on the stage in the service of the restoration, soon showed its absolute superiority to all political parties.

Caesar could not but become convinced of this through his practical party experience. Accordingly, he matured the momentous resolution of making the military machine itself serve his ideals, and of erecting the commonwealth he envisaged by the power of the rootless soldiers. With this design he concluded in 71 B.C. the league with the generals of the opposite party, which, despite their acceptance of the democratic program, yet brought the party and Caesar himself to the brink of destruction. With the same design he himself came forward eleven years afterwards as a military dictator.

It was done in both cases with a certain naïveté, with faith in his ability to found a free commonwealth, if not by the swords of others, at any rate by his own. We perceive without difficulty that this faith was fallacious, and that no one calls up an evil spirit without becoming himself enslaved to it. But the greatest men are not those who err the least. If after so many centuries we still bow before what Caesar willed and did, it is not because he desired and gained a crown (which is fundamentally as unimportant as the crown itself), but rather because his mighty ideal of a free commonwealth under one ruler never forsook him, and preserved him even as monarch from sinking into vulgar royalty.

The election of Caesar as consul for 59 B.C. was carried without difficulty by the united parties. The aristocracy had to rest content with giving him a colleague by means of a slush fund to which the whole order of lords contributed, and which excited surprise even in that most corrupt period. The colleague in question was Marcus Bibulus, whose narrow-minded obstinacy was regarded as energy in conservative circles, and whose good intentions at least were not at fault if the genteel lords did not get a fit return for their patriotic expenditure.

As consul, Caesar first proposed the measures of his confederates, among which the question of land for the Asiatic veterans was by far the most important. The agrarian law projected for this purpose by Caesar generally followed the outlines of the proposal introduced the year before at the suggestion of Pompey but not carried. Only the Italian domain land was earmarked for distribution—that is, substantially the territory of Capua; and if this should not suffice, other Italian estates were to be purchased at their legal, taxable value, using the revenue of the new eastern provinces. All existing property rights thus remained unaffected.

The individual allotments were small, with the recipients of land to be poor citizens, fathers of at least three children. Thus the dangerous principle that rendering military service gave a claim to landed estate was not laid down, but, in line with reasonable past practice, the land distributors were urged to give special consideration to old soldiers as well as to temporary lessees ejected from their holdings. The execution of the measure was entrusted to a commission of twenty, from whose number Caesar specifically asked to be excluded.

It was hard for the opposition to resist this proposal. Undeniably, after the creation of the provinces of Pontus and Syria the state should be in a position to forego the rents from the Campanian leases. It was unwarranted to withhold one of the finest districts of Italy, and one peculiarly fitted for small holdings, from private enterprise. And finally, it was as unjust as it was ridiculous to withhold municipal rights from the township of Capua, after extending the franchise to all Italy. The whole proposal bore the stamp of moderation, honesty, and solidity, dexterously combined with democratic objectives. In substance, the new law amounted to the re-establishment of the Capuan colony founded in the time of Marius and done away with by Sulla.

Caesar also gave all possible consideration to legal forms. He put the new agrarian law, as well as the proposal to ratify collectively the ordinances issued by Pompey in the East, and the petition of the tax farmers for

remission of a third of the sums payable by them, before
the Senate for approval, and declared himself ready to
entertain and discuss amendments.

That body now had a chance to convince itself how
foolishly it had acted in driving Pompey and the equites
into the enemy's arms by refusing these requests. Perhaps
it was the secret realization of this that drove the highborn lords to the most vehement opposition, in sour contrast to the calm demeanor of Caesar. They rejected the
agrarian law nakedly and without discussion. The decree
as to Pompey's arrangements in Asia found quite as little
favor in their eyes. Cato attempted, in accordance with
the disreputable custom of Roman parliamentary debate,
to kill the proposal regarding the tax farmers by prolonging his speech up to the legal hour for closing the sitting.
When Caesar threatened to have the stubborn man arrested, this proposal too was at length rejected.

Of course all the proposals were now brought before
the citizens. Without deviating far from the truth, Caesar
could tell the multitude that the Senate had scornfully rejected most rational and necessary proposals submitted
respectfully to it, simply because they came from the
democratic consul. When he added that the aristocrats
were plotting to procure rejection of the proposals, and
summoned the citizens, especially Pompey himself and his
old soldiers, to stand by him against fraud and force,
this too was by no means a mere invention. The aristocracy, headed by the weak and obstinate Bibulus and the
dogmatic fool Cato, actually intended to push the matter
to open violence. Pompey, pressed by Caesar to proclaim
his position, on this one occasion declared bluntly that if
any one should venture to draw the sword he too would
grasp his, and in that case would not leave the shield at
home. Crassus expressed himself to the same effect. The
old soldiers of Pompey were directed to appear on the
day of the vote (which in fact primarily concerned them)
with arms under their dress.

The nobility left nothing undone to frustrate the proposals of Caesar. Each day when Caesar appeared before the people, his colleague Bibulus interrupted with the well-known political observations about the weather, which were supposed to suspend all public business. Caesar did not trouble himself about the skies, but continued to prosecute his terrestrial occupation. The tribunician veto was interposed, but Caesar contented himself with disregarding it. Bibulus and Cato then sprang to the rostra, harangued the multitude, and instigated the usual riot. Caesar ordered that they should be led away by lictors from the Forum, and took care that no harm should befall them, for it was to his interest that this political comedy should continue.

Notwithstanding all the chicanery and blustering by the nobility, the agrarian law, the confirmation of the Asiatic arrangements, and the remission to the tax farmers were adopted by the citizens, and the commission of twenty, with Pompey and Crassus at its head, was elected and installed in office. All their exertions had gained the aristocracy nothing, save that their blind and spiteful antagonism had strengthened the bonds of the coalition, and their energy, which they were soon to need for more important matters, was exhausted on these trivial affairs. They congratulated each other on their patriotic courage as evidenced by the declaration of Bibulus that he would rather die than yield, and the peroration which Cato still continued to deliver when in the hands of the lictors. Otherwise, they resigned themselves to their fate.

The consul Bibulus shut himself up for the rest of the year in his house, at the same time intimating that his pious intention was to watch the skies on all the days appropriate for public assemblies during that year. His colleagues once more admired the great man who, as Ennius had said of the old Fabius, "saved the state by wise delay," and followed his example. Most of them, Cato included, no longer appeared in the Senate, but within their

four walls helped their consul to fret over the fact that
the history of the world went on in spite of political as-
trology. To the public this passive attitude of the consul
and the aristocracy appeared, as well it might, a political
abdication. As for the coalition, it was naturally very well
content that it was left to take its further steps almost
undisturbed.

The most important of these steps was deciding the
future position of Caesar. Constitutionally it devolved
on the Senate to fix the functions of the second consular
year of office before the election of the consuls took place.
Accordingly it had, anticipating the election of Caesar,
selected for him for 58 B.C. two provinces in which the
governor would be limited to building roads and other
public works. Since this was of course out of the question,
it was agreed among the confederates that Caesar should
obtain by decree of the people an extraordinary command
modeled on the Gabinio-Manilian laws. Since Caesar had
publicly declared that he would introduce no proposal on
his own behalf, the tribune Publius Vatinius submitted the
proposal to the citizens, who naturally gave their unconditional assent.

By this means Caesar obtained the governorship of
Cisalpine Gaul and the command of the three legions stationed there, which were already experienced in border
warfare under Lucius Afranius, as well as the same rank
of propraetor for his adjutants as those of Pompey had
enjoyed. This post was granted to him for five years, a
longer period than ever before assigned to a general
whose appointment had any definite limits. The country
of the Transpadanes, which for years had supported the
democratic party and Caesar in particular in the hope of
securing the franchise, formed the main portion of his
province. His jurisdiction extended south as far as the
Arno and the Rubicon, and included Luca and Ravenna.
Subsequently Caesar's official district was enlarged by
the province of Narbo with its one legion, a resolution

adopted by the Senate on the proposal of Pompey to prevent this command also from passing to Caesar by extraordinary popular decree.

Caesar's goal was thus attained. As no troops could constitutionally be stationed in Italy proper, the commander of the legions of northern Italy and Gaul dominated both Italy and Rome for the next five years, and he who was master for five years was master for life. The consulship of Caesar had attained its object. As a matter of course, the new holders of power did not neglect to keep the multitude in good humor by games and amusements of all sorts, and they embraced every opportunity of filling the exchequer. In the case of the king of Egypt, for instance, the decree of the people which recognized him as legitimate ruler was sold to him by the coalition at a high price, and other dynasts and communities acquired charters and privileges in like manner.

The arrangements also seemed sufficiently secure. The consulship was, at least for the next year, in safe hands. The public believed at first that it was destined for Pompey and Crassus. However, the holders of power preferred to elect two subordinate but trustworthy associates, Aulus Gabinius, the best among Pompey's adjutants, and Lucius Piso, who was less important but was Caesar's father-in-law. Pompey personally was to watch over Italy, where as head of the commission of twenty he administered the agrarian law and furnished nearly 20,000 citizens, mainly veterans from his army, with land in the territory of Capua. Caesar's northern Italian legions served to back him against opposition in the capital.

There existed no immediate prospect of a rupture among the holders of power. The laws issued by Caesar as consul, which Pompey was at least as interested in maintaining as Caesar, constituted a guarantee of a continuing breach between Pompey and the aristocracy (whose heads, especially Cato, continued to treat these laws as void) and thereby a guarantee of the existence of the coalition. Moreover, its chiefs were drawn closer by personal bonds. Caesar had honestly and faithfully kept his word to his confederates without trimming or cheating, and in particular had fought as dexterously and energetically for the agrarian law proposed in Pompey's interest as if it had been his own. Pompey was not insensible to upright dealing and good faith, and was kindly disposed towards the man who had helped rescue him from the sorry part of a suppliant which he had been playing for three years.

Frequent and familiar intercourse with a man as irresistibly amiable as Caesar did what more was needed to convert the alliance of interests into an alliance of friendship. The result and the pledge of this friendship—and at the same time, a public announcement of the newly established joint rule which could hardly be misunderstood—was the marriage of Pompey with Caesar's only daughter, three-and-twenty years of age. Julia, who had inherited the charm of her father, lived in the happiest domestic relations with her husband, who was nearly twice her age. The citizens, longing for rest and order after so many troubles and crises, saw in this marital alliance the guarantee of a peaceful and prosperous future.

The more firmly and closely the alliance was thus cemented between Pompey and Caesar, the more hopeless grew the cause of the aristocracy. They felt the sword suspended over their heads, and they knew Caesar sufficiently to have no doubt that he would, if necessary, use it without hesitation. "On all sides," wrote one of them, "we are checkmated. We have already through fear of death or banishment despaired of 'freedom'; every one sighs, no one ventures to speak." More the confederates could not desire. But though the majority of the aristocracy was in this desirable frame of mind, there was, of course, no lack of aristocratic Hotspurs. Hardly had Caesar completed his consulship when two of the most violent aristocrats, Lucius Domitius and Gaius Memmius, proposed in a full Senate the annulling of the Julian laws.

This indeed was simply a piece of folly which redounded only to the benefit of the coalition. When Caesar himself now insisted that the Senate investigate the validity of the laws assailed, the latter could not but formally recognize their legality. As may readily be conceived, however, the holders of power used this as a new opportunity to make an example of some of the most notable and noisiest of their opponents, thereby assuring that the remainder would adhere to the policy of sighing in silence. At first the coalition had hoped that the change of the agrarian law, which as usual required all the senators to swear to uphold the new law on pain of forfeiting their political rights, would induce its most vehement opponents to banish themselves by refusing the oath. But these did not show themselves so compliant. Even the rigid Cato submitted to the oath, and his Sancho Panzas followed.

A second and far from honorable attempt to threaten the leading aristocrats with criminal impeachments and drive them into exile, on account of an alleged plot to murder Pompey, was frustrated by the incapacity of the instruments. The informer, one Vettius, exaggerated and contradicted himself so grossly, and the tribune Vatinius (who directed the foul scheme) showed his complicity with Vettius so clearly, that it was found advisable to strangle the latter in prison and let the matter drop. This occasion, however, produced sufficient evidence of the total disorganization of the aristocracy and the boundless alarm of the genteel lords: even a man like Lucius Lucullus threw himself in person at Caesar's feet and publicly declared that he found himself compelled by reason of his great age to withdraw from public life.

Ultimately, therefore, the democrats were content with a few isolated victims. It was of primary importance to

remove Cato, who made no secret of his conviction as to
the nullity of all the Julian laws, and who was a man
to act as he thought. Such a man Cicero certainly was not,
and they did not bother to fear him. But the victorious
democratic party, which played the leading part in the
coalition, could not possibly leave unpunished the judicial
murder of December 5, 63 B.C., which it had so loudly
and justly censured. Had it wished to bring to account the
real authors of the fatal decree, it ought to have seized
not the pusillanimous consul, but that section of the die-
hard aristocracy which had egged on the timorous man
to the execution. But legally it was not the consul's ad-
visers but the consul himself who was responsible, and it
was the gentler course to charge the consul alone and
leave his senatorial colleagues out of it. For this reason
the charge directed against Cicero describes the decree
of the Senate, by virtue of which he ordered the execution, as supposititious.

Even against Cicero the holders of power would gladly
have avoided steps that attracted attention. However, he
could not prevail on himself either to give to those in
power the guarantees which they required, or banish himself from Rome under one of several feasible pretexts, or
even keep silent. With sincere alarm and the utmost desire to avoid any offense, he still did not have enough self-
control to be prudent. He could not keep quiet when a
petulant witticism stung him, or when the praise of so
many noble lords evoked in his brainless conceit the sono-
rous eloquence of the plebeian advocate.

The execution of the measures against Cato and Cicero
was committed to the loose and dissolute but clever and
audacious Publius Clodius, a bitter enemy of Cicero for
years. In order to satisfy that enmity and play the part of
a demagogue, Clodius had hastily converted himself from
a patrician into a plebeian during the consulship of Caesar, and was then chosen as tribune of the people for the
year 58 B.C. To support Clodius, the proconsul Caesar

remained in the vicinity of the capital till the blow was struck against the two victims. In line with the instructions which he had received, Clodius proposed that the citizens entrust Cato with the regulation of the complicated municipal affairs of the Byzantines and with the annexation of the kingdom of Cyprus. The latter had like Egypt fallen to the Romans by the testament of Alexander II; but unlike Egypt, it had not bought off the Roman annexation, and its king had also once given personal offense to Clodius. As for Cicero, Clodius proposed a law which characterized the execution of a citizen without trial and sentence as a crime punishable by banishment.

Cato was thus removed on an honorable mission, while Cicero was given the gentlest possible punishment and, moreover, was not designated by name in the proposal. But the holders of power did not refuse themselves the pleasure, on the one hand, of punishing a notoriously timid and shifty politician for the conservative energy which he had displayed, while on the other they invested the bitter opponent of all governmental interferences by the citizens, and of all extraordinary commands, with just such a command conferred by decree of the citizens themselves. With similar humor the proposal regarding Cato was based on the ground of his abnormal virtue, which made him appear pre-eminently qualified to execute so delicate a commission as confiscating the considerable royal treasure of Cyprus without embezzlement.

Both proposals bear the same stamp of respectful deference and cool irony which generally marked Caesar's bearing with reference to the Senate. They met with no resistance. It was naturally unavailing that the majority of the Senate, seeking to protest in some way against the mockery and censure of their decree regarding Catiline, put on public mourning, and that Cicero himself, now that it was too late, besought mercy on his knees from Pompey. He had to banish himself even before the passing of the law which barred him from his native land.

Cato likewise did not venture to provoke sharper measures by declining the commission which he had received,
but accepted it and embarked for the East. What was
most immediately necessary was done, and Caesar too
might leave Italy to devote himself to more serious tasks.

*The situation which Caesar found upon his arrival in
Gaul in the spring of 58 B.C. was a difficult one. The
Celtic culture of Gaul, prevented by the Romans from
expanding further south-westward, was showing signs of
disintegration under the blows of the Germans advancing
from the east. This pressure had already dislodged the
Helvetian tribe of Celts from their accustomed territory
and sent them in search of new land in the interior of
Gaul. Caesar chastised the Helvetii and sent them back to
their former terrain. Then he crushed a major German
invasion—and thereby for the first time established the
Rhine as the Roman boundary against the Germans.*

*Thus began the eight years of complicated warfare (58
through 51 B.C.) which accomplished the conquest of all
Gaul and saw the beginnings of the Roman dominion over
Britain. The detailed story of the numerous campaigns of
those years—full of Roman victories, though frequently
accompanied by perils and sometimes by disaster—has
often been told, most notably by Caesar himself in his
Gallic Wars. The consequences were tremendous. "Centuries elapsed before men understood that Caesar had not
merely conquered a new province for the Romans, but
had laid the foundations for the Romanizing of the
west," comments Mommsen. "That there is a bridge connecting the past glory of Greece and Rome with the
prouder fabric of modern history; that Western Europe
is Romanic, and Germanic Europe classic; that the names
of Themistocles and Scipio have a very different sound
for us than those of Asoka and Salmanazar; that Homer
and Sophocles are not merely attractive to the literary*

botanist, but bloom for us in our own garden—all this is
the work of Caesar."

But the still vaster work of Caesar—pulling down the
structure of the Roman republic, and thereby laying the
foundation of the Roman empire—was yet to come.

X
JOINT RULE OF POMPEY
AND CAESAR

Among the democratic chiefs who from the time of Cae-
sar's consulship were recognized almost officially as the
joint rulers of the commonwealth, in the public view Pompey clearly occupied the first place. It was before him,
whom the Optimates called "the private dictator," that
Cicero prostrated himself in vain. Against him were directed the sharpest sarcasms of Bibulus, and the most envenomed conversational arrows in the private chambers
of the opposition.

This was only to be expected. According to the facts before the public, Pompey was indisputably the first general
of his time, while Caesar was a dexterous political leader
and orator of undeniable talents, but notoriously unwar-
like and indeed of effeminate temperament. Such opinions
had long been current, and it could not be expected that
the highborn rabble would trouble itself to discover the
real state of affairs and abandon established platitudes because of obscure feats of heroism on the Tagus. Caesar
obviously played the part of a mere adjutant who executed for his chief the work which Flavius, Afranius, and
other less capable instruments had attempted unsuccessfully.

Even his governorship did not seem to change this situation. Afranius had but recently occupied a quite similar
position without thereby acquiring any special importance. In previous years several provinces at once had repeatedly been placed under one governor, and often far
more than four legions had been united in one hand. As
matters were again quiet beyond the Alps and the German
prince Ariovistus was recognized by the Romans as a
friend and neighbor, there was no prospect of conducting
a war of any moment there. It was natural to compare
Pompey's position under the Gabinio-Manilian laws with
that which Caesar had obtained by the Vatinian, and the
comparison was all to Caesar's disadvantage. Pompey
ruled over nearly the whole Roman empire, Caesar over
two provinces. Pompey had the soldiers and the treasures

of the state almost absolutely at his disposal, while Caesar had only the sums assigned to him and an army of 24,000 men. Pompey himself could choose the time of his retirement, while Caesar's command was given to him for a limited though long period. Pompey, in short, had been entrusted with the most important undertakings by sea and land; Caesar was sent north to watch over the capital from upper Italy and insure that Pompey might rule it undisturbed.

But when Pompey was appointed by the coalition to be ruler of the capital, he undertook a task far exceeding his powers. Pompey understood nothing about ruling except how to command. The waves of agitation in the capital were simultaneously swelled by past and future revolutions. The problem of ruling such a city—quite comparable to the Paris of the nineteenth century—without an armed force was infinitely difficult, and for that stiff and stately soldier altogether insoluble. As a result, matters soon reached such a pitch that friends and foes, both equally inconvenient to him, could do as they pleased so far as he was concerned. After Caesar's departure the coalition still ruled the destinies of the world, but not the streets of the capital.

The Senate, too, which still carried on a sort of nominal government, allowed matters to take their natural course, partly because the coalition's sympathizers in that body lacked instructions from the regents, partly because the angry opposition kept aloof out of indifference or pessimism, but chiefly because the whole aristocratic class began to feel, if not to understand, its utter impotence. For the moment there was nowhere in Rome any determined government, any real authority. Men were living in an interregnum between the ruin of the aristocratic and the rise of the military rule. As the Roman commonwealth has illustrated the different political principles more purely than any other state in ancient or modern times, so it exhibited political anarchy with unenviable clarity.

It is a strange coincidence that in the same years when Caesar was creating beyond the Alps a work for the ages, there was enacted in Rome one of history's most extravagant political farces. The new regent of the commonwealth did not rule, but shut himself up in his house and sulked in silence. The former half-deposed government likewise did not rule but sighed, sometimes privately amid the confidential circles of the villas, sometimes in chorus in the senate house. That section of the citizens who still yearned for freedom and order was disgusted with the reign of confusion, but utterly lacking leaders or counsel it maintained a passive attitude, not only avoiding political activity, but keeping as far aloof as possible from the political Sodom.

On the other hand the rabble never had a merrier arena. The number of little great men was legion. Demagoguery became quite a trade, with its professional insignia—the threadbare mantle, the shaggy beard, the long streaming hair, the deep bass voice—and not infrequently its rich rewards. For declamations the tried tricks of the theater were much in demand. Greeks and Jews, freedmen and slaves, were the most regular attenders and the loudest shouters in the public assemblies, where frequently only a minority of those voting consisted of citizens constitutionally entitled to do so.

The real power lay with the armed bands, the battalions of anarchy recruited by adventurers of rank from gladiatorial slaves and blackguards. Their possessors had from the outset been numbered mostly among the popular party; but since the departure of Caesar, who alone understood how to lead and control the democrats, all discipline had crumbled and every partisan practiced politics on his own. Even now these men fought with most pleasure under the banner of freedom; but strictly speaking, they were neither of democratic nor of antidemocratic views. They inscribed on the indispensable banner first the name of the people, then that of the Senate or of a party

chief. Clodius, for instance, fought or professed to fight
in turn for the ruling party, for the Senate, and for Crassus. The leaders of these bands kept to their colors only
in the persecution of their personal enemies—as in the
case of Clodius against Cicero and Milo against Clodius—where their partisan position served merely as an
instrument in private feuds. We might as well seek to set
a charivari to music as to write the history of this political
witches' revel; nor is it of any moment to enumerate all
the murders, besiegings of houses, acts of incendiarism
and other scenes of violence within the capital, or to
reckon up how often the gamut was traversed from hiss-
ing and shouting to spitting and trampling and thence to
throwing stones and drawing swords.

The principal performer in this rascally theater was
Publius Clodius, whose services the regents had already
used against Cato and Cicero. Left to himself, this influential, talented, energetic, and truly noteworthy partisan
pursued during his tribunate an ultrademocratic policy.
He gave the citizens free grain, restricted the right of
the censors to stigmatize immorality, and prohibited the
magistrates from obstructing the comitial machinery by
religious formalities. He set aside the limits which shortly
before had been imposed on the right of association for
the purpose of checking the political gangs, and he re-
established the "street-clubs," which with their almost
military street-by-street setup were nothing else than a
formal organization of the whole free and slave proletariat of the capital.[1] Of course these exertions in behalf
of freedom did not exclude a traffic in decrees of the citizenry. Like Caesar himself, Caesar's ape did a thriving
business in governorships and other posts great and small,
and sold the sovereign rights of the state to subject kings
and cities.

■

1. Clodius also (Mommsen notes in the original) even proposed a law in
later years to give full political rights to all freedmen and many slaves.

Pompey looked on all these things unmoved, but if he did not perceive how seriously he thus compromised himself, his opponent did. Clodius had the cheek to dispute with the regent of Rome on a trifling question of sending back a captive Armenian prince, and the dispute soon became a formal feud which revealed Pompey's utter helplessness. The head of the state sought to meet the partisan with his own weapons, only wielded with far less dexterity. Having been tricked by Clodius regarding the Armenian prince, he offended him in turn by releasing Clodius' enemy Cicero from exile, and thus converted his opponent into an implacable foe. If the gangs of Clodius made the streets unsafe, the victorious general likewise set slaves and pugilists to work. In the street battles which ensued the general naturally was worsted by the demagogue, and Cato was kept almost constantly under siege in his garden by Clodius and his comrades. Not the least remarkable feature of this strange spectacle was that the regent and the rogue vied in courting the favor of the fallen government. Pompey, partly to please the Senate, permitted Cicero's recall, while Clodius on the other hand declared the Julian laws null and void, and called on Marcus Bibulus publicly to testify to their having been unconstitutionally passed.

Naturally no positive result could come from this dark imbroglio, for its most distinctive character was its utter pointlessness. Even a man of Caesar's genius had to learn by experience that agitation was completely worn out, and that the way to the throne no longer lay through demagoguery. It was nothing more than a historical makeshift if now, in the interregnum between republic and monarchy, some whimsical fellow dressed himself in the prophet's mantle and staff which Caesar had laid aside, and parodied the great ideals of Gaius Gracchus. The so-called party from which this democratic agitation proceeded had so little substance that afterwards it did not even play a part in the decisive struggle.

It cannot even be said that this anarchy kindled among neutral citizens a desire for a strong government based on military power. Quite apart from the fact that such neutral citizens were chiefly to be found outside Rome, and thus were not directly affected by the rioting in the capital, everyone who could be so influenced had already been thoroughly converted to the principle of authority by former experiences, especially the Catilinarian conspiracy. Those who were really alarmed were far more apprehensive of the gigantic crisis accompanying the overthrow of the constitution, than of the mere continuance of superficial anarchy in the capital. Its only noteworthy result was the painful position of Pompey due to the attacks of the Clodians, which had a material share in determining his further steps.

Much as Pompey hated taking the initiative, on this occasion he was compelled by the change of his position towards both Clodius and Caesar to depart from his previous inaction. The disgraceful situation to which Clodius had reduced him at length must arouse even his sluggish nature to hatred and anger. But far more important was the change which took place in his relations with Caesar. Of the two regents, Pompey had utterly failed in the functions which he had undertaken, while Caesar had the skill to turn his official position to an account which left all calculations and all fears far behind. Without troubling much about permission, Caesar had doubled his army by levies in his southern province inhabited mainly by Roman citizens. Instead of keeping watch over Rome from Northern Italy, he had crossed the Alps with this army, crushed in the bud a new Cimbrian invasion, and within two years (58-57 B.C.) had carried the Roman arms to the Rhine and the Channel.

In the face of such facts the aristocratic tactics of ignoring and disparaging him were scarcely suitable. He who had often been scoffed at as effeminate was now the idol of the army, the celebrated victory-crowned hero, whose fresh triumphs outshone the faded laurels of Pompey, and to whom even the Senate as early as 57 B.C. accorded far greater honors than had ever fallen to Pompey. Pompey's relation to his former adjutant was precisely that of the latter towards him after the Gabinio-Manilian laws. Caesar was now the hero of the day and the master of the most powerful Roman army; Pompey was an ex-general who had once been famous.

It is true that no open collision had yet occurred between father-in-law and son-in-law, but every political alliance is inwardly broken when the relative power proportions of the parties are mutually altered. While the quarrel with Clodius was merely annoying, the change in the position of Caesar involved a very serious danger for Pompey. Just as Caesar and his confederates had formerly sought a military support against him, he now found himself compelled to seek a military support against Caesar. This required laying aside his haughty privacy and coming forward as a candidate for some extraordinary magistracy, which would enable him to match or exceed the power of the governor of the two Gauls.

His tactics, like his position, were exactly those of Caesar during the Mithradatic war. To balance the military power of a superior but still remote adversary by obtaining a similar command, Pompey required in the first instance the official machinery of government. A year and a half ago this had been absolutely at his disposal. The regents then ruled the state both through the comitia, which absolutely obeyed them as the masters of the street, and through the Senate, which was energetically overawed by Caesar. As representative of the coalition in Rome and as its acknowledged head, Pompey could doubtless have obtained from the Senate and from the citizens any decree he wished, even if it were against Caesar's interest. But the awkward quarrel with Clodius had cost Pompey the command of the streets, and he could not expect to carry a proposal in his favor in the popular

assembly. Things were not quite so unfavorable for him
in the Senate; but even there it was doubtful whether
after such long and fatal inaction he still held the majority firmly enough in hand to procure the decree he needed.

The position of the Senate also, or rather of the nobility generally, had meanwhile undergone a change. From
the very fact of its complete abasement it drew fresh energy. In the coalition of 60 B.C. various things had come
to light for which the times were by no means yet ripe.
The exit of Cato and Cicero (which public opinion un-
erringly referred to the regents, however much they kept
in the background and even professed to lament it) and
the marriage relationship between Caesar and Pompey
suggested, with disagreeable clarity, monarchical banish-
ments and family alliances. The larger public too, which
stood more aloof from political events, observed the
foundations of the future monarchy coming more and
more distinctly into view.

From the moment it became clear that Caesar's object
was not a modification of the republican constitution, but
that the question was the life or death of the republic,
many of the best men who had hitherto supported the
popular party and honored Caesar as its head must inevitably have passed over to the opposite side. It was no
longer only in salons and country houses that men talked
of the "three dynasts" and the "three-headed monster."
The dense crowds of people listened to Caesar's consular
orations without a sound, and not a hand stirred to ap-
plaud when the democratic consul entered the theater.
But they hissed when one of the tools of the regents
showed himself in public, and even staid men applauded
when an actor uttered an antimonarchic sentence or an
allusion against Pompey. When Cicero was banished, it
is said that twenty thousand citizens, mostly of the middle
classes, put on mourning after the Senate's example.
"Nothing is now more popular," remarks a letter of this
period, "than hatred of the popular party."

The regents dropped hints that through such opposition the equites might easily lose their new special places in the theater, and the populace its free grain. People therefore became somewhat more guarded in expressing their displeasure, but the feeling remained the same. The lever of money was applied with better success. Caesar's gold flowed in streams. Apparently rich men whose affairs were in disorder, influential ladies who were financially embarrassed, insolvent young nobles, merchants and bankers in difficulties, all either went in person to Gaul with the view of drawing from the fountainhead, or applied to Caesar's agents in the capital; and Caesar rarely rejected any outwardly respectable man, though he avoided dealing with vagabonds who were utterly lost. In addition Caesar undertook considerable building in the capital, by which men of all ranks from consular down to common porter were able to profit, and also expended immense sums for public amusements. Pompey did the same on a more limited scale, building the capital's first theater of stone, and celebrating its dedication with a magnificence never before seen.

Such measures naturally influenced a number of men who were inclined towards opposition, especially in the capital, and reconciled them somewhat to the new order of things. But the core of the opposition was not to be reached by this system of corruption. Every day showed more and more clearly how deep the existing constitution was rooted in the people, and how little the politically neutral groups, especially in country towns, were inclined to favor monarchy or even simply to suffer its coming.

If Rome had had a representative constitution, the discontent of the citizens would have found its natural expression in the elections, and would have grown in force by such expression. Under existing circumstances nothing was left for the constitutionalists but to place themselves under the Senate, which, degraded though it might be, was still the representative and champion of the legitimate

republic. Thus it transpired that the Senate, now that it
had been overthrown, suddenly found at its disposal an
army far larger and more faithful than when in its power
and splendor it overthrew the Gracchi and under the protection of Sulla's sword restored the state.

The aristocracy felt this, and began to bestir itself
afresh. Just then Marcus Cicero, after having bound himself not only to join the do-nothing faction in the Senate
but also to work with all his might for the regents, had
secured their permission to return. Although Pompey in
this matter only made an incidental concession to the oligarchy, intending first to play a trick on Clodius, and second to acquire in the fluent consular a tool rendered pliant
by sufficient blows, Cicero's return was seized as an opportunity for republican demonstrations just as his banishment had been a demonstration against the Senate. With
all possible solemnity, and protected against the Clodians
by the band of Titus Annius Milo, the two consuls at the
Senate's behest submitted a proposal to the citizens to
permit Cicero's return, and the Senate urged all supporters of the constitution to be present for the vote. An
unusual number of worthy men, especially from the country towns, gathered in Rome on the day of the voting
(August 4, 57 B.C.). Cicero's journey from Brundisium
to the capital gave occasion for a series of similar manifestations of public feeling. The new alliance between the
Senate and the constitutionally minded citizens was thus
publicly proclaimed, and helped not a little to revive the
shaken courage of the aristocracy.

Pompey's helplessness in the presence of these daring
demonstrations, as well as the undignified and almost
ridiculous position which he had assumed in his fight with
Clodius, discredited both him and the coalition. Thus the
section of the Senate which adhered to the regents was
left demoralized and helpless by his singular ineptitude,
and could not prevent the republican-aristocratic party
from regaining complete ascendency in the Senate. This

party's game was still by no means hopeless for a courageous and dexterous player. It now had what it had not
possessed for a century—firm popular support. If it
trusted the people and itself, it might attain its objective
in the shortest and most honorable way. Why not attack
the regents openly and avowedly? Why should not an
eminent and resolute man at the head of the Senate cancel
the extraordinary powers as unconstitutional and summon
the republicans of Italy to arms against the tyrants? It
was possible perhaps in this way once more to restore the
rule of the Senate. The republicans would thus be playing
a bold game, but perhaps in this case (as often) the most
courageous resolution might have been at the same time
the most prudent.

Since the indolent aristocracy of this period was
scarcely capable of so simple and bold a resolution, there
was another and perhaps surer way, or at any rate one
better adapted to the character and nature of these constitutionalists: they might work to set the two regents at
odds, and thereby ultimately attain to the helm themselves. The relations between the two rulers had become
altered and relaxed, now that Caesar's preponderant
power had compelled Pompey to seek a new position of
command. It was probable that if he obtained it, a rupture would occur in one way or another and give rise to a
struggle between them. If Pompey was unsupported his
defeat was scarcely doubtful, and the constitutional party
would then find itself ruled by one master instead of two.
But if the nobility employed against Caesar the same
means by which he had won his previous victories, and
made an alliance with the weaker competitor, then the
victory—given a general like Pompey, and an army such
as that of the constitutionalists—would probably fall to
the coalition. To settle matters with Pompey after the
victory, judging from his proven political incapacity,
could not be an especially difficult task.

The course of events thus naturally suggested an understanding between Pompey and the republican party. Whether such an understanding could be reached, and what shape the confused relations of the two regents and the aristocracy were to assume, came up for discussion in the autumn of 57 B.C., when Pompey proposed that the Senate entrust him with extraordinary official power. He once more based his proposal, as eleven years earlier, on the price of bread in the capital, which had again (as just before the Gabinian law) reached an oppressive height. Whether it had been forced up by manipulation, as Clodius sometimes charged to Pompey and sometimes to Cicero, and these in turn charged to Clodius, cannot be determined. The continuance of piracy, the emptiness of the public chest, and the negligent and disorderly supervision of the grain distribution were already quite sufficient by themselves to produce scarcities of bread in a great city dependent almost solely on overseas supplies. Pompey's plan was to get the superintendence of all matters relating to grain throughout the empire, and, to this end, to secure on the one hand the unlimited disposal of the Roman state-treasure, and on the other hand an army and fleet, as well as a command which was superior in each Roman province to that of the governor. In short, he sought an improved edition of the Gabinian law, to which the conduct of the pending Egyptian war would naturally have been added as the conduct of the Mithradatic war was added to the pirate roundup.

However much the opposition to the new dynasts had gained ground, when the proposal was discussed in 57 B.C. the majority of the Senate was still under the constraint of the terror excited by Caesar. It obsequiously accepted the project in principle on the motion of Marcus Cicero, who was expected to give (and gave) this first proof of the pliancy which exile had taught him. But in settling the details very material changes were made in the original plan, which the tribune Gaius Messius had submitted. Pompey obtained neither a free hand with the treasury, nor legions and ships of his own, nor even an authority superior to that of the governors. The senators contented themselves with granting him considerable sums, fifteen adjutants, and full proconsular power in all affairs relating to grain supply throughout the Roman dominions for the next five years. This decree, moreover, would have to be confirmed by the citizenry.

There were many reasons which led to this alteration, almost equivalent to a rejection, of the original plan. Even the most timid must surely hesitate to invest Caesar's colleague not merely with equal but with superior authority in Gaul itself. There was the concealed opposition of Pompey's hereditary enemy and reluctant ally Crassus, to whom Pompey himself largely attributed the failure of his plan. The republican opposition in the Senate was hostile to any decree which even nominally enlarged the authority of the regents. Finally, and most important, there was the incompetence of Pompey himself, who even when compelled to act could not make himself acknowledge his own actions, but chose always to bring forward his design incognito by means of friends, while he himself in his well-known modesty declared his willingness to be content with even less. No wonder that they took him at his word, and gave him less.

Pompey was nevertheless glad to have found at least a serious employment, and above all a fitting pretext for leaving the capital. He succeeded, moreover, in providing it with ampler and cheaper grain supplies, although not without the provinces severely feeling the reflex effect. But he had missed his real object. The proconsular title, which he had a right to bear in all the provinces, remained an empty name so long as he had no troops of his own. Accordingly he soon afterwards had a second proposition made to the Senate, that it should charge him with restoring the expelled king of Egypt, if necessary by force of arms. But the more evident became his urgent need of the Senate, the less respectfully were his wishes received. It was immediately discovered in the Sibylline oracles that it was impious to send a Roman army to Egypt, whereupon the pious Senate almost unanimously resolved to avoid armed intervention. Pompey was already so humbled that he would have accepted the mission even without an army. But in his incorrigible dissimulation he left this also to be requested only by his friends, and he spoke and voted for sending another senator. Of course the Senate rejected a proposal which wantonly risked a life so precious to his country; and the ultimate issue of the endless discussions was the resolution not to interfere in Egypt at all.

These repeated repulses which Pompey met in the Senate (and still worse, had to accept without retaliation) were naturally regarded by the public as so many victories for the republicans and defeats for the regents. Accordingly, the tide of republican opposition was always on the increase. Already the elections for 56 B.C. had gone but partly for the dynasts. Caesar's candidates for the praetorship, Publius Vatinius and Gaius Alfius, had failed, while two decided adherents of the fallen government, Gnaeus Lentulus Marcellinus and Gnaeus Domitius Calvinus, had been elected, the former as consul and the latter as praetor. For 55 B.C. the consulship was sought by Lucius Domitius Ahenobarbus, whose election it was difficult to prevent owing to his influence in the capital and his colossal wealth, and who clearly would not be content with a concealed opposition.

The comitia thus rebelled, and the Senate chimed in. The latter solemnly deliberated over an opinion which Etruscan soothsayers of acknowledged wisdom had furnished upon request respecting certain signs and wonders. The celestial revelation announced that through dissension among the upper classes the whole power over the army and treasury threatened to pass to one ruler, and the state was faced with loss of freedom (the gods seemed to point primarily at the proposal of Gaius Messius). The republicans soon descended from heaven to earth. The law as to the domain of Capua and the other laws issued by Caesar as consul had been constantly described by them as null and void, and an opinion had been expressed in the Senate as early as 57 B.C. that it was necessary to cancel them on account of their irregularity. Then, on April 6, 56 B.C., the consular Cicero proposed in a full Senate that the Campanian land distribution be debated on May 15.

It was the formal declaration of war, and all the more significant because it came from one of those men who only show their colors when they think that they can do so with safety. Evidently the aristocracy felt that the moment had come for beginning the struggle not with Pompey against Caesar, but against the regency generally. What would further follow might easily be seen. Domitius made no secret that he intended as consul to propose to the citizens the immediate recall of Caesar from Gaul. An aristocratic restoration was at work, and with the attack on the colony of Capua the nobility threw down the gauntlet to the regents.

Caesar, although receiving detailed daily accounts of events in the capital, and, when military considerations allowed, watching their progress from as nearby as possible, had not up to then openly interfered. But now war had been declared against his colleague and especially against him; he was compelled to act, and he acted quickly. He happened to be in the neighborhood, for the aristocracy had not even found it advisable to delay the rupture until he had crossed the Alps. Early in April of 56 B.C. Crassus left the capital to make the necessary arrangements with his more powerful colleague. He found Caesar in Ravenna, from whence both proceeded to Luca. There they were joined by Pompey, who had departed from Rome soon after Crassus, ostensibly for the purpose of procuring supplies of grain from Sardinia and Africa. The most noted adherents of the regents, such as Metellus Nepos the proconsul of Hither Spain, Appius Clau-

dius the propraetor of Sardinia, and many others, followed them. A hundred and twenty lictors and upwards
of two hundred senators were counted at this conference,
a new monarchical Senate in contradistinction to the republican.

In every respect the decisive voice lay with Caesar. He
used it to re-establish and consolidate the existing joint
rule on a new basis of more equal distribution of power.
The governorships of most importance from a military
point of view, next to that of the two Gauls, were assigned to his two colleagues, the two Spains to Pompey,
Syria to Crassus. These offices were to be secured to them
by decree of the people for five years (54-50 B.C.), with
suitable military and financial support. On the other hand
Caesar demanded the prolongation of his command,
which expired with the year 54 B.C., to the close of
49 B.C., as well as the prerogative of increasing his legions to ten and of making the state pay for the troops
he arbitrarily levied. Pompey and Crassus were promised
a second consulship for the next year (55 B.C.) before
they departed for their governorships, while Caesar reserved the right to administer the supreme magistracy a
second time after the end of his governorship in 48 B.C.,
when the ten years' interval legally required between two
consulships should have elapsed. The military support
which Pompey and Crassus needed all the more urgently
in the capital, now that Caesar's legions originally intended for this purpose could not be withdrawn from
Transalpine Gaul, was to be found in new legions they
were to raise for the Spanish and Syrian armies, but were
not to despatch from Italy until they found it convenient
to do so.

The main questions were thus settled, and such subordinate matters as the tactics to be followed against the opposition in the capital, the regulation of the candidacies
for the ensuing years, etc., did not long detain them. The
great master of mediation composed with his wonted ease

the personal differences which stood in the way of an agreement, and compelled the most refractory elements to act in concert. An understanding befitting colleagues was re-established, externally at least, between Pompey and Crassus. Even Publius Clodius was induced to keep himself and his pack quiet, and to give no further annoyance to Pompey—not the least marvelous feat of the mighty magician.

The circumstances reveal that this whole settlement proceeded not from a compromise among independent and rival regents meeting on equal terms, but solely from the good will of Caesar. Pompey appeared at Luca in the painful position of a powerless refugee who comes to ask aid from his opponent. Whether Caesar chose to dismiss him and declare the coalition dissolved, or to receive him and let the league continue just as it stood, Pompey was in either case politically annihilated. If he did not in this case break with Caesar, he became the powerless dependent of his confederate. If on the other hand he did break with Caesar and, which was not very probable, effected even now a coalition with the aristocracy, the last-minute alliance between opponents concluded under pressure of necessity was so little formidable that Caesar need hardly put himself out to avert it. A serious rivalry on the part of Crassus with Caesar was utterly impossible.

It is difficult to say what motives induced Caesar to surrender his superior position and to grant voluntarily the second consulate and a military command—concessions which he had refused his rival even at the consummation of the league in 60 B.C., and which the latter had since (with the evident intent of being armed against Caesar) vainly striven to attain without Caesar's help and even against his will. To be sure, it was not Pompey alone that was placed at the head of an army, but also Pompey's old enemy and Caesar's long-time ally Crassus; and undoubtedly Crassus obtained his respectable military position merely as a counterpoise to Pompey's new power. Nevertheless, Caesar lost greatly when his rival exchanged his former powerlessness for an important command.

It is possible that Caesar did not yet feel himself sufficiently master of his soldiers to lead them confidently in a war against the established government, and was therefore anxious not to be forced into civil war now by being recalled from Gaul. But whether civil war came or not depended at the moment far more on the aristocracy of the capital than on Pompey. This would have been at most a reason for Caesar not breaking openly with Pompey, so that the opposition might not be emboldened by this breach, but not a reason for conceding what was conceded. Purely personal motives may have contributed to the result. It may be that Caesar recollected how he had once stood in a similar position before Pompey, and had been saved from destruction only by Pompey's (pusillanimous, it is true, rather than magnanimous) retirement. It is probable that Caesar hesitated to break the heart of his beloved daughter who was sincerely attached to her husband, for in his soul there was room for much besides the statesman.

But the decisive reason was doubtless the consideration of Gaul. Caesar (as distinct from his biographers) regarded the subjugation of Gaul not as an incidental enterprise useful for gaining the crown, but as one on which depended his country's external security and internal reorganization—in short, its future. That he might complete this conquest undisturbed, and not be obliged to take on at that moment the settlement of Italian affairs, he unhesitatingly gave up his superiority over his rivals and granted Pompey sufficient power to settle matters with the Senate and its adherents.

This was a grave political blunder, if Caesar had no other object than to become king of Rome as quickly as possible. But the ambition of that rare man was not confined to the vulgar aim of a crown. He had the boldness to prosecute side by side, and to complete, two equally vast labors—the arranging of the internal affairs of Italy, and the winning of new and fresh soil for Italian civilization. These tasks of course interfered with each other, and his Gallic conquests hindered much more than helped him on his way to the throne. Postponing the Italian revolution until 48 B.C., instead of settling it in 58 B.C., bore bitter fruit for him. But as statesman as well as general Caesar was that kind of daring player who, confident of himself and despising his opponents, gave always great and sometimes extravagant odds.

It was now the turn of the aristocracy to wage war as boldly as they had declared it. But there is no more pitiable spectacle than cowardly men who have the misfortune to take a bold resolution. They had simply exercised no foresight at all. It seemed to have occurred to nobody that Caesar would possibly stand his ground, or that even now Pompey and Crassus would again combine with him more closely than ever. This seems incredible, but it becomes intelligible when we glance at the leaders of the constitutional opposition in the Senate. With Cato still absent, the most influential man in the Senate was Marcus Bibulus, the hero of passive resistance, the most obstinate and stupid of all consulars. The aristocracy had taken up arms, only to lay them down as soon as the adversary merely put his hand to the sheath.

The mere news of the conferences in Luca sufficed to suppress all thought of serious opposition and to bring the mass of the timid—that is, the immense majority of the Senate—back to their duty as subjects, which in an unhappy hour they had abandoned. There was no further talk of the scheduled discussion to consider the validity of the Julian laws. The legions raised by Caesar on his own behalf were charged to the public chest by senatorial decree. The attempts, while arranging for the next consular provinces, to take away one or both Gauls from Caesar by decree were rejected by the Senate near the end of May, 56 B.C.

Thus the corporation did public penance. In secret the individual lords, one after another, thoroughly frightened at their own temerity, came to make their peace and vow unconditional obedience—none more quickly than Marcus Cicero, who repented too late of his perfidy, and with regard to the most recent period of his life clothed himself with titles of "honor" which were more appropriate than flattering. (*"Me asinum germanum fuisse"*—"I have been a complete ass.") Of course the regents agreed to be pacified. They refused nobody pardon, for there was nobody worth making an exception over. How suddenly the tone in aristocratic circles changed, after the resolutions of Luca became known, may be seen by comparing the pamphlets given forth by Cicero shortly before with that which he caused to be issued as public evidence of his repentance and his good intentions.

The regents could thus arrange Italian affairs at their pleasure and more fully than before. Italy and the capital obtained what amounted to a garrison (although not assembled in arms) and one of the regents as commandant. Of the troops levied for Syria and Spain by Crassus and Pompey, those destined for the East took their departure. But Pompey caused the two Spanish provinces to be administered by his lieutenants with the garrison already there, while he furloughed the officers and soldiers of the legions nominally raised for dispatch to Spain, and remained himself with them in Italy.

Doubtless the tacit public resistance increased, the more clearly men perceived that the regents were working to end the old constitution and, with as much gentleness as possible, to accommodate the existing government and administration to the forms of monarchy. But they submitted, because they were obliged to submit. First, all the more important matters, particularly those relating to military affairs and external relations, were disposed of without consulting the Senate, sometimes by decree of the people and sometimes at the mere good pleasure of the rulers. The arrangements agreed on at Luca regarding the military command of Gaul were submitted directly to the citizens by Crassus and Pompey, those relating to Spain and Syria by the tribune of the people Gaius Trebonius, and in other instances the more important governorships were frequently filled by decree of the people. Caesar had already shown that the regents did not need any consent to increase their troops at pleasure, nor did they hesitate to borrow troops. Caesar, for instance, received support from Pompey for the Gallic war, and Crassus from Caesar for the Parthian war. The Transpadanes, who possessed under the existing constitution only Latin rights, were treated by Caesar during his administration practically as full citizens of Rome.

While formerly the organization of newly acquired territories had always been managed by a senatorial commission, Caesar organized his extensive Gallic conquests according to his own judgment, and, without having received any further powers, founded colonies such as Novum-Comum (Como), with 5,000 colonists. Piso conducted the Thracian, Gabinius the Egyptian, Crassus the Parthian war, without consulting the Senate, and without even the usual reports to that body. In like manner triumphs and other marks of honor were accorded without the Senate being asked about them.

Obviously this did not arise from a mere neglect of forms, which would be still less understandable since in the great majority of cases no senatorial opposition was to be expected. On the contrary, it was a well-calculated design to cut off the Senate from military arrangements and high policy, and to restrict it to financial questions and internal affairs. Even opponents plainly discerned this and protested against this conduct of the regents so far as they could, by means of senatorial decrees and criminal actions. While the regents thus in the main set aside the Senate, they still made some use of the less dangerous popular assemblies, though taking care that the lords of the street should not obstruct the plans of the lords of the state. In many cases, however, they dispensed even with this empty shadow, and employed openly autocratic forms. The humbled Senate had to submit to its position whether it would or not. The leader of the compliant majority continued to be Marcus Cicero. He was useful for his lawyer's talent of finding reasons, or at any rate words, for everything; and there was a genuine Caesarian irony in employing the man, by means of whom mainly the aristocracy had conducted their demonstrations against the regents, as the mouthpiece of servility. Accordingly the regents pardoned him for his brief desire to kick against the pricks, having previously assured themselves of his complete submissiveness. His brother had been obliged to become an officer in the Gallic army, thus also becoming a hostage. Pompey had compelled Cicero himself to accept a nominal deputy position under him, which furnished a means for politely banishing him at any moment. Clodius had doubtless been instructed to leave him meanwhile at peace, but Caesar no more discarded Clodius on account of Cicero than he discarded Cicero on account of Clodius; thus the great savior of his country, and the equally great hero of liberty, entered into an antechamber rivalry for whose illustration there was unfortunately no Roman Aristophanes.

Not only was the same rod, which already had once descended on him so severely, kept in suspense over Cicero's head; golden fetters were also laid upon him. Amid his serious financial embarrassment, the interest-free loans of Caesar, and the joint overseership of those buildings which occasioned the circulation of enormous sums in the capital, were in a high degree welcome to him. Many an immortal oration was nipped in the bud by the thought of Caesar's agent, who might present a bill to him after the close of the sitting. Consequently he vowed "in future to ask no more after right and honor, but to strive for the favor of the regents," and "to be as flexible as an earlap." They used him accordingly as what he was good for, an advocate. In this capacity he had on various occasions to defend his very bitterest foes at a higher bidding, especially in the Senate, where he often served as the organ of the dynasts and submitted the proposals "to which others probably consented, but not he himself." Indeed, as recognized leader of the party of spinelessness, he even attained a certain political importance. The regents dealt with the other members of the governing corporation accessible to fear, flattery, or gold in the same way as they had dealt with Cicero, and succeeded in keeping them on the whole in subjection.

Certainly there remained a section of their opponents who at least kept to their colors, and who were neither to be terrified nor won over. The regents had become convinced that exceptional measures, such as those once used against Cato and Cicero, did their cause more harm than good, and that it was a lesser evil to tolerate an inconvenient republican opposition than to convert their opponents into martyrs. Therefore they allowed Cato to return near the end of 56 B.C., and thenceforward both in the Senate and in the Forum, often at the peril of his life, he offered a continuous opposition to the regents which was doubtless honorable, but unhappily was at the same time ridiculous.

The regents allowed him, in the debate on the proposals of Trebonius, to push matters once more to a hand-to-hand conflict in the Forum, and to submit to the Senate a proposal that the proconsul Caesar should be given over to the Usipetes and Tencteri on account of his perfidious conduct toward those barbarians. They were patient when Marcus Favonius, Cato's Sancho Panza, after the Senate had adopted the resolution to charge the legions of Caesar to the state-chest, sprang to the door of the senate house and proclaimed to the streets the danger to the country; when the same person in his scurrilous fashion called the white bandage which Pompey wore round his

weak leg a displaced diadem; when the consular Lentulus
Marcellinus, on being applauded, called out to the assembly to make diligent use of this privilege of expressing
their opinion now while they were still allowed to do so;
when the tribune of the people Gaius Ateius Capito con-
signed Crassus, with all the formalities of the theology of
the day, publicly to the evil spirits on the occasion of his
departure for Syria.

These were, on the whole, vain demonstrations of an
irritated minority. Yet the little party from which they issued was to this degree important, that on the one hand
it fostered and gave the watchword to the republican opposition fermenting in secret, and on the other hand now
and then dragged the majority of the Senate (which cherished at bottom quite the same sentiments with reference
to the regents) into isolated actions against them. For
even the majority felt the need of giving vent to their suppressed indignation, at least sometimes and in subordinate
matters, especially (after the manner of those who are reluctantly servile) by exhibiting their resentment towards
the great foes in rage against the small. Wherever it was
possible, a gentle blow was administered to the instruments of the regents. Thus Gabinius was refused the
thanksgiving festival that he asked, and Piso was recalled
from his province. Thus mourning was put on by the Senate, when the tribune of the people Gaius Cato hindered
the elections for 55 B.C. as long as the consul Marcellinus, who belonged to the constitutional party, was in office. Even Cicero, however humbly he always bowed before the regents, issued an equally envenomed and insipid
pamphlet against Caesar's father-in-law.

But these feeble signs of opposition by the senatorial
majority, and the ineffectual resistance of the minority,
show only the more clearly that the government had now
passed from the Senate to the regents as it had once
passed from the citizens to the Senate. The Senate was already not much more than a monarchical council of state

also employed to absorb the antimonarchical elements. "No man," the adherents of the fallen government complained, "is of the slightest account except the three. The regents are all-powerful, and they take care that no one shall remain in doubt about it. The whole Senate is virtually transformed and obeys the dictators; our generation will not live to see a change of things." They were living in fact no longer under the republic, but under monarchy.

But if the guidance of the state was at the absolute disposal of the regents, there remained still a political domain separated in some measure from the government proper, which was more easy to defend and more difficult to conquer—the field of ordinary magisterial elections, and that of the jury courts. It is clear that the latter do not fall directly under politics, but everywhere, and above all in Rome, partly reflect the spirit of the times. The elections of magistrates were certainly a part of the government of the state. But since at this time the state was administered substantially by extraordinary magistrates or by men wholly without title, and even the supreme magistrates, if they belonged to the antimonarchical party, were not able in any tangible way to influence the state machinery, the ordinary magistrates more and more resembled mere puppets. When in fact even those who were most disposed to opposition described themselves frankly and correctly as powerless ciphers, their elections therefore sank into mere demonstrations. Thus, after the opposition had already been wholly dislodged from the proper field of battle, hostilities might nevertheless be continued in the field of elections and of processes.

The regents spared no pains to become victors in this field also. As to the elections, they had already settled at Luca the lists of candidates for the next years, and they left no means untried to carry the candidates agreed upon there. They expended their gold primarily for the purpose of influencing the elections. A great number of soldiers

were dismissed annually on furlough from the armies of
Caesar and Pompey to take part in the voting at Rome,
and Caesar himself was wont to guide and watch over the
election campaigns from as near a point in Upper Italy as
possible.

Yet the object was but very imperfectly attained. For
55 B.C. Pompey and Crassus were indeed elected consuls,
in agreement with the arrangements at Luca, and Lucius
Domitius, the only candidate of the opposition who persevered, was set aside. But this had been effected only by
open violence, on which occasion Cato was wounded and
other extremely scandalous incidents occurred. In the next
consular elections, despite all the exertions of the regents,
Domitius was actually elected, and Cato also now prevailed in the race for the praetorship, which Caesar's tool
Vatinius had won the previous year to the scandal of the
whole citizenry. At the elections for 53 B.C. the opposition succeeded in so indisputably convicting the regency
candidates (along with others) of the most shameful
electioneering intrigues that the regents, on whom the
scandal recoiled, could not do otherwise than abandon
them.

These repeated and severe defeats of the dynasts in the
elections may be traceable in part to the unmanageable-
ness of the rusty machinery, to the incalculable accidents
of the polling, to the opposition at heart of the middle
classes, and to the various private considerations that interfere in such cases and often strangely clash with those
of party. But the main cause lies elsewhere. The elections
were at this time essentially in the power of the different
clubs into which the aristocracy had grouped themselves.
The system of bribery was organized by them on the most
extensive scale and with the utmost care. The same aristocracy which was represented in the Senate also ruled the
elections. But while in the Senate it yielded grudgingly,
here it worked and voted, in secret and secure from all
reckoning, wholeheartedly against the regents. That the

nobility's influence in this field was by no means broken by the strict law against electioneering intrigues, which Crassus as consul in 55 B.C. caused to be confirmed by the citizens, is proved by the elections of the succeeding years.

The jury courts caused equally great difficulty to the regents. As they were then composed, the decisive voice lay chiefly with the middle class, though the senatorial nobility was also influential. The setting of a high property qualification for jurymen under a law proposed by Pompey in 55 B.C. is a remarkable proof that the opposition to the regents had its center in the middle class proper, and that the great capitalists showed themselves as usual more compliant. Nevertheless the republican party was not yet deprived of all hold in the courts, and it was never weary of directing political impeachments, not indeed against the regents themselves, but against their prominent instruments. This warfare of prosecutions was waged the more keenly since by custom the duty of accusation belonged to the senatorial youth, and, as may readily be conceived, there was more of republican passion, fresh talent, and bold delight in attack to be found among these youths than among the older members of their order.[2]

On the whole, therefore, in the sphere of the popular elections and of the jury courts it was the regents who fared worst. The controlling factors here were less tangible, and therefore more difficult to be terrified or corrupted, than the direct organs of government and administration. The holders of power encountered here, especially in the popular elections, the tough energy of a close oligarchy grouped in cliques, which is by no means finally disposed of when its rule is overthrown, and which is the more difficult to vanquish the more covert its action. They

2. In the original Mommsen observes that the regents could still often protect their creatures, as Caesar protected Vatinius. But Gabinius was pursued so implacably by the aristocracy and the great capitalists that he was eventually exiled.

also encountered, especially in the jury courts, the repugnance of the middle classes towards the new monarchical rule. Thus they suffered in both quarters a series of defeats. The election victories of the opposition had, it is true, merely the value of demonstrations, since the regents possessed and employed the means of practically annulling any magistrate whom they disliked. However, the criminal trials in which the opposition secured condemnations deprived them, in a way keenly felt, of useful auxiliaries. As things stood, the regents could neither set aside nor adequately control the popular elections and the jury courts; and the opposition, however much it felt itself constrained even here, maintained to a certain extent the field of battle.

It proved, moreover, a still more difficult task to encounter the opposition in another field, to which it turned with greater zeal the more it was dislodged from direct political action. This was literature. Even the judicial opposition was also a literary one, and indeed pre-eminently so, for the orations were regularly published and served as political pamphlets. The arrows of poetry hit their mark still more rapidly and sharply. The lively youth of the high aristocracy, and still more energetically perhaps the cultivated middle class in the Italian country towns, waged the war of pamphlets and epigrams with zeal and success. There fought side by side on this field the genteel senator's son Gaius Licinius Calvus (82-48 B.C.), who was as much feared as an orator and pamphleteer as a versatile poet, and the municipals of Cremona and Verona, Marcus Furius Bibaculus (102-c.20 B.C.) and Quintus Verleius Catullus (87 to about 54 B.C.), whose elegant and pungent epigrams flew swiftly and surely like arrows through Italy.

An oppositional tone prevails throughout the literature of these years. It is full of indignant sarcasm against the "great Caesar," "the unique general," against the affectionate father-in-law and son-in-law who ruin the whole globe in order to let their dissolute favorites parade the spoils of the long-haired Celts through the streets of Rome, to furnish royal banquets with the booty of the farthest isles of the west, and as rich rivals to supplant honest youths at home in the favor of their mistresses. There is in the poems of Catullus and the other fragments of the literature of this period something of that fervor of personal and political hatred, of that republican agony overflowing in riotous humor or stern despair, which are more prominently and powerfully apparent in Aristophanes and Demosthenes.

The most sagacious of the three rulers at least saw well that it was as impossible to despise this opposition as to suppress it by word of command. So far as he could, Caesar rather tried personally to win over the more notable authors. Cicero himself had his literary reputation to thank in large part for the respectful treatment which he received especially from Caesar. But the governor of Gaul did not disdain to conclude a special peace even with Catullus himself, through the intervention of his father who had become personally known to him in Verona; and the young poet, who had just heaped upon the powerful general the bitterest and most personal sarcasms, was treated with the most flattering distinction. In fact, Caesar was gifted enough to meet his literary opponents on their own field and to publish (as an indirect way of repelling manifold attacks) a detailed report on the Gallic wars, which set forth with happily assumed naïveté the necessity and constitutional propriety of his military operations.

But it is freedom alone that is absolutely and exclusively poetical and creative; it and it alone is able, even in its most wretched caricature and with its dying breath, to inspire fresh enthusiasm. All the sound elements of literature were, and remained, antimonarchical. If Caesar himself could venture on this field without proving a failure, the reason was merely that even now he still cherished at heart the magnificent dream of a free commonwealth, although he was unable to transfer it either to his adversaries or to his adherents. Practical politics was not more absolutely controlled by the regents than literature by the republicans.

It became necessary to take serious steps against this opposition, which though powerless was becoming ever more troublesome and audacious. The condemnation of Gabinius at the end of 54 B.C. apparently tipped the scale. The regents agreed to introduce a dictatorship, though only a temporary one, and by means of this to carry new coercive measures especially concerning the elections and the jury courts. Pompey, as the regent on whom primarily devolved the government of Rome and Italy, was charged with the execution of this resolve. Accordingly, it was marked by his characteristic awkwardness in resolution and action, as well as his singular incapacity to speak out frankly even where he would and could command.

Toward the close of 54 B.C. the demand for a dictatorship was hinted to the Senate, though not by Pompey himself. Its ostensible ground was the continuance of the system of clubs and bands in the capital, which by acts of bribery and violence certainly exercised the most pernicious pressure on the elections as well as on the jury courts, and kept the city in a perpetual state of disturbance. We must allow that this rendered it easy for the regents to justify their exceptional measures. But, as may well be conceived, even the servile majority shrank from granting what the future dictator seemed to shrink from asking openly. When the unparalleled agitation regarding the elections for the consulship of 53 B.C. led to the most scandalous scenes, so that the elections were postponed a full year beyond the fixed time and took place only after a seven months' interregnum in July of 53, Pompey found in this state of things the desired occasion for indicating distinctly to the Senate that the dictatorship was the only means of cutting, if not of loosing, the knot. Even then, however, the decisive word of command was not spoken. Perhaps it would have remained long un-uttered had not the most audacious partisan of the republican opposition, Titus Annius Milo, stepped into the field at the consular elections for 52 B.C. as a candidate opposing the regency's choices, Quintus Metellus Scipio and Publius Plautius Hypsaeus, both of whom were closely connected with Pompey personally and thoroughly devoted to him.

Milo, endowed with physical courage, with a certain talent for intrigue and for contracting debt, and above all with an ample amount of native assurance which had been carefully cultivated, had made himself a name among the political adventurers of the day. He was the greatest bully in his trade next to Clodius, and naturally therefore at deadly odds with the latter. As this latter Achilles of the streets had been acquired by the regents and with their permission was again playing the ultrademocrat, the Hector of the streets became as a matter of course an aristocrat! The republican opposition, which now would have concluded an alliance with Catiline himself, readily acknowledged Milo as their legitimate champion in all riots. In fact, the few successes which they achieved in this field of battle were the work of Milo and his well-trained band of gladiators. So Cato and his friends in return supported the candidacy of Milo for the consulship. Even Cicero could not avoid recommending one who had been his enemy's enemy and his own protector during many years; and as Milo himself spared neither money nor violence, his election seemed certain.

For the regents this would have been not only a new and keenly felt defeat but also a real danger, for the bold partisan would surely not allow himself as consul to be reduced to insignificance so easily as Domitius and the other opposition respectables. It happened that this Achilles and Hector accidentally encountered each other not far from the capital on the Appian Way, and a fray arose

between their respective bands, in which Clodius himself
received a sword cut on the shoulder and was compelled
to take refuge in a neighboring house. This had occurred
without orders from Milo. However, as the matter had
gone so far and as the storm now had to be encountered
in any case, the whole crime seemed to Milo more desirable and less dangerous than the half. Therefore he ordered his men to drag Clodius forth from his lurking
place and to put him to death.

The street leaders of the regents' party—the tribunes
Titus Munatius Plancus, Quintus Pompeius Rufus, and
Gaius Sallustius Crispus—saw in this occurrence a golden
opportunity to thwart the candidacy of Milo and carry
the dictatorship of Pompey. Since the dregs of the populace, especially the freedmen and slaves, had lost in Clodius their patron and future deliverer, the requisite excitement was easily aroused. After the bloody corpse had
been exhibited at the orators' platform in the Forum and
the appropriate speeches had been made, the riot broke
out.

The seat of the perfidious aristocracy was apparently
destined as the funeral pile of the great liberator, for the
mob carried the body to the senate house and set the
building on fire. Thereafter the multitude proceeded to
Milo's house, keeping it under siege till his band drove off
the assailants by discharges of arrows. They then passed
on to the houses of Pompey and his consular candidates,
saluting the former as dictator and the latter as consuls,
and thence to the house of the interrex Marcus Lepidus,
on whom devolved the conduct of the consular elections.
When the latter, as his duty dictated, refused to make
the immediate arrangements for the elections which the
clamorous multitude demanded, he was kept under siege
in his house for five days.

But the instigators of these scandalous scenes had over-
acted their part. Certainly their lord and master sought
to employ this favorable episode not merely to set aside

Milo, but also to seize the dictatorship. However, he wished to receive it from the Senate, not from a mob of bludgeon-men. Pompey brought up troops to put down the anarchy in the capital, which had become intolerable to everybody. At the same time he now demanded what he had hitherto requested, and the Senate complied. It was merely an empty subterfuge that on the proposal of Cato and Bibulus the proconsul Pompey, retaining his former offices, was nominated as "consul without colleague" instead of dictator.

Thus in legal possession of full power, Pompey proceeded energetically against the republican party which was powerful in the clubs and the jury courts. The existing enactments as to elections were repeated and enforced by a special law, while another one, retroactive to 70 B.C., increased the penalties hitherto imposed. Still more important was the enactment that the governorships, by far the more important and especially the more lucrative half of official life, should be conferred on the consuls and praetors only after a waiting period of five years. Such an arrangement of course could only take effect after four years, which made the filling of the governorships during that period substantially dependent on special decrees of Senate, and thus in turn practically on the person or group ruling the Senate at the moment.

The jury commissions were left in existence, but limits were put to the right of counter-plea, and (perhaps still more important) freedom of speech in the courts was limited; for both the number of the advocates and the length of speeches were restricted by setting a maximum, and the prevailing bad practice of adducing character witnesses in favor of the accused, in addition to the witnesses as to the facts, was prohibited. The obsequious Senate further decreed, on Pompey's suggestion, that the nation had been endangered by the quarrel on the Appian Way. Accordingly, a special commission was appointed for all crimes connected with it, the members of which were directly nominated by Pompey. An attempt was also made to give the office of censor a serious importance once more, and thereby to purge the deeply disordered citizenry of the worst rabble.

All these measures were adopted under pressure of the sword. In consequence of the Senate's declaration that the country was in danger, Pompey called to arms the men capable of service throughout Italy and made them swear allegiance for all contingencies. An adequate and trustworthy corps was temporarily stationed at the Capitol, and at every stirring of opposition Pompey threatened armed intervention. During the proceedings at the trial regarding Clodius' murder a guard was stationed, contrary to all precedent, over the place of trial itself.

The scheme for reviving the censorship failed, because among the servile majority of the Senate no one possessed sufficient moral courage and authority even to become a candidate. On the other hand Milo was condemned by the jurymen (on April 8, 52 B.C.), and Cato's candidacy for the consulship the following year was frustrated. The literary opposition received through the new judicial ordinance a blow from which it never recovered, for the dreaded forensic eloquence was thereby driven from the field of politics, and thus felt the restraints of monarchy. Of course, opposition had not disappeared either from the minds of the great majority of the nation or even wholly from public life: to effect that end the popular elections, the jury courts, and literature must have been not merely restricted, but annihilated. Indeed, in these very transactions Pompey by his unskilfulness and perversity helped the republicans to gain even under his dictatorship several triumphs which he felt severely.

The special measures which the rulers took to strengthen their power were of course officially characterized as enactments made on behalf of public tranquility and order, and every citizen who did not desire anarchy was described as substantially concurring in them. But Pompey pushed this transparent fiction so far that instead of putting safe partisans on the special commission for investigating the recent tumult, he chose the most respectable men of all parties, even including Cato. He also applied his influence over the court primarily to maintain order, and to make it impossible for his adherents as well as for his opponents to indulge in the disturbances customary in the courts of this period.

This neutrality of the regent was recognizable in the verdicts of the special court. The jurymen did not venture to acquit Milo himself. However, most of the subordinate defendants belonging to the republican opposition were acquitted, while condemnation inexorably befell those who had aided Clodius (or in other words the regents) including not a few of Caesar's and Pompey's own most intimate friends—even Hypsaeus, his candidate for the consulship, and the tribunes of the people Plancus and Rufus, who had directed the riot in Pompey's interest.

That Pompey did not prevent their condemnation, in the interest of appearing impartial, was one specimen of his folly. A second was that in unimportant matters he violated his own laws to favor his friends, for example appearing as a character witness in the trial of Plancus, and in fact protecting from condemnation several accused persons such as Metellus Scipio who were closely connected with him. As usual, here also he wished to accomplish opposite things. In attempting to satisfy simultaneously the duties of the impartial regent and of the party chief, he fulfilled neither the one nor the other, being justly regarded by public opinion as a despot, and with equal justice by his adherents as a leader who either could not or would not protect his followers.

But although the republicans were still stirring and were even refreshed by an isolated success here and there, chiefly through the blunders of Pompey, the regency's objective in proposing the dictatorship was largely at-

tained, the reins were drawn tighter, the republican party
was humbled, and the new monarchy was strengthened.
The public began to reconcile itself to the latter. When
Pompey recovered from a serious illness, his restoration
was celebrated throughout Italy with the accompanying
demonstrations of joy which are usual on such occasions
in monarchies. The regents showed themselves satisfied.
On August 2, 52 B.C., Pompey resigned his dictatorship
and shared the consulship with his friend Metellus Scipio.

Drawing of Julius Caesar at beginning of chapter, Bettmann Archive

Even before Pompey's temporary assumption of the political dictatorship, however, the ruling triumvirate had been reduced to a simple partnership by the death of Crassus in one of the fateful campaigns of Roman history. The conference at Luca in 56 B.C. had given Crassus the governorship of Syria, together with an army thought sufficient to regulate affairs in the East. When he arrived in Syria early in 54 B.C. he found that hostilities had already begun with the Parthians, partly because of Pompey's failure to arrange a workable peace with the Parthian state. But even Crassus' burning ambition to become a great conqueror did not prevent him from pausing for months in Asia Minor to despoil a few rich temples and carry out other lucrative schemes, and not until 53 B.C. did he lead his army into the field.

Crassus made the fatal decision to march his army straight across the desert to reach the Parthian forces reportedly poised for flight. This error was matched by an equally significant tactical decision by the Parthians, to dispense entirely with their infantry in favor of heavily armored cavalry. In two successive desert battles at Carrhae and Sinnaca the Roman army of 40,000 was utterly destroyed, less than one-fourth escaping death or capture; and among the slain was Crassus. This signal proof that a well-led Asiatic army on the right terrain was more than a match for the hitherto invincible legions seemed to shake the Roman supremacy throughout the East. But political dissension among the Parthians, plus better Roman leadership in a theater of war quite different from the uncharted desert, enabled the Romans to turn back the Parthian invasion of western Asia Minor and once again stabilize the Roman rule there.

In Rome, meanwhile, the volcano of revolution was again whirling upward its clouds of stupefying smoke. The Romans began to have no longer a soldier or a de-

narius to be employed against the public foe, no longer a
thought of the destinies of nations. One of the most dreadful signs of the times was that the huge national disaster
of Carrhae and Sinnaca gave the politicians of that day
far less concern than the wretched tumult on the Appian
road in which, a couple of months after Crassus, Clodius
the partisan leader perished; but it is easily conceivable
and almost excusable. The breach between the two regents, long felt as inevitable and often announced as near,
was now assuming a terrifying immediacy. Like the boat
of the ancient Greek mariners' tale, the Roman ship of
state now found itself between two great rocks moving
towards each other. Its crew, expecting at any moment the
crash of collision, was paralyzed by nameless dread as
they were borne deeper into the whirlpool; and all eyes
were fastened there as no one gave a glance to the right
or the left.

After Caesar had at the conference of Luca made considerable concessions to Pompey, and the regents had thus
placed themselves substantially on an equal footing, their
relation was not without the outward appearance of dura-
bility—so far as a division of the monarchical power can
ever be lasting. It was another question whether the regents, at least for the present, were determined to keep
together and mutually to acknowledge without reservation their rank as equals. That this was the case with Caesar, insofar as he had acquired the interval necessary
for the conquest of Gaul at the price of equalization with
Pompey, has been already set forth. But Pompey was
hardly ever, even provisionally, a true partner in the joint
enterprise. His was one of those mean and petty natures
towards which it is dangerous to practice generosity. To
his paltry spirit it appeared certainly a point of prudence
to supplant at the first opportunity his reluctantly acknowledged rival, and his mean soul thirsted after retaliation on Caesar for the humiliation which he had suffered
through Caesar's indulgence.

But while it is probable that Pompey, in keeping with his dull and sluggish nature, never formally consented to let Caesar assume an equal rank, yet the design of breaking up the alliance doubtless grew upon him little by little. At any rate the public, which usually saw through Pompey's views and intentions better than he did himself, could not be mistaken in thinking that with the death of the beautiful Julia (who died in the bloom of womanhood in the autumn of 54 B.C., and was soon followed to the tomb by her only child) the personal tie between her father and her husband was broken. Caesar attempted to re-establish these ties by asking for himself the hand of Pompey's only daughter, and offered Octavia, his sister's grand-daughter, who was now his nearest relative, in marriage to his fellow regent. But Pompey left his daughter to her existing husband Faustus Sulla, the son of Lucius Sulla, and he himself married the daughter of Quintus Metellus Scipio.

The personal breach had unmistakably begun, and it was Pompey who drew back his hand. The populace expected that a political breach would soon follow; but the understanding continued for a time to exist, at least in public affairs. The reason was that Caesar did not wish publicly to dissolve the relation before completing the conquest of Gaul, and Pompey did not wish to dissolve it before the governing authorities and Italy were entirely humbled by his receipt of the dictatorship. It is novel but understandable that under these circumstances the regents supported each other. After the near-disaster of Aduatuca in Gaul in 54 B.C., Pompey lent Caesar one of his Italian legions that had been dismissed on furlough, while Caesar granted his consent and his moral support to Pompey in the repressive measures which the latter took against the stubborn republican opposition.

Only after Pompey had procured at the beginning of 52 B.C. the undivided consulship and an influence in the capital outweighing that of Caesar, and after all the men capable of bearing arms in Italy had tendered their military oath to him personally and in his name, did he resolve to break formally with Caesar as soon as possible. The design quickly became quite apparent. That the prosecutions which followed the tumult on the Appian Way landed with harsh and unerring severity on Caesar's old democratic partisans might perhaps pass as mere awkwardness. That the new law against electioneering intrigues, which was retroactive to 70 B.C., included also the dubious proceedings in Caesar's campaign for the consulship might likewise be nothing more, although not a few Caesarians thought that they perceived in it a definite design.

But people could no longer shut their eyes, however willing they might be to do so, when Pompey did not select as his consular colleague his former father-in-law, as was fitting under the circumstances and was demanded in many quarters, but chose his new father-in-law Scipio, a puppet wholly dependent on him. Still less could they ignore it when Pompey got the governorship of the two Spains continued to him for five more years (that is, to 45 B.C.), plus a considerable sum appropriated from the state chest for the payment of his troops—not only without securing for Caesar a like prolongation of command and a similar grant of money, but even while laboring to effect Caesar's recall before the end of the agreed-upon term.

These encroachments were unmistakably calculated to undermine Caesar's position and eventually overthrow him. The moment could not be more favorable. Caesar had conceded so much to Pompey at Luca only because Crassus and his Syrian army would necessarily, in the event of any rupture with Pompey, be thrown into Caesar's scale; for Crassus, who since Sulla's day had been deeply hostile to Pompey and almost as long politically and personally allied with Caesar, and whose peculiar character would have made him content with being the new king's banker, could always be counted on by Caesar, who could have no apprehension at all of seeing Crassus confronting him as an ally of his enemies. The catastrophe of June of 53 B.C., by which Crassus and his army perished in Syria, was therefore a terribly severe blow for Caesar also. A few months later the national insurrection in Gaul, just when it had seemed completely subdued, blazed up more violently than ever, and Caesar for the first time was pitted against an equal opponent in the Arvernian king Vercingetorix.

Once again fate had been working for Pompey. Crassus was dead, all Gaul was in revolt, Pompey was practically dictator of Rome and master of the Senate. What might have happened if now, instead of merely intriguing against Caesar, he had compelled the citizens or the Senate to recall Caesar at once! But Pompey never understood how to take advantage of fortune. He heralded the breach clearly enough: already in 52 B.C. his acts left no doubt about it, and in the spring of the following year he openly expressed his intention to break with Caesar. But he did not make the break, and allowed months to slip away unemployed.

But however Pompey might delay, the crisis was incessantly urged on by the force of circumstances. The impending war was not a struggle between republic and monarchy (for that had been virtually decided years before) but a struggle between Pompey and Caesar for the possession of the crown of Rome. However, neither of the pretenders could have profited by uttering this plain truth, which would merely have driven into the opposing camp all those respectable citizens who desired the continuance of the republic and believed in its possibility. The old battle cries of Gracchus and Drusus, Cinna and Sulla, worn and meaningless as they were, still remained good enough for watchwords in the struggle of the two generals contending for the sole rule; and though for the moment both Pompey and Caesar ranked themselves officially with the so-called popular party, it was a foregone conclusion that Caesar would inscribe on his banner the people and democratic progress, Pompey the aristocracy and the legitimate constitution.

Caesar had no choice. He had from the outset been an earnest democrat. The monarchy as he envisioned it differed more in outward form than in reality from the Gracchan government of the people; and he was too magnanimous and too profound a statesman to conceal his colors and to fight under any other flag than his own. The immediate advantage which this battle cry brought to him was doubtless trifling: it was confined mainly to the circumstance that he was thereby relieved of the inconvenience of directly naming the kingly office, and thus alarming his own adherents and the mass of the lukewarm by that detested word. The democratic banner yielded little further positive gain, since the ideals of Gracchus had been rendered infamous and ridiculous by Clodius. Where was there now (with the possible exception of the Transpadanes) any important group which would have been induced by democratic battle cries to take part in the struggle?

This state of affairs would have decided Pompey's part in the impending struggle, even if it had not been self-evident that he could enter it only as the general of the legitimate republic. Nature had destined him above all men to be a member of an aristocracy, and nothing but accident and selfish motives had carried him into the democratic camp as a deserter. That he should now revert to his Sullan traditions was not merely fitting, but in every way advantageous. Threadbare as was the democratic cry, the conservative slogan could not but have the more potent effect if it proceeded from the right man. Perhaps the majority, at any rate the best of the citizens, belonged to the constitutional party; and its numerical and moral strength might well influence powerfully, perhaps decisively, the impending struggle of the pretenders.

All that was lacking was a leader. Marcus Cato, its present head, fulfilled the functions of leadership (as he understood them) amid daily peril to his life and perhaps without hope of success. His fidelity to duty deserves respect, but to be the last at a forlorn post is commendable in the soldier, not in the general. He lacked the skill either to organize or to bring into timely action the powerful reserve which had sprung up almost spontaneously in Italy for the party of the overthrown government. For good reason he had never made any pretension to military leadership, on which everything ultimately depended. If instead of this man, who knew not how to act either as party chief or general, a leader of the political and military stature of Pompey should raise the banner of the existing constitution, the citizens of Italy would necessarily flock towards it in crowds, that under it they might help to fight against the kingship of Caesar if not for the kingship of Pompey.

To this was added another consideration at least as important. It was characteristic of Pompey, even when he had formed a resolve, not to be able to find his way to its execution. While he knew perhaps how to conduct war but certainly not how to declare it, the Catonian party, although assuredly unable to conduct it, was able and most willing to supply grounds for the war against the impending monarchy. According to Pompey's intention, he would keep himself aloof and in his peculiar way now talk as though he would immediately depart for his Spanish provinces, now make preparations as though he would set out to take over the command on the Euphrates. Meanwhile the legitimate governing board, the Senate, was to break with Caesar, declare war against him, and entrust the conduct of it to Pompey. Then, yielding to the general desire, he was to come forward as the protector of the constitution against demagogic-monarchical plots, as an upright man and champion of the existing order of things against the profligates and anarchists, as the duly installed gen-

eral of the Senate against the Imperator of the street, and
so once more save his country.

Thus Pompey gained by the alliance with the conservatives a second army (in addition to his personal adherents) and a suitable war manifesto—advantages, to be
sure, which were purchased at the high price of combining with those who were in principle opposed to him. Of
the countless evils involved in this coalition, the only immediate one (though a very grave one) was that Pompey
surrendered the power of commencing hostilities against
Caesar when and how he pleased, and made himself dependent on all the accidents and caprices of an aristocratic
corporation.

Thus the republican opposition, after having been
obliged for years to play the mere spectator with no more
voice than a whisper, was now brought back onto the political stage by the impending rupture between the regents.
It consisted primarily of the men rallied round Cato, who
were resolved in any case to struggle for the republic and
against the monarchy, and the sooner the better. The pitiful outcome of the attempt made in 56 B.C. had taught
them that by themselves they were in a position neither
to conduct war nor even to begin it. It was known to everyone that while the entire Senate was with a few isolated exceptions averse to monarchy, the majority would
restore the oligarchic government only if it might be restored without danger—in which case there would be a
long time to wait.

Faced by the regents on the one hand, and on the other
by this indolent majority which above all things desired
peace at any price, and which was averse to any decided
action and most of all to a rupture with one or other of
the regents, the only possible way for Cato's group to restore the old rule lay in a coalition with the less dangerous
of the rulers. If Pompey acknowledged the oligarchic constitution and offered to fight for it against Caesar, the republican opposition must recognize him as its general, and

in alliance with him compel the timid majority to a declaration of war. That Pompey was scarcely earnest in his fidelity to the constitution could indeed escape nobody. But undecided as he was in everything, he had by no means arrived at Caesar's clear and firm conviction that the first business of the new monarch must be to sweep away once and for all the oligarchic lumber. In any event the war would train a really republican army and really republican generals. After the victory over Caesar there would be more favorable prospects of setting aside not merely one of the monarchs, but the monarchy itself. Desperate as was the cause of the oligarchy, Pompey's offer to become its ally was the most favorable arrangement possible for it.

The alliance between Pompey and the Catonian party was concluded with comparative rapidity. Already during the dictatorship of Pompey a remarkable rapprochement had taken place between them. His whole behavior in the Milonian crisis, his abrupt repulse of the mob that offered him the dictatorship, his distinct declaration that he would accept this office only from the Senate, his unrelenting severity against all disturbers of the peace and especially against the ultrademocrats, the surprising complaisance with which he treated Cato and those who shared Cato's views, appeared as much calculated to please the men of order as to offend Caesar. On their side Cato and his followers, instead of combating with their wonted sternness the proposal to confer the dictatorship on Pompey, had made it their own with but trifling changes of form, so that Pompey received the undivided consulship primarily from the hands of Bibulus and Cato.

While the Catonian party and Pompey had thus at least a tacit understanding as early as the beginning of 52 B.C., the alliance was in effect formally concluded when the consular elections for 51 B.C. went not to Cato himself, but (along with an insignificant man belonging to the Senate majority) to one of Cato's most decided ad-

herents, Marcus Claudius Marcellus. Marcellus was no
furious zealot and still less a genius, but a steadfast and
strict aristocrat, just the right man to declare war if war
was to be begun with Caesar. Under the circumstances this
election, so surprising after the recent repression of the republican opposition, can hardly have occurred without the
consent or at least the tacit permission of the regent of
Rome. Slowly and clumsily, as was his wont, but steadily
Pompey moved toward the rupture.

On the other hand it was not Caesar's intention to fall
out with Pompey at this moment. He could not indeed
seriously desire to share the ruling power permanently
with any colleague, least of all with a second-rater like
Pompey. Beyond doubt he had long resolved after the
conquest of Gaul to take the sole power for himself, if
need be by force of arms. But a man like Caesar, in whom
the officer was thoroughly subordinate to the statesman,
could not fail to perceive that regulating the political organism by force of arms also disorganizes it deeply and
often permanently. Therefore he could not but seek to
solve the difficulty, if at all possible, without open civil
war. And even if civil war were unavoidable, he could not
wish to be driven to it when the rising of Vercingetorix
in Gaul, imperiling all that had been obtained, occupied
him without interruption from the winter of 53-52 B.C.
to the winter of 52-51 B.C., and when Pompey and the
constitutional party were dominant in Italy.

Accordingly he sought to preserve relations with Pompey and to attain, by peaceful means if at all possible, to
the consulship for 48 B.C. that had already been promised to him at Luca. If after a conclusive settlement of
Celtic affairs he should then be placed at the head of the
state, the decided superiority which he held over Pompey
even more as a statesman than as a general might enable
him to outmaneuver the latter in the senate house and in
the Forum without special difficulty. Perhaps it was possible to find for his awkward, vacillating, and arrogant ri-

val some sort of honorable and influential position where he might be content to sink into obscurity. The repeated attempts of Caesar to keep himself related to Pompey by marriage may have been designed to pave the way for such a solution, and to settle the old quarrel through the succession of offspring inheriting the blood of both competitors. The republican opposition would then remain without a leader and therefore probably quiet, and peace would be preserved.

If this should not be successful, and if there should be (as was certainly possible) a necessity for resorting to arms, Caesar would as consul in Rome dispose of the compliant majority of the Senate. He could then impede or perhaps frustrate the coalition of the Pompeians and the republicans, and conduct the war far more suitably and more advantageously than if now as proconsul of Gaul he gave orders to march against the Senate and its general. Certainly the success of this plan depended on Pompey being good-natured enough to let Caesar still obtain the consulship for 48 B.C. assured to him at Luca. But even if it failed, it would have the advantage that Caesar had given practical and repeated evidence of the most yielding disposition. On the one hand time would thus be gained for attaining his objectives in Gaul, while on the other his opponents would be left with the odium of initiating the rupture and consequently the civil war—which was of the utmost importance for Caesar with respect to the majority of the Senate and the mercantile party, and even more with regard to his own soldiers.

On these views he acted. To be sure, through new levies in the winter of 52-51 B.C. he increased the number of his legions to eleven, including the one borrowed from Pompey. But at the same time he expressly and openly approved of Pompey's conduct during the dictatorship and the restoration of order in the capital, rejected the warnings of officious friends as calumnies, reckoned every day by which he succeeded in postponing the conflict a gain, overlooked whatever could be overlooked and bore whatever could be borne. He adhered immovably only to one decisive demand: that when his governorship expired at the end of 49 B.C. he should have his second consulship, permissible under the law and promised to him by his colleague.

This demand became the battlefield of the diplomatic war which now began. If Caesar were compelled either to resign his office of governor before the last day of December, 49 B.C., or to postpone the assumption of the consulship in the capital beyond January 1st, there would be a gap between the governorship and the consulate when he would be without office and consequently liable to criminal impeachment—which according to law could not be brought against one who was in office. In such event the public had good reason to prophesy for him the fate of Milo, because Cato had for long been ready to impeach him and Pompey was a more than doubtful protector.

To attain that object Caesar's opponents had a very simple device. According to the election laws every candidate for the consulship was obliged to appear personally before the presiding magistrate for his name to be inscribed in the official list of candidates before the election —that is, half a year before entering an office. It had probably been taken for granted in the conferences at Luca that Caesar would be released from this obligation, which was purely formal and was very often dispensed with. But the decree to that effect had not yet been issued, and, as Pompey now controlled the official machinery, Caesar depended in this respect on the good will of his rival.

Pompey incomprehensibly abandoned this completely secure position of his own accord. With his consent and during his dictatorship the personal appearance of Caesar was dispensed with by a tribunician law. However, when the new election laws were issued soon afterwards, the obligation of candidates to appear personally was repeated in general terms, and no exception was added in favor of those exempted by earlier legislation. Strictly speaking, the privilege granted to Caesar was canceled by the later general law. Caesar complained, and the requisite clause was subsequently added but not confirmed by special decree of the people, so that this enactment by mere insertion could only be looked on *de jure* as null and void. Where Pompey, therefore, might have simply stuck to the law, he preferred first to make a spontaneous concession, then to recall it, and lastly to cloak this recall in a most disloyal manner.

While in this way the shortening of Caesar's governorship was attempted indirectly, the regulations as to governorships issued at the same time sought the same object directly. The ten years for which the governorship had been granted to Caesar, in the last instance through the law proposed by Pompey himself together with Crassus, ran according to the usual mode of reckoning from March 1, 59 B.C., to the last day of February, 49 B.C. However, according to the earlier practice, the proconsul or propraetor had the right of taking over his provincial post immediately after the termination of his consulship or praetorship. Thus the successor of Caesar was to be nominated not from the urban magistrates of 50 B.C., but from those of 49 B.C., who therefore could not take over before January 1st, 48 B.C. So far Caesar still had during the last ten months of the year 49 B.C. a right to his command, not on the ground of the Pompeio-Licinian law, but according to the old rule that a command with a set term still continued after its expiration until the arrival of the successor. But now the new legislation of 52 B.C. granted the governorships not to the outgoing consuls and praetors, but to those who had served five or more years ago. This interval between the civil magistracy and the command, instead of the previous immediate sequence, made it no longer difficult to fill every legally vacant governorship immediately, so that the change of command for the Gallic provinces could take place on March 1, 49 B.C., instead of January 1 of 48 B.C.

The pitiful dissimulation and procrastinating artifice of Pompey are mixed in these arrangements in a remarkable manner with the wily formalism and the constitutional erudition of the republican party. Years before these legal weapons could be used they had been duly prepared, on the one hand to compel Caesar, by sending his successors, to resign his command on the day when his term under Pompey's own law expired (that is, on March 1), and on the other hand, if Caesar declined to resign, to enable the Senate to treat as null and void any votes cast for him in the elections. Caesar, not in a position to hinder these moves in the game, kept silent and let things take their own course.

Gradually the slow constitutional procedure unfolded itself. According to custom the Senate had to deliberate on the governorships of the year 49 B.C., so far as they went to former consuls, at the beginning of 51 B.C., and so far as they went to former praetors, at the beginning of 50 B.C. That earlier deliberation gave the first occasion to discuss the nomination of new governors for the two Gauls in the Senate, and thus the first occasion for open collision between the constitutional party supported by Pompey and the senatorial supporters of Caesar. The consul Marcus Marcellus accordingly introduced a proposal to give the two Gallic provinces as of March 1, 49 B.C., to the two consulars who were to be provided with governorships for that year.

The long-repressed indignation burst forth in a torrent once the sluice was opened, and everything that the Catonians were meditating against Caesar came forth in open discussion. For them it was a settled point that the right granted Caesar by exceptional law to announce his candidacy for the consulship *in absentia* had been canceled by a subsequent decree of the people, and that the reservation inserted in the latter was invalid. The Senate should in their opinion instruct this magistrate, now that the subjugation of Gaul was completed, to discharge immediately the soldiers who had served out their time. The cases where Caesar had bestowed citizenship rights and established colonies in Upper Italy were described by them as unconstitutional. In confirmation of this view Marcellus ordained that a respected senator of the Caesarian colony of Comum, who was entitled to lay claim to Roman citizenship even if his city had only Latin rights, should receive the punishment of scourging, which was admissible only in the case of noncitizens.

Caesar's supporters (among whom the most notable was Galus Vibius Panou, formerly an officer in Caesar's army and now tribune of the people) affirmed in the Senate that both equity and the state of Gallic affairs demanded not only that Caesar should not be recalled ahead of time, but that he should be allowed to retain the command along with the consulship. Beyond doubt they pointed out that a few years earlier Pompey had in the same way combined the Spanish governorships with the consulship; that even at the present time, besides the important office of superintending the supply of food to the capital, he held the supreme command in Italy in addition to the Spanish; and that in fact all the men of Italy capable of bearing arms had been sworn in by him and had not yet been released from their oath.

The process began to take shape, but by no means rapidly. The majority of the Senate, seeing the breach approaching, allowed no sitting capable of issuing a decree to take place for months, and further months were lost through the solemn procrastination of Pompey. At length the latter broke the silence and ranged himself, in his usual reserved and vacillating fashion but plainly enough, on the side of the constitutional party against his former ally. He summarily rejected the demand of the Caesarians that their master should be allowed to combine the consulship and the proconsulship. This demand, he added with blunt coarseness, seemed to him no better than if a son should offer to flog his father. He also approved in principle the proposal of Marcellus, insofar as he too declared that he would not allow Caesar directly to attach the consulship to the proconsulship.

However, he also hinted (although without making any binding declaration on the point) that they would perhaps grant Caesar admission to the elections for 49 B.C. without requiring a personal appearance, as well as the continuance of his governorship at the utmost to November 13, 49 B.C. But in the meantime the incorrigible procrastinator consented to the postponement of the nomination of successors to the last day of February, 50 B.C., which Caesar's representatives had asked probably on the ground of a clause of the Pompeio-Licinian law forbidding senatorial discussion of successors before the beginning of a magistrate's last year of office.

To this end the decrees of the Senate were issued on September 29, 51 B.C. The filling of the Gallic governorships was placed on the agenda for March 1, 50 B.C. But already the Senate was attempting to break up the army of Caesar (just as had formerly been done by decree of the people with the army of Lucullus) by inducing his veterans to apply to the Senate for their discharge. Caesar's supporters canceled these decrees, as far as they constitutionally could, by their tribunician veto. But Pompey distinctly declared that the magistrates were bound unconditionally to obey the Senate, and that intercessions and similar antiquated formalities would produce no change.

The aristocratic party, whose organ Pompey now made himself, thus betrayed its intention, in the event of a victory, of revising the constitution to remove everything which had even the semblance of popular freedom. Indeed, this was doubtless the reason why it did not avail itself of the comitia at all in its attacks against Caesar. The coalition between Pompey and the constitutional party was thus formally proclaimed, and sentence was evidently already passed on Caesar, with the date of its issuance simply postponed. The elections for the following year proved thoroughly adverse to him.

During these party maneuvers of his antagonists preparatory to war, Caesar had succeeded in quelling the Gallic insurrection and restoring peace in the whole subject territory. As early as the summer of 51 B.C., under the convenient pretext of defending the frontier but obviously because the legions in Gaul began to be unnecessary there, he moved one of them to northern Italy. He could not avoid perceiving now, if he had not earlier, that he would not be able to avoid drawing the sword against his fellow citizens. Nevertheless, as it was highly desirable to leave the legions for a further time in barely pacified Gaul, he still sought to procrastinate; and being well acquainted with the Senate majority's extreme love of peace, he did not abandon the hope of still restraining them from declaring war despite the pressure from Pompey.

He did not even hesitate to make great sacrifices, if only he might for the present avoid open variance with the supreme governing board. In the spring of 50 B.C. the Senate upon Pompey's suggestion requested that Pompey and Caesar each furnish a legion for the impending Parthian war, and in accordance with this resolution Pompey demanded back from Caesar the legion lent to him some years before, so as to send it also to Syria. Caesar complied with the double demand, because neither the opportuneness of the senatorial decree nor the justice of Pompey's demand could in themselves be disputed, and keeping within the bounds of the law and of formal loyalty was more important to Caesar than a few thousand soldiers. The two legions came without delay and placed themselves at the disposal of the government. However, instead of sending them to the Euphrates, the latter kept them at Capua in readiness for Pompey; and the public once more had the opportunity of comparing Caesar's conciliatory efforts with his opponent's perfidious preparation for war.

For the discussions with the Senate Caesar had succeeded in purchasing not only one of the two consuls of
the year, Lucius Aemilius Paullus, but above all the tribune of the people Gaius Curio, probably the most eminent
among the many outstanding profligates of this epoch.
He was unsurpassed in refined elegance, in fluent and
clever oratory, in dexterity of intrigue, and in that energy
which in the case of vigorous but vicious characters be-
stirs itself only the more powerfully amid the pauses of
idleness. He was also unsurpassed in the dissoluteness of
his life, in his talent for borrowing (his debts were estimated at 60,000,000 sesterces) and in his moral and political want of principle. He had previously offered himself to be bought by Caesar and had been rejected. The
talent which he thereafter displayed in his attacks on Caesar induced the latter to buy him up: the price was high,
but the commodity was worth the money.

In the first months of his tribunate Curio had played
the independent republican, and thundered against both
Caesar and Pompey. He cashed in with rare skill on the
apparently impartial position which this gave him, when
in March of 50 B.C. the proposal for filling the Gallic
governorships for the next year came up anew for discussion in the Senate. He expressed complete approval of
the decree, but asked that it should at the same time be
extended to Pompey and his extraordinary commands.
His arguments—that a constitutional state of things
could be brought about only by doing away with all exceptional positions, that Pompey as merely entrusted by
the Senate with the proconsulship could still less than
Caesar refuse obedience to it, and that the removal of but
one of the two generals would only increase the danger
to the constitution—carried complete conviction to superficial politicians and to the public at large. Further,
Curio's declaration that he intended to prevent any one-
sided proceedings against Caesar by the veto constitution-

ally belonging to him met with much approval in and out of the Senate.

Caesar at once consented to Curio's proposal and offered to resign his governorship and command at any moment, provided Pompey would do the same. (He might safely do so, for Pompey without his Italo-Spanish command was no longer formidable.) Pompey for that same reason could not avoid refusing. His reply—that Caesar must first resign, and that he meant speedily to follow the example thus set—was still more unsatisfactory in that he did not even specify a definite date for his retirement. Again the decision was delayed for months, as Pompey and the Catonians, perceiving the dubious humor of the majority of the Senate, did not venture to bring Curio's proposal to a vote. Caesar employed the summer in pacifying the regions which he had conquered, in holding a great review of his troops on the Scheldt, and in making a triumphal march through the province of North Italy, which was entirely devoted to him. Autumn found him in Ravenna, the southern frontier town of his province.

At length the vote on Curio's proposal could no longer be delayed, and it yielded a signal defeat of the party of Pompey and Cato. By a margin of 370 to 20 the Senate resolved that the proconsuls of Spain and Gaul should both be called upon to resign, and with boundless joy the good citizens of Rome heard the glad news of Curio's achievement. Pompey was thus recalled by the Senate no less than Caesar; but while Caesar was ready to comply with the command, Pompey flatly refused obedience. The presiding consul Gaius Marcellus, cousin of Marcus Marcellus and like the latter belonging to the Catonian party, addressed a severe lecture to the servile senatorial majority; it was certainly vexatious to be beaten in their own camp, and beaten by a phalanx of poltroons. But where was victory to come from under a leader who, instead of bluntly dictating his orders to the senators, resorted in his later years once more to the instructions of a professor of rhetoric, that with rekindled eloquence he might encounter the youthful vigor and brilliant talents of Curio?

The coalition, thus defeated in the Senate, was in a most painful position. The Catonian section, which had undertaken to push matters to a rupture and to carry the Senate along with them, now saw their vessel vexingly stranded on the sandbanks of the indolent majority. Their leaders had to listen to the bitterest reproaches from Pompey. He pointed out emphatically and with entire justice the dangers of the seeming peace; and though it depended on himself alone to cut the knot by rapid action, his allies knew very well that they could never expect this from him, and that it was for them to fulfill their promise of bringing matters to a crisis. After the champions of the constitution and of senatorial government had already declared the constitutional rights of the citizens and of the tribunes of the people to be meaningless formalities, they now found themselves driven by necessity to treat the constitutional decisions of the Senate itself in a similar manner and, as the legitimate government would not let itself be saved with its own consent, to save it against its will. This was nothing new; both Sulla and Lucullus had been obliged to carry every energetic resolution conceived in the interest of the government with a high hand irrespective of it, just as Cato and his friends now proposed to do. The machinery of the constitution was in fact utterly obsolete, and the Senate was now (as the comitia had been for centuries) nothing but a worn-out wheel slipping constantly out of its track.

It was rumored in October of 50 B.C. that Caesar had moved four legions from Transalpine into Cisalpine Gaul and stationed them at Placentia. This transfer of troops was within the prerogative of the governor; Curio moreover proved to the Senate the utter groundlessness of the rumor; and that body rejected the proposal of the consul Gaius Marcellus to give Pompey orders to march against Caesar on the strength of it. Yet Marcellus, in concert with the two consuls elected for 49 B.C. who likewise belonged to the Catonian party, by virtue of their own official authority requested the general to put himself at the head of the two legions stationed at Capua, and to call the Italian militia to arms at his discretion. A more casual authorization for beginning a civil war can hardly be conceived, but people had no longer time to trouble over such secondary matters, and Pompey accepted the mission. The military preparations began, and Pompey left the capital in December of 50 B.C. in order personally to forward them.

Caesar had completely attained his object of putting the onus for starting the civil war on his opponents. He had, while himself keeping on legal ground, compelled Pompey to declare war, and to declare it not as representative of the legitimate authority, but as general of an openly revolutionary minority of the Senate which had overawed the majority. This result was not to be reckoned of slight importance, although the masses were not deceived for a moment as to the fact that the war concerned other things than questions of formal law. Now that war had been declared, it was to Caesar's interest to strike as soon as possible. His opponents were just beginning to mobilize, and even the capital was not occupied. In ten or twelve days an army three times as strong as Caesar's troops in Upper Italy could be collected at Rome; but it might not be impossible to surprise the undefended city, or even perhaps by a rapid winter campaign to seize all Italy, and thus preempt the best resources of his opponents before they could be brought to bear.

The sagacious and energetic Curio, who after resigning his tribunate had immediately gone to Caesar at Ravenna, vividly represented this state of affairs to his master—though Caesar hardly needed convincing that longer delay now could only be injurious. However, to forestall any complaints by his antagonists he had brought no troops to Ravenna itself. Thus he could do nothing for the present but order his whole force to set out posthaste; and he had to wait till at least the one legion stationed in Upper Italy reached Ravenna. Meanwhile he sent a communication to Rome which by its extreme submissiveness still further compromised his opponents in public opinion, and perhaps even, by his show of hesitation, tempted them to slacken their preparations against him.

In this communication Caesar dropped all the counter-demands which he formerly made on Pompey, and offered both to resign the governorship of Transalpine Gaul, and to dismiss eight of his ten legions, at the term fixed by the Senate. He declared himself content if the Senate would grant him either the governorship of Cisalpine Gaul and Illyria with one legion, or that of Cisalpine Gaul alone with two, not until his accession to the consulship, but only until after the close of the consular elections for 48 B.C. Thus he consented to those proposals which at the beginning of the discussions the senatorial party and even Pompey himself had pronounced satisfactory, and showed himself ready to remain in a private position between his election to the consulship and his accession to office.

Whether Caesar was in earnest in these astonishing concessions; whether he had confidence that he would be able to win against Pompey even after granting so much; or whether he reckoned that his opponents had already gone too far to find in these conciliatory proposals more than a proof that Caesar regarded his own cause as lost—can no longer be determined with certainty. The likelihood is that Caesar committed the fault of playing too bold a game, rather than the worse fault of promising something he did not intend to perform. If, strangely

enough, his proposals had been accepted, he would probably have made good his word.

Curio undertook once more to represent his master in
the lion's den. In three days he made the journey from
Ravenna to Rome. When the new consuls Lucius Lentulus
and Gaius Marcellus the younger assembled the Senate
for the first time on January 1, 49 B.C., Curio delivered
in a full meeting the letter addressed by the general to
the Senate. In Curio's absence, the leadership of the Caesarian party in Rome had devolved upon the tribunes
Marcus Antonius [Mark Antony], well known to the city
gossip-chroniclers as Curio's friend and accomplice in
all his follies, but also as a brilliant cavalry officer in the
Egyptian and Gallic campaigns, and Quintus Cassius,
Pompey's former quaestor. Both insisted on the immediate reading of the dispatch. The grave and clear words
in which Caesar set forth, with all the irresistible force of
truth, the imminence of civil war, the general wish for
peace, the arrogance of Pompey, and his own yielding disposition; the proposals for compromise whose moderation doubtless surprised his own partisans; the distinct
declaration that this was the last time that he should offer
his hand for peace—all these made the deepest impression.

In spite of the dread inspired by the numerous soldiers
of Pompey who flocked into the capital, the sentiment of
the majority was so unmistakable that the consuls did
not dare to let it find expression. Regarding Caesar's renewed proposal that both generals resign their commands
simultaneously, regarding all the conciliatory suggestions
in his letter, and regarding the proposal made by Marcus
Caelius Rufus and Marcus Calidius that Pompey be urged
to depart immediately for Spain, the consuls refused to
permit a vote—as in their capacity of presiding officers
they were entitled to do. Even the proposal to defer a decision until the Italian levy was called up and could pro-

tect the Senate—made by Marcus Marcellus, who although a vehement partisan was simply not so blind to
military realities as his party—was not allowed to be
brought to a vote. Pompey let it be known through his
usual mouthpiece, Quintus Scipio, that he was determined
to take up the cause of the Senate now or never, and that
he would let it drop if they delayed longer. The consul
Lentulus said flatly that even the decision of the Senate
was no longer controlling, and that if it should persevere
in its cowardice, he would himself act and with his powerful friends take the necessary steps.

Thus overawed, the majority decreed what was commanded. Caesar was ordered at a definite and not distant
day to give up Transalpine Gaul to Lucius Domitius
Ahenobarbus, and Cisalpine Gaul to Marcus Servilius
Nonianus, and to dismiss his army, failing which he
should be regarded a traitor. When the tribunes of Caesar's party made use of their right of veto against this
resolution, not only were they (as they at least asserted)
threatened in the senate house itself by the swords of
Pompeian soldiers, and forced, in order to save their
lives, to flee in slaves' clothing from the capital: the sufficiently overawed Senate also treated their constitutional
interferences as an attempt at revolution, declared the
country in danger, and in the usual forms called the whole
citizenry to take up arms and all magistrates faithful to
the constitution to place themselves at the head of the
armies.

Now it was enough. When Caesar was informed by the
tribunes who had fled to his camp of the reception which
his proposals had met in the capital, he called together the
soldiers of the thirteenth legion, which meanwhile had
arrived from its cantonments near Tergeste (Trieste)
at Ravenna, and unfolded before them the state of things.
It was not merely the man of genius versed in the knowledge of men's hearts, whose brilliant eloquence shone
forth in this gripping crisis of his own and the world's

destiny. It was not even the generous and victorious commander-in-chief addressing soldiers whom he himself had called to arms, and who for eight years had followed his banners with daily increasing enthusiasm. There spoke, above all, the energetic and consistent statesman, who had now for nine-and-twenty years defended the cause of freedom in good times and bad; who had braved for it the daggers of assassins and the executioners of the aristocracy, the swords of the Germans and the waves of the unknown ocean, without ever yielding or wavering; who had torn to pieces the Sullan constitution, overthrown the rule of the Senate, and furnished the defenseless and unarmed democracy with protection and arms by means of the struggle beyond the Alps. And he spoke not to the Roman public, whose republican enthusiasm had been long burnt down to ashes and dross, but to the young men from the towns and villages of Northern Italy, who still felt freshly and purely the mighty influence of the thought of civic freedom; who were still capable of fighting and dying for ideals; who had themselves received for their country in a revolutionary way from Caesar the citizenship which the Roman government had refused; whom Caesar's fall would leave once more at the mercy of the fasces, and who already possessed practical proofs of how the oligarchy proposed to use these against the Transpadanes.

Such were the listeners before whom such an orator pointed out the thanks which the nobility were preparing for the general and his army in return for the conquest of Gaul; the contemptuous setting aside of the comitia; the overawing of the Senate; the sacred duty of protecting with armed hand the tribunate of the people wrested five hundred years ago by their fathers arms in hand from the nobility, and of keeping the ancient oath, which their ancestors had sworn for themselves as for their children's children, that they would man by man stand firm even unto death for the tribunes of the people. And when he,

the leader and general of the popular party, summoned
the soldiers of the people, now that conciliatory means
had been exhausted and concession had reached its utmost
limits, to follow him in the last, the inevitable, the decisive struggle against the equally hated and despised,
equally perfidious and incapable, and in fact ludicrously
incorrigible aristocracy, not an officer or a soldier could
hold back. The order was given for the march. At the
head of his vanguard Caesar crossed the narrow brook
separating his province from Italy, which the constitution
forbade the proconsul of Gaul to pass. When after nine
years' absence he trod once more the soil of his native
land, he trod at the same time the path of revolution.
"The die was cast."

Arms were thus to decide which of the two men who had jointly ruled Rome was to be its first sole ruler. Let us see what were Caesar's and Pompey's comparative resources for waging the impending war.

Caesar's power rested primarily on the unlimited authority which he enjoyed in his own party. If the ideas of democracy and of monarchy met together in it, this was not the result of an accidentally formed coalition which might be accidentally dissolved. On the contrary, the very nature of a democracy without a representative constitution demanded that democracy and monarchy should find their highest and ultimate expression in Caesar. In political as in military matters the first and the final decision lay with Caesar. However highly he honored any serviceable instrument, it remained an instrument still. In his own party Caesar was surrounded not by confederates but by military-political adjutants, who as a rule had risen from the army, and who as soldiers were trained never to ask the reason why but unconditionally to obey. For this reason, at the outbreak of the civil war only one of Caesar's officers and soldiers refused him obedience; and the fact that that one was the foremost of all serves simply to confirm this view of Caesar's relation to his adherents.

Titus Labienus had shared all Caesar's troubles of the dark times of Catiline as well as all the luster of the Gallic conquest. He had regularly held independent command, and frequently led half the army. As the oldest, ablest, and most faithful of Caesar's adjutants, he was also beyond question highest in position and honor. As late as 50 B.C. Caesar had entrusted to him the supreme command in Cisalpine Gaul, partly to put this confidential post into safe hands and partly to highlight the views of Labienus in his campaign for the consulship. But from this very position Labienus entered into communication with the opposite party, moved to Pompey's headquarters when hostilities began in 49 B.C., and fought through the whole struggle with unparalleled bitterness against his old friend and master.

We are not sufficiently informed either as to the character of Labienus or as to the special circumstances of his changing sides. In the main, however, his case certainly presents nothing but further proof of the fact that a military chief can rely far more confidently on his captains than on his marshals. To all appearances Labienus was one of those persons in whom military efficiency is combined with utter incapacity as statesmen. Consequently, if they unfortunately choose or are compelled to take part in politics, they exhibit those strange paroxysms of giddiness of which the history of Napoleon's marshals supplies so many tragicomic examples. He may well have felt himself entitled to rank alongside Caesar as the second chief of the democracy, and the rejection of his claim may have sent him over to the opposing camp. His case illustrated for the first time the gravity of the evil, that Caesar's treatment of his officers as mere adjutants did not permit the rise of men fitted to undertake a separate command, while at the same time he urgently needed such men amid the easily foreseeable spread of the struggle throughout the empire. But this disadvantage was far outweighed by that unity of leadership which was the primary condition of success, and a condition which could be preserved only at such a cost.

This unity of leadership acquired its full power through the efficiency of its instruments, first of all the army. It still numbered nine legions of infantry, or at the most 50,000 men. All of these, however, had faced the enemy, and two-thirds had served in all the campaigns against the Celts. The cavalry consisted of German and Noric mercenaries, whose usefulness and trustworthiness had been proved in the war against Vercingetorix. Eight years of the most varied warfare against the Celtic nation (which was brave, although militarily quite inferior to the Italian) had given Caesar the opportunity of organizing his army as he alone knew how to organize it.

The whole efficiency of the soldier presupposes physical vigor. In Caesar's levies more regard was had to the strength and activity of the recruits than to their means or morals. But the serviceableness of an army, like that of any other machine, depends above all on the ease and quickness of its movements; and the soldiers of Caesar attained a perfection rarely reached and probably never surpassed in their constant readiness for immediate departure and in their rapidity of marching. Courage, of course, was valued above everything. Caesar practiced with unrivaled mastery the art of stimulating *esprit de corps,* so that the eminence accorded to particular soldiers and divisions appeared desirable even to those who were lower in the hierarchy of valor. He weaned his men from fear by often—where it could be done without serious danger—keeping his soldiers ignorant of an approaching battle, allowing them to meet the enemy unexpectedly.

But obedience was on a parity with valor. The soldier was required to do what he was bidden without asking why. Many an aimless fatigue was imposed on him solely as training in the difficult art of blind obedience. The discipline was strict but not harassing. It was exercised with unrelenting vigor when the soldier was in the presence of the enemy. At other times, however, especially after victory, the reins were relaxed; and if an otherwise efficient soldier then wished to indulge in perfumery or deck himself with elegant arms and the like, or even if he were guilty of outrages or irregularities of a very questionable kind—provided only his military duties were not immediately affected—the foolery and the crime were allowed to pass, and the general lent a deaf ear to the complaints of the provincials on such points. Mutiny, on the other hand, was never pardoned in the instigators or even in the guilty corps itself.

But the true soldier ought to be capable, brave, and obedient willingly and spontaneously, and it is the privilege of gifted natures alone to impel the animated machine which they govern to a joyful service by means of example and of hope, and especially by the consciousness of being turned to suitable use. As the officer who demands valor from his troops must himself have looked danger in the face, Caesar even when general found opportunity of drawing his sword and using it like the best. Moreover, in activity and fatigue he was constantly far more demanding of himself than of his soldiers.

Caesar also took care that victory, whose fruits are doubtless primarily for the general, should arouse the hope of personal gain in his soldiers. We have already mentioned that he knew how to arouse enthusiasm in his soldiers for the democratic cause, so far as the times still permitted enthusiasm, and that the political equalization of the Transpadane country (the native land of most of his soldiers) with Italy proper was one of the announced objects of the struggle. Of course material recompense was not wanting, both special rewards for distinguished feats of arms and general rewards for every efficient soldier. The officers had their portions, the soldiers received presents, and the most lavish gifts were promised for the triumph.

Above all, Caesar as a true commander understood how to awaken in every single component, large or small, of the mighty machine the consciousness of its suitable application. The ordinary man, destined for service, is ever willing to be an instrument if he feels that a master guides him. Everywhere and at all times the eagle eye of the general rested on the whole army, rewarding and punishing with impartial justice, and directing the action of each toward the good of all. There was no experimenting or trifling with the sweat and blood of the humblest; but for that very reason, where necessary, unconditional devotion even to death was required.

Without allowing each individual to see the whole plan of action, Caesar yet permitted each to catch such glimpses of the political and military connection of things that he might be recognized—even idealized—by his soldiers as a statesman and a general. He treated his soldiers throughout not as equals, but as men entitled to demand and able to endure the truth, who had to trust the assurances of their general without thinking of deception or listening to rumors; as comrades through long years of warfare and victory, among whom hardly any one was not known to him by name and in the course of so many campaigns had not formed a more or less personal relation to the general; as good companions, with whom he talked and dealt confidentially with the cheerful elasticity peculiar to him; as followers, to requite whose services and to avenge whose wrongs and death he regarded as a sacred duty.

Perhaps there never was an army which was so perfectly what an army ought to be—a machine able and willing for its ends, in the hand of a master who transfers to it his own elasticity. Caesar's soldiers were, and felt themselves, a match for a tenfold superior force—in connection with which it should not be overlooked that under the Roman tactics, intended solely for hand-to-hand conflict and especially for combat with the sword, the practiced Roman soldier showed far greater superiority over the novice than is the case today.

But still more than by superiority of valor the adversaries of Caesar were humbled by the unswerving fidelity of the soldiers for their general. It is perhaps without a parallel in history that when the general summoned his soldiers to follow him into a civil war, with the single exception of Labienus no Roman officer or soldier deserted him. His opponents' hopes for extensive desertion were thwarted as ignominiously as were their earlier attempts to break up his army. Labienus himself appeared in the camp of Pompey with a band of Celtic and German horsemen, but without a single legionary. Indeed, the soldiers, as if to show that the war was quite as much their affair as their general's, agreed among themselves that for the duration they would forego their pay, which Caesar had promised to double on the outbreak of the civil war, and would meanwhile support their poorer comrades from the general means. In addition, every subaltern officer equipped and paid a trooper out of his own purse.

While Caesar thus had certain essentials—unlimited political and military authority and a trustworthy army ready for the fight—his power only extended over a very limited space. It was based essentially on the province of Upper Italy. This region was not merely the most populous Italian district, but was also devoted to the democratic cause as its own. The feeling which prevailed there is shown by the conduct of a division of recruits from Opitergium, which not long after the outbreak of the war in Illyrian waters, surrounded on a wretched raft by the war vessels of the enemy, allowed themselves to be shot at all day until sunset without surrendering, when the survivors put themselves to death with their own hands during the following night. It is easy to conceive what might be expected of such a population. As they had already granted Caesar the means of more than doubling his original army, so after the war's outbreak numerous recruits presented themselves for the ample levies that were immediately instituted.

In Italy proper, on the other hand, the influence of Caesar was not even remotely comparable to that of his opponents. Although he had the skill by dexterous maneuvers to put the Catonian party in the wrong, and had sufficiently commended the justice of his cause to all who sought a pretext either to remain neutral, like the majority of the Senate, or to embrace his side, like his soldiers and the Transpadanes, the mass of the citizenry naturally did not allow themselves to be misled. When the commandant of Gaul put his legions in motion against

Rome, they regarded Cato and Pompey as the defenders of the legitimate republic and Caesar as the democratic usurper, despite all legalistic explanations. Moreover, people in general expected from the nephew of Marius, the son-in-law of Cinna, and the ally of Catiline a repetition of the Marian and Cinnan horrors and a realization of Catiline's intended saturnalia of anarchy. To be sure, Caesar certainly gained allies through this expectation, for the political refugees immediately put themselves at his disposal in a body, the ruined men saw in him their deliverer, and the lowest rabble were thrown into a ferment on the news of his advance. But such friends are more dangerous than foes.

In the provinces and the dependent states Caesar had even less influence than in Italy. Transalpine Gaul as far as the Rhine and the Channel obeyed him, and the colonists of Narbo as well as the Roman settlers in Gaul were devoted to him. But in the Narbonese province itself the constitutional party had numerous adherents, and even the newly conquered regions were far more a burden than a benefit to Caesar in the impending civil war. In fact, for a good reason he used no Celtic infantry at all in that war, and but little cavalry. In the other provinces, and in the neighboring partly or wholly independent states, Caesar had indeed attempted to procure support, had lavished rich presents on the princes, had caused great buildings to be erected in various towns, and had granted them financial and military assistance. But not much had been gained by such means, and the relations with the German and Celtic princes along the Rhine and the Danube—particularly the connection with the Noric king Voctio, so important for the recruiting of cavalry—were probably the only such ties of any importance to him.

While Caesar thus entered the struggle only as commandant of Gaul, without other essential resources than efficient adjutants, a faithful army, and a devoted province, Pompey began it as *de facto* head of the Roman commonwealth, in full possession of all the resources of the legitimate government of the great Roman empire. But while his political and military position was far more considerable, it was also far less definite and firm. The unity of leadership which automatically went with Caesar's position was inconsistent with the nature of a coalition; and although Pompey, too much of soldier to deceive himself as to its importance, attempted to force it on the coalition and had himself nominated by the Senate as sole and absolute generalissimo by land and sea, yet the Senate itself could not be set aside politically nor hindered from an occasional and therefore doubly injurious interference with the military command. The recollection of twenty years' war waged between Pompey and the constitutional party with envenomed weapons on both sides; the mutual and ill-concealed feeling that the first consequence of victory would be a rupture between the victors; the well-justified contempt which each entertained for the other; the pitiful number of respectable and influential men in the ranks of the aristocracy, and the intellectual and moral inferiority of almost all who took part in the struggle—all these together produced among Caesar's opponents a reluctant and refractory co-operation which contrasted sadly with the harmonious and compact action on the other side.

While all the disadvantages attending the coalition of naturally hostile powers were thus felt in unusual degree by Caesar's antagonists, this coalition was still a formidable power. It alone commanded the sea, all ports, all ships of war, and all the materials for equipping a fleet. The two Spains—the home of Pompey's power just as the two Gauls were the home of Caesar's—were faithful to their master and under able and trustworthy administrators. All the other provinces except for the two Gauls were governed by recently appointed men who were safely under the influence of Pompey and the active Senate minority. The protectorates all took decisive part against Caesar and in favor of Pompey. The most important princes and cities had the closest personal relations with Pompey by virtue of his manifold activities.[1]

As for Italy, the great majority of the citizens were, as already noted, opposed to Caesar—especially, of course, the whole aristocracy with its very considerable following, but also in nearly equal degree the great capitalists, who could not hope in the event of a thorough reform of the commonwealth to preserve their partisan jury courts and their monopoly of extortion. Of equally antidemocratic sentiments were the small capitalists, the landholders and generally all classes that had anything to lose; but in these groups the cares of the next rent term and of sowing and reaping outweighed, as a rule, every other consideration.

The army at Pompey's disposal consisted chiefly of the Spanish troops, seven wholly trustworthy legions inured to war, to which might be added the weak and scattered forces in Syria, Asia, Macedonia, Africa, Sicily, and elsewhere. In Italy there were under arms at the outset only the two legions recently transferred by Caesar, whose effective strength did not amount to more than 7,000 men. Their trustworthiness was also more than doubtful, because, levied in Cisalpine Gaul and being old comrades-in-arms of Caesar, they were highly indignant at the unbecoming intrigue by which they had been made to change camps, and they recalled with longing their general who had magnanimously paid them on their departure the presents which were promised to every soldier for the triumph. But apart from the Spanish troops who might arrive in Italy the following spring either by land via Gaul or by sea, the men of the three legions still remaining from the levies of 55 B.C. as well as the Italian levy sworn to allegiance in 52 B.C. could be recalled from

■

1. In the original Mommsen enumerates many of the dependent kingdoms in some way beholden to Pompey.

their furlough. Including these, the number of troops at Pompey's disposal in Italy, without counting the seven legions in Spain and those scattered in other provinces, amounted to ten legions or about 60,000 men.

Thus it was no exaggeration at all when Pompey asserted that he had only to stamp his foot to cover the ground with armed men. It is true that a brief interval was required to render these soldiers available, but the arrangements for this purpose as well as for organizing the new levies ordered by the Senate were already everywhere in progress. Immediately after the decisive decree of the Senate on January 7, 49 B.C., in the dead of winter the most eminent aristocrats set out to hasten the calling up of recruits and the preparation of arms. The lack of cavalry was much felt, as they had been accustomed to rely wholly on the provinces, especially the Celtic ones, for this arm. To make at least a beginning, three hundred gladiators belonging to Caesar were taken from the fencing schools of Capua and mounted. However, the step met with such general disapproval that Pompey disbanded this troop and levied in its place 300 horsemen from the mounted slave herdsmen of Apulia.

The state treasury, being at its usual low ebb, was supplemented from the local treasuries and even from the temple treasures of the municipalities.

Under these circumstances the war opened at the beginning of January, 49 B.C. Of troops capable of marching Caesar had not more than a legion—5,000 infantry and 300 cavalry—at Ravenna, which by highway was some 240 miles from Rome. Pompey had two weak legions—7,000 infantry and a small squadron of cavalry—under the orders of Appius Claudius at Luceria, from which the highway distance to the capital was about the same. The other troops of Caesar, not counting the raw divisions still being formed, were stationed half on the Sâone and Loire, the other half in Belgica, while Pompey's Italian reserves were already arriving from all sides at their rendezvous. Long before even the first of Caesar's Transalpine divisions could arrive in Italy, a far superior army would surely be ready to receive it.

It seemed folly, with a band the size of Catiline's and for the moment without any effective reserve, to assume the aggressive against a superior and hourly increasing army under an able general; but it was a folly in the spirit of Hannibal. If the beginning of the struggle were postponed till spring, the Spanish troops of Pompey would assume the offensive in Transalpine and his Italian troops in Cisalpine Gaul; and Pompey, a match for Caesar in tactics and his superior in experience, was a formidable antagonist in such an ordered campaign. For the moment, however, accustomed as he was to operate slowly and surely with superior masses, Pompey might be disconcerted by a wholly improvised attack. And while the suddenness of the war and the toil of a winter campaign could not greatly distress Caesar's thirteenth legion, after its severe trials in Gaul, these same burdens might well disorganize the Pompeian corps consisting of old soldiers of Caesar or of ill-trained recruits still in the course of formation.

Accordingly Caesar advanced into Italy. Two highways led south at that time from the Romagna: the Aemilio-Cassian, from Bononia over the Apennines to Arretium and Rome; and the Popillio-Flaminian, which led from Ravenna along the coast of the Adriatic to Fanum, where one branch ran westward through the Furlo pass to Rome, another southward to Ancona and thence onward to Apulia. On the former Marcus Antonius advanced as far as Arretium, on the latter Caesar himself pushed forward. Resistance was nonexistent: the aristocratic recruiting officers had no military skill, their bands of recruits were not yet soldiers, and the inhabitants of the country towns were only anxious to avoid a siege. When Curio with 1,500 men approached Iguvium, a couple of thousand Umbrian recruits assembled there took flight at the mere word of his approach, and similar results on a small scale took place everywhere.

Caesar had to choose whether he would march against Rome, only 130 miles from his cavalry at Arretium, or against the legions encamped at Luceria. He chose the latter plan, to the boundless consternation of the enemy. Pompey received the news of Caesar's advance at Rome, and seemed at first disposed to defend the capital; but when the tidings arrived of Caesar's entrance into the Picenian territory and of his first successes there, he ordered Rome's evacuation. A panic, augmented by the false report that Caesar's cavalry had reached the gates, came over the world of quality. The senators, warned that every one remaining in the capital would be treated as Caesar's accomplice, streamed through the gates in crowds. The consuls so totally lost their senses that they did not even secure the treasury; and when Pompey urged them to fetch it, for which there was still time, they replied that they deemed it safer if first he occupied Picenum.

All was perplexity. Consequently, a great council of war was held in Teanum Sidicinum, at which Pompey, Labienus, and both consuls were present. First, Caesar's proposals of accommodation were again submitted. Even now he declared himself ready to dismiss his army, hand over his provinces to his successors, and become a candidate in the regular way for the consulship, provided Italy were disarmed and Pompey departed for Spain. The answer was that if Caesar immediately returned to his province, they would procure the disarming of Italy and the departure of Pompey by a senatorial decree to be duly passed in the capital.

Perhaps this reply was intended not as a transparent deceit but as an acceptance; in reality, however, it was the opposite. The personal conference which Caesar desired with Pompey the latter had to decline, to avoid provoking still more the constitutional party's distrust by the appearance of a new coalition with Caesar. As for the management of the war, it was agreed in Teanum that Pompey should take the command of the troops stationed at Luceria, on whom everything depended notwithstanding their untrustworthiness; that he should advance with these into Picenum, his own and Labienus' native country; and that he should personally call the general levy there to arms (as he had done thirty-five years ago) and attempt at the head of the faithful Picentine cohorts and the veterans formerly under Caesar to halt the enemy's advance.

Everything thus depended on whether Picenum held out until Pompey could come to its defense. Already Caesar's reunited army had penetrated into it along the coast road by way of Ancona. Here, too, preparations were in full swing. In the northernmost Picenian town, Auximum, a considerable band of recruits was collected under Publius Attius Varus. However, at the urging of the municipality Varus evacuated the town even before Caesar appeared, and a handful of Caesar's soldiers dispersed the troop not far from Auximum after a brief conflict—the first in the war. In like manner soon afterwards Gaius Lucilius Hirrus evacuated Camerinum with 3,000 men, and Publius Lentulus Spinther quit Asculum with 5,000. The men, thoroughly devoted to Pompey, for the most part willingly abandoned their houses and farms and followed their leaders over the frontier. But the district itself was already lost when the officer sent by Pompey for the initial defense, Lucius Vibullius Rufus—no genteel senator, but a soldier experienced in war—arrived there. He had to content himself with taking the six or seven thousand recruits away from the incapable recruiting officers, and conducting them to the nearest rendezvous.

The appointed meeting place for the levies of the Albensian, Marsian and Paelignian territories was Corfinium, and there were assembled nearly 15,000 recruits from the most warlike and trustworthy regions of Italy, the flower of the constitutional army still in course of formation. Vibullius arrived there several days before Caesar, and there was nothing to prevent him from immediately obeying Pompey's instructions and conducting the rescued Picenian recruits together with those assembled at Corfinium to join the main army in Apulia. But the commandant in Corfinium was Lucius Domitius, Caesar's designated successor in Transalpine Gaul and one of the most narrow-minded and stubborn Roman aristocrats. He not only refused to comply with Pompey's orders, but also prevented Vibullius from departing with the men from Picenum. So firmly did he believe that Pompey only delayed from obstinacy, and must necessarily come to his relief, that he made no serious preparations for a siege, and did not even gather into Corfinium the bands of recruits quartered in surrounding towns.

Pompey, however, did not appear, and for good reason. While he might perhaps use his two untrustworthy legions as a reserve for the Picenian general levy, he could not oppose Caesar with them alone. A few days later, on February 14, Caesar arrived, having been joined in Picenum by the twelfth legion and near Corfinium by the eighth, both from beyond the Alps. Besides these, three new legions had been formed partly from Pompeians who had been captured or had presented themselves voluntarily, and partly from the recruits that were being levied everywhere. Thus Caesar before Corfinium already headed an army of 40,000 men, half of whom had seen service.

So long as Domitius hoped for Pompey's arrival he prepared to defend the town. But when Pompey's letters had at length undeceived him, he resolved not to persevere at the forlorn post (which would have rendered the greatest service to his party) nor even to capitulate, but rather, while informing the common soldiers that relief was close at hand, to escape with his officers of quality the following night. Yet he could not even carry this pretty scheme into effect, for the confusion of his behavior betrayed him. When part of the men began to mutiny, the Marsian recruits wished to fight against the mutineers, believing such infamy on the part of their general to be impossible. They too were obliged reluctantly to recognize the truth of the accusation, whereupon the whole garrison arrested its staff and handed it, themselves, and the town over to Caesar on February 20. The corps of 3,000 at Alba, and 1,500 recruits assembled in Tarracina, thereupon laid down their arms as soon as Caesar's patrols of horsemen appeared; a third division of 3,500 men in Sulmo had previously been compelled to surrender.

Pompey had given up Italy as soon as Caesar occupied Picenum. However, he wished to delay his embarkation to the last moment to save as much of his force as possible. Accordingly he set out slowly for Brundisium, the nearest seaport. Thither came the two legions of Luceria and such recruits as Pompey had been able hastily to collect in the deserted Apulia, as well as the troops raised by the consuls and other commissioners in Campania. There also gathered a number of political fugitives, including the most respected senators and their families. The embarkation began, but the vessels at hand would not in one trip carry the whole multitude, which still amounted to 25,000 persons. No course remained but to divide the army, of which the larger part set out on March 4. With the smaller remainder (some 10,000 men) Pompey awaited at Brundisium the return of the fleet; for however desirable Brundisium might be for an eventual reinvasion of Italy, the place could not be held permanently against Caesar.

Meanwhile Caesar arrived and the siege began. Caesar attempted first to close the mouth of the harbor against the returning fleet by moles and floating bridges. But Pompey armed the trading vessels in the harbor, and managed to prevent the closing until the fleet appeared.

Then Pompey, with great dexterity and in spite of the vigilance of the besiegers and the hostility of the inhabitants, managed to evacuate every last soldier from the town unharmed and transport them to Greece. Caesar's further pursuit, like the siege, failed for want of ships.

Thus, in a two-month campaign without a single serious engagement, Caesar had so broken up an army of ten legions that less than the half of it had with great difficulty escaped in a confused flight across the sea. The whole Italian peninsula, including the capital with the state chest and all the stores accumulated there, had fallen to the victor. The beaten party had reason to bewail the terrifying rapidity, sagacity, and energy of the "monster."

But it may be questioned whether Caesar gained or lost by his conquest of Italy. Militarily, no doubt, considerable resources were both denied his opponents and rendered available for him. Even in the spring of 49 B.C. his army embraced, in consequence of the levies instituted everywhere, a considerable number of new legions in addition to the nine old ones. On the other hand, however, it now became necessary not only to establish a considerable garrison, but also to take measures against the closing of the overseas traffic contemplated by his opponents, and against the famine which consequently threatened the capital. Thus Caesar's already amply complex military task was complicated further still.

Financially, it was certainly important that Caesar had the good fortune to seize the state treasury in the capital. But the principal sources of income and particularly the revenues from the East were still in the hands of his enemies, and the greatly increased demands of the army and the new obligation to provide for the starving population of the capital meant that the considerable sums which were found quickly melted away. Caesar soon found himself compelled to appeal to private credit, but since it seemed that he could not possibly depend long on this resource, extensive confiscations were generally anticipated as the next step.

Still more serious political difficulties were created by the conquest of Italy. Fear of an anarchical revolution was universal among the propertied classes. Friends and foes saw in Caesar a second Catiline, Pompey believing or pretending to believe that Caesar had been driven to civil war by the impossibility of paying his debts. While this was patently absurd, Caesar's antecedents were in fact anything but reassuring, and still less reassuring was the aspect of the retinue around him. Individuals of the most questionable reputation, notorious personages like Quintus Hortensius, Gaius Curio, and Marcus Antonius (the latter was the stepson of the Catilinarian Lentulus, who was executed on the orders of Cicero) were its most prominent members. The highest posts were bestowed on men who had long ceased even to reckon up their debts, and who not only kept dancing-girls—which others did also—but appeared publicly with them. Was there any wonder that even grave and politically impartial men expected amnesty for all exiled criminals, canceling of creditor's claims, comprehensive mandates of confiscation, proscription, murder—nay, even a plundering of Rome by the Gallic soldiery?

But in this respect the "monster" deceived his foes as well as his friends. As soon as Caesar occupied the first Italian town, Ariminum, he prohibited all common soldiers from appearing armed within the walls, and the country towns, whether friendly or hostile, were protected from all injury. When the mutinous garrison surrendered Corfinium late in the evening, Caesar disregarded every military consideration by postponing the town's occupation until the following morning solely to avoid abandoning the citizens to the nocturnal invasion of his exasperated soldiers. The common soldiers among Caesar's prisoners, presumably indifferent to politics, were incorporated into his own army; the officers were not merely spared but freely released without distinction and without the exaction of pledges, and all which they claimed as private property was promptly handed over without any strict investigation of their claims. Lucius Domitius himself was thus treated, and even the money and baggage which Labienus had left behind was sent after him to the enemy's camp.

Despite his painful financial embarrassment, the immense estates of his opponents were not touched. Indeed, Caesar preferred to borrow from friends, rather than stir up the possessors of property even by exacting the formally admissible but practically antiquated land tax. The victor regarded only the less difficult half of his task as solved with the victory: it could be consolidated, according to his own expression, only by the unconditional pardon of the vanquished. Accordingly, during the whole march from Ravenna to Brundisium he incessantly renewed his efforts to bring about a personal conference with Pompey and a tolerable compromise.

But if the aristocracy had previously refused to listen to any reconciliation, their unexpected and disgraceful emigration raised their wrath to madness, and the wild threats of the defeated contrasted strangely with the victor's moderation. The communications from the emigrants' camp to their friends in Italy were full of projects for confiscations and proscriptions, for purifying the Senate and the state, compared with which the Sullan restoration was child's play, and which even the moderates of their own party heard with horror.

This contrast between the frantic passion of impotence and the wise moderation of power produced its effect. The whole group more concerned with material than political interests threw itself into Caesar's arms. The country towns idolized "the uprightness, the moderation, the prudence" of the victor; and even opponents conceded that these demonstrations of respect were sincere. The great capitalists, the tax farmers, and the jurymen showed no special desire, after the shipwreck of the constitutional party in Italy, to entrust themselves further to the same pilots. Capital came out of hiding, and "the rich lords resorted again to their daily task of writing their rent rolls."

Even the great majority of the Senate, at least numerically speaking—for few of the nobler and more influential senators were included—had disregarded the orders of Pompey and the consuls by staying in Italy, some even in the capital itself; and they acquiesced in Caesar's rule. His moderation, well calculated even in its apparent excess, attained its object by partly allaying the trembling anxiety of the propertied classes. This was doubtless an incalculable gain for the future, for the prevention of anarchy—and the scarcely less dangerous fear of anarchy—was indispensable to the future reorganization of the commonwealth.

But at the moment this moderation was more dangerous for Caesar than renewing the Cinnan and Catilinarian fury would have been: while it did not convert enemies into friends, it converted friends into enemies. Caesar's Catilinarian adherents were indignant at being denied murder and pillage, and these audacious and desperate personages, some of them men of talent, would likely prove cross and intractable. The republicans, on the other hand, were neither converted nor propitiated by the conqueror's leniency. According to the Catonian party's creed, duty towards what they called their fatherland superseded every other consideration; even one who owed freedom and life to Caesar remained duty bound to take up arms or at least to plot against him. The lukewarm constitutionalists were no doubt willing to accept peace and protection from the new monarch. Nevertheless, they ceased not to curse both monarchy and monarch at heart.

The more clearly the change of the constitution became manifest, the more distinctly the great majority of the citizens—both in the capital with its keener taste for

political excitement, and among the more energetic country population—awoke to a consciousness of their republican sentiments. The friends of the constitution in Rome
reported truthfully to their brethren in exile that all
classes and all persons at home favored Pompey. The
discontent among these circles was increased by the moral
pressure which the more notable and decided emigrants
exercised over the humbler and more lukewarm multitude. The conscience of the honorable man smote him
for staying in Italy, while the half-aristocrat fancied
himself among the plebeians if he did not go into exile,
or even if he took his seat in the Caesarian Senate of nobodies. The victor's extreme clemency gave increased political importance to this silent opposition. Since Caesar
abstained from terrorism, it seemed as if his secret opponents could show their dislike for his rule without much
risk.

Thus Caesar soon experienced remarkable treatment
at the hands of the Senate. He had begun the struggle to
liberate the overawed Senate from its oppressors. This
done, he wished to obtain Senate approval of his acts, and
full powers for continuing the war. For this purpose the
tribunes belonging to his party convoked the Senate on
April 1. The meeting was fairly well-attended, but the
more notable of the senators remaining in Italy were absent, including even Marcus Cicero, the former leader of
the servile majority, and Caesar's own father-in-law Lucius Piso.

Still worse, those present were cool to Caesar's proposals. When he spoke of full power to continue the war,
one of the only two consulars present, Servius Sulpicius
Rufus, a timid man who desired nothing but a quiet death
in bed, suggested that Caesar would deserve well of his
country if he abandoned the thought of carrying the war
to Greece and Spain. When Caesar thereupon requested
the Senate at least to transmit his peace proposals to

Pompey, there was no opposition to the request itself, but the threats of the emigrants had so terrified the neutrals that no one was found to carry the olive branch.

Thus, through the aristocracy's disinclination to help build the monarch's throne, and through the same inertness which Caesar had shortly before used to frustrate Pompey's legal nomination as generalissimo in the civil war, he too was now thwarted in a like request. Other impediments also arose. Caesar wished to be named as dictator, in order to regularize his position in some kind of way. But his wish was not granted because constitutionally such a magistrate could only be appointed by one of the consuls, and the attempt of Caesar to buy the consul Lentulus (whose disordered finances made him a good prospect) proved a failure.

Furthermore, the tribune of the people Lucius Metellus lodged a protest against all Caesar's acts, and threatened to protect personally the public chest when Caesar's men came to empty it. Caesar could not avoid ordering the inviolable person pushed aside as gently as possible. Otherwise, however, he continued to abstain from all violent steps. He declared to the Senate (just as the constitutional party had done shortly before) that he had desired to regulate matters legally with the help of the supreme authority, but since this help was refused he could dispense with it.

Without more ado about the Senate and legal formalities, he gave the temporary administration of the capital to the praetor Marcus Aemilius Lepidus as city prefect, and made the necessary arrangements for the administration of the provinces that obeyed him. Even amid the din of the gigantic struggle, and despite Caesar's lavish promises, it still made a deep impression on the multitude when they first saw in their free Rome the monarch wielding a monarch's power and breaking open the treasury doors with his soldiers. But the time had passed when popular feelings determined the course of events. The decision lay with the legions, and a few hurt feelings more or less were unimportant.

Caesar hastened to resume the war, for he intended to maintain the offensive to which he owed his initial successes. The position of his antagonist was singular. After the original plan of invading the two Gauls simultaneously from Italy and Spain had been frustrated by Caesar's initiative, Pompey had intended to go to Spain. There he had a very strong position. The army, amounting to seven legions, included a large number of Pompey's veterans, and years of fighting in the Lusitanian mountains had hardened both soldiers and officers. Among its captains Marcus Varro was simply a celebrated scholar and a faithful partisan; but Lucius Afranius had fought with distinction in the East and in the Alps, and Marcus Petreius, the conqueror of Catiline, was an officer as dauntless as he was able. While in the Further province Caesar still had various adherents from the time of his governorship, the more important province of the Ebro was attached by ties of veneration and gratitude to Pompey, who twenty years before had commanded there during the Sertorian war, and after the war's end had organized it anew.

After the Italian disaster Pompey could have done nothing better than proceed to Spain with the rescued remnant of his army, and then advance at the head of his whole force to meet Caesar. But unfortunately he had, in the hope of saving the troops in Corfinium, tarried in Apulia so long that he was compelled to embark from nearby Brundisium instead of from the Campanian ports. Why, as master of the sea and Sicily, he did not revert to his original plan cannot be determined. Whether the short-sighted and distrustful aristocracy showed no desire to entrust themselves to the Spanish troops and population, the fact is that Pompey remained in the East, and Caesar might choose to attack either the army being organized in Greece under Pompey's own command, or that ready for battle under his lieutenants in Spain. Caesar decided for the latter, and as soon as the Italian campaign ended had collected on the lower Rhone nine of his best legions, 6,000 cavalry—partly men picked by Caesar himself in the Celtic cantons, partly German mercenaries— and a number of Iberian and Ligurian archers.

But his opponents had also been active. Lucius Domitius had proceeded from Corfinium—as soon as Caesar had released him—with his attendants and with Lucius Vibullius Rufus to Massilia (Marseilles), and had actually induced that city to declare for Pompey and to refuse passage to Caesar's troops. Of the Spanish legions the two least trustworthy were left behind under the command of Varro in the Further province, while Afranius and Petreius set out with the five best, reinforced by 40,000 Spanish infantry and 5,000 Spanish cavalry. Their objective, in accordance with Pompey's orders transmitted by Vibullius, was to close the Pyrenees against the enemy.

Meanwhile Caesar arrived in Gaul and, as the siege of Massilia still detained him, he immediately dispatched most of his troops on the Rhone—six legions and the cavalry—along the great road via Narbo (Narbonne) to Rhode in order to reach the Pyrenees first. The movement was successful. When Afranius and Petreius arrived at the passes, they found them already occupied by the Caesarians. They then took up a position at Ilerda (Lerida) between the Pyrenees and the Ebro, a town lying twenty miles north of the Ebro on the right bank of one of its tributaries, the Sicoris (Segre), which was crossed by only one solid bridge hard by Ilerda. South of Ilerda the mountains which adjoin the left bank of the Ebro approach close to the town; to the northward there stretches on both sides of the Sicoris a level plain commanded by the hill on which the town is built.

For an army which had to submit to a siege it was an

excellent position. But the defense of Spain, once the line of the Pyrenees had been lost, could only be undertaken in earnest behind the Ebro; and as no secure communication was established between Ilerda and the Ebro, and no bridge existed over the latter stream, the retreat from the temporary to the true defensive position was not sufficiently secured. The Caesarians established themselves above Ilerda in the delta between the Sicoris and the Cinga (Cinca) rivers, which join below Ilerda. But the attack began in earnest only after Caesar arrived in the camp on June 23. Under the walls of the town the struggle was maintained with equal exasperation and valor on both sides and with frequent alternations of success. However, the Caesarians did not attain their object—to establish themselves between the Pompeian camp and the town and thereby capture the stone bridge. Consequently their communications with Gaul depended solely on two bridges hastily thrown over the Sicoris about eighteen or twenty miles upstream, as the river at Ilerda itself was too considerable to be bridged.

The floods resulting from the melting snows swept away these temporary bridges. As there were no vessels for crossing the highly swollen rivers, and the restoration of the bridges was temporarily impracticable, the Caesarian army was confined to the narrow space between the Cinga and the Sicoris; while the left bank of the Sicoris, and with it the road by which the army communicated with Gaul and Italy, were exposed almost undefended to the Pompeians, who passed the river partly by the town bridge and partly by swimming on skins in the Lusitanian fashion. It was the season shortly before harvest, when the old produce was almost used up and the new was not yet gathered; and the narrow strip between the two streams was soon denuded of food. In the camp actual famine prevailed (a modius of wheat cost 50 denarii) and dangerous diseases broke out; whereas on the left bank there were accumulated provisions and varied supplies, as well as troops of all sorts—reinforcements of cavalry and archers from Gaul, officers and soldiers from furlough, foraging parties returning—totalling 6,000 men. The Pompeians attacked this mass with superior force and drove it with great loss to the mountains, while the Caesarians on the right bank were obliged to remain passive spectators of the unequal conflict.

The communications of the army were thus in the hands of the Pompeians. In Italy the reports from Spain suddenly ceased, and the suspicious rumors which began to circulate were not far from the truth. Had the Pompeians followed up their advantage energetically they could not have failed either to wipe out the mass crowded on the left bank of the river, which was scarcely capable of resistance, or at least to drive it back towards Gaul and occupy this bank so completely that not a man could cross the river without their knowledge. But both points were neglected. The isolated bands were pushed aside with loss, but neither destroyed nor completely beaten back, and the prevention of the crossing of the river was left substantially to the river itself.

Thereupon Caesar formed his plan. He ordered portable boats of a light wooden frame and osier work lined with leather, like those used in the Channel by the Britons and subsequently by the Saxons, to be prepared in camp and transported in wagons to where the bridges had stood. On these frail barks the other bank was reached unopposed and the bridge re-established without much difficulty. The road connecting with it was thereupon quickly cleared, and the eagerly expected supplies conveyed to the camp. Caesar's happy idea thus rescued the army from its immense peril. Then the Caesarian cavalry, which far surpassed the enemy's in efficiency, began to scour the country on the left bank of the Sicoris. The most considerable Spanish communities between the Pyrenees and the Ebro, and even several south of the Ebro, passed over to Caesar's side.

The supplies of the Pompeians were sharply reduced by Caesar's foraging parties and the defection of the neighboring communities. They resolved to retire behind the line of the Ebro, and began hastily to form a bridge of boats over the Ebro below the mouth of the Sicoris. Caesar sought to cut off the retreat of his opponents over the Ebro and to detain them in Ilerda; but so long as the enemy held the bridge at Ilerda and he had neither ford nor bridge there, he could neither distribute his army over both banks of the river nor invest Ilerda. His soldiers therefore worked day and night to lessen the river's depth by canals drawing off the water, so that the infantry could wade across. But the preparations of the Pompeians were finished sooner than those of the Caesarians. When the former began their march towards the Ebro along the left bank of the Sicoris, the canal project seemed not far enough advanced to permit an infantry crossing. Therefore Caesar ordered only his cavalry to pass the stream and, by clinging to the enemy rear, to detain and harass them.

But when Caesar's legions saw in the gray morning light the enemy's columns which had been retiring since midnight, they discerned with the sure instinct of veterans the strategic importance of this retreat, which would compel them to follow their antagonists into distant regions filled with hostile troops. At their own request the general ventured to lead the infantry into the river, and although the water reached up to the shoulders of the men, it was crossed without accident. It was high time. If the narrow plain separating the town of Ilerda from the mountains enclosing the Ebro were once traversed and the Pompeians entered the mountains, their retreat to the Ebro could no longer be prevented. Notwithstanding the constant cavalry attacks which greatly delayed their march, they had already approached within five miles of the mountains when, having been on the march since midnight and unspeakably exhausted, they abandoned their original plan of crossing the whole plain in one day and pitched their camp. Here the infantry of Caesar overtook them in the evening and encamped opposite to them during the night. The nocturnal march which the Pompeians had at first contemplated was abandoned from fear of night cavalry attacks. On the following day also both armies remained immovable, occupied only in reconnoitering the country.

Early on the third morning Caesar's infantry began a movement through the pathless mountains alongside of the road, that they might turn the enemy's position and bar the route to the Ebro. The object of the strange march, which seemed at first to turn back towards the camp before Ilerda, was not at once perceived by the Pompeian officers. When they discerned it, they sacrificed camp and baggage and advanced by a forced march along the highway to gain the crest of the ridge before the Caesarians. But it was already too late: when they came up, the compact enemy masses were already posted on the highway itself. A desperate attempt to discover other routes to the Ebro over the steep mountains was frustrated by Caesar's cavalry, which surrounded and cut to pieces the Lusitanian troops sent forth for that purpose.

Had a battle taken place between the Caesarians and the Pompeian army—which was utterly demoralized with the enemy cavalry in its rear and the infantry in front—the issue was scarcely doubtful, and the opportunity for fighting presented itself several times. But Caesar made no use of it, and with some difficulty restrained the impatient eagerness of his confident soldiers. In any event the Pompeian army was strategically lost, and Caesar wished to avoid weakening his army and further envenoming the bitter feud by useless bloodshed. The day after he had succeeded in cutting off the Pompeians from the Ebro, the soldiers of the two armies had begun to fraternize and to negotiate respecting surrender. Indeed, the terms asked by the Pompeians, especially as to the sparing of their officers, had already been conceded by Caesar when Petreius with his escort consisting of slaves and Spaniards came upon the negotiators and caused all the Caesarians whom he could reach to be put to death. Nevertheless the Pompeians who had come to Caesar's camp were sent back unharmed, and he persevered in seeking a peaceful solution.

Ilerda, where the Pompeians still had a garrison and considerable supplies, now became the point which they sought to reach; but with the hostile army in front and the Sicoris between them and the fortress, they marched without coming nearer to their object. Their cavalry became gradually so afraid that the infantry had to take them into the center and legions had to be set as the rearguard. The procuring of water and forage became more and more difficult, and they had to kill the beasts of burden which could no longer be fed. At length the wandering army was formally inclosed between the Sicoris and the enemy's force, which drew rampart and trench around it. It attempted to cross the river, but Caesar's German horsemen and light infantry anticipated it by occupying the opposite bank.

No bravery or fidelity could now delay the inevitable capitulation, which occurred on August 2, 49 B.C. Caesar granted to officers and soldiers their lives and liberty and the property they still retained, plus restoring what had been already taken from them, the full value of which he undertook personally to repay to his own soldiers. While he had compulsorily enrolled in his army the recruits captured in Italy, he honored these old legionaries of Pompey by the promise that no one should be compelled to serve under Caesar against his will. He required only that each should give up his arms and go home. Accordingly about a third of the soldiers, who were natives of Spain, disbanded at once, while the Italians were discharged on the borders of Transalpine and Cisalpine Gaul.

On the breaking up of this army Hither Spain fell into the power of the victor. In Further Spain, where Marcus Varro held the chief command for Pompey, it seemed to him advisable when he learned of the disaster of Ilerda that he should throw himself into the insular town of Gades, carrying thither for safety the considerable sums collected by confiscating the treasures of the temples and the property of prominent Caesarians, the substantial fleet he had raised, and the two legions entrusted to him. But on the mere rumor of Caesar's arrival the most notable towns of the province (such as Corduba, Carmo, and Gades itself), long attached to Caesar, drove away the Pompeian garrisons or induced them to revolt. One of Varro's two legions also set out of its own accord for Hispalis, and passed over to Caesar's side along with the town. When at length even Italica closed its gates against Varro, he resolved to capitulate. About the same time Massilia also submitted.

The year 49 B.C. also saw two further Caesarian successes and one major defeat. The capture of Sardinia by Quintus Valerius and of Sicily by Gaius Curio helped forestall the starvation of Italy which Pompey was planning by naval blockade. But Curio's further expedition to Africa came to grief, after some initial successes, when he and his forces were surrounded and wiped out by the army of Pompey's ally, King Juba of Numidia.

How far these events of 49 B.C. interfered with Pompey's general plan of campaign, and particularly what part in that plan was assigned to the important Spanish corps after the loss of Italy, can only be determined by conjecture. That Pompey intended to come by way of Africa and Mauretania to the aid of his army in Spain was simply a romantic and beyond doubt groundless rumor circulating in the camp at Ilerda. More likely he still kept to his earlier plan of attacking Caesar from both sides in Transalpine and Cisalpine Gaul even after losing Italy, and meditated a combined attack at once from Spain and Macedonia. The Spanish army was presumably meant to remain on the defensive at the Pyrenees till the fully organized Macedonian army was ready to march. Then both would have started simultaneously and joined forces either on the Rhone or on the Po, while the fleet, it may be conjectured, would have attempted a landing in Italy proper.

On this supposition Caesar apparently prepared himself to meet an attack on Italy. One of his ablest officers, the tribune Marcus Antonius, commanded there with propraetorian powers. The southeastern ports of Sipus, Brundisium, and Tarentum, where a landing might first be expected, received a garrison of three legions. Besides this Quintus Hortensius, the degenerate son of the well-known orator, collected a fleet in the Tyrrhenian Sea, and Publius Dolabella a second fleet in the Adriatic, partly to support the defense of Italy and partly to transport the intended expedition to Greece. In the event of a Pompeian land penetration into Italy, Marcus Licinius Crassus, the eldest son of Caesar's old colleague, was to conduct the defense of Cisalpine Gaul, and Marcus Antonius' younger brother that of Illyricum.

But the expected attack was long in coming. Not until midsummer of 49 B.C. did the conflict begin in Illyria. There Caesar's lieutenant Gaius Antonius with his two legions was on the island of Curicta (Veglia in the gulf of Quarnero), and Caesar's admiral Publius Dolabella with forty ships lay in the narrow arm of the sea between this island and the mainland. Pompey's admirals in the Adriatic, Marcus Octavius with the Greek division of the fleet and Lucius Scribonius Libo with the Illyrian, attacked Dolabella's squadron, destroyed all his ships, and cut off Antonius on his island. To rescue him, a corps under Basilus and Sallustius came from Italy and the squadron of Hortensius from the Tyrrhenian Sea. But neither the former nor the latter was able to effect anything in the presence of the far superior enemy fleet.

The legions of Antonius had to be abandoned to their fate. Provisions came to an end, the troops became troublesome and mutinous. Except for a few divisions which succeeded in reaching the mainland on rafts, the corps, still fifteen cohorts strong, laid down their arms and were conveyed to Macedonia to be incorporated into the Pompeian army, while Octavius was left to complete the subjugation of the undefended Illyrian coast. The Dalmatae, the most powerful tribe in these regions, the important insular town of Issa (Lissa), and other townships embraced the party of Pompey. But the adherents of Caesar maintained themselves in Salonae (Spalato) and Lissus (Alessio); and the former town not merely sustained with courage a siege which reduced it to extremities, but made so effective a sally that Octavius raised the siege and sailed off to Dyrrhachium to pass the winter.

The success achieved in Illyricum by the Pompeian fleet, though not inconsiderable, had little influence on the campaign as a whole. Moreover, it appears miserably small when we consider that Pompey's land and naval activity during the whole eventful year of 49 B.C. was confined to this single feat of arms, and that from the East, where the general, the Senate, the second great army, the principal fleet, the immense military and still more extensive financial resources of the republicans were united, no intervention at all took place in the crucial struggle in the West. The scattering of the forces in the eastern empire, the general's method of never operating except with superior masses, his cumbrous and tedious movements, and the discord of the coalition may perhaps partly explain (though not excuse) the inactivity of his land forces. But that the fleet, which commanded the Mediterranean without a rival, should have thus done nothing to influence the course of affairs—nothing for

Spain, next to nothing for Massilia, nothing to defend Sardinia, Sicily, Africa, or, if not to reoccupy Italy, at least to obstruct its supplies—gives some inkling of the well-nigh inconceivable confusion and perversity which must have prevailed in the Pompeian camp.

The net result of this campaign was corresponding. Caesar's offensive against Spain was completely successful, that against Sicily and Africa partly so. Pompey's plan of starving Italy was thwarted mainly by the capture of Sicily, and his general plan of campaign was frustrated completely by the destruction of the Spanish army, while in Italy only a very small portion of Caesar's defensive arrangements had met any test. Notwithstanding the painful losses in Africa and Illyria, Caesar came out of the first year of the war decisively victorious.

However, if nothing material was done from the East to hinder Caesar's subjugation of the west, efforts at least were made towards political and military consolidation during the ignominious respite. The great rendezvous of Caesar's opponents was Macedonia. There headed Pompey himself and the mass of the emigrants from Brundisium. There also came the other refugees from the West—Marcus Cato from Sicily, Lucius Domitius from Massilia, and especially a number of the best officers and soldiers of the broken Spanish army, headed by its generals Afranius and Varro.

In Italy emigration gradually became among the aristocrats a question not merely of honor but also of fashion, and it obtained a fresh impulse through the unfavorable accounts of Caesar's position before Ilerda. Not a few of the lukewarm and the political trimmers went over by degrees, even Marcus Cicero at last persuading himself that he did not adequately discharge his duty as a citizen by writing a dissertation on concord. The Senate of emigrants at Thessalonica, where official Rome pitched its interim abode, numbered nearly 200 members, including many venerable old men and almost all the consulars.

But emigrants indeed they were. This Roman Coblenz was a pitiful spectacle of high pretensions and paltry performances, with unseasonable reminiscences and still more unseasonable recriminations, political perversities and financial embarrassments. It was a matter of little moment that, while the old structure was crumbling, they were painstakingly watching over every ornamental scroll and speck of rust in the constitution. After all, it was simply ridiculous when the genteel lords had pangs of conscience about calling their deliberative assembly "the Senate," and cautiously entitled it "the three hundred," or when they launched tedious investigations as to whether a curiate law could be legitimately enacted beyond the ring-wall of Rome.

Far worse traits were the indifference of the lukewarm and the narrow stubbornness of the ultras. The former would neither act nor keep silent. If asked to perform some definite task for the common good, with the inconsistency of the weak they regarded the suggestion as a malicious attempt to compromise them, and either did not do what was ordered or did it halfheartedly. At the same time, of course, with their know-it-all attitude after it was too late and their over-wise impracticalities, they perpetually hindered those who were acting. Their daily work consisted of criticizing, ridiculing, and bemoaning every occurrence great or small, and in unnerving and discouraging the multitude by their own sluggish hopelessness.

While these displayed the prostration of weakness, the ultras blatantly exhibited the exaggeration of action. They made no attempt to conceal that the price of any peace negotiation was Caesar's head. Every attempt towards peace, which Caesar continued to make, was tossed aside without examination, or used only to cover insidious attempts on the lives of Caesar's envoys. That Caesar's declared partisans had forfeited life and property was a matter of course, but the neutrals fared little better.

Lucius Domitius, the bumbler of Corfinium, gravely proposed in council that the senators who had fought in Pompey's army should decide whether those who had remained neutral, or had emigrated but not entered the army, should be acquitted, fined, or punished by the forfeiture of life and property. Another of these ultras formally charged Lucius Afranius with corruption and treason for his defective defense of Spain.

Among these deep-dyed republicans political theory assumed almost the character of a religious faith. Accordingly, they detested Pompey, his personal adherents, and their own more lukewarm partisans still more, if possible, than their open opponents, displaying all the dull obstinacy of hatred that characterizes orthodox theologians; and they were mainly to blame for the numberless and bitter quarrels which distracted the emigrant army and Senate. Nor did they confine themselves to words. Marcus Bibulus, Titus Labienus, and others of this clique carried out their theory by causing captured officers or soldiers of Caesar's army to be executed en masse— which, it may be assumed, did not make Caesar's troops fight less fiercely. If the counterrevolution in favor of the republic, for which all the elements existed, did not break out in Italy during Caesar's absence, the reason in the opinion of Caesar's discerning opponents lay chiefly in the general dread of the unbridled fury of the republican ultras after the restoration.

The better men in the Pompeian camp were in despair over this frantic behavior. Pompey, himself a brave soldier, spared the prisoners as far as he could. But he was too pusillanimous and in too awkward a position to prevent or even to punish all such atrocities as a commander-in-chief should. Marcus Cato, the only man who at least carried moral consistency into the struggle, attempted with more energy to check such proceedings. He induced the emigrant Senate to prohibit by special decree the pillage of subject towns and the killing of a citizen except in battle. The able Marcus Marcellus had similar views. No one, indeed, knew better than Cato and Marcellus that the extreme party would carry out their ghastly threats, if necessary defying all the decrees of the Senate. If even now the ultras could not be tamed despite all considerations of prudence, people might expect after their victory a reign of terror from which Marius and Sulla themselves would have recoiled in horror. We can understand why Cato professed himself more afraid of the victory than of the defeat of his own party.

Military preparation in the Macedonian camp was in the hands of Pompey as commander-in-chief. His position, always anomalous, had become still worse through the unfortunate events of 49 B.C. In the eyes of his partisans he was mainly to blame for this result. This judgment was in many respects unjust. Much of the misfortune endured was chargeable to the perversity and insubordination of his lieutenants, especially Lucius Domitius and the consul Lentulus. From the moment Pompey took charge of the army he had led it with skill and courage, and had saved very considerable forces from the debacle. That he was not a match for Caesar's superior genius—a fact now recognized by all—could not fairly be made a matter of reproach. But results alone decided men's judgment. Trusting in Pompey the constitutional party had broken with Caesar, and the pernicious consequence of this breach recoiled upon Pompey. While no attempt was made to change the supreme command, owing to the notorious military incapacity of all the other chiefs, confidence in the commander-in-chief was paralyzed.

These painful consequences of the defeats were heightened by the injurious influences of the emigration. Among the refugees were a number of efficient soldiers and capable officers, especially those from the former Spanish army. But the number who came to serve and fight was small, while the number of generals of quality who called themselves proconsuls and Imperators with as good title as Pompey, and of genteel lords who endured active military service more or less reluctantly, was alarmingly great. These introduced the capital's mode of life into the camp, with no benefit to the army. The tents of such grandees were graceful bowers, the ground elegantly covered with fresh turf, the walls clothed with ivy; silver plate stood on the table, and the winecup often circulated even in broad daylight. Those fashionable warriors formed a singular contrast with Caesar's daredevils, who ate coarse bread and, lacking that, devoured even roots, and who swore that they would rather chew the bark of trees than flee from the enemy.

Moreover, Pompey's actions were hampered by the necessity of consulting with a senatorial governing board personally hostile to him, and this embarrassment was sharply increased when the Senate of emigrants took up its abode almost in his very headquarters, displaying there all the venom of the emigrants in its sittings. And finally, there was nowhere any man of mark who could throw his own weight into the scale against these preposterous doings. Pompey himself was intellectually far too second-rate, and far too hesitating, awkward, and reserved. Marcus Cato would have had the requisite moral authority, plus the good will to support Pompey with it. But Pompey, instead of seeking his aid, jealously kept him in the background, and preferred (for instance) to commit the highly important chief command of the fleet to that totally incapable Marcus Bibulus.

While Pompey thus handled his political position with characteristic perversity, outdoing himself to worsen an already bad situation, on the other hand he devoted himself with commendable zeal to organizing the considerable but scattered forces of his party. The flower of his force was composed of the troops brought from Italy. From these, supplemented by the Illyrian prisoners of war and the Romans domiciled in Greece, five legions were formed. Three others came from the East—the two Syrian legions made up of the remains of Crassus' army, and one formed out of the two weak legions hitherto stationed in Cilicia.

Nothing prevented the withdrawal of these corps of occupation. On the one hand the Pompeians had an understanding with the Parthians, and might even have had an alliance if Pompey had not indignantly refused the price they demanded for it—cession of the Syrian province which Pompey himself had added to the empire. On the other hand Caesar's plan of dispatching two legions to Syria, and inducing the Jews once more to revolt by means of the prince Aristobulus kept a prisoner in Rome, was frustrated partly by the death of Aristobulus and partly by other causes. New Pompeian legions were also raised, one from the veteran soldiers settled in Crete and Macedonia, and two from the Romans of Asia Minor. To all these were added 2,000 volunteers, derived from the remains of the Spanish select corps and other similar sources, and the contingents of subject allies. The cavalry (except for a noble guard, more respectable than militarily important, formed from the young aristocracy of Rome, and the Apulian slave herdsmen whom Pompey had mounted) consisted exclusively of contingents from Roman provinces and protectorates and totaled some 7,000 men.[2]

Finally, Pompey's fleet was very considerable. It consisted partly of the Roman transports brought from Brundisium or subsequently built, partly of the war vessels of the king of Egypt, of the Colchian princes, of the Cilician dynast Tarcondimotus, of the cities of Tyre, Rhodes, Athens, Corcyra, and generally of all the Asiatic and Greek maritime states. It numbered nearly 500 sail, of which the Roman vessels formed a fifth. Immense

2. In the original Mommsen describes the origin of the light troops and cavalry brought into the Pompeian army.

stores of food and military supplies were accumulated in Dyrrhachium. The warchest was well filled, for the Pompeians possessed the principal sources of revenue and turned to their own account the resources of the satellite princes, the senators of distinction, the tax farmers, and generally of the whole Roman and non-Roman population within their reach. Every device that the reputation of the legitimate government and the much renowned protectorship of Pompey over kings and peoples could put in motion in Africa, Egypt, Macedonia, Greece, Western Asia and Syria was applied for the protection of the Roman republic. The title "King of Kings" given to Pompey in his camp, and the report which circulated in Italy that Pompey was arming the Getae, Colchians, and Armenians against Rome, could hardly be called exaggerations.

Altogether, Pompey commanded an army of 7,000 cavalry and eleven legions (of which, it is true, five at most could be described as veteran) and a fleet of 500 sail. The temper of the soldiers, for whose provisioning and pay Pompey gave adequate care, and to whom the most abundant rewards were promised after victory, was consistently good, and in several of the most efficient divisions even excellent. However, much of the army consisted of new recruits whose training, however zealously pressed, still took time. As a whole the force was imposing, but of a somewhat motley character.

The commander-in-chief's plan was that the army and fleet should be fully mobilized by the winter of 49-48 B.C. along the coast and in the waters of Epirus. The admiral Bibulus had already arrived with 110 ships at his new headquarters, Corcyra. On the other hand the land army, whose headquarters during the summer had been at Berrhoea on the Haliacmon, had not yet arrived, but was moving slowly along the great highway from Thessalonica toward the west coast to the future headquarters at Dyrrhachium. The two legions which Metellus Scipio was bringing up from Syria wintered at Pergamus in Asia, and were expected in Europe only toward the spring. In fact, all their movements were proceeding so leisurely that for the moment the ports of Epirus were guarded, except for the fleet, merely by their own civic defenses and the levies of the adjoining districts.

It thus remained possible for Caesar, despite the Spanish war, to take the offensive also in Macedonia, and he at least was not slow to act. He had long ago ordered the collection of war vessels and transports in Brundisium, and there he sent the greater portion of his select troops after the Spanish victory and the fall of Massilia. The unparalleled exertions which Caesar thus required from his soldiers thinned their ranks more than conflict had done, and the mutiny of one of the four oldest legions, the ninth, on its march through Placentia indicated the dangerous temper of the army. But Caesar's presence of mind and personal authority gained the mastery, and nothing impeded the embarkation from this quarter.

However, the want of ships which had prevented the pursuit of Pompey in March of 49 B.C. threatened to frustrate this expedition also. The war vessels which Caesar had ordered built in the Gallic, Sicilian, and Italian ports were not yet ready, or at any rate not on the spot. His Adriatic squadron had been destroyed the previous year at Curicta, and he found at Brundisium not more than twelve ships of war and scarcely transports enough to carry at once a third of the twelve legions and 10,000 cavalry intended for Greece. The considerable enemy fleet dominated the Adriatic and especially all the mainland and island harbors on its eastern coast.

Under these circumstances it is a question why Caesar did not march through Illyria, a route which obviated any naval threat and was also shorter for his troops, most of whom came from Gaul, than the route by Brundisium. It is true that Illyria was rugged and poor, but it was traversed by other armies soon afterward, and this obstacle can hardly have daunted the conqueror of Gaul. Perhaps he feared that during the troublesome march through Illyria Pompey might convey his whole force over the Adriatic to Italy, thereby changing places with Caesar—though such a rapid response was scarcely to be expected from his slow-moving antagonist. Perhaps Caesar originally favored the maritime route on the theory that his fleet could meanwhile be brought to respectable strength, and, when after returning from Spain he learned the true situation in the Adriatic, it was too late to change his plan. Perhaps—and in view of Caesar's quick and decisive temperament it is even highly probable—he found himself irresistibly tempted by the fact that the still-undefended Epirote coast would certainly be covered by the enemy in a few days, and a bold stroke might thwart once more his antagonist's whole plan.

Whatever his reasoning, on January 4th of 48 B.C. Caesar set sail from Brundisium with six legions, greatly thinned by toil and sickness, and 600 horsemen. It was a counterpart to his foolhardy Britannic expedition, but at least the first throw was fortunate. The coast of Epirus was reached in the middle of the Acroceraunian (Chimara) cliffs, at the little-frequented roadstead of Paleassa (Paljassa). The transports were seen both from the harbor of Oricum (creek of Avlona) where a Pompeian squadron of eighteen sail was lying, and from the headquarters of the hostile fleet at Corcyra; but the first group considered itself too weak, and the second was not ready to sail, so that Caesar's initial force landed without hindrance. While the vessels at once returned to bring over the second, Caesar that same evening scaled the Acroceraunian mountains. His first successes were as great as the enemy's surprise. The Epirote militia offered no resistance, the important seaports of Oricum and Apollonia along with a number of smaller towns were taken, and Dyrrhachium, the chief Pompeian arsenal filled with supplies but only feebly garrisoned, was in the utmost danger.

The rest of the campaign did not measure up to this brilliant beginning. Bibulus subsequently made up for some of his negligence by redoubling his exertions. He not only captured and burned nearly thirty of the returning transports, but also established along the whole occupied coast a most careful watch, despite the inclement season of the year and the necessity of bringing everything for the guardships, even wood and water, from Corcyra. In fact, his successor Libo (for Bibulus soon succumbed to the unwonted fatigues) even blockaded the port of Brundisium for a time until lack of water dislodged him from the little island facing it which he had seized. As a result, the second part of the army could not be brought over to Caesar, nor did he succeed in capturing Dyrrhachium. Pompey learned through one of Caesar's peace envoys of his plan to invade the Epirote coast, and thereupon accelerated his march to reach that important arsenal in the nick of time.

Caesar's situation was critical. Although he extended his range in Epirus as far as his slight strength permitted, the subsistence of his army remained difficult and precarious, while the enemy's mastery of the sea and its possession of the stores at Dyrrhachium gave him plenty of everything. With an army presumably little above 20,000 strong he could not challenge Pompey with at least twice that number. He had to deem himself fortunate that Pompey did not immediately force a battle, but went methodically to work and took up winter quarters between Dyrrhachium and Apollonia on the right bank of the Apsus, facing Caesar on the left, in order that after his eastern legions arrived in the spring he might overwhelm the enemy.

Thus months passed. If the arrival of better weather, which brought the enemy strong reinforcements plus the free use of his fleet, found Caesar still in the same position he was surely lost, with his weak band wedged in among the rocks of Epirus between the immense fleet and the trebly superior land army of the enemy; and already the winter was drawing to a close. His sole hope still depended on his transport fleet. It was hardly to be hoped that it could steal or fight its way through the blockade, but after the first voluntary foolhardiness this second gamble was mandatory. How desperate Caesar regarded his situation is shown by his scheme—when the fleet still did not come—to sail alone in a fishing boat across the Adriatic to Brundisium to fetch it. The plan was only abandoned because no mariner could be found to undertake the daring voyage.

But his personal appearance was not needed to induce his faithful lieutenant in Italy, Marcus Antonius, to make a last effort to save his master. Once more the transport fleet, with four legions and 800 horsemen on board, sailed from Brundisium, and fortunately a strong south wind carried it past Libo's galleys. But the same wind which saved the fleet also blew it past the camps of Caesar and Pompey to the north of Dyrrhachium towards Lissus, which town fortunately still adhered to Caesar. When it sailed past Dyrrhachium the Rhodian galleys started in pursuit, and hardly had Antonius' ships arrived at Lissus when the enemy's squadron appeared. But just at this moment the wind suddenly veered, and drove the pursuing galleys partly back into the open sea and partly on the rocky coast. Through the most marvellous good fortune the landing of the second convoy had also been successful.

Antonius and Caesar were still some four days' march from each other, separated by Dyrrhachium and the whole enemy army. But Antonius fortunately made the perilous march around Dyrrhachium and joined Caesar, who had gone to meet him, on the right bank of the Apsus. Pompey, after vainly attempting to prevent the junction and to force Antonius' corps to fight alone, took up a new position at Asparagium on the river Genusus (Skumbi), which flows parallel to the Apsus between the latter and the town of Dyrrhachium, and there remained once more immovable. Caesar felt himself now strong enough to give battle, but Pompey declined it. On the other hand Caesar with his fast-marching infantry deceived his adversary, just as at Ilerda, by getting between the enemy's camp and its base at Dyrrhachium.

The chain of the Graba Balkan, which stretches from east to west on the Adriatic and ends in the narrow tongue of land at Dyrrhachium, sends off a lateral branch in a southwesterly direction some fourteen miles east of Dyrrhachium. This branch then turns crescent-like towards the sea, and with the main chain encloses a small plain extending round a cliff on the seashore. Here Pompey now took up his camp, and, although Caesar's army kept the land route to Dyrrhachium closed against him, his fleet kept in constant communication with the town and he was amply and easily supplied from it. Among the Caesarians, notwithstanding strong detachments scouring the back country, and despite all the general's exertions to organize a system of transport and thereby a regular supply, there was such scarcity that flesh, barley, and even roots very frequently had to take the place of the customary wheat.

As his phlegmatic opponent still did not act, Caesar sought to occupy the heights which enclosed the plain held by Pompey, in order at least to hinder the enemy's superior cavalry and to operate with more freedom against Dyrrhachium, and if possible to compel his opponent either to fight or sail away. Nearly half of Caesar's troops were detached to the interior, and it seemed almost quixotic for the rest to attempt virtually to besiege an army perhaps twice as strong, concentrated in position, and resting on the sea and the fleet. Yet Caesar's veterans by infinite exertions surrounded the Pompeian camp with a chain of posts sixteen miles long. To this inner line was afterward added a second outer one, to protect against attacks from Dyrrhachium and against attempts to turn their position, so easily executed with the aid of the fleet.

Pompey attacked portions of these entrenchments more

than once with a view to breaking the enemy line if possible, but he did not attempt to prevent the investment by a battle. Instead he constructed entrenchments around his own camp, connecting them by lines. Both sides sought to push forward their trenches as far as possible, and the earthworks advanced but slowly amid constant conflicts. At the same time skirmishes took place on the opposite side of Caesar's camp with the garrison of Dyrrhachium. Caesar hoped to seize the fortress with the help of some of its garrison, but was prevented by the enemy fleet. There was incessant fighting at different points—on one of the hottest days at six places simultaneously—and as a rule the tried valor of the Caesarians had the advantage. Once, for instance, a single cohort maintained itself in its entrenchments against four legions for several hours until support came up. No notable success was achieved by either side, yet the effects of the investment gradually became oppressive to the Pompeians. The stopping of the rivulets flowing down from the heights compelled them to be content with poor and scanty wellwater. Still more troublesome was the lack of fodder for the horses, which the fleet could not supply adequately. Numbers died, and it was no use to transport them by water to Dyrrhachium since fodder was also lacking there.

Pompey could not delay much longer freeing himself from his disagreeable position. He was informed by Celtic deserters that the Caesarians had failed to build a cross-wall along the beach between their two chains of entrenchments 600 feet apart, and on this he formed his plan. While Caesar's inner line was attacked by legions from the camp, and the outer line by light troops landed from the sea beyond the enemy's entrenchments, a third division landed in the space between the two lines and attacked the embattled defenders in the rear. The entrenchment next to the sea was taken, and its garrison fled in wild confusion. With difficulty Marcus Antonius, the commander of the next trench, succeeded in limiting the Pompeian advance; but apart from the considerable loss, the entrenchment along the sea remained in enemy hands and the line was broken.

Caesar the more eagerly seized the opportunity soon afterward of attacking with the bulk of his infantry a Pompeian legion which had incautiously become isolated. But it resisted valiantly, and as the battleground was intersected by mounds and ditches, Caesar's right wing along with the cavalry missed its way. Instead of supporting the left in attacking the Pompeian legion, it got into a narrow trench that led from one of the old camps towards the river. Pompey, who came up hastily with five legions to aid his troops, found the two enemy wings separated and one of them in a forlorn position. A panic seized the Caesarians at his advance, and all plunged into disorderly flight. That the matter ended with merely the loss of 1,000 of Caesar's best soldiers, and not the complete defeat of his army, was due simply to the fact that Pompey also could not freely deploy his forces on the broken ground, and to the further fact that from fear of a stratagem he at first held back his troops.

Even so, these days were fraught with mischief for Caesar. Not only had he endured the most serious losses and surrendered at one blow his entrenchments, the result of four months of gigantic labor; the recent engagements had put him back exactly where he started. Pompey's elder son Gnaeus had in a bold attack partly burnt and partly carried off Caesar's few ships of war in the port of Oricum, and soon afterward had set fire to the transport fleet left behind in Lissus. Thus all possibility of reinforcement by sea from Brundisium was lost. The pent-up Pompeian cavalry now poured over the adjacent country and threatened to make the already difficult task of provisioning Caesar's army utterly impossible. Caesar's daring enterprise of mounting an offensive without ships, against an enemy in command of the sea and resting on his fleet, had totally failed. In the present theater of war he found himself facing an impregnable defensive position, and unable to attack effectively either Dyrrhachium or the hostile army. Pompey alone could now choose the most favorable circumstances to attack an antagonist already wrestling with grave problems of supply.

XIII
CIVIL WAR: PHARSALUS
AND THAPSUS

The war had reached a crisis. Hitherto *Pompey had, to* all appearances, played the game of war without a particular plan, adjusting his defense to the exigencies of each attack; nor was this to be censured, for protracting the war enabled him to harden his recruits, bring up his reserves, and make fuller use of his superior Adriatic fleet. Caesar was beaten both tactically and strategically. True, this defeat did not have the effect which Pompey might reasonably expect; the soldierly energy of Caesar's veterans prevented an immediate break-up of the army by hunger and mutiny. But it seemed to depend solely on Pompey, by judiciously following up his victory, to reap its full fruits.

It was up to Pompey to take the aggressive, and he was resolved to do so. He had three different ways of rendering his victory fruitful. The first and simplest was to assail the vanquished army and, if it departed, to pursue it. Secondly, Pompey might leave Caesar himself and his best troops in Greece and cross in person with the main army to Italy (as he had long been preparing to do) where the feeling was decidedly republican, and where Caesar's forces, after the departure of the best troops and their commander for Greece, would not be of much moment. Lastly, the victor might turn inland, effect a junction with the legions of Metellus Scipio, and attempt to capture Caesar's troops stationed in the interior. These latter had, immediately after the arrival of the second convoy from Italy, sent strong detachments to Aetolia and Thessaly to procure supplies, and had ordered two legions under Gnaeus Domitius Calvinus to advance on the Egnatian highway towards Macedonia, to intercept and if possible defeat in detail Scipio's force advancing on the same road from Thessalonica.

Calvinus and Scipio had already approached within a few miles of each other when Scipio suddenly turned southward. Then, rapidly crossing the Haliacmon (Inje Karasu) and leaving his baggage there under Marcus Fa-

vonius, he penetrated into Thessaly to attack Caesar's
legion of recruits under Lucius Cassius Longinus, engaged
in subduing the countryside. But Longinus retired over the
mountains toward Ambracia to join the detachment under Gnaeus Calvisius Sabinus sent by Caesar to Aetolia;
and Scipio could only send his Thracian cavalry in pursuit, for Calvinus threatened his reserve left under Favonius on the Haliacmon with the same fate which he had
intended for Longinus. So Calvinus and Scipio met on the
Haliacmon, and encamped opposite each other for a considerable time.

Pompey might choose among these plans, while Caesar
had no choice. After the unfortunate engagement at Dyrrhachium he retreated toward Apollonia, and Pompey
followed. The march from Dyrrhachium to Apollonia,
along a difficult road crossed by several rivers, was no
easy task for a defeated army pursued by the enemy; but
the dexterous leadership of their general and the indestructible marching energy of the soldiers compelled Pompey after four days to give up the pursuit as useless. He
now had to decide between the Italian expedition and the
march into the interior. However attractive the former
might seem, and though various voices urged it, he preferred not to abandon Scipio's corps, especially since he
hoped by this march to lay hands on the corps of Calvinus.

Calvinus at the moment was on the Egnatian road at
Heraclea Lyncestis between Pompey and Scipio, and further distant from Caesar than from the great Pompeian
army. Moreover, he knew nothing of the events at Dyrrhachium and of his perilous position, since after Caesar's
defeat the whole countryside inclined to Pompey and Caesar's messengers were everywhere seized. Not until the
enemy's main force was a few hours away did Calvinus
learn the true state of affairs from the enemy's advanced
posts themselves. A quick departure southward towards
Thessaly averted his imminent destruction, and Pompey

had to be content with liberating Scipio from his position of peril.

Caesar had meanwhile arrived unmolested at Apollonia. Immediately after the disaster at Dyrrhachium he had resolved to transfer the struggle from the coast into the interior, to get beyond the reach of the enemy's fleet —the ultimate cause of his previous failure; the march to Apollonia had only been intended to place his wounded in safety and to pay his soldiers there, where his depots were stationed. This done, he set out for Thessaly, leaving garrisons behind in Apollonia, Oricum, and Lissus. Calvinus' corps had likewise started towards Thessaly, where Caesar could also more easily join forces with the two legions of reinforcements under Quintus Cornificius coming from Italy, this time overland through Illyria.

Ascending by difficult paths in the valley of the Aous and crossing the mountain chain which separates Epirus from Thessaly, Caesar arrived at the Peneus. Calvinus was likewise directed thither, and the junction of the two armies, thus accomplished by the shortest and least exposed route, took place at Aeginium not far from the source of the Peneus. The first Thessalian town (Gomphi) before which the united army arrived closed its gates. It was quickly stormed and given up to pillage, and the other terrified towns of Thessaly submitted as soon as Caesar's legions merely appeared. Amid these marches and conflicts, and with the help of the supplies—albeit not too ample—which the region afforded, the traces and recollections of past calamitous days gradually vanished.

The victories of Dyrrhachium had thus borne little immediate fruit for the victors. Pompey's unwieldy army and numerous cavalry had not been able to follow his nimble enemy into the mountains; Caesar like Calvinus had escaped from pursuit, and the two stood securely united in Thessaly. Perhaps it would have been best if Pompey had now embarked straightway for Italy, where success was scarcely doubtful. But only a division of the

fleet departed for Sicily and Italy. In the coalition camp
the war was regarded as so completely won at Dyrrhachium that it only remained to seek out and capture the
defeated army. Their former overcaution was succeeded
by still less-justified arrogance. They ignored the fact that
they had, strictly speaking, failed in the pursuit; that they
had to encounter a refreshed and reorganized army in
Thessaly; and that there was grave risk in leaving the sea,
renouncing the support of the fleet, and following their
antagonist to a battlefield of his choice. They were simply
resolved at any price to fight with Caesar, and therefore
to get at him as soon as possible and by the most convenient way. Cato took command of the garrison of eighteen
cohorts at Dyrrhachium, and the 300 ships of war at
Corcyra. Pompey and Scipio proceeded by different routes
to the lower Peneus, and met at Larisa.

South of Larisa is a plain intersected by a tributary of
the Peneus, the Enipeus; Caesar's army lay on the left
bank of the latter stream near the town of Pharsalus,
while Pompey pitched his camp opposite to Caesar on the
right bank of the Enipeus along a gradual slope. Pompey's entire army was assembled, while Caesar still expected the arrival of nearly two legions now stationed under Quintus Fufius Calenus in Greece, and the two legions
of Cornificius en route from Italy via Illyria. Pompey's
army, numbering eleven legions (47,000 men) and 7,000
horse, was more than double Caesar's in infantry, and
seven times as numerous in cavalry. Fatigue and conflicts
had so decimated Caesar's troops that his eight legions
numbered not over 22,000 men under arms—well under
half their normal size. Pompey's victorious army, provided with a countless cavalry and ample supplies, had
provisions in abundance, while Caesar's troops had difficulty keeping alive, and could only hope for better supplies from the approaching harvest. The Pompeian soldiers, who had learned in the last campaign to know war
and trust their leader, were in the best of humor.

All military considerations on Pompey's side favored engaging in the decisive battle soon, since they had now confronted Caesar in Thessaly; and the emigrant impatience of the genteel officers and others with the army doubtless made such reasoning invincible in the war council. Since Dyrrhachium these lords had regarded their triumph as established fact. Already they were contending among themselves over Caesar's supreme pontificate, and sending instructions to Rome to hire houses at the Forum for the next elections. When Pompey hesitated to cross the rivulet separating the two armies, which Caesar with his much weaker force did not venture to pass, great indignation was aroused. Pompey, it was said, only delayed in order to play somewhat longer his part of Agamemnon, ruling over so many consulars and praetorians.

Pompey yielded. Caesar, under the impression that matters would not come to a battle, had just formed a plan of turning the enemy's flank, and for that purpose was about to set out towards Scotussa. But he likewise arrayed his legions for battle when he saw the Pompeians preparing to offer it on his bank.

Thus the battle of Pharsalus was fought on August 9, 48 B.C., on almost the same field where a victory over Philip of Macedonia a hundred and fifty years before had laid the foundation of Rome's dominion in the East. Pompey rested his right wing on the Enipeus, Caesar resting his left on the broken ground in front of the river. The two other wings were stationed out in the plain, covered in each case by cavalry and light troops. Pompey's plan was to keep his infantry on the defensive, while his cavalry scattered the weak enemy horse, mixed with light infantry after the German fashion, and then took Caesar's right wing in the rear. Pompey's infantry courageously sustained the first charge, and the engagement there came to a stand. Labienus likewise dispersed Caesar's cavalry after a brave but brief resistance, and deployed his force to the left with the view of turning the infantry.

But Caesar, foreseeing his cavalry defeat, had stationed behind it some 2,000 of his best legionaries. As the enemy's horsemen, driving those of Caesar before them, galloped along and around the line, they suddenly came upon this select corps advancing intrepidly against them and, rapidly thrown into confusion by the unexpected and unusual infantry attack, galloped at full speed from the field of battle. The victorious legionaries cut to pieces the now defenseless enemy archers, then rushed at Pompey's left wing and began on their part to turn it. At the same time Caesar's reserve advanced along the whole line to the attack. The unexpected defeat of the Pompeian army's best arm not only raised the courage of their opponents, but broke that of the army and above all that of the general. When Pompey, who from the outset distrusted his infantry, saw his horsemen gallop off, he rode back at once to the camp without even awaiting the outcome of the general attack ordered by Caesar. His legions began to waver and soon to retire over the brook into the camp, which was not accomplished without severe loss.

The day was thus lost and many an able soldier had fallen, but Pompey's army was still substantially intact, and his situation was far less perilous than Caesar's after the defeat at Dyrrhachium. But while Caesar had learned that fortune loves to withdraw herself at certain moments even from her favorites, in order to be won back through their perseverance, Pompey knew fortune only as the constant goddess, and despaired when she withdrew. Caesar's grander nature only developed mightier energies in the face of adversity; Pompey's inferior soul under similar pressure sank into the abyss of despondency. As once in the Sertorian war Pompey had been on the point of abandoning his post when faced by a superior opponent, so now, when he saw his legions retire over the stream, he threw from him the fatal general's scarf and rode off by the nearest route to the sea.

His discouraged and leaderless army—for Scipio, although recognized by Pompey as colleague in supreme command, was general-in-chief in name only—hoped to find protection behind the camp walls, but Caesar allowed it no rest. The obstinate resistance of the Roman and Thracian camp guard was speedily overcome, and the mass was compelled to withdraw in disorder to the heights above the camp. It attempted by moving along these hills to reach Larisa; but Caesar's troops, heeding neither booty nor fatigue and advancing by better paths in the plain, intercepted the route of the fugitives. In fact, when late in the evening the Pompeians suspended their march, their pursuers were even able to draw an entrenched line excluding them from the only water in the neighborhood.

So ended the day of Pharsalus. The enemy's army was not only defeated, but annihilated: 15,000 of the enemy lay dead or wounded on the field of battle, while the Caesarians missed only 200 men. The Pompeians who remained together, amounting still to nearly 20,000 men, surrendered the next morning. Only isolated troops (including, it is true, the officers of most note) sought a refuge in the mountains, and nine of the eleven enemy eagles were handed over to Caesar. Caesar, who on the very day of the battle had reminded his soldiers to remember the fellow citizen in the foe, did not treat the captives as did Bibulus and Labienus; nevertheless he too now found it necessary to exercise some severity. The common soldiers were incorporated in the army, fines or confiscations were inflicted on the men of better rank, and the captured senators and equites of note with few exceptions suffered death. The time for clemency was past, and the longer the civil war lasted, the more remorseless and implacable it became.

Some time elapsed before the consequences of August 9, 49 B.C., could be fully discerned. First was the passing over to Caesar's side of all those who had supported the party vanquished at Pharsalus merely as the more powerful; the defeat was so decisive that the victor was joined by everyone not willing or obligated to fight for a lost cause. All the cities, kings, and peoples who had hitherto been Pompey's vassals now recalled their naval and military contingents, and declined to receive the refugees of the beaten party.[1] Almost the sole exceptions were the little town of Megara, which allowed itself to be besieged and stormed by the Caesarians, and King Juba of Numidia, who after his victory over Curio awaited with still greater certainty the long-expected annexation of his kingdom by Caesar, and was thus tied to the defeated party for better or worse.

Just as the protectorates submitted to the victor of Pharsalus, the tail of the constitutional party—all who had joined it halfheartedly or, like Marcus Cicero and his ilk, merely danced around the aristocracy like the witches around the Brocken [2]—hastened to come to terms with the new monarch, who with contemptuous indulgence readily and courteously granted their petition. But the flower of the defeated party made no compromise. The aristocracy was done for, but the aristocrats could never be converted to monarchy. The highest revelations of humanity are perishable: the once-true religion may become a lie, the most blessed political system a curse. But even a dying gospel still finds confessors. If such a faith cannot move mountains like faith in the living truth, yet it remains true to itself to the end, and does not depart from the earth until it has dragged its last priests and partisans along with it, and a new generation, freed from those shadows of the dead past, rules over a world that has renewed its youth.

1. The original here adds a list, including the Bosporan king Pharnaces, who seized the chance to grab some adjoining territory.
2. The German mountain designated by legend as the witches' meeting place.

So was it in Rome. Into whatever abyss of degeneracy the aristocratic rule had now sunk, it had once been a great political system. The sacred fire by which Italy had been conquered and Hannibal vanquished continued to glow, though somewhat dim and dull, in the Roman nobility so long as that nobility existed, and rendered impossible a cordial understanding between the men of the old regime and the new monarch. A large part of the constitutional party submitted outwardly, and recognized the monarchy so far as to accept pardon from Caesar and to retire as much as possible into private life—which, however, ordinarily was not done without the mental reservation of thereby preserving themselves for better days. This course was chiefly followed by the partisans of lesser note, but the able Marcus Marcellus, who had brought about the rupture with Caesar, judiciously and voluntarily banished himself to Lesbos. However, in most of the genuine aristocracy passion was more powerful than cool reflection—no doubt with the help of self-deception as to their prospects and fear of the victor's vengeance.

No one probably judged the situation with such painful clarity, free from fear or hope, as Marcus Cato. Completely convinced that after Ilerda and Pharsalus monarchy was inevitable, and courageous enough to accept that bitter truth and act upon it, he hesitated whether the constitutional party ought even to continue a war which would necessarily require sacrifices for a lost cause by many who knew not why they fought. And when he resolved to oppose the monarchy not for victory, but for a speedier and more honorable fall, he sought to draw no one into this war who chose to survive the republic's fall and accept the monarchy. He believed that so long as the republic had been merely threatened, it was his right and duty to compel the lukewarm to take part in the struggle. Now, he felt it senseless and cruel to force the individual to share the republic's ruin. Not only did he himself discharge every one who desired to return to Italy; when the wildest of the partisans, Gnaeus Pompey the younger, insisted on executing these people and Cicero in particular, Cato alone by his moral authority prevented it. Pompey also had no desire for peace. Had he deserved to hold the position he occupied, he might have perceived that an aspirant to a crown cannot return to the ordinary beaten track, and that there is no place left on earth for one who has failed in that aim. But Pompey was hardly too noble-minded to ask a favor which the victor would have perhaps been magnanimous enough to grant. On the contrary, he was probably too mean to do so. Whether he could not decide to trust himself to Caesar, or whether in his usual vague way, after the first impression of the disaster of Pharsalus had worn off, he began to cherish new hope, Pompey was resolved to continue the struggle and seek yet another battlefield.

Thus, despite Caesar's efforts by prudence and moderation to appease the fury of his opponents and lessen their number, the struggle went on without a break. But almost all the leading men had fought at Pharsalus; and while none were killed except Lucius Domitius Ahenobarbus, their flight scattered them in so many directions that they were unable to mount a common plan for continuing the campaign. Most of them found their way, partly through the desolate mountains of Macedonia and Illyria and partly by the aid of the fleet, to Corcyra, where Marcus Cato commanded the reserve left behind.

Here a council of war took place under the presidency of Cato, at which Metellus Scipio, Titus Labienus, Lucius Afranius, Gnaeus Pompey the younger, and others were present; but the commander-in-chief's absence and the painful uncertainty as to his fate, as well as the party's internal dissensions, prevented any common agreement, and eventually each took the course he felt most suitable for himself or for the common cause. Among the many

straws to which one might cling, it was in fact highly difficult to say which one would keep above water longest.
Macedonia and Greece were lost by the battle of Pharsalus. It is true that Cato (who had immediately evacuated Dyrrhachium on the news of the defeat) still held
Corcyra, and Rutilius Lupus the Peloponnesus, for the
constitutional party. For a moment it seemed as if the
Pompeians would make a stand at Patrae in the Peloponnesus, but the accounts of the advance of Calenus sufficed
to frighten them from that quarter. There was also no
serious attempt to maintain Corcyra. The Pompeian
squadrons despatched to the Italian and Sicilian coasts
after the victories at Dyrrhachium had achieved not unimportant successes against Brundisium, Messana and
Vibo, and at Messana had burnt the whole fleet being
fitted out for Caesar. However, the ships involved, mostly
from Asia Minor and Syria, were recalled by their communities after Pharsalus, so that the expedition came to
an end of itself.

In Asia Minor and Syria there were at the moment no
troops of either party, except for the Bosporan army of
Pharnaces which had taken possession, ostensibly on Caesar's behalf, of various regions belonging to his opponents. In Egypt there was still a considerable Roman
army formed of the troops left behind by Gabinius, and
thereafter recruited from Italian vagrants and Syrian or
Cilician banditti; but the recall of the Egyptian vessels
soon made it evident that the court of Alexandria had no
intention of standing by the defeated party or even placing its troops at their disposal.

Somewhat more favorable prospects presented themselves in the West. In Spain, Pompeian sympathies were
so strong among the population that the Caesarians had
to give up their planned attack against Africa, and an insurrection seemed inevitable as soon as a leader of note
appeared on the peninsula. In Africa the coalition—or
rather King Juba of Numidia, who was the true regent

there—had been arming unmolested since the autumn of
49 B.C.

Thus, while the whole East was lost by the coalition at
Pharsalus, it might continue the war honorably perhaps
in Spain and certainly in Africa; for to claim the aid of
the Numidian king, who had been a subject of Rome,
against revolutionary fellow citizens was no act of treason, though doubtless a painful humiliation. Those who
gave up right or honor in this conflict of despair might
move outside the law and commence hostilities as robbers. They might enter into alliance with independent
neighboring states, and introduce the public foes into the
civil strife. And finally, they might give lip service to the
monarchy while seeking to restore the legitimate republic
by the assassin's dagger.

That the vanquished should withdraw and renounce the
new monarchy was at least a natural expression of their
desperate position. The mountains and above all the sea
had long been for the ancient world the asylum not only
of all crime, but also of intolerable misery and of oppressed right. It was natural for Pompeians and republicans to wage a defiant war from the mountains and the
sea against the monarchy of Caesar, which had ejected
them, and especially natural for them to take up piracy
on a grand scale with more compact organization and
more definite aims. Even after the recall of the eastern
squadrons they still possessed a considerable fleet, while
Caesar had as yet virtually no vessels of war. Their connection with the Dalmatae, who had risen against Caesar
in their own interest, plus their control over the most important seas and seaports, presented most advantageous
prospects for a small-scale naval war. Sulla's hunting out
of the democrats had ended in the Sertorian insurrection,
a conflict waged first by pirates and then by robbers which
ultimately became a serious war. So possibly, if Cato's
aristocrats or Pompey's adherents showed as much spirit
and fire as the Marian democracy, and if a true sea king

was to be found among them, a commonwealth independent of the monarchy of Caesar and perhaps a match for it might still arise on the unconquered sea.

Far more contemptible was the idea of dragging an independent neighboring state into the Roman civil war to effect a counterrevolution. Law and conscience condemn the deserter more severely than the robber, and a victorious gang of bandits finds its way back into a commonwealth more easily than emigrants who march back with the public foe. Besides, it was scarcely probable that a restoration could be effected in this way. The only state from which support could be sought was the Parthian; and it was at least doubtful whether it would adopt the republican cause, and most improbable that it would fight for that cause against Caesar.

The time for republican conspiracies had not yet come.

While the remnant of the defeated party was thus driven helplessly about by fate, with even those determined to continue the struggle knowing not how or where to do so, Caesar, resolving and acting as quickly as ever, laid everything aside to pursue Pompey—the only opponent whom he respected as an officer, and the one whose capture would probably have paralyzed half (and perhaps the more dangerous half) of his opposition. With a few men he crossed the Hellespont, where his single bark encountered an enemy fleet destined for the Black Sea and captured the entire crews, who were stupefied by the news of Pharsalus. As soon as the most necessary preparations were made, he then hastened to the East in pursuit of Pompey.

The latter had gone from the Pharsalian battlefield to Lesbos, whence he brought away his wife and his second son Sextus, and had sailed onward round Asia Minor to Cilicia and thence to Cyprus. He might have joined his partisans at Corcyra or in Africa; but repugnance toward his aristocratic allies and the thought of the reception which awaited him there, after the day of Pharsalus and above all after his disgraceful flight, seem to have induced him to prefer the Parthian king to Cato. While employed in collecting money and slaves from the Roman revenue farmers and merchants in Cyprus, and in arming a band of 2,000 slaves, he learned that Antioch had declared for Caesar and thereby closed the route to the Parthians. So he sailed instead to Egypt, where a number of his old soldiers served in the army, and where the situation and rich resources of the country would allow him time and opportunity to reorganize the war.

In Egypt, after the death of Ptolemy Auletes his children, Cleopatra, about sixteen years of age, and Ptolemy Dionysus, about ten, had jointly ascended the throne as consorts according to their father's will. But soon the brother, or rather his guardian Pothinus, had driven the sister out and compelled her to seek a refuge in Syria, whence she made preparations to get back to her paternal kingdom. Ptolemy and Pothinus with the whole Egyptian army were at Pelusium to protect the eastern frontier against her, when Pompey cast anchor at the Casian promontory and requested permission to land. The Egyptian court, long informed of the disaster at Pharsalus, was about to refuse when the king's tutor Theodotus pointed out that Pompey would then probably employ his connections in the Egyptian army to instigate rebellion, and that it would be safer, and also more politic towards Caesar, if they used this opportunity to do away with Pompey. Political reasonings of this sort were potent arguments among statesmen of the Hellenic world.

Achillas, the general of the royal troops, and some of Pompey's former soldiers went in a boat to his vessel, inviting him to come to the king and, as the water was shallow, to enter their barge. As he was stepping ashore, the military tribune Lucius Septimius stabbed him from behind under the eyes of his wife and son, who were compelled to watch the murder from the deck of their ship without the means of rescue or revenge. Thus on September 28, 48 B.C., the very same day on which thirteen years before he had entered the capital in triumph over Mithradates, the man who for a generation had been called the Great, and who for years had ruled Rome, died on the inhospitable Casian shore by the hand of one of his old soldiers.

A good officer, but otherwise limited in both intellect and heart, for thirty years fate had with superhuman constancy allowed him to shine in solving a series of easy tasks. He had been permitted to pluck all laurels planted and fostered by others, and had been presented with every opportunity for obtaining the supreme power—only to reveal an example of spurious greatness without parallel in history. Of all pitiful parts, the most pitiful is to pass for more than one really is; it is the inevitable fate of monarchy, for scarcely once in a thousand years does a man arise who is a king not merely in name but in fact. If this disproportion between appearance and reality had not been so marked in Pompey, one might gravely reflect that it was indeed he who was in a certain sense the first of the series of Roman monarchs.

When Caesar followed Pompey's trail into the roadstead of Alexandria, it was all over. With deep agitation he turned away when the murderer brought to his ship the head of the man who had been his son-in-law and for long years his colleague, and whom he had come to Egypt to capture alive. The dagger of the rash assassin canceled the question of how Caesar would have dealt with a captive Pompey. But while humane sympathy, which still found a place alongside ambition in Caesar's great soul, enjoined that he should spare his former friend, his interest also required that he demolish Pompey otherwise than by execution. For twenty years Pompey had been the acknowledged ruler of Rome, and a dominion so deeply rooted does not perish with the ruler's death. The death of Pompey did not break up the Pompeians, but merely replaced an aged, incapable, and worn-out chief

with his sons Gnaeus and Sextus, both young and active
and the second a man of decided capacity. Thus hereditary pretendership attached itself at once to the newly
founded hereditary monarchy like a parasite, and it was
very doubtful whether by this change Caesar did not lose
more than he gained.

Caesar now had nothing further to do in Egypt, and
both Romans and Egyptians expected him to apply himself immediately to the subjugation of Africa and to the
huge task of organization awaiting him after victory. But
Caesar was faithful to his custom of regulating matters
once and for all while on the spot. Being firmly convinced
that no resistance was to be expected either from the Roman garrison or the Egyptian court, and being moreover
in urgent pecuniary embarrassment, he landed in Alexandria with the two amalgamated legions (numbering
3,200 men and 800 Celtic and German cavalry) and took
up his quarters in the royal palace. There he proceeded to
collect the necessary funds and to regulate the Egyptian
succession, ignoring the saucy remark of Pothinus that
Caesar should not neglect his own important affairs for
such petty matters.[3]

But a storm was secretly brewing. Alexandria like
Rome was a cosmopolitan city, hardly inferior to the latter in numbers, and far superior to it in commercial spirit,
skill of handicraft, and a taste for science and art. Its
citizens had a lively sense of their own national importance; and if there was no political feeling, there was at
least a turbulent spirit which induced them to riot in the
streets as regularly and heartily as today's Parisians. One
may therefore conceive their feelings when they saw the
Roman general ruling in the palace of the Lagids and
their kings accepting the award of his tribunal. Pothinus

■

3. Here a further brief section of the original cites Caesar's forbearance
toward the Egyptians in money matters, and describes his cession of the
Egyptian crown jointly to the intermarried brother and sister Cleopatra
and Ptolemy Dionysus.

and the boy-king, both of whom resented the peremptory demand for the payment of old favors as well as the intervention in the throne dispute (which could only redound in favor of Cleopatra), ostentatiously sent the treasures of the temples and the gold plate of the king to be melted at the mint in order to satisfy the Roman demands. With increasing indignation the Egyptians—who were pious to the point of superstition, and who rejoiced in the world-renowned magnificence of their court as if it were their own possession—beheld the bare walls of their temples and the wooden cups on the table of their king.

The Roman army of occupation, essentially denationalized by its long abode in Egypt and many intermarriages with Egyptian women, and which moreover numbered many former Pompeians and runaway Italian criminals and slaves in its ranks, was also indignant at Caesar, who had obliged it to suspend its action on the Syrian frontier, and at his handful of haughty legionaries. The tumult at the landing, when the multitude saw the Roman axes carried into the old palace, and the numerous assassinations of his soldiers in the city, had shown Caesar the immense danger to his small force in the presence of that exasperated multitude. But it was difficult to depart at this season because of the prevailing northwest winds, and the attempt to embark might easily bring the outbreak of the insurrection. Besides, it was not Caesar's nature to leave without finishing his work.

Accordingly he ordered reinforcements from Asia at once, and meanwhile made a show of the utmost self-possession. Never was there greater gaiety in his camp than at Alexandria; and while the beautiful and clever Cleopatra was not sparing of her charms in general, and least of all towards her judge, Caesar also appeared to value most his victories won over beautiful women. It was a merry prelude to near-disaster. Led by Achillas and, as was afterwards proved, at the secret orders of the king and his guardian, the Roman army of occupa-

tion appeared unexpectedly in Alexandria. As soon as
the citizens saw that it had come to attack Caesar, they
made common cause with the soldiers.

With a presence of mind which partly atoned for his
earlier foolhardiness Caesar hastily collected his scattered men, seized the king and his ministers, and entrenched himself in the royal residence and the adjoining
theater. There being no time to save the war fleet stationed in the principal harbor immediately in front of the
theater, he ordered that it be set on fire and that Pharos,
the island with the lighthouse commanding the harbor, be
occupied by means of boats. Thus at least a restricted
position for defense was secured, and the way kept open
for supplies and reinforcements. At the same time orders
were issued to the commandant of Asia Minor as well
as to the nearest subject countries, the Syrians and Na-
bataeans, the Cretans and the Rhodians, to send troops
and ships in all haste to Egypt.

Meanwhile the insurrection, now led by the princess
Arsinoë and her confidant the eunuch Ganymedes, had
free range throughout Egypt and in most of the capital.
In the streets of the latter there was daily fighting, but
Caesar was unsuccessful in gaining freer scope and breaking through to the fresh-water lake of Marea which lay
behind the town, where he could have provided himself
with water and forage. At the same time, the Alexandrians were unable to deprive the besieged of all drinking
water; for when the Nile canals in Caesar's part of the
town had been spoiled by introducing salt water, drink-
able water was unexpectedly found in wells dug on the
beach.

As Caesar could not be overcome by land, the besiegers
exerted themselves to destroy his fleet and cut him off
from his sea-borne supplies. The island with the lighthouse, and the mole connecting this with the mainland,
divided the harbor into western and eastern halves,
which were in communication with each other through

two arched openings in the mole. Caesar commanded the island and the eastern harbor, while the mole and the western harbor were held by the citizens; and, as the Alexandrian fleet had been burnt, his vessels sailed freely in and out. The Alexandrians, after having vainly attempted to introduce fire-ships from the western into the eastern harbor, equipped with the remnant of their arsenal a small squadron, and with this blocked the way of Caesar's vessels when these were towing in a fleet of transports with a legion that had arrived from Asia Minor; but the excellent Rhodian mariners of Caesar mastered the enemy.

Not long afterwards, however, the citizens captured the lighthouse island, and from that point totally closed the narrow and rocky mouth of the eastern harbor for larger ships. Thus Caesar's fleet was compelled to remain in the open roads before the eastern harbor, and his communication with the sea hung only on a weak thread. Caesar's fleet, attacked in that roadstead repeatedly by the superior naval force of the enemy, could neither shun the unequal conflict, since the loss of the lighthouse island closed the inner harbor against it, nor yet withdraw, for losing the roadstead would have cut Caesar off from the sea. Though the brave legionaries supported by the skilled Rhodian sailors consistently triumphed in these conflicts, the Alexandrians renewed and augmented their naval armaments with unwearied perseverance. The besieged had to fight as often as it pleased the besiegers, and a single victory for the latter would have left Caesar totally hemmed in and probably lost.

It was imperative to recover the lighthouse island. A double attack, made by boats from the harbor side and by the war vessels from the seaboard, recaptured both the island and the lower part of the mole. Caesar ordered the attack stopped at the mole's second arch opening, and at that point closed the mole from the city by a transverse wall. But when a violent conflict arose around the

entrenchers, the Roman troops left undefended the part
of the mole adjoining the island. An Egyptian force
landed there unexpectedly, attacked in the rear the Roman soldiers and sailors crowded on the mole at the
transverse wall, and drove the whole mass in wild confusion into the sea. Roman ships rescued some, but most
—including about 400 soldiers and a still larger number
of sailors—were drowned. The general himself was obliged to seek refuge in his ship, and when this sank from
overloading, he had to save himself by swimming to another. But the severe loss was amply compensated by re-
covery of the lighthouse island, which together with the
mole as far as the first arch opening remained in Caesar's
hands.

At last the longed-for relief arrived. Mithradates of
Pergamum, an able warrior of the school of King Mithradates of Pontus (whose natural son he claimed to be),
led a motley army by land from Syria—Ityraeans of the
prince of the Libanus, Bedouins of Jamblichus, Jews under their leader Antipater, and contingents of the petty
chiefs and communities of Cilicia and Syria. From Pelusium, which Mithradates had the good fortune to occupy
the day he arrived, he took the great road toward Memphis with the view of crossing the Nile before it divides
into its many mouths in the Delta. During this movement
his troops received substantial support from the Jewish
peasants who were settled in large numbers in this part
of Egypt.

The Egyptians, headed by the young king Ptolemy
(whom Caesar had released in the vain hope of quench-
ing the insurrection), dispatched an army to detain
Mithradates on the Nile's farther bank. This army fell in
with the enemy beyond Memphis at the so-called Jews'-
camp, between Onion and Heliopolis. Nevertheless
Mithradates, trained in Roman-style maneuvering and en-
camping, succeeded in fighting his way to the opposite
bank at Memphis. Caesar, as soon as he received word of

the relieving army's arrival, conveyed part of his troops in ships to the end of the lake of Marea west of Alexandria, and marched round this lake and up the Nile to meet Mithradates advancing down the river.

The junction took place without enemy hindrance. Caesar then followed the retreating king into the Delta, and, notwithstanding the deep canal in front of the Egyptian vanguard, overthrew it at the first onset and immediately stormed the Egyptian camp. It lay at the foot of a rise between the Nile—from which only a narrow path separated it—and marshes difficult of access. Caesar ordered the camp assailed simultaneously from the front and from the flank on the path along the Nile, while a third detachment was to ascend unseen the heights behind the camp. The victory was complete. The camp was taken, and those Egyptians who did not fall to the sword were drowned in attempting to escape to the fleet on the Nile. In one of the overladen boats, the young king also disappeared beneath the waters of his native stream.

Immediately after the battle Caesar advanced at the head of his cavalry from the land side straight into the part of the capital occupied by the Egyptians. In mourning attire, with the images of their gods in their hands, the enemy received him and sued for peace; and the legionaries left behind, when they saw him return as victor, welcomed him with boundless joy. The fate of the city, which had ventured to thwart his plans and which had brought the master of the world within a hairsbreadth of destruction, lay in Caesar's hands. But he was too much of a ruler to be vengeful, and dealt with the Alexandrians as with the citizens of Massilia. Pointing to their devastated city deprived of its granaries, its world-renowned library, and other important public buildings through the burning of the fleet, he exhorted the inhabitants to cultivate earnestly the arts of peace alone, and to heal the wounds which they had inflicted on themselves.

For the rest, he contented himself with granting the

Jews of Alexandria the rights enjoyed by the Greek population, and with replacing the Roman army of occupation, which at least nominally obeyed the kings of Egypt,
by a formal garrison composed of the two besieged legions plus a third which afterwards arrived from Syria,
under a commander chosen by himself. He purposely selected for this position of trust a man whose birth made
it impossible for him to abuse it—Rufio, an able soldier
but the son of a freedman. Cleopatra and her younger
brother Ptolemy obtained the sovereignty of Egypt
under the Roman protection. The princess Arsinoë was
carried off to Italy, to prevent her from serving again as
a pretext for revolt by the Egyptians, who in Oriental
fashion were as devoted to their dynasty as they were indifferent towards individual dynasts. Cyprus again became a part of the Roman province of Cilicia.

This insignificant Alexandrian insurrection, of slight
importance compared with the world-shaking events then
taking place in the Roman state, had nonetheless a momentous influence in that it compelled the one man who
was everything, and without whom nothing could be settled, to forego his proper tasks from October of 48 B.C.
to March of 47 in order to fight alongside Jews and Bedouins against a city rabble. The results of personal rule
began to appear. The monarchy had arrived, but the
monarch was absent and the wildest confusion reigned
everywhere. For the moment the Caesarians were, like
the Pompeians, without leadership. Everywhere matters
were decided partly by the ability of the individual officers,
but most of all by accident.[4]

Indeed, matters were in a serious state in Africa, where
the constitutional party had ruled absolutely from the
start of the civil war. Until the battle of Pharsalus, King

■

---

4. A short section here omitted describes Caesar's lightning conquest of
King Pharnaces of Pontus, who took advantage of the Roman civil war to
expand his dominions, and some not inconsiderable successes by the Pompeians in Illyria and on the Adriatic coast.

Juba had been the *de facto* ruler there. He had vanquished Curio, and his flying horsemen and numberless
archers were the main strength of the army. Beside him
the Pompeian governor Varus played so subordinate a
role that he even had to deliver the Roman captives from
Curio's army to the king, and look on while they were
executed or transported into the interior.

After the battle of Pharsalus a change took place. Except for Pompey, no leader of the defeated party thought
of flight to the Parthians. As little did they attempt to
hold the sea with their united resources; the efforts of
Marcus Octavius in Illyrian waters were isolated and
without permanent success. The great majority of republicans and Pompeians headed for Africa, where alone an
honorable and constitutional warfare might still be waged
against the usurper. There gradually gathered the fragments of the army scattered at Pharsalus, the troops that
had garrisoned Dyrrhachium, Corcyra, and the Peloponnesus, and the remains of the Illyrian fleet. There met the
second commander-in-chief Metellus Scipio, Pompey's
two sons Gnaeus and Sextus, the republican political
leader Marcus Cato, and the able officers Labienus, Afranius, Petreius, and Octavius.

If the resources of the emigrants had diminished, their
fanaticism had if possible even increased. Not only did
they continue to murder their prisoners, and even Caesar's officers under flag of truce. King Juba, who combined the partisan's exasperation with the fury of the
half-barbarous African, even laid down the maxim that
the citizens of every community suspected of sympathiz-
ing with the enemy should be exterminated and their
town burnt—a theory applied in practice against some unfortunate townships. In fact, it was solely due to Cato's
energetic intervention that the flourishing provincial capital Utica, which like Carthage of old had long been eyed
jealously by the Numidian kings, did not meet the same
fate, and that only precautionary measures were taken

against its citizens, who were not unjustly accused of Caesarian leanings.

As neither Caesar nor any of his lieutenants made the smallest move against Africa, the coalition had ample time to reorganize politically and militarily. First, it was necessary to fill the post of commander-in-chief left open by Pompey's death. King Juba was not disinclined to retain the position which he had held in Africa up to the battle of Pharsalus. Indeed, he bore himself no longer as a Roman vassal but as an ally or even as a protector, and took it upon himself, for example, to coin Roman silver money with his name and device. He even proposed to be the sole wearer of purple in the camp, and suggested that the Roman commanders lay aside their purple mantle of office. Metellus Scipio also demanded the supreme command because Pompey had recognized him on an equal footing, though more because Pompey was his son-in-law than on military grounds. A like demand was raised by Varus as provincial governor—self-nominated, it is true —since the war was to be waged in his province. And lastly, the army desired for its leader the propraetor Marcus Cato.

Obviously the army was right. Cato was the only man with the requisite devotion, energy, and authority for the difficult office. If he was no military man, it was infinitely better to appoint a nonmilitary man who understood how to listen to reason and make his subordinates act, than an officer of untried capacity like Varus or one of tried incapacity like Metellus Scipio. But the decision fell at length on this same Scipio, and it was Cato himself who mainly determined that decision.

He did so not because he felt unequal to such a task, or because his vanity found satisfaction in declining rather than accepting. Still less was it because he loved or respected Scipio, with whom he was at odds personally, and who despite his notorious inefficiency had attained influence merely through being Pompey's father-in-law. He did it simply and solely because in his obstinate legal formalism he chose to let the republic founder according to law rather than save it in an irregular way. When after the battle of Pharsalus he met Marcus Cicero at Corcyra, he had offered to hand over the Corcyran command to the latter—who still held the rank of general from his Cilician administration—as the ranking officer according to the letter of the law. By this readiness he had driven almost to despair the unfortunate advocate, who now cursed his military laurels a thousand times; but he also astonished all men of the least perspicacity.

The same principles were applied now when something more was at stake. Cato weighed the question of the new commander-in-chief as if the matter involved a field at Tusculum, and adjudged it to Scipio. By this sentence both his own and Varus' candidacy were set aside. But it was also he alone who resisted with energy the claims of King Juba, and made him feel that the Roman nobility came to him not as a suppliant might approach a Parthian king, beseeching aid at the hands of a protector, but as men entitled to command and require aid from a subject. In view of the state of the Roman forces in Africa Juba could not avoid lowering his claims to some extent, although the weak Scipio agreed that his troops should be paid from the Roman treasury, and that the province of Africa should be ceded to him in the event of victory.

Alongside the new commander-in-chief the Senate of the "three hundred" again emerged. It established itself in Utica, replenishing its thinned ranks by admitting the wealthiest and most esteemed men of the equestrian order.

Military preparations were energetically pushed, chiefly through the zeal of Cato, and every man capable of arms, even freedmen and Libyans, was enrolled in the legions. So many hands were withdrawn from agriculture that many of the fields were untended, but the result was certainly imposing. The heavy infantry numbered fourteen legions, of which two were already raised by Varus, eight others formed partly from the refugees and partly from provincial conscripts, and four were legions of Juba armed in the Roman manner. The heavy cavalry, consisting of Celts and Germans who came with Labienus and sundry others incorporated in their ranks, was 1,600 strong without counting Juba's cavalry squadron equipped in Roman style. The light troops consisted of mounted bowmen, a host of archers on foot, and innumerable Numidians riding without bridle or rein and armed merely with javelins. To these might be added Juba's 120 elephants and the fleet of 55 sail commanded by Publius Varus and Marcus Octavius.

The urgent want of money was somewhat remedied through self-taxation by the Senate, which was the more productive since the richest African capitalists had been induced to enter it. Grain and other supplies were accumulated in immense quantities in defensible fortresses, while at the same time open townships were swept as clean of stores as possible. The absence of Caesar, the troublesome temper of his legions, and the ferment in Spain and Italy gradually raised men's spirits, and fresh hopes of victory began to replace the recollection of the Pharsalian defeat.

The time Caesar lost in Egypt nowhere revenged itself more severely than here. Had he proceeded to Africa immediately after Pompey's death, he would have found a weak, disorganized, and frightened army under hopelessly divided leaders. Now, owing especially to Cato's energy, there was in Africa an army equal in size to that defeated at Pharsalus, led by generals of note, and under a regulated superintendence.

An evil star seemed to preside over this African expedition of Caesar. Even before embarking for Egypt he had made certain preparatory arrangements in Spain and Italy looking toward the African war, but all these had yielded nothing but mischief. From Spain, according to Caesar's arrangement, the governor of the southern province Quintus Cassius Longinus was to cross with four legions to Africa and, after joining forces with King Bogud of West Mauretania, was to advance with him toward Numidia and the Roman province of Africa. But that army destined for Africa included a number of native Spaniards and two former Pompeian legions; Pompeian sympathies also prevailed in the province, and the unskilful and tyrannical behavior of the Caesarian governor was not suited to allay them. A formal revolt took place, with troops and towns taking part for or against the governor. Those who had risen against Caesar's lieutenant were on the point of openly displaying the Pompeian banner, and Pompey's elder son Gnaeus had already embarked for Spain to capitalize on this favorable development, when the disavowal of the governor by the most respectable Caesarians and the interference of the commander of the northern province suppressed the insurrection in the nick of time.

Gnaeus Pompey, who had lost time en route in vainly attempting to establish himself in Mauretania, came too late. Gaius Trebonius, whom Caesar sent to Spain to relieve Cassius in the fall of 47 B.C., met with absolute obedience everywhere, but amid these blunders nothing was done from Spain against the republicans in Africa. Indeed, because of these complications King Bogud of West Mauretania, who as Caesar's ally might at least have hindered King Juba, had been called away with his troops to Spain.

Still more serious were the disturbances among the troops collected at Caesar's orders in southern Italy for transporting to Africa. They were mainly the old legions which had founded Caesar's throne in Gaul, Spain, and Thessaly. Their spirit had not been improved by victories, and had been utterly disorganized by long repose in Lower Italy. The almost superhuman demands which the general had made on them, whose effects were only too apparent in their fearfully thinned ranks, left even in these men

of iron a secret rancor which required only time and quiet
to set in ferment. The only man with influence over them
had been absent and almost unheard-of for a year. Their
commanding officers were far more afraid of the soldiers
than the soldiers of them, and overlooked in the conquerors of the world every outrage and every breach of
discipline.

When the orders to embark for Sicily arrived, requiring the soldier to exchange the luxurious ease of Campania for a third campaign certainly as difficult as those
of Spain and Thessaly, the reins, too long relaxed and
now too suddenly tightened, snapped asunder. The legions
refused to obey till the promised presents were paid to
them, scornfully repulsed the officers sent by Caesar, and
even threw stones at them. An attempt to extinguish the
incipient revolt by increased promises not only had no success, but the soldiers set out in masses to demand fulfillment of the promises from the general in the capital. Several officers who attempted to restrain them were slain.

It was a formidable danger. Caesar ordered the gates
occupied by the few soldiers who were in the city, to ward
off at least for the moment the justly feared pillage, and
suddenly appeared among the furious bands demanding
to know what they wanted. They exclaimed: "Discharge!"
In a moment the request was granted. Caesar added that
regarding the presents promised to his soldiers at his
triumph, as well as the lands which he had not promised
but had destined for them, they might apply to him on the
day when he and the other soldiers celebrated their triumph. In the triumph itself they could not participate,
having been previously discharged.

The mutineers were not prepared for this turn of
events. Convinced that they were essential for the African campaign, they had demanded their discharge only
so that, if it were refused, they might attach their own
conditions to further service. Half shaken in their belief
as to their own indispensability; too awkward to bring the

negotiation back to the proper channel; shamed by Caesar's fidelity to his word even toward soldiers who had forgotten their allegiance, and by his generosity which even now granted more than he had ever promised; deeply affected at the prospect of being mere civilian spectators of the triumph of their comrades; shocked at being no longer called "comrades" but "citizens," a form of address which from his mouth sounded so strangely, destroying in one blow the whole pride of their past soldierly career; and besides all this, under the spell of the man whose presence had an irresistible power—the soldiers stood mute and lingering awhile, till from all sides a cry arose to be permitted again to be called Caesar's soldiers. Caesar, after allowing himself to be sufficiently entreated, granted the permission, but the ringleaders in the mutiny had their triumphal presents reduced by a third. History knows no greater psychological masterpiece, nor one more completely successful.

This mutiny harmed the African campaign, at least by considerably delaying its start. When Caesar arrived at Lilybaeum, the port of embarkation, the ten legions destined for Africa were far from ready, and the experienced troops were farthest behind. However, hardly had six legions (five were newly formed) arrived together with the necessary war vessels and transports, when Caesar put to sea with them.

The enemy fleet, which because of the prevailing autumn gales was drawn up on the beach of an island in front of the bay of Carthage, did not oppose the passage. But the same storms scattered Caesar's fleet, and when he availed himself of the opportunity of landing not far from Hadrumetum (Susa), he could disembark only some 3,000 men, mostly recruits, and 150 horsemen. His attempt to capture Hadrumetum, strongly occupied by the enemy, miscarried, but Caesar possessed himself of two seaports near each other, Ruspina (Monastir near Susa) and Little Leptis. Here he entrenched himself; but his position was so insecure that he kept his cavalry in the ships, and the ships provisioned with water and ready for sea, in order to re-embark instantly if he were attacked by a superior force. This, however, was not necessary, for just at the right time the ships driven out of their course arrived.

The very next day Caesar, whose army suffered from want of grain because of the activities of the Pompeians, undertook with three legions an expedition into the interior. But on the march he was attacked not far from Ruspina by the corps which Labienus had brought up to dislodge Caesar from the coast. As Labienus had only cavalry and archers, and Caesar almost nothing but infantry, the legions were quickly surrounded and exposed to the enemy's missiles without being able to retaliate or attack successfully. No doubt the deploying of the entire line relieved once more the flanks, and spirited charges saved the honor of their arms. But a retreat was unavoidable, and had Ruspina not been so near, the Moorish javelin might have done the work of the Parthian bow at Carrhae.

Caesar, now fully convinced of the difficulty of the impending war, did not again expose his untried soldiers, disheartened by the new mode of fighting, but awaited the arrival of his veterans. The interval was employed in providing a counterpoise to the enemy's crushing superiority in long-range weapons. The use of men from the fleet as light horsemen or archers availed little, but Caesar succeeded in mobilizing against Juba the Gaetulian pastoral tribes wandering on the southern slope of the Atlas mountains toward the Sahara. The blows of the Marian and Sullan period had reached even these peoples, and their indignation against Pompey, who had made them subordinate to the Numidian kings, rendered them from the outset favorably inclined to the heir of the mighty Marius, of whose Jugurthan campaign they still had a lively recollection. The Mauretanian kings, Bogud in Tingis and

Bocchus in Iol, were Juba's natural rivals and to a certain extent long since in alliance with Caesar. Further, there still roamed in the border region between the kingdoms of Juba and Bocchus the last of the Catilinarians, Publius Sittius, who eighteen years before had transformed himself from a bankrupt Italian merchant into a leader of Mauretanian freebooters, and since then had acquired both a name and a body of retainers amid the Libyan quarrels. Bocchus and Sittius together fell on Numidia, occupying the important town of Cirta; and their attack, as well as that of the Gaetulians, compelled King Juba to send part of his troops to his southern and western frontiers.

Caesar's situation, however, continued amply unpleasant. His army was crowded into a space of six square miles, and though the fleet conveyed grain, the want of fodder was as keenly felt by Caesar's cavalry as by that of Pompey before Dyrrhachium. The light troops of the enemy, notwithstanding all Caesar's exertions, remained so immeasurably superior that it seemed almost impossible for him to invade the interior even with veterans. If Metellus Scipio had abandoned the coast towns, he might perhaps have achieved a victory like those which the Parthians won over Crassus and Juba over Curio, and he could at least have endlessly protracted the war. Every consideration suggested this plan of campaign. Even Cato, although far from a strategist, counseled its adoption, and offered at the same time to lead a corps to Italy and call the republicans to arms—which amid the utter confusion there might very well have met with success. But Cato could only advise, and the commander-in-chief Scipio decided that the war should be fought along the coast.

This was a blunder not only because they thereby abandoned a sure-fire strategy, but also because much of their own army, as well as the civilian populace in the new theater of hostilities, was in a dangerous mood. The fearfully strict recruitment, the seizure of supplies, the devas-

tation of the smaller townships, and the general feeling
that they were being sacrificed for an already lost alien
cause had exasperated the native population against the
republicans; and the acts of terror against any community
merely suspected of indifference had raised this exasperation to bitter hatred. The African towns which could declared for Caesar, and desertion spread among the
numerous Gaetulians and Libyans serving in the light
troops and even in the legions of the republicans. But
Scipio persevered with all the obstinacy of folly. He
marched his entire force from Utica to Ruspina and Little
Leptis, furnished Hadrumetum to the north and Thapsus
to the south with strong garrisons, and in concert with
Juba, who likewise appeared before Ruspina with all his
troops not required to defend his frontier, offered battle
repeatedly to the enemy.

Caesar, however, was determined to wait for his veteran legions. As one after another arrived, Scipio and
Juba lost their desire for a pitched battle, and Caesar
could not compel one because of his marked inferiority
in light cavalry. Nearly two months passed in skirmishing near Ruspina and Thapsus, devoted chiefly to establishing outposts and discovering the concealed store-pits
common in the country. Caesar, compelled by the enemy's
horse to keep to the heights or to cover his flanks by
entrenchments, gradually accustomed his soldiers to the
new mode of fighting during this laborious and protracted
warfare. Friend and foe hardly recognized the brilliant
general in this cautious tactician who trained his men
carefully and often in person; and they became almost
puzzled by his masterly skill in delay.

At last Caesar, having received his final reinforcements,
made a lateral movement towards Thapsus. Scipio had
strongly garrisoned this town, thereby committing the
blunder of offering his opponent an easy point of attack.
He soon committed a second and less excusable one of
attempting to rescue Thapsus, thus giving battle on

ground where the infantry would be decisive. Immediately along the shore opposite Caesar's camp the legions of Scipio and Juba appeared, their front ranks ready for fighting while the rear were occupied in forming an entrenched camp. At the same time the garrison of Thapsus prepared for a sally.

Caesar's camp guard sufficed to repulse the latter. His veteran legions, correctly judging the enemy from their disorderly array, compelled a trumpeter to sound the attack while the enemy entrenching was still going on, and even before the general gave the signal. The whole line advanced headed by Caesar himself, who, when he saw his men attack without waiting for his orders, galloped forward to lead them. The right wing, in advance of the other divisions, frightened the elephants opposed to it (this was the last great battle in which these animals were employed) by throwing bullets and arrows, so that they wheeled round on their own ranks. The covering force was cut down, the enemy left wing broken, and the whole line overthrown. The defeat was the more destructive since the new enemy camp was not yet ready and the old one somewhat distant. Both were successively captured almost without resistance.

The mass of the defeated army threw away their arms and sued for quarter, but Caesar's soldiers were no longer those who had readily refrained from battle before Ilerda and honorably spared the defenseless at Pharsalus. The habit of civil war and the rancor left by the mutiny asserted themselves terrifyingly at Thapsus. If the hydra which they fought always put forth new energies, if the army hurried from Italy to Spain to Macedonia to Africa, if the longed-for repose never came, the soldier not unreasonably charged this state of affairs to Caesar's unseasonable clemency. Swearing to remedy the general's neglect, he ignored the pleas of his disarmed fellow citizens as well as the commands of Caesar and his officers. The fifty thousand corpses that covered the battlefield of Thapsus

—including several Caesarian officers known as secret opponents of the new monarchy, who were cut down by their own men—showed how the soldier procures his own repose. The victorious army's dead on that April 6th of 46 B.C. numbered no more than fifty.

The battle of Thapsus ended the African struggle as completely as Pharsalus a year and a half before had terminated that in the East. Cato as commandant of Utica convoked the Senate, set forth the state of affairs, and asked those assembled to decide whether to yield or defend themselves to the last man, urging only that all resolve and act together. The more courageous view found several supporters, who proposed to free all slaves capable of bearing arms. However, Cato rejected this as an illegal encroachment on private property, and suggested instead a patriotic appeal to the slave owners. But this fit of resolution soon passed over, and the assembly, now composed largely of African merchants, agreed to capitulate. When Faustus Sulla and Lucius Afranius arrived in Utica with a strong division of cavalry from the field of battle, Cato still made an attempt to hold the town through them. But he indignantly rejected their demand to wipe out the untrustworthy citizens of Utica, choosing to let the last stronghold fall undefended into the hands of the monarch rather than profane the republic's dying moments by such a massacre.

After he had, partly by his authority and partly by liberal largesses, checked so far as he could the fury of the soldiery against the unfortunate Uticans; after he had with touching solicitude furnished the means for flight to those who preferred not to trust Caesar's mercy, and to those who wished to remain the opportunity for capitulating under the most tolerable conditions; and after having thoroughly satisfied himself that he could render to no one any further aid, he retired to his bedchamber and plunged his sword into his breast.

Few of the other fugitive leaders escaped. The cavalry

that fled from Thapsus encountered the bands of Sittius, and were cut down or captured by them. Their leaders Afranius and Faustus were delivered up to Caesar, and were slain in a tumult by his veterans when he did not order their immediate execution. Metellus Scipio with the fleet of the defeated party fell into the power of the cruisers of Sittius and, when they were about to lay hands on him, stabbed himself. King Juba, not unprepared for such an issue, had resolved to die in a way which he felt befitted a king, and had readied an enormous funeral pyre in the market place of Zama which was intended to consume himself, his treasures, and the dead bodies of the entire citizenry of the town. But the inhabitants, showing no desire to become mere decorations at his funeral rites, closed the city gates against the king when he appeared, accompanied by Marcus Petreius.

King Juba, one of those natures that become savage amid a life of dazzling and insolent enjoyment, and concoct even out of death an intoxicating feast, resorted with his companion to one of his country houses. There, after a copious banquet, he challenged Petreius to fight him to death in single combat. But the conqueror of Catiline himself suffered death at the hand of the king, who thereupon caused himself to be stabbed by one of his slaves. The few men of eminence who escaped, such as Labienus and Sextus Pompey, followed the latter's elder brother to Spain and sought, like Sertorius before them, a last refuge as robbers and pirates in the shores and mountains of that still half-conquered land.

Caesar regulated the affairs of Africa without resistance. As Curio had already proposed, the kingdom of Massinissa was broken up, with the most eastern portion united with the kingdom of Bocchus, while the faithful Bogud was rewarded with considerable gifts. Cirta and the surrounding district, hitherto held under Juba's supremacy by the prince Massinissa and his son Arabion, were conferred on Publius Sittius, so that he might settle

his half-Roman bands there. But at the same time this
district, plus by far the largest and most fertile portion
of Juba's kingdom, was united as "New Africa" with the
older province of Africa. Thus the empire undertook the
defense of the country against the roving desert tribes,
instead of entrusting it (like the republic) to a dependent
king.

The struggle of Pompey and the republicans against
the monarchy thus ended, after four years, in the complete victory of the new monarch. Doubtless the monarchy
could be dated not from the battles of Pharsalus and
Thapsus, but from the moment when Pompey and Caesar
had established their joint rule and overthrown the previous aristocratic constitution. Yet it was only those bloody
baptisms of August 9, 48 B.C., and April 6, 46 B.C., that
set aside the joint rule so different from absolute dominion, and conferred recognition and status on the new
monarchy. Risings of pretenders and republican conspiracies might provoke new commotions, perhaps even new
revolutions and restorations. But the five-hundred-year-
old continuity of the republic had been broken, and
throughout the Roman empire monarchy had acquired
the legitimacy of established fact.

That the constitutional struggle was at an end was proclaimed by Marcus Cato when he fell on his sword at
Utica. For many years he had been the foremost defender
of the legitimate republic against its oppressors, continuing the struggle long after he had abandoned any hope of
victory. But now the struggle itself had become impossible.
The republic which Lucius Brutus had founded was dead,
never to be revived; what on earth were the republicans
to do now? When the treasure was carried off the sen-
tinels were thereby relieved; and who could blame them
if they departed? There was more nobility, and above all
more judgment, in Cato's death than there had been in his
life.

Cato was anything but a great man. But with all that shortsightedness, that perversity, that dry prolixity, and those spurious phrases which have stamped him for all time as the ideal of unreflecting republicanism and the favorite of all who make it their hobby, he was yet the only man who honorably and courageously championed the great doomed system in its last struggle. Just because the shrewdest lie feels itself inwardly annihilated by the simple truth, and because the dignity and glory of human nature ultimately depend not on shrewdness but on honesty, Cato has played a greater part in history than many men of far superior intellect. It only heightens the tragic significance of his death that he was himself a fool; indeed, it is just because Don Quixote is a fool that he is a tragic figure. And it is moving fact that on this vast stage, where so many great and wise men had moved and acted, the fool was destined to give the epilogue.

He did not die in vain. That the last republican departed as the first monarch came was the fearfully striking protest of the republic against the monarchy, a protest which ripped aside all the so-called constitutional character of Caesar's monarchy, and exposed its shibboleth of the reconciliation of parties as a hypocritical screen behind which despotism flowered. The unrelenting warfare of political plots and literary accusations which the ghost of the republic waged against the monarchy for centuries, from Cassius and Brutus down past Thrasea and Tacitus, was the legacy of the dying Cato to his enemies.

This republican opposition drew from Cato its whole attitude—stately, transcendental in its rhetoric, pretentiously rigid, hopeless, and faithful unto death. Accordingly, it began immediately after his death to worship as a saint the man who in his lifetime was not infrequently a laughingstock and a scandal. But the greatest mark of respect was the involuntary homage paid by Caesar, when he made an exception to the contemptuous clemency with which he was wont to treat all his opponents. In the case of Cato alone, Caesar pursued him even beyond the grave with that energetic hatred which practical statesmen are wont to feel towards antagonists who oppose them on the ground of principles which they regard as equally dangerous and impracticable.

XIV

THE OLD REPUBLIC
AND THE NEW
MONARCHY: I

The new monarch of Rome, the first ruler over the whole Graeco-Roman civilization, Gaius Julius Caesar, was in his fifty-sixth year (he was probably born on July 12, 102 B.C.) when the battle at Thapsus, the last in a long chain of momentous victories, placed in his hands the power to decide the world's future. Few men have had their elasticity so thoroughly tested as Caesar, sole creative genius of Rome and the last produced by the ancient world, which accordingly followed the path he marked for it until its sun was set. Sprung from one of Latium's oldest noble families, tracing back its lineage to the heroes of the Iliad and the kings of Rome, he spent his boyhood and young manhood like the typical genteel youth of that epoch. He had tasted both the sweet and the bitter in the cup of fashionable life, had recited and declaimed, had attempted literature and verses in his idle hours, had pursued love affairs of every sort, and had learned all the mysteries of shaving, curls, and ruffles pertaining to the dandyism of the day, as well as the still more mysterious art of always borrowing and never paying.

But the flexible steel of that nature was proof against even these dissipations, for Caesar maintained unimpaired both his bodily vigor and his elasticity of mind and heart. In fencing and riding he was a match for any of his soldiers, and his proficiency at swimming saved his life at Alexandria. The incredible rapidity of his journeys, usually made at night for the sake of gaining time (in sharp contrast to Pompey's procession-like slowness), astonished his contemporaries and was not the least among the causes of his success.

The mind was like the body. His remarkable intuitive powers revealed themselves in the precision and practicality of all his arrangements, even regarding situations which he himself had not seen. His memory was matchless, and he could easily carry on several occupations simultaneously with equal self-possession. Although a gentleman, a man of genius, and a monarch, he had still a heart. All his life he cherished the purest veneration for his mother Aurelia, his father having died early. To his wives and above all to his daughter Julia he displayed an honorable affection, which was not without influence even on political affairs. He maintained warm and faithful relations with the ablest and most excellent men of his time, high and low, each after his kind. As he never abandoned any of his partisans after the unfeeling manner of Pompey, but adhered to his friends unswervingly through good times and bad, several of these, such as Aulus Hirtius and Gaius Matius, even after his death gave noble testimonies of their attachment to him.

If in so harmoniously organized a nature any one aspect stands out, it is that he disdained everything theoretical or ideological. Caesar was of course a man of passion, for without passion there is no genius; but his passion was never stronger than he could control. Song and love and wine had taken lively possession of his spirit in the season of his youth, but they did not penetrate to the core of his nature. Literature occupied him long and earnestly; but while Alexander could not sleep for thinking of the Homeric Achilles, Caesar in his sleepless hours mused on the inflections of Latin nouns and verbs. He made verses, as everybody then did, but they were weak. On the other hand, he was interested in astronomy and natural science. While wine continued to be Alexander's destroyer of care, the temperate Roman, after the revels of his youth were over, avoided it entirely.

Around him, as around all those whose youth has felt the dazzling luster of woman's love, fainter gleams continued ever to linger. Even in later years he had love adventures and successes with women, and retained a certain foppishness in his appearance—or, to speak more correctly, a pleasing consciousness of his own manly beauty. He carefully covered his baldness, which he felt keenly, with the laurel chaplet that he wore in public in later years; and he would doubtless have traded some of his victories for the return of his youthful locks. But however much he enjoyed the society of women, he allowed them no measure of influence over him. Even his much-censured relation to Cleopatra only served to mask a political weakness.

Caesar was thoroughly a realist and a man of sense; and whatever he undertook was pervaded and guided by the cool sobriety which is the most characteristic mark of his genius. To this he owed the power of living energetically in the present, undisturbed either by recollection or by expectation; to this he owed the capacity of acting at any moment with fullest vigor, and of applying his whole genius even to the smallest enterprise; to this he owed the many-sided power with which he grasped and mastered whatever understanding can comprehend and will can compel; to this he owed the self-possessed ease with which he dictated his writings as well as projected his campaigns; to this he owed the "marvelous serenity" which remained steadily with him through good and evil days; to this he owed his complete independence, uninfluenced by favorite, by mistress, or even by friend.

As a result of this clarity of judgment Caesar never formed illusions regarding the power of fate and the ability of man; in his case the friendly veil was lifted which conceals the inadequacy of man's works. Prudently as he laid his plans and considered all possibilities, he never forgot that in all things fortune (that is to say, accident) must bestow success. With this may be connected the circumstance that he so often played a desperate game, especially again and again risking his person with daring indifference. As occasionally the most sagacious men enter into a pure game of hazard, so Caesar's rationalism at some points made contact with mysticism.

Such gifts could not fail to produce a statesman. From early youth, accordingly, Caesar was a statesman in the truest sense, with the highest aim which a man is allowed to set for himself—the political, military, intellectual, and moral regeneration of his own deeply decayed nation, and of the still more deeply decayed Hellenic nation joined to his own. The hard school of thirty years' experience changed his views as to how this aim might be reached, but his aim itself remained constant both in time of hopeless humiliation and of unlimited power, both when as demagogue and conspirator he stole toward it by paths of darkness, and when as joint ruler and then as sole monarch he worked at his task before the eyes of the world.

All the permanent measures that Caesar set in motion at the most scattered times take their places in the great building plan. Therefore we cannot properly speak of his isolated achievements, for he did nothing isolated. With justice men admire the inimitable simplicity of Caesar the author, and the unique purity and beauty of his language. With justice the greatest masters of war have praised Caesar the general, who with a singular disregard for routine and tradition always discerned the mode of warfare by which the given enemy could be conquered, and which was thus the right one; who with prophetic certainty found the proper means for every end; who after defeat stood ready for battle like William of Orange, and invariably ended the campaign with victory; who managed the rapid movement of masses—that element of warfare which distinguishes military genius from mere ordinary ability—with unsurpassed perfection, and found the means of victory not in massive forces but in the celerity of their movements, not in long preparation but in rapid and daring action even with inadequate means.

But all these were with Caesar mere secondary matters. He was no doubt a great orator, author, and general, but he became each of these merely because he was a consummate statesman. The soldier especially played in him an altogether subsidiary part, and it is one of his principal distinctions from Alexander, Hannibal, and Napoleon that he began his public life not as an officer but as a politician. He had originally intended to reach his object, like Pericles and Gaius Gracchus, without the use of force, and for eighteen years as leader of the popular party he confined himself exclusively to political plans and intrigues. Then, reluctantly convinced at the age of forty that military support was necessary, he had put himself at the head of an army.

It was therefore natural that he should ever remain more statesman than general—just like Cromwell, who also transformed himself from opposition leader into military chief and democratic king, and who in general, little as the prince of Puritans seems to resemble the dissolute Roman, is yet in his development, his objectives, and his achievements perhaps the closest to Caesar of all modern statesmen. Even in his mode of warfare this improvised generalship is apparent. Just as Napoleon's campaigns against Egypt and England clearly exhibit the artillery lieutenant who had risen to command, so Caesar's similar enterprises betray the demagogue transformed into a general. A dyed-in-the-wool officer would hardly have been prepared, for political reasons not altogether compelling, to ignore military considerations as Caesar did on several occasions, most strikingly in his landing in Epirus. Several of his acts are therefore censurable from a military viewpoint; but what the general loses, the statesman gains.

The statesman's task is as universal as was Caesar's genius. He undertook the most varied things, but all without exception bore on the one great object to which he faithfully and consistently devoted himself, and he never preferred one aspect of this great activity to another. A master of the art of war, he did his utmost to avert civil strife and, when it nevertheless began, to earn laurels with the least possible spilling of blood. Although the founder of a military monarchy, he was uniquely successful in preventing the formation of a hierarchy of mar-

shals or a government of praetorians. If he had a preference for any one form of service to the state, it was for
the sciences and arts of peace rather than for those of
war.

The most remarkable peculiarity of his action as a
statesman was its perfect harmony. In reality, all the conditions for this most difficult of human functions were
united in Caesar. A thorough realist, he never allowed the
images of the past to disturb him. For him nothing was of
value in politics but the living present and the law of reason—just as in his grammarian's role he ignored historical and antiquarian research, recognizing nothing but the
living language and the rule of symmetry. A born ruler,
he governed the minds of men as the wind drives the
clouds, and compelled the most heterogeneous natures to
his service—the plain citizen and the rough subaltern, the
genteel matrons of Rome and the fair princesses of Egypt
and Mauretania, the brilliant cavalry officer and the cal-
culating banker.

His talent for organization was marvelous. No statesman ever compelled alliances, no general ever collected
an army, out of such unyielding and refractory elements,
and kept them together with the firmness that Caesar displayed in cementing his coalitions and his legions. Never
did a regent judge his instruments, and assign to each its
appropriate place, with so acute an eye.

He was monarch, but he never played the king. Even
when absolute lord of Rome he deported himself like the
party leader, pliant and smooth, easy and charming in
conversation, complaisant towards everyone, seeming to
wish nothing more than to be the first among his peers.
Caesar entirely avoided the blunder into which so many
similar men have fallen, of carrying into politics the military tone of command. However much occasion his disagreeable relations with the Senate gave for it, he never
resorted to outrages such as that of the eighteenth Bru-

maire.[1] Caesar was monarch, but he was never seized with the giddiness of the tyrant. He is perhaps the only one among the earth's great who in large matters and small never acted from impulse or caprice, but always according to his duty as ruler, and who might look back on his life and doubtless find erroneous calculations to deplore, but no false step of passion to regret. There is nothing in Caesar's life even remotely comparable to those aberrant excesses, such as the murder of Clitus or the burning of Persepolis, which the history of Alexander records.

He is, in sum, perhaps the only great man who preserved to the end the statesman's touch for discriminating between the possible and the impossible, and was not broken by that most difficult task for greatly gifted natures—the task of recognizing, when on the pinnacle of success, its natural limits. What was possible he performed, never ignoring the possible good for the sake of the impossible better, never disdaining at least to provide palliatives for evils that were incurable. But when he recognized that fate had spoken, he always obeyed. Alexander on the Hyphasis, Napoleon at Moscow, turned back because they had to, and were indignant at destiny for granting merely limited successes even to its favorites. Caesar turned back voluntarily on the Thames and on the Rhine; and even on the Danube and the Euphrates he thought not of world conquest, but merely of practical frontier regulation.

Such was this unique man, so easy and yet so infinitely difficult to describe. His whole nature is transparent clarity, and tradition preserves more copious information about him than about any of his peers in the ancient world. Our conceptions of such a person may well vary in shallowness or depth, but they cannot be truly different.

1. The date, according to the revolutionary French calendar, on which Napoleon Bonaparte seized the state power.

The grand figure has exhibited the same essential features to every inquirer of the least discernment, and yet no one has succeeded in reproducing it to the life. The secret lies in its perfection. As a man no less than as a historical figure, Caesar occupies a position where the great contrasts of existence meet and balance. Of mighty creative power and yet at the same time of the most penetrating judgment; no longer a youth and not yet an old man; of the highest energy of will and the highest capacity of execution; filled with republican ideals and at the same time born to be a king; a Roman in the deepest essence of his nature, and yet called to reconcile and combine in himself as well as in the outer world the Roman and Hellenic cultures—Caesar was the entire and perfect man.

Accordingly, we miss in him more than in any other historic figure what are called characteristic features, which are in reality mere deviations from the natural course of human development. What in Caesar passes for such at first glance is seen, on closer observation, to be the peculiarity not of the individual but of the epoch. His youthful adventures, for instance, were common to all his more gifted contemporaries of like position, and his unpoetical but strongly logical temperament was the temperament of Romans in general. It was also part of Caesar's humanity that he was completely controlled by considerations of time and place; for there is no abstract humanity, and the living man cannot but occupy a place in a given nationality and culture. Caesar was a perfect man just because more than any other he placed himself amid the currents of his time, and because more than any other he epitomized the essential peculiarity of the Roman nation—practical aptitude as a citizen. His Hellenism was only the Hellenism which had long been intimately blended with the Italian nation.

In this very circumstance, however, lies the difficulty, perhaps the impossibility, of depicting Caesar to life. As the artist can paint everything save consummate beauty, so the historian, when once in a thousand years he encounters perfection, can only be silent. For normality is doubtless capable of being described, but only by the negative notion of the absence of defect. Nature's secret, whereby she combines normality and individuality in her most finished productions, is beyond expression. We can only deem fortunate those who beheld this perfection, and gain some faint conception of it from the reflected luster which rests imperishably on the creations of so great a nature.

True, these also bear the stamp of the times. The Roman hero stood beside his youthful Greek predecessor not as an equal but as a superior, but meantime the world had grown old and faded. Caesar's course was no longer, like that of Alexander, a joyous marching toward an infinitely remote goal. He built on and with ruins, and was content to establish himself as securely as possible within the ample yet limited scope assigned to him. With reason, therefore, the dreamers of succeeding ages have passed over the unpoetical Roman, while investing Alexander with the golden luster of poetry and the rainbow hues of legend. But with equal reason the political life of nations has for two thousand years reverted again and again to the lines which Caesar drew; and the fact that the peoples to whom the world belongs still designate their highest monarchs by his name is at once deeply significant and a source of shame.

If the old and totally vicious state of things was to be expunged and the commonwealth renovated, it was necessary first of all that the country be effectively pacified and the rubbish of the recent catastrophe cleared away. In this work Caesar adopted the principle of reconciling the existing parties—or, to put it more correctly (for where irreconcilable antagonisms exist we cannot speak of real reconciliation) the principle that the arena where the nobility and the people had hitherto contended was to be abandoned by both parties, which were to meet together on the ground of the new monarchical constitution.

First of all, therefore, the older quarrels of the republican past were regarded as finished forever. While Caesar ordered that Sulla's statues, which had been thrown down by the mob on the news of the battle of Pharsalus, should be re-erected, thus recognizing that history alone should sit in judgment on that great man, at the same time he canceled the last of Sulla's exceptional laws, recalled the exiles banished during the Cinnan and Sertorian troubles, and restored the children of the outlaws to eligibility to office. In like manner all those were restored who early in the recent catastrophe had lost their Senate seats or their civil rights through sentence of the censors or political processes, especially through impeachments based on the exceptional laws of 52 B.C. Only those who had killed for money remained under attainder (as was reasonable), and Milo, the most daring henchman of the senatorial party, was excluded from the general pardon.

Far more difficult than the settlement of these past questions was the treatment of the existing parties, Caesar's own democratic adherents and the overthrown aristocracy. It was understandable that the former should be, if possible, still less satisfied than the latter with Caesar's conduct after victory and with his summons to abandon the old political arena. Caesar himself doubtless desired the same general outcome that Gaius Gracchus had contemplated, but the objectives of the Caesarians were no longer those of the Gracchans. The Roman popular party had gradually been driven from reform to revolution, from revolution to anarchy, from anarchy to a war against property. They celebrated among themselves the memory of the reign of terror, and now adorned Catiline's tomb, as formerly that of the Gracchi, with flowers and garlands. They had placed themselves under Caesar's banner because they expected him to succeed where Catiline had failed.

But as it speedily became plain that Caesar had no intention of following Catiline's course, and that the most which debtors might expect was some alleviation of payment and modification of procedure, the indignant partisans loudly inquired, For whom had the popular party conquered? This rabble high and low, chagrined at the miscarriage of their intended Saturnalia, began first to flirt with the Pompeians, and then during Caesar's absence (from January 48 to autumn of 47 B.C.) to instigate a second civil war within the first.

The praetor Marcus Caelius Rufus, a good aristocrat and bad payer of debts, a man of some talent and much culture, and, as a vehement and fluent orator, one of Caesar's most zealous champions in the Forum, on his own responsibility proposed a law which granted debtors an interest-free respite of six years. When he was opposed in this step, he proposed a second law canceling all claims arising out of loans and current house rents; whereupon the Caesarian Senate deposed him from office.

It was on the eve of the battle of Pharsalus, when the balance seemed to incline to the side of the Pompeians. Rufus entered into communication with Milo, the old street fighter for the aristocracy, and the two contrived a counterrevolution whose banner combined the republican constitution with the cancellation of creditors' claims and the manumission of slaves. Milo left his place of exile in Massilia and called the Pompeians and the slave herdsmen to arms in the region of Thurii, while Rufus made arrangements to seize the town of Capua by armed slaves. But the latter plan was detected before its execution and frustrated by the Capuan militia. Quintus Pedius, who advanced with a legion into the territory of Thurii, scattered the plundering band there, and the fall of the two leaders put an end to the scandal.

Nevertheless, the following year (47 B.C.) a second fool, the tribune Publius Dolabella, equally insolent but far less talented than his predecessor, reintroduced the law as to creditors' claims and house rents. Then, with his colleague Lucius Trebellius, he sought to support his view (it was the last time) with demagogic incitement. There were street riots and serious frays between the armed bands on both sides until the commandant of Italy, Marcus Antonius, ordered the military to interfere; and Caesar's early return from the East put a complete stop to the preposterous proceedings. Caesar attributed so little importance to these brainless projects that after some time he even received Dolabella again into favor. Against such a rabble, engaged not in political activity but solely in a bandit war against property, the mere existence of a strong government is sufficient; and Caesar did not deign to curry favor for his monarchy by concerning himself with alarmist apprehensions over these communists of that day.

While Caesar thus could and did leave the popular party to continue its already far-advanced disintegration, the aristocratic party possessed much greater vitality. His object here was not to bring about its dissolution—which time alone could effect—but to begin and pave the way for it by a nice blend of repression and conciliation. Among minor measures, from a natural sense of propriety, Caesar avoided exasperating the fallen party by empty sarcasm. He did not celebrate a triumph over his conquered fellow citizens, and he mentioned Pompey often and always with respect, causing his overthrown statue to be put back after the senate house had been restored.

Caesar assigned the narrowest possible limits to political prosecutions. There was no inquiry into the various communications between the constitutional party and nominal Caesarians. Caesar himself threw into the fire unread the piles of papers found in the enemy's headquar-

ters at Pharsalus and Thapsus, and spared himself and
the country from political processes against suspected individuals. Further, all the common soldiers who had followed their Roman or provincial officers into the contest
against Caesar came off with impunity, except for Roman
citizens who had served in the army of King Juba; their
property was confiscated as penalty for their treason.

Even to the officers of the conquered party Caesar had
granted unlimited pardon up to the close of the Spanish
campaign of 49 B.C.; but he became convinced that he
had gone too far, and that the removal of at least the
leaders was inevitable. He therefore set up the rule that
every one who had served as an officer in the enemy's
army or had sat in the opposition-senate after Ilerda forfeited his property and his political rights, and was banished from Italy for life. If he did not survive the war,
his property was forfeited to the state. But those who had
formerly accepted pardon from Caesar and were later
found in the ranks of the enemy thereby forfeited their
lives.

These rules, however, were materially modified in
practice. The death sentence was carried out only against
a very few of the numerous backsliders. In property confiscations not only were all the estate's debts as well as
widows' claims for their dowries paid off (as was reasonable), but a part of the estate was also left to the children of the deceased. Lastly, not a few of those liable to
banishment and confiscation of property were pardoned
entirely or got off with fines, like the African capitalists
who were impressed into the senate of Utica. And even
the others almost without exception had their freedom
and property restored, if they could only bring themselves
to petition Caesar to that effect. Indeed, several who declined to do so, such as the consular Marcus Marcellus,
received pardon unasked, and ultimately in 44 B.C. a general amnesty was issued for all who were still unrecalled.

The republican opposition submitted to pardon, but it

was not reconciled. Discontent with the new order and exasperation against the ruler were general. There was no further opportunity for open political resistance, and it is hardly worth noting that some opposition tribunes acquired the republican crown of martyrdom by an intervention against those who had called Caesar king. But republicanism expressed itself all the more decidedly as an inner opposition, and in secret agitation and plotting. Not a hand stirred when the Imperator appeared in public. There were abundant wall placards and sarcastic verses full of bitter and telling popular satire against the new monarchy. When a comedian ventured on a republican allusion, he was saluted with the loudest applause. Praise of Cato was the most fashionable theme of opposition pamphleteers, and their writings found a more grateful audience because literature itself was no longer free.

Indeed, Caesar even now combated the republicans on their own ground. He and his abler confidants replied to the Cato literature with Anticatones, and the republican and Caesarian scribes fought round the dead hero of Utica like the Trojans and Greeks round the body of the Trojan Patroclus. But as a matter of course the Caesarians had the worst of this conflict, where the public with its thoroughly republican feelings was judge. No course remained but to overawe the authors. On this account well-known and dangerous literary men, such as Publius Nigidius Figulus and Aulus Caecina, had more difficulty in obtaining permission to return to Italy than other exiles, while the opposition writers in Italy were subjected to a practical censorship whose restraints were all the more annoying because the punishment to be dreaded was utterly arbitrary.

The underground machinations against the new monarchy will be set forth in another connection. Here it is sufficient to say that risings of pretenders as well as of republicans were incessantly brewing throughout the Roman empire; that the flames of civil war, kindled now by Pompeians and now by republicans, again burst forth brightly at various places; and that in the capital there was perpetual conspiracy against the life of the monarch. But Caesar could not be induced by these plots even to surround himself with a permanent bodyguard, and usually contented himself with making known the detected conspiracies by public placards.

However much Caesar was wont to treat his personal safety with daring indifference, he could not conceal from himself the serious danger which this mass of malcontents represented to his creations. Yet disregarding the urgent warnings of his friends, and without deluding himself as to the implacability of the opponents to whom mercy was granted, he persevered with marvelous composure and energy in pardoning by far the greater number of them. He did so neither from the chivalrous magnanimity of a proud man, nor from the sentimental mercy of effeminacy, but from the statesmanlike consideration that vanquished parties are disposed of more quickly and less injuriously by their absorption into the state than by any attempt to wipe them out or to banish them from the commonwealth.

Caesar's high purposes required the constitutional party itself, which in fact embraced not only the aristocracy but all the elements of a free national spirit among the Italian citizenry. His schemes, which sought to renovate the antiquated state, needed the whole mass of talent, culture, and hereditary and self-acquired distinction comprehended within this party, and in this sense he may well have regarded the pardoning of his opponents as the finest reward of victory. Accordingly the most prominent chiefs were indeed removed, but full pardon was not withheld from men of the second and third rank, especially younger men. These were not, moreover, allowed to sulk in passive opposition, but by more or less gentle pressure were made to take an active part in the new administration and to accept honors and offices from it.

As with Henry the Fourth and William of Orange, so Caesar's greatest difficulties began only after the victory. Every revolutionary conqueror learns by experience that if after vanquishing his opponents he would not remain a mere party chief like Cinna and Sulla, but would like Caesar, Henry the Fourth, and William of Orange substitute the common welfare for his own party's necessarily one-sided program, there is a point when he faces the united hostility of all parties including his own; and the purer his ideal the more this is true. The constitutionalists and the Pompeians paid homage with their lips, yet at heart hated the monarchy or at least the dynasty. The degenerate populists were in open rebellion from the moment they perceived that Caesar's goals were by no means their own. Even Caesar's personal adherents murmured when they found that their chief was establishing not a bandit state but a monarchy equal and just toward all, and that their personal gains were to be diminished by the raising up of the vanquished. This reorganization of the commonwealth was acceptable to no party, and had to be imposed on his associates no less than on his opponents.

Caesar's own position was in this sense weaker than before his victory, but what he lost the state gained. By annihilating the parties, while not simply sparing the partisans but allowing every man of talent or even merely of good family to hold office regardless of his political past, he focused on his great design the massed energies of the state; and the voluntary or compulsory participation of men of all parties in the same work imperceptibly led the nation over to the newly prepared ground. Nor was he misled by the fact that this reconciliation was for the moment only external, and that there was much less agreement about the new state of things than about hatred for Caesar. He knew well that antagonisms lose their keenness when brought into outward union, and that only thus can the statesman assist the working of time, which alone can heal such strife by laying the old generation in the grave. Still less did he inquire who hated him or meditated his assassination. Like every genuine statesman he served not for reward, nor even for the love of the people, but sacrificed the favor of his contemporaries for the blessing of posterity, and above all for the opportunity to save and renew his nation.

In describing in detail the method by which this transition from the old to the new was effected, we must first of all recollect that Caesar came to complete rather than to begin. The plan of a new political framework suited to the times, long ago projected by Gaius Gracchus, had been maintained by his adherents and successors with more or less spirit and success but ever without wavering. Caesar, from the outset almost by hereditary right the head of the popular party, had for thirty years borne its banner without ever changing or concealing his colors, and he remained the democrat even when monarch. As he accepted without limitation (except for the preposterous projects of Catiline and Clodius) the heritage of his party; as he displayed the bitterest personal hatred for the aristocracy and the genuine aristocrats; and as he retained unchanged the essential ideas of Roman democracy—alleviation of the burdens of debtors, transmarine colonization, gradual equalization of the classes comprising the state, and emancipation of the executive power from the Senate—to this extent his monarchy differed so little from the older democracy that on the contrary that democracy attained its completion and fulfilment by means of his monarchy.

For this monarchy was not an Oriental despotism, but a monarchy such as Gaius Gracchus had wished to found and Pericles and Cromwell founded—the representation of the nation by the man in whom it puts supreme and unlimited confidence. The ideas which underlay Caesar's work were not strictly new, but to him belongs their realization, which after all is the main point. To him belongs the grandeur of execution, which would probably have surprised the brilliant builder himself if he could have seen it. For it has always commanded the deepest admiration of everyone who has observed it, whether as living reality or in the mirror of history, whatever his historical epoch or political convictions, limited only by his ability to comprehend human and historical greatness.

At this point, however, it is proper to express once and for all what the historian ever tacitly assumes, and to protest against the custom—common alike to simplicity and perfidy—of using historical praise and censure as phrases of general application with no regard for circumstances. The present case involves construing the judgment of Caesar into a judgment of what is called Caesarism. It is true that history ought to instruct the present, but not in the vulgar sense, as if by simply turning over the leaves one could diagnose the ills of the present from the records of the past, and derive from these the specifics for a prescription. It is instructive only so far as observing older cultures reveals the organic conditions of civilization generally—the fundamental forces everywhere alike, the manner of their combination everywhere different—and leads and encourages men not to slavish imitation but to independent reproduction.

In this sense the history of Caesar and of Roman Imperialism, with all the unsurpassed greatness of the master worker, with all the historical necessity of the work, is in truth a sharper censure of modern autocracy than could be written by the hand of man. According to the same natural law by which the smallest organism infinitely surpasses the most artistic machine, every constitution, however defective, which expresses the free will of the majority infinitely surpasses the most brilliant and humane absolutism; for the former is capable of growth and therefore living, while the latter is what it is and therefore dead.

This law of nature demonstrates itself all the more completely in the Roman military monarchy, in that under the impulse of its creator's genius, and in the absence of all foreign pressures, that monarchy developed in purer form than in any similar state. From Caesar's time, as Gibbon has shown long ago, the Roman system had only an external coherence, repeating itself only mechanically; while internally, even under Caesar it was utterly withered and dead. If in its early stages, and above all in Caesar's own soul, the hopeful dream of combining free popular development and absolute rule was still cherished, the government of the highly gifted emperors of the Julian house soon taught men a terrible lesson in how far it was possible to hold fire and water in the same vessel.

Caesar's work was salutary and necessary not because it was or could be a blessing in itself. But given the social organization of antiquity based on slavery and utterly foreign to republican-constitutional representation, and under the organization of the urban constitution which during five hundred years had ripened into oligarchic absolutism, an absolute military monarchy was both a logical necessity and the least of evils. When the slave-holding aristocracy of Virginia and the Carolinas shall have carried matters as far as their predecessors in Sullan Rome, Caesarism will there too be legitimized at the bar of history; [2] where it appears under other circumstances it is at once a caricature and a usurpation. But history will not deny the true Caesar his due honor, because her verdict in the presence of bad Caesars may lead fools astray and give rogues occasion for lying and fraud. She too is a Bible; and if she cannot any more than the Bible hinder the fool from misunderstanding and the devil from quoting her, she too will be able to requite them both.

2. When this was written—in the year 1857—no one could foresee how soon the mightiest struggle and the most glorious victory as yet recorded in human annals would save the United States from this fearful trial, and secure the future existence of an absolute self-governing freedom not to be permanently kept in check by any local Caesarism.—T. M. [This entire passage repudiating Caesarism was added to the second edition.]

The position of the new supreme head of the state appears formally, at least at the outset, as a dictatorship. Caesar took it up first after his return from Spain in 49 B.C., then laid it down again after a few days and waged the decisive campaign of the following year simply as consul. But in the autumn of that year after the battle of Pharsalus he reverted to the dictatorship and had it repeatedly entrusted to him, at first for an undefined period, but from January 1, 45 B.C., as an annual office, and then in January or February of 44 B.C. for the duration of his life, so that in the end he pointedly dropped the earlier reservation as to laying down the office and formally expressed his life tenure in the new title of *dictator perpetuus*.

This dictatorship, both in its initial transitory and its second enduring phase, was not that of the old constitution, but the supreme office devised by Sulla. It was an office whose functions were fixed not by the constitutional ordinances regulating the supreme single magistracy, but by special decree of the people granting the holder the power to project laws and to regulate the commonwealth, an unlimited official prerogative which superseded the republican partition of powers. It was a mere elaboration of this general prerogative when the holder of power was entrusted by separate acts with the right of deciding on war and peace without consulting the Senate and the people, with the independent disposal of armies and finances, and with choosing provincial governors.

Caesar could accordingly assume prerogatives which lay outside the proper functions of the magistracy, and even outside the traditional power of the state. It appears almost as a concession on his part that he abstained from nominating the magistrates in place of the comitia, limiting himself to proposing a proportion of the praetors and of the lower magistrates, and that he had himself empowered by special decree of the people to create patricians, which was not at all permissible according to use and custom.

For other magistracies the dictatorship in effect left no room. Caesar did not himself fill the censorship, but he doubtless made full use of censorial rights, particularly the important right of nominating senators. He frequently held the consulship alongside the dictatorship, once even without colleague. But he refused to attach it permanently to his person, and he ignored the pleas for him to undertake it for a five- or even a ten-year term.

Caesar had no need to undertake the superintendence of religion, since he was already pontifex maximus. Membership in the college of augurs was conferred on him as a matter of course, along with an abundance of old and new honors, such as the title of "father of the fatherland," giving his name to the month of his birth, and other courtly manifestations which ultimately developed into outright deification. Two of these arrangements deserve to be singled out. First, Caesar was given the same personal inviolability as the tribunes of the people; and second, the title of Imperator was granted to him permanently alongside his other official designations.

Men of judgment will need no proof that Caesar intended to impose his supreme power permanently on the commonwealth, or that he chose a simple and fitting name for the new institution; for if it is a blunder to create names without power, it is scarcely less of an error to set up the substance of power without a name. Only it is not easy to determine what final shape Caesar had in mind, partly because in this period of transition it is difficult to distinguish the scaffolding from the permanent structure, and partly because his worshipful followers anticipated their master's nod and loaded him (doubtless to his disgust) with a multitude of powers and honors.

Least of all could the new monarchy act through the consulship, just because its elective character could hardly be separated from it. Moreover, Caesar obviously labored to downgrade this hitherto supreme office into an empty title, and subsequently, when he accepted it, he gave it away to persons of secondary rank before the year expired. The dictatorship came most frequently and clearly into prominence, but probably only because Caesar wished to use it in its old significance of an extraordinary presidency for surmounting extraordinary crises. On the other hand it was far from suitable for the new monarchy, for it was inherently marked with an exceptional and unpopular character, and a democratic statesman could hardly be expected to choose a permanent organizational form which had been created by the most gifted champion of the opposition.

The new name of Imperator, on the other hand, seemed in every respect a more appropriate title for the monarchy, just because in this context it was entirely new, and without apparent reason for its introduction. The new wine might not be put into old bottles. Here is a new name for the new thing, summing up most pregnantly what the democratic party had already expressed (though less precisely) in the Gabinian law as the function of its chief—the concentration and perpetuation of official power in the hands of a popular chief independent of the Senate. On Caesar's coins, especially those of the last period, we find the title of Imperator prevailing, and in Caesar's law as to political crimes the monarch seems to have been designated by this name. Thus later generations came to connect the monarchy with the name of Imperator. To give this new office both a democratic and religious sanction, Caesar probably intended to combine in it the tribunician power along with the supreme pontificate.

Unquestionably the new organization was not meant to be limited to its founder's lifetime. But Caesar did not succeed in settling the thorny problem of the succession, and it must remain moot whether he planned to institute some sort of election of a successor, such as marked the early Roman kings, or whether he wished to make the supreme office hereditary, as his adopted son subsequently claimed. It is not improbable that he had some notion of combining the two systems, and of arranging the succession (as did Cromwell and Napoleon) so that the ruler should be succeeded by his son; but if he had no son, or the son did not seem suitable, the ruler might choose his successor by adoption.

In law the new office of Imperator was based on the position which the consuls or proconsuls occupied outside Rome, so that primarily the military command, but along with it the supreme judicial and administrative power, were comprehended in it. But the Imperator's authority exceeded that of the consular-proconsular, being not only unlimited in time and space and held for life, but also operative in the capital. Unlike the consul, the Imperator could not be checked by colleagues of equal power, and all the restrictions gradually imposed on the original supreme power did not apply to the Imperator.

In a word, this new office of Imperator was nothing else than the re-establishment of the old kingship; for it was those very limitations of power as regards time, place, colleagues, and the co-operation of the Senate or the community which distinguished the consul from the king. Hardly a trait of the new monarchy is lacking from the old: the union of the supreme military, judicial, and administrative authority in the hands of the prince; religious leadership of the commonwealth; the right of issuing ordinances with binding power; the reduction of the Senate to an advisory council; the revival of the patriciate and of the city praefecture.

But still more striking than these analogies is the internal similarity of the ancient Roman monarchy of Servius Tullius and the monarchy of Caesar. If those old kings of Rome with all their plenitude of power had yet been rulers of a free community and protectors of the commons against the nobility, Caesar too had not come to destroy liberty but primarily to break the intolerable yoke of the aristocracy. Nor need it surprise us that Caesar, anything but a political antiquarian, went back five hundred years to find the model for his new state. Since the highest office of the Roman commonwealth had always remained a kingship restricted by a number of special laws, the idea of the regal office itself had by no means become obsolete. At various periods and from very different sides—in the decemviral power, in the Sullan regency, and in Caesar's own dictatorship—the regal power had in fact recurred during the republic. Indeed, by a certain logical necessity, whenever exceptional powers seemed needed there emerged, as distinct from the usual limited *imperium,* the unlimited *imperium* which was simply nothing else than the regal power.

Lastly, surface considerations also recommended this recurrence to the former kingly position. Mankind has infinite difficulty in achieving new creations, and therefore cherishes established forms as sacred heirlooms. Accordingly Caesar judiciously connected himself with Servius Tullius, just as subsequently Charlemagne connected himself with Caesar, and Napoleon attempted at least to connect himself with Charlemagne. He did so not covertly and secretly, but like his successors in the most open manner possible. Indeed, the very object of this connection was to find a clear, national, and popular form of expression for the new state. From ancient times there stood on the Capitol the statues of those seven kings, whom the conventional history of Rome was wont to bring on the stage; Caesar ordered his own to be erected beside them as the eighth. He appeared publicly in the costume of the old kings of Alba. In his new law as to political crimes, the principal departure from the law of Sulla was that alongside and on a level with the collective community was placed the Imperator, as the living personal expression of the people. In the formula used for political oaths the genius of the Imperator was added to the Jupiter and

Penates of the Roman people. The outward badge of monarchy was, according to the universal view of antiquity, the image of the monarch on the coins; from the year 44 B.C. the head of Caesar appears on those of the Roman state.

There could accordingly be no complaint that Caesar left the public in the dark as to his view of his position. As distinctly and as formally as possible, he came forward as king of Rome. It is conceivable (although not probable, and in any case unimportant), that he intended to designate his office not by the new title of Imperator but by the old one of King. Even in his lifetime many of his enemies and friends were of the opinion that he intended to have himself expressly so nominated. Indeed, several of his most vehement adherents suggested in different ways and at different times that he should assume the crown—most strikingly Marcus Antonius, when as consul he offered the diadem to Caesar before all the people in February of 44 B.C.

But Caesar rejected all these proposals at once. If at the same time he took steps against those who used these incidents to stir republican opposition, it by no means follows that he was not sincere in his rejection. The assumption that he encouraged these invitations, in order to prepare the multitude for the unfamiliar spectacle of the Roman diadem, utterly misjudges the mighty power of the sentimental opposition with which Caesar had to reckon. This opposition could not be rendered more compliant, but on the contrary gained strength from the fact that Caesar himself recognized its power. It may have been the uncalled-for zeal of his followers that occasioned these incidents. It may also be that Caesar permitted or even suggested the scene to Antonius, to bring the inconvenient gossip to a sharp halt by a refusal before the eyes of the citizens, a refusal which was inserted at his command in the state calendar and which therefore could hardly be revoked. The probability is that Caesar appreciated both the value of a convenient title as well as the popular prejudice which focuses on the names of things regardless of their essence. Thus he was resolved to avoid the name of king—tainted with an ancient curse, and connoting to the Romans of his time the despots of the East rather than their own Numa and Servius—and to appropriate the substance of the regal office under the title of Imperator.

But whatever title he gave himself in his thoughts, the sovereign ruler was there, and accordingly the court gathered itself at once with its usual accompaniments of pomp, insipidity, and emptiness. Caesar appeared in public not in the consular robe bordered with purple stripes, but in the all-purple robe regarded by antiquity as the proper regal attire. Seated on his golden chair, and without rising from it, he reviewed the solemn procession of the Senate. The festivals commemorating his birthday, his victories, and his vows filled the calendar. When Caesar came to the capital, his principal servants marched forth in troops to escort him over a considerable distance. To be near him began to be of such importance that rents rose in the quarter of the city where he dwelt. Personal interviews with him became so difficult, because of the multitude of individuals soliciting audience, that Caesar often found it necessary to communicate in writing even with his intimate friends, and persons of the highest rank sometimes had to wait for hours in his antechamber.

People felt, more clearly than Caesar liked, that they no longer approached a fellow citizen. There arose a monarchical aristocracy, to a remarkable degree both new and old, which sprang from the idea of overshadowing the aristocracy of the oligarchy by that of royalty, the nobility by the patriciate. The patrician body still existed, although without important privileges as an order, in the guise of a tight aristocratic guild. But as it could receive no new families it had dwindled away over the centuries, and by Caesar's time no more than fifteen or sixteen patrician clans still survived. Caesar, himself sprung from one of them, received by popular decree the right of creating new patrician families, thus establishing, in contrast to the republican nobility, a new patrician aristocracy which met all the requisites of a monarchical privileged order—the charm of antiquity, complete dependence on the government, and total insignificance. On all sides the new sovereignty revealed itself.

Under a monarch thus practically unlimited there was little room for a constitution, and still less for continuing the old commonwealth based on legal co-operation of the citizens, the Senate, and the several magistrates. Caesar reverted completely to the old tradition: the citizen-assembly remained alongside the king the supreme expression of the sovereign people's will; the Senate reverted to its original function of advising the ruler when requested; and the ruler again concentrated in his person the whole executive authority, with no independent official by his side any more than was true of the ancient kings.

For legislation the democratic monarch adhered to the primitive Roman maxim that the people alone, in concert with the king convoking them, had the power to regulate the commonwealth; and Caesar had his enactments regularly sanctioned by decree of the people. To be sure, the energy and authority, half-moral and half-political, which the yea or nay of those old warrior assemblies had carried could not again be instilled into the so-called comitia of this period. The co-operation of the citizens in legislation, which under the old constitution had been extremely limited but real and living, was under the new one a mere shadow. Thus there was no need of special restrictive measures against the comitia, many years' experience having shown that every government—oligarchical as well as the monarchical—easily kept on good terms with this formal sovereign. These Caesarian comitia were practically important only in so far as by retaining in principle the sovereignty of the people they constituted a protection against absolutism. But at the same time Caesar also revived the other maxim of the old state law, that the command of the sole magistrate is unconditionally valid so long as he holds office, and that while legislation no doubt belongs only to the king and the citizens in concert, the royal edict is equivalent to law at least till the abdication of its author.

While the democratic king thus conceded to the community at least a formal share of sovereignty, it was by no means his intention to divide his authority with the previous governing body, the Senate. Caesar's Senate was to be (in a quite different way from the later Senate of Augustus) merely a supreme state council with which he consulted as to laws, and in whose name the more important administrative ordinances might be issued; for cases in fact occurred where senatorial decrees were issued unbeknownst to any of the senators who were recorded as present at their preparation.

There were no serious legal obstacles to reducing the Senate to its original deliberative position, which it had overstepped more *de facto* than *de jure*. However, it was necessary for Caesar to protect himself from practical resistance, for the Roman Senate was as much the focus of the opposition to Caesar as the Attic Areopagus was to Pericles. Chiefly for this reason the number of senators, which had normally amounted at most to six hundred and had been greatly reduced by the recent crises, was raised by extraordinary supplement to nine hundred. At the same time, to keep it at least up to this mark, the number of quaestors to be nominated annually—that is, members annually admitted to the Senate—was raised from twenty to forty.

The extraordinary reinforcement of the Senate was undertaken by the monarch alone, while for the annual additions he secured a permanent influence through the law that the electoral colleges were required to vote for the first twenty quaestorship candidates who were recommended by the monarch. Besides, the crown could confer the honorary rights of the quaestorship or any superior office, and thus a seat in the Senate, even to individuals not formally qualified. The extraordinary appointments naturally went in the main to adherents of the new order, and introduced, along with equites of respectable standing, various dubious and plebeian personages into the proud corporation—former senators removed by the censor or expelled because of a judicial sentence, foreigners from Spain and Gaul who to some extent had to learn their Latin in the Senate, subaltern officers who had not previously received even the equestrian ring, sons of freedmen or of men who followed dishonorable trades, and similar elements.

The exclusive circles of the nobility, who naturally took bitterest offense at this change in the composition of the Senate, saw it as an intentional corruption of the institution itself. Caesar was not capable of such a self-destructive policy, but he was as determined not to be governed by his council as he was convinced of the necessity of its existence. They might more correctly have discerned in these actions his intention to change the Senate's exclusively oligarchic character, and to make it once more what it had been in olden days—a state council representing all classes through their most intelligent elements, and not necessarily excluding the man of humble birth or even the foreigner. Just as the ancient kings introduced noncitizens, so Caesar introduced non-Italians into his senate.

While the nobility's rule was thus set aside and its existence undermined, and while the Senate in its new form was merely a tool of the monarch, autocracy took firm root in the whole administration of the state, and the executive power was concentrated in the hands of the monarch. First, the Imperator decided in person every important question. Caesar was able to carry on personal government to an extent we puny men can hardly conceive, and for more general reasons than his unparalleled rapidity and decisiveness. When we see Caesar, Sulla, Gaius Gracchus, and Roman statesmen in general displaying a capacity for work that transcends our notions of human powers, the reason lies not in any change in human nature but in the different organization of the modern household. The Roman house was a machine in which even the mental powers of the slaves and freedmen yielded their produce to the master; and a master who knew how to govern these worked as it were with countless minds. It was the *beau ideal* of bureaucratic centralization, which our countinghouse system indeed strives zealously to imitate, but still lags as far behind its prototype as the modern power of capital falls short of the power of ancient slavery.

Caesar knew how to profit by this advantage. Wherever any post demanded special confidence, we see him filling it, so far as other considerations at all permitted, with his slaves, freedmen, or followers of humble birth. His works show what such an organizing genius could accomplish with such an instrument; but how these marvelous feats were achieved in detail we have no adequate answer. Bureaucracy resembles manufacture in this respect, that the work done does not appear as that of the individual who made it, but as that of the factory in which it was produced. This much only is clear, that Caesar had no assistant who exerted a personal influence over his work or was even initiated into the whole plan. Not only was he the sole master; he also worked without skilled helpers, merely with common laborers.

In strictly political affairs Caesar avoided so far as possible any delegation of functions even as to details. Where it was inevitable, as when he needed a principal representative in Rome during his frequent absences, the person chosen was, significantly, not the monarch's legal deputy, the prefect of the city, but a confidant without official status, usually Caesar's banker, the cunning and pliant Phoenician merchant Lucius Cornelius Balbus from

Gades. In administration Caesar was above all careful to take over the keys of the treasury—which the Senate had seized from the fallen kings, and through which it had established its government—and to entrust them only to servants absolutely and exclusively devoted to him. The monarch's private wealth remained, of course, strictly separate from the property of the state. But Caesar took in hand the whole financial and monetary system, and conducted it as he and other Roman grandees were wont to manage their estates. The levying of provincial taxes, and also largely the coining of money, were entrusted to the Imperator's slaves and freedmen to the exclusion of men of the senatorial order—a momentous step, from which in time grew the important class of procurators and the "imperial household."

On the other hand, the governorships, now more than ever military commands after their financial functions had been taken over by the new imperial tax receivers, did not go to the monarch's retainers except in the case of Egypt alone. The country of the Nile, geographically isolated and politically centralized in the extreme, was better suited than any other district to break off permanently from the central power, as witness the repeated attempts by hard-pressed Italian party chiefs to establish themselves there during the recent crisis. Probably just this consideration induced Caesar not to declare the land a province, but to leave the harmless Lagid dynasty there. This is surely the reason why the command of the legions stationed in Egypt were not entrusted to a man of the Senate (or, in other words, to the former government) but was treated as a menial office like taxgathering.

In general, however, Caesar felt that Roman soldiers should not, like Oriental armies, be commanded by lackeys. The more important governorships were thus normally entrusted to exconsuls, the less important to expraetors; and the five-year interval prescribed by the law of 52 B.C. was probably set aside, so that the governorship followed hard on the heels of the term of office in Rome. On the other hand the distribution of the governorships, hitherto arranged sometimes by decree of the people or Senate, sometimes by agreement among the magistrates or by lot, passed over to the monarch. As the consuls were often induced to resign before the end of their year, to make room for replacement consuls (*consules suffecti*) ; as the number of praetors annually nominated was raised from eight to sixteen, with half being nominated by the Imperator (as in the case of the quaestors) ; and as the Imperator reserved the right of nominating titular praetors and titular quaestors—Caesar therefore never lacked a sufficient number of acceptable candidates for the governorships. Their recall was of course left to the regent's discretion, though as a rule the consular governor did not remain more than two years or the praetorian more than one year in his province.

Lastly, as for the administration of the capital city, the Imperator for a time evidently intended to entrust this also to magistrates nominated by him. He revived the old city lieutenancy of the kings, and during several absences of indefinite duration he committed the administration of the capital to one or more such lieutenants nominated by him without consulting the people. These lieutenants united in themselves all the administrative functions including even the right of coining money with their own name, although of course not with their own likeness. In 47 B.C. and in the first nine months of 45 there were neither praetors nor curule aediles nor quaestors; even the consuls were not nominated until near the end of the former year, and in the latter Caesar was consul without colleague.

This looks quite like an attempt to revive the old regal authority inside Rome, limited only by the democratic past of the new monarch: in other words, an attempt to abolish the consulship, the censorship, the praetorship, the curule aedileship, and the quaestorship, leaving only the prefect of the city during the king's absence and the tribunes and plebeian aediles appointed for protecting popular freedom. But Caesar subsequently abandoned this, neither accepting the royal title himself nor canceling those venerable names interwoven with the glorious history of the republic. The consuls, praetors, aediles, tribunes, and quaestors substantially retained their previous formal powers, but within a totally altered situation.

The foundation political idea of the republic was the identification of the Roman empire with the city of Rome, and by this token the city's magistrates were treated as magistrates of the empire. In Caesar's monarchy this view fell into abeyance. The magistrates of Rome governed thenceforth only the first among the empire's many municipalities, the consulship especially becoming a purely titular post of practical importance only because of the major governorship appended to it.

Thus the fate which the Roman community had been accustomed to visit on the vanquished now befell itself, and its sovereignty over the empire was converted into a limited communal freedom within the Roman state. Like the praetors and quaestors, the plebeian aediles were doubled in number and two new "grain aediles" (*aediles ceriales*) were added to superintend the supplies of the capital. Candidates for those offices were chosen by the community, without the restriction that marked the consuls and perhaps also the tribunes of the people and plebeian aediles. In general the ancient safeguards of popular freedom were not touched—but this, of course, did not prevent a refractory tribune of the people from being seriously interfered with and, in fact, deposed and erased from the roll of senators. As the Imperator was thus in all more important questions his own minister, as he controlled the finances by his servants and the army by his adjutants, and as the old republican offices were again converted into municipal magistracies, the autocracy was sufficiently established.

In the spiritual hierarchy Caesar made little material alteration.[3] If the Roman state religion had served to support the ruling oligarchy, it might render the same service to the new monarchy; thus the Senate's conservative religious policy was transferred to the new king. When the conservative Varro published about this time his *Antiquities of Divine Things,* the great fundamental repository of Roman theology, he was allowed to dedicate it to the Pontifex Maximus Caesar. The faint luster still adhering to the worship of Jove shone round the newly established throne, and the old national faith became in its dying stages the instrument, however hollow and feeble, of a Caesarian papacy.

In judicial matters the old regal jurisdiction was reestablished. The king had once judged criminal and civil cases without being legally bound in the former to respect an appeal to the people for mercy, or in the latter to delegate the decision to jurymen. In like fashion Caesar claimed the right of bringing any case to his own bar, and disposing of it personally or (in his absence) through his city lieutenant. In fact we find him, quite after the manner of the ancient kings, now sitting publicly in judgment in the Forum on Roman citizens accused of high treason, now holding a judicial inquiry in his house regarding dependent kings similarly accused. Thus the only special privilege of Roman citizens seems to have consisted in the publicity of the judicial procedure. But exercise of this kingly judicial right, although Caesar discharged its duties with impartiality and care, was naturally limited to exceptional cases.

In criminal and civil cases the former republican judicial practices were substantially retained. Criminal cases

---

3. The original describes here a few minor religious changes.

were disposed of before various jury commissions competent to the crimes, civil cases partly before the court of inheritance (the *centumviri*) and partly before the single *iudices*. Judicial proceedings were supervised in the capital chiefly by the praetors, in the provinces by the governors. Even under the monarchy political crimes continued to be referred to a jury commission. The new ordinance which Caesar issued precisely specified the punishable acts, excluded all prosecution of opinions, and fixed banishment rather than death as the penalty. The jurymen were chosen not exclusively from the Senate, as the oligarchy wished, nor solely from the equestrian order, as the strict Gracchians would have desired, but on the basis of the compromise law of Cotta, with an eye to reconciling the parties. However, in line with Pompey's law of 55 B.C., the *tribuni aerarii* who came from the lower ranks of the people were set aside by the requirement that jurymen must own property of at least 400,000 sesterces. Thus senators and equites now divided the judicial functions which had so long been an apple of discord between them.

Any case might be initiated either before the king's bar or before the competent republican tribunal, the latter of course taking precedence in any conflict; but a sentence handed down by either tribunal finally disposed of the case. Even the monarch might not overturn the verdict of a qualified juryman except (as under the law of the republic) where corruption, violence, or similar circumstances warranted canceling the juryman's sentence. On the other hand, the principle that an injured person might appeal any magisterial decree to the magistrate's superior probably obtained sufficient currency as to give rise to the later imperial appellate jurisdiction. Perhaps all the magistrates, at least all the provincial governors, were regarded as subordinates of the ruler, so that any of their decrees might be appealed to him.

These innovations, even the most important of which (the general right of appeal) cannot be reckoned as an absolute improvement, by no means remedied all the evils in the Roman administration of justice. Criminal procedure cannot be sound in any slave state, since the task of proceeding against slaves lies at least *de facto* in the hands of the master. The Roman master naturally punished his slave only if the crime rendered the slave useless or disagreeable to him: slave criminals were treated somewhat like oxen addicted to goring, and, as the latter were sold to the butcher, so were the former sold to fight in the arena. But even criminal procedure against free men, which had always been partly a political process, had amid the recent disorderly generations become transformed from a grave legal proceeding into a factional fight employing favor, money, and violence.

The blame rested jointly on all parties—magistrates, jurymen, litigants, even the public as spectators. But the most incurable wounds were inflicted by the lawyers. As the parasitic plant of courtroom eloquence flourished, all ideas of right and wrong vanished, and the distinction between opinion and evidence (so difficult for the public to understand) disappeared from Roman criminal practice. "An ordinary defendant," says an experienced Roman advocate of this period, "may be accused of any crime whether he has committed it or not, and will certainly be condemned." Numerous pleadings in criminal cases have come down to us from this epoch, and hardly one of them makes even a serious attempt to define the crime and present the proof or counterproof.

That the contemporary civil procedure was in many ways likewise unsound goes without saying. It too suffered from the intrusions of party politics, as for instance in the process of Publius Quinctius in 83-81 B.C., where the most contradictory decisions were given depending on whether Cinna or Sulla had the ascendency in Rome; and the advocates, frequently nonjurists, also added abundant confusion both intentionally and unintentionally. But in the nature of such cases political considerations became involved only exceptionally, and lawyers' quibbles could not so easily erode natural ideas of right. Accordingly, the civil pleadings handed down from this period, while not meeting our stricter tests of effectiveness, are yet far less libelous and more judicious than the contemporary speeches in criminal causes.

If Caesar retained Pompey's curb on the eloquence of advocates, or even strengthened it, nothing was lost; and much was gained when better-selected and better-superintended magistrates and jurymen were nominated and the flagrant corruption and intimidation of the courts came to an end. But the sacred sense of right and the reverence for the law, which it is difficult to destroy in the minds of the multitude, is still more difficult to replace. Though the legislator did away with various abuses, he could not heal the root of the evil; and it was doubtful whether time, which cures everything curable, would in this case bring relief.

The Roman military system of this period was in nearly the same condition as that of Carthage in Hannibal's time. The governing classes furnished only officers, the subjects, plebeians, and the provincials the army. Financially and militarily the general was almost independent of the central government, and in fortune or misfortune was left substantially to himself and the resources of his province. Civic and even national spirit had vanished from the army, and *esprit de corps* alone was left as an inner bond. The army had ceased to be an instrument of the commonwealth. Politically it had no viewpoint of its own, though it was doubtless able to adopt that of the master who commanded it. Militarily, under its usual miserable leaders it degenerated into a useless rabble, but under the right general it attained a military perfection which the citizen army could never match.

The officer class especially had degenerated. The higher ranks, senators and equites, grew more and more unused to arms. Where formerly there had been a zealous competition for the posts of staff officers, now every man of equestrian rank who chose to serve was sure of a military tribuneship; several of these posts had to be filled with men of humbler origin; and any man of quality who still served sought at least to finish his term in Sicily or some other province where he was sure not to face the enemy. Officers of ordinary bravery and efficiency were stared at as prodigies, Pompey especially becoming the object of a military idolatry by his contemporaries which displayed their own unfitness. As a rule the staff gave the signal for desertion and mutiny; in spite of the culpable indulgence of the commanders, proposals for cashiering officers of rank were daily occurrences. We still possess the picture drawn (not without irony) by Caesar's own hand of the situation at his headquarters when orders were given to march against Ariovistus: of the cursing and weeping, the preparation of wills, and even the presentation of requests for furlough.

Among the soldiers no trace of the better classes could any longer be found. The general legal obligation to bear arms still existed, but the levy, if resorted to alongside of enlisting, took place in the most irregular manner. Numerous persons liable to serve were wholly passed over, while those once inducted were retained beneath the eagles for thirty years and longer. The Roman citizen-cavalry was merely a sort of mounted noble guard, whose perfumed cavaliers and exquisite highbred horses only appeared in the festivals of the capital. The so-called citizen-infantry was a troop of mercenaries swept together from the lowest ranks of the population. The subjects furnished all the cavalry and the light troops, and came to be more and more extensively employed in the infantry as well. The post of centurion, on which the efficiency of the legions essentially depended, and which according to the military constitution was to be filled by soldiers rising from the ranks, was not merely conferred as a favor, but often sold to the highest bidder. Because of the government's bad financial management and the venality and fraud of nearly all the magistrates, the payment of the soldiers was extremely defective and irregular.

The inevitable result was that the Roman armies frequently pillaged the provincials, mutinied against their officers, and ran away from the enemy. Instances occurred where considerable armies, such as the Macedonian army of Piso in 57 B.C., though undefeated were utterly ruined by such misconduct. Capable leaders such as Pompey, Caesar, and Gabinius doubtless formed able and effective, and to some extent exemplary, armies out of these materials. But these armies belonged far more to their general than to the commonwealth. The still more complete decay of the Roman navy—which had remained an object of antipathy to the Romans and had never been fully nationalized—scarcely needs mention. Here, too, everything that could be injured had been reduced to ruin under the oligarchic government.

Caesar's reorganization of the Roman military system was substantially limited to tightening and strengthening the reins of discipline, which had been relaxed under the previous negligent and incapable supervision. The system as a whole seemed to him neither to need nor to be capable of radical reform; therefore he accepted the elements of the army just as Hannibal had accepted them. His ordinance setting three years' mounted service (i.e., as an officer), or six years of service on foot, as a prerequisite for holding a municipal magistracy or sitting in the municipal council before the thirtieth year, proves indeed that he wished to attract the better classes to the army. But it also proves with equal clarity that amid the steady decline of martial spirit he felt it no longer possible to associate unconditionally the holding of an honorary office with the completion of military service. This also explains why Caesar did not try to re-establish the Roman citizen-cavalry. The levy was better arranged, the time of service regulated and shortened, but otherwise the infantry of the line continued to come chiefly from the lower orders of the Roman citizens, the cavalry and the light infantry from the subjects. It is surprising that nothing was done to reorganize the fleet.

The untrustworthy character of the cavalry compelled Caesar to adopt the innovation—which doubtless seemed hazardous to him—of enlisting hired foreigners, especially Germans. Another innovation was the appointment of adjutants of the legion (*legati legionis*). Hitherto the legions had been led by military tribunes, nominated partly by the citizens and partly by the governor concerned. Six tribunes were placed over each legion, the command alternating among these; and only as a temporary and extraordinary measure was a single commandant appointed by the general. In later times these adjutants of legions, or colonels, appear as a permanent institution, nominated no longer by the governor whom they obey but by the supreme command in Rome; and both changes seem to stem from Caesar's arrangements in connection with the Gabinian law. This important new step was inserted in the military hierarchy partly because of the need for a more energetic centralization of the command, and partly because of the lack of capable superior officers, but chiefly in order to provide a counterpoise to the governor by associating with him one or more colonels nominated by the Imperator.

The most essential change in the military system was the installation of the Imperator as a permanent military head. Superseding the previous unmilitary and incapable governing corporation, he united in his hands the whole control of the army, and thus converted a largely nominal supervision into a real and energetic supreme command. We are not properly informed as to the relation between this supreme command and the special commands hitherto omnipotent in their respective spheres. Probably the relation between the praetor and the consul, or the consul and the dictator, provided a pattern. Thus, while the governor remained the supreme military authority in his province, the Imperator was entitled to assume it for himself or his delegates at any moment; and while the governor's authority was confined to the province, that of the Imperator extended over the whole empire.

Furthermore, it is extremely probable that the nomination of military tribunes and centurions (so far as it had hitherto belonged to the governor) as well as the new adjutants passed directly into the hands of the Imperator. In like manner the arrangement of the levies, the granting of leaves of absence, and the more important criminal cases may also have devolved upon the commander-in-chief. With the regulated control by the Imperator, and with the governors' powers thus limited, there was little need to fear that the armies might become disorganized or converted into the private troops of their respective officers.

But however decided were the indications of military monarchy, and however distinctly Caesar reserved the supreme command for himself, he was nevertheless quite disinclined to base his authority on the army. No doubt he deemed a standing army necessary, but only because the state's geographical position required comprehensive regulation of the frontiers and permanent frontier garrisons. Both during the recent civil war and earlier, he had worked at the tranquilizing of Spain, and had established strong frontier defensive positions along the great African desert and on the Rhine. He also made similar plans for the regions of the Euphrates and the Danube. Above all he designed an expedition against the Parthians to avenge the defeat of Carrhae. He had scheduled three years for this war, and was resolved to settle accounts thoroughly yet cautiously with these dangerous enemies once for all. In like manner he had formed the scheme of attacking King Burebistas of the Getae (Goths), who was extending his power on both sides of the Danube, and of protecting Italy in the northeast by border districts similar to those which he had created in Gaul.

On the other hand, there is no evidence that Caesar contemplated like Alexander a career of victory extending indefinitely. It is indeed said that he had intended to march from Parthia to the Caspian to the Black Sea, and thence along its northern shores to the Danube; to annex all Scythia and Germany as far as the Northern Ocean (which according to the notions of those days was not so far from the Mediterranean); and to return home through Gaul. But no credible authority vouches for the existence of these fantastic projects. The Roman state already included a mass of barbaric elements difficult to control, and for centuries to come had more than enough to do in assimilating them. Hence such conquests, even granting their military practicability, would have been nothing but blunders far more brilliant and far worse than Alexander's Indian expedition. Judging both from Caesar's conduct in Britain and Germany, and from the conduct of those who became his political heirs, it is highly probable that Caesar (like Scipio Aemilianus) called on the gods not to increase the empire but to preserve it. His schemes of conquest apparently restricted themselves to a stabilization of the frontier—measured, it is true, on his own great scale—which should secure the line of the Euphrates and replace the fluctuating and militarily useless boundary of the empire on the northeast by establishing and rendering defensible the line of the Danube.

If it is merely probable that Caesar ought not to be designated a world conqueror in the same sense as Alexander and Napoleon, it is quite certain that his design was not to found his new monarchy primarily on the army. He did not seek to place the military authority above the civil, but to incorporate it into, and as far as possible subordinate it to, the civil commonwealth. The invaluable pillars of a military state, those old and far-famed

Gallic legions, were honorably dissolved just because of the incompatibility of their *esprit de corps* with a civil commonwealth, and their glorious names were perpetuated only in newly founded urban communities. The soldiers who were allotted land by Caesar on their discharge were not, like those of Sulla, settled together in quasimilitary colonies of their own, but, especially in Italy, were isolated as much as possible and scattered throughout the peninsula. Only in the case of the Campanian land remaining for disposal was it impossible to avoid a concentration of the old soldiers of Caesar.

The difficult task of keeping the soldiers of a standing army within the civil community was attacked in various ways. The former arrangement merely prescribing certain years of service, which might be interrupted by temporary discharge, was retained, which occasioned a faster turnover in the army. Soldiers who had served out their terms were regularly settled as agricultural colonists. And perhaps most important, the army was kept away from Italy and centers of civil and political life, and directed toward what Caesar considered the soldier's only proper place— that is, on the frontier, where he might ward off the foreign foe.

The true criterion of a military state—the development of a privileged corps of guards—is not to be found with Caesar. Although a special bodyguard for the general on active duty had long existed, under Caesar this fell completely into disuse. His praetorian cohort seems to have consisted essentially of orderlies rather than a select corps, and consequently was never an object of jealousy to the troops of the line. Even less as king than as general would Caesar tolerate a bodyguard. Although well aware of the lurking assassins who constantly beset him, he rejected the Senate's proposal to create a select guard, soon dismissed the Spanish escort which he had used at first in the capital, and contented himself with the retinue of lictors traditional for Roman supreme magistrates.

However much of his and his party's ideal—to found a Periclean government in Rome not on the sword but on the confidence of the nation—Caesar had been obliged to abandon in the struggle, he continued to strive against the idea of a military monarchy with an energy almost without parallel in history. This too was certainly an impracticable ideal, and the only instance in which the earnest longing of that vigorous mind was more powerful than its clear judgment. The government which Caesar had in mind was not only by necessity highly personal, and thus as likely to perish with its author as the creations of Pericles and Cromwell. Amid the deep disorganization of the nation, it was incredible that even for his lifetime the eighth king of Rome would succeed like his seven predecessors in ruling his fellow citizens merely through law and justice; and it was equally improbable that he would again successfully incorporate the standing army, which in the last civil war learned its power and unlearned its obedience, as a controllable part of civil society.

Anyone who has calmly considered the extent to which respect for law had disappeared from top to bottom of Roman society must regard the former hope as almost a dream. If with the Marian military reform the soldier had generally ceased to be a citizen, the Campanian mutiny and the battlefield of Thapsus showed with painful clarity what kind of support the army now lent to the law. Even the great democrat could scarcely hold in check the powers which he had unchained. At his signal thousands of swords still flew from the scabbard, but they were no longer equally ready at that signal to return to the sheath.

Fate is mightier than genius. Caesar sought to restore the civil commonwealth, and became the founder of the military monarchy which he abhorred. He overthrew the regime of aristocrats and bankers only to put a military regime in its place, and the commonwealth continued as before to be tyrannized and exploited by a privileged minority. And yet it is a privilege of the highest natures thus creatively to err. The brilliant failures of great men to achieve their ideals form the best treasures of nations. It was Caesar's work that the Roman military state did not become a police state till after the lapse of several centuries; it is due to him that the Roman emperors, however little they otherwise resembled the great founder of their sovereignty, mainly employed the soldier not against the citizen but against the public foe, and esteemed both nation and army too highly to set the latter as constable over the former.

The regulation of financial matters was of slight difficulty, because of the empire's immense magnitude and the absence of any extensive public borrowing. If the state had been in constant financial embarrassment, the fault was not chargeable to inadequate revenues, which in recent years had immensely increased. To the earlier estimated income of 200,000,000 sesterces, 85,000,000 more were added by the creation of the provinces of Bithynia-Pontus and Syria. This increase, along with the other new or augmented sources of income (especially the constantly increasing yield of the taxes on luxuries), far outweighed the loss of rent from the Campanian public lands. Besides, immense windfalls had been brought into the treasury through Lucullus, Metellus, Pompey, Cato and others.

The cause of the state's financial embarrassments lay partly in increased ordinary and extraordinary expenditures, partly in poor management. Under the former head, the distribution of grain in the capital claimed almost exorbitant sums. Through its extension by Cato in 63 B.C. the yearly expenditure for that purpose amounted to 30,000,000 sesterces, and after 58 B.C., when the nominal price hitherto paid was abolished, it swallowed up a fifth of the state revenues. The military budget also had risen through the need for new garrisons in Cilicia, Syria, and Gaul. The extraordinary expenditures included the great cost of the navy, on which, for example, five

years after the great pirate roundup of 67 B.C., 34,000,-
000 sesterces were expended at once. In addition, very
considerable sums were consumed in wars and warlike
preparations, such as 18,000,000 sesterces paid to Piso
merely for outfitting his Macedonian army, 24,000,000
sesterces annually to Pompey for the maintenance and
pay of the Spanish army, and similar sums to Caesar for
the Gallic legions.

But considerable as were these demands, the Roman
treasury would probably have been able to meet them had
not its once efficient administration been affected by the
universal laxness and dishonesty of the age. The treasury
often had to suspend payments merely through failure to
collect its outstanding claims. The two quaestors placed
over it—young men annually changed—contented themselves at best with inaction; while the permanent staff,
once so justly esteemed for its integrity, now perpetuated
the worst abuses, more especially since such posts had
come to be bought and sold.

As soon, however, as the financial threads were concentrated in the cabinet of Caesar, new life and stricter
order at once pervaded all the wheels and springs of that
great machine. The two innovations of Gaius Gracchus
that ate like a gangrene into the Roman financial system
—the leasing of the direct taxes, and the distribution of
grain—were partly abolished and partly revised. Caesar,
unlike his predecessor, did not seek to hold the nobility
in check by the great capitalists and the populace of the
capital, but to set them aside and to deliver the commonwealth from all parasites of whatever rank.

Therefore in these two important questions he followed
Sulla rather than Gaius Gracchus. The leasing system was
continued for indirect taxes, for which it was very old
and (under the Roman financial maxim which Caesar retained inviolable, that tax collection should at any cost be
kept simple and manageable) absolutely could not be dispensed with. But the direct taxes were thenceforth uni-

versally made either taxes in kind to be supplied directly to the state, as in the case of the African and Sardinian deliveries of grain and oil, or converted, like the revenues of Asia Minor, into fixed money payments whose collection was entrusted to the tax districts themselves. The grain distribution in the capital had hitherto been regarded as a profitable prerogative of the community which ruled, and which therefore had to be fed by its subjects. Caesar set aside this infamous principle, but it could not be overlooked that only these largesses protected a multitude of destitute citizens from starvation. To this extent Caesar retained them. Under the Sempronian law ~~as reaffirmed by Cato every citizen settled~~ in Rome could legally claim free bread grain, and the list of recipients had risen to 320,000. This number was reduced, by excluding all individuals otherwise provided for, to 150,000, which was fixed once and for all as the maximum. At the same time the list was revised annually, so that places vacated by removal or death might be again filled by the most needy applicants.

By thus converting a political privilege into a provision for the poor, a unique moral and historical principle came into being. Civil society but slowly and gradually perceives its interdependence of interests. In earlier antiquity the state protected its members from the public enemy and the murderer, but it need not protect its helpless fellow citizens from a worse enemy, want. Greek civilization first developed, in the Solonian and post-Solonian legislation, the principle that the community was obligated to provide for its invalids and indeed for its poor generally. Caesar first transformed a restricted Greek municipal practice into an organic state institution, and converted what had been a burden and a disgrace for the commonwealth into the first of those institutions, now as countless as they are beneficial, where the depth of human compassion contends with the depth of human misery. In addition to these fundamental reforms a thorough revision of income and expenditures took place. Not a few communities and even whole districts were exempted from taxation, either indirectly by receiving the Roman or Latin franchise, or directly by special privilege. Still more communities had their taxes lowered; and Asia, the most oppressed province of all, was not only granted direct taxation but had also a third of these remitted. New revenues, as from the communities subdued in Illyria and especially in Gaul—the latter alone paid 40,000,000 sesterces per year—were fixed throughout on a low scale.

On the other hand, various towns such as Little Leptis in Africa had their taxes raised as a penalty for their wartime conduct. The very lucrative Italian harbor-tolls so recently abolished were instituted all the more readily, in that this tax fell primarily on luxuries imported from the East. To these new or revived sources of ordinary income were added the extraordinary sums which accrued as a result of the civil war: the booty collected in Gaul; the stock of cash in the capital; the treasures taken from the Italian and Spanish temples; the sums raised in the shape of forced loans, compulsory presents, or fines from dependent communities and rulers; the pecuniary penalties imposed by judicial sentence, or simply by sending an order to pay, on individual wealthy Romans; and above all things the proceeds from the estates of defeated opponents.

How productive were these extraordinary sources may be seen from the fact that the African capitalists who sat in the opposition-Senate were fined 100,000,000 sesterces, while 70,000,000 more were received from the sale of Pompey's property. This course was necessary because the power of the beaten nobility rested in great measure on their colossal wealth, and could be effectually broken only by imposing on them the costs of the war. But Caesar somewhat mitigated the odium of the confiscations by channeling their proceeds solely to the state. Unlike Sulla, who overlooked any act of fraud in his favorites, Caesar rigorously exacted the purchase price even from his most faithful adherents, such as Marcus Antonius.

Expenditures were lowered first of all by considerably restricting the distribution of grain. The supply to the poor of the capital, as well as the kindred supply of oil newly introduced by Caesar for the Roman baths, was in great part supported by contributions in kind from Sardinia and especially from Africa, and was thus kept wholly or largely separate from the state treasury. On the other hand regular military expenditures were increased partly by augmenting the standing army, and partly by raising the legionary's pay from 480 to 900 sesterces annually. Both these latter steps were in fact indispensable. There was a total want of any real frontier defense, whose prerequisite was a considerable increase of the army. Doubling the soldier's pay was doubtless employed by Caesar to attach his soldiers firmly to him, but it was introduced permanently for a very different reason. The former pay of 1⅓ sesterces per day had been fixed in very ancient times, when money had an altogether different value than in Caesar's day. In a period when day laborers in the capital earned an average of 3 sesterces, it could be retained only because the soldier entered the army chiefly for the sake of the perquisites, largely illicit, of military service. The first precondition to a serious reform in the military system, and to ending those irregular gains of the soldier which mainly burdened the provincials, was a suitable increase in pay; and fixing it at 2½ sesterces may be regarded as a necessary and beneficial step, despite the great burden thereby imposed on the treasury.

It is difficult to conceive of the extraordinary expenses which Caesar undertook voluntarily or otherwise. The wars themselves consumed enormous sums, and similar amounts were required to fulfil the promises which he had been obliged to make during the civil war. It was a bad example, and one unhappily not soon forgotten, that every common soldier received 20,000 sesterces for his participation, and every citizen in the capital 300 sesterces for his nonparticipation. But Caesar, having once pledged his word, was too much of a king to break it. Besides, he satisfied innumerable demands of honorable liberality, and put immense sums into building, which had been shamefully neglected during the last years of the republic. The cost of his buildings in the capital, executed partly during the Gallic campaigns and partly afterwards, was reckoned at 160,000,000 sesterces. The net result of Caesar's financial administration is expressed in the fact that, while he fully met all equitable claims, nevertheless by March of 44 B.C. 700,000,000 sesterces lay in the public treasury and 100,000,000 in his own—a sum ten times that in the treasury in the republic's palmiest days.

But difficult as it was, the task of breaking up the old parties and furnishing the new commonwealth with an appropriate constitution, an efficient army, and well-ordered finances was not the hardest part of Caesar's work. Real regeneration of the Italian nation required a reorganization that would transform all parts of the great empire— Rome, Italy, and the provinces. Let us endeavor here also to delineate the old state of things, as well as the beginnings of a new and more tolerable time.

The good stock of the Latin nation had long since wholly disappeared from Rome. By its very nature, a capital loses its municipal and even its national stamp more quickly than any subordinate community. There the upper classes speedily withdraw from urban public life, in order to find their home in the state as a whole rather than in a single city. There are inevitably concentrated the foreign settlers, the fluctuating population of travelers for pleasure or business, the mass of the indolent, lazy, criminal, financially and morally bankrupt (and for that very reason cosmopolitan) rabble. All this applied preeminently to Rome. The rich Roman frequently regarded his town house merely as a lodging. When the urban municipal offices were converted into imperial magistracies, when the civic assembly became the governing assembly of the empire, and when smaller self-governing tribal or other associations were not tolerated within the capital, then all true community life ceased for Rome. From all the empire people flocked to Rome for speculation, for debauchery, for intrigue, for training in crime, or even to hide there from the eye of the law.

While these evils arose partly from the very nature of a capital, they were accompanied by others more accidental and perhaps still more grave. There has perhaps never existed a great city so thoroughly lacking means of support as Rome. Importation on the one hand, and home manufacture by slaves on the other, made any free industry impossible from the outset. The radical evil pervading all the societies of antiquity—slavery—showed its consequences most conspicuously in the capital. Nowhere were such masses of slaves accumulated as in the city palaces of the great families or the wealthy upstarts. Nowhere were the peoples of three continents mingled as in Rome's slave population—Syrians, Phrygians and other half-Hellenes with Libyans and Moors, Getae and Iberians with the mounting influx of Celts and Germans. The demoralization inseparable from the absence of freedom, and the terrible inconsistency between formal and moral right, were far more glaringly apparent in the partially or wholly cultivated city slave than in the rural serf who tilled the field in chains like a fettered ox.

Still worse than the slave masses, however, were those who had been *de jure* or simply *de facto* released from slavery—a mixture of mendicant rabble and rich parvenus, no longer slaves and not yet citizens, economically and even legally dependent on their masters, but with the pretensions of free men. These freedmen were drawn above all toward the capital, where various profits could be had and where retail trade as well as the minor handicrafts were almost wholly in their hands. Their influence on elections is well known, and their leading part in the street riots is evident from the ordinary signal by which these were virtually proclaimed by the demagogues—the closing of shops and places of business.

The government not only did nothing to counteract this corruption, but even encouraged it from selfish policy. The judicious law which prohibited individuals condemned for a capital offense from dwelling in the city was winked at by the negligent police. The urgently needed supervision of popular associations was at first neglected, and afterwards was even forbidden as an unwarranted restriction of popular freedom. The public festivals had so increased that the seven ordinary ones alone—the Roman, the Plebeian, those of the Mother of the Gods, of Ceres, of Apollo, of Flora, and of Victoria—lasted altogether sixty-two days; and to these were added the gladiatorial games and numerous other extraordinary amusements. The duty of providing grain at low prices—unavoidable with such a proletariat living wholly from hand to mouth—was treated with the most unscrupulous frivolity, and the fluctuations in the price of bread grain were incredible. These grain distributions formed as it were an official invitation to every citizen proletarian who was destitute of food and disinclined to work to move to the capital.

The bad seed yielded a corresponding harvest. The political system of clubs and bands, and the religious worship of Isis and similar pious extravagances, had their roots in this state of things. People constantly faced want, and not unfrequently utter famine. Nowhere was life less secure than in the capital, whose sole unique trade was murder professionally prosecuted by banditti. Luring the prospective victim to Rome was the preliminary to assassination, and no one ventured into the countryside near the capital without an armed retinue.

The city's outward condition corresponded to this inward disorganization, and seemed a keen satire on the aristocratic government. Nothing was done to regulate the Tiber, except that the single bridge was rebuilt of stone at least as far as the Tiber-island. No more was done toward leveling the city of the Seven Hills, except perhaps where rubbish accumulation effected some improvement. The wretchedly kept streets were crooked, narrow, and steep, the footpaths small and ill-paved. The ordinary houses, poorly built of brick to a giddy height, were constructed mostly by speculative builders for the account of small proprietors, by which means the former became enormously rich while the latter were reduced to beggary. Like isolated islands amid this dreary sea rose the splendid palaces of the rich, which pre-empted the space for smaller houses just as their owners pre-empted the rights of lesser men in the state. The marble pillars and Greek statues of these palaces formed a striking contrast to the decaying temples, whose images were still in great part carved of wood.

Official supervision of streets, of river banks, of fires, or of building was almost unknown. If the government troubled itself at all about the frequent floods, conflagrations, and collapses, it was only to ask the state theologians for their advice on the true meaning of such signs and wonders. If we try to imagine a London with the slave population of New Orleans, with the police of Constantinople, with the nonindustrial character of modern Rome, and the political ferment of Paris in 1848, we can get some idea of the republican glory whose departure the sulky letters of Cicero and his associates deplore.

Caesar sought to help rather than deplore. Rome remained, of course, a cosmopolitan city. Any attempt to give it a specifically Italian character would not only have been impracticable, but also would not have suited Caesar's plan. Just as Alexander found an appropriate capital for his Graeco-Oriental empire in the Hellenic, Jewish, Egyptian and above all cosmopolitan city of Alexandria, so the capital of the new Romano-Hellenic empire, situated between East and West, was to be not an Italian community but the denationalized capital of many nations. For this reason Caesar tolerated the worship of the newly introduced Egyptian gods alongside Father Jove, and even allowed the Jews to practice their strange foreign ritual in the capital. However offensive was the motley mixture of Rome's parasitic population, he nowhere opposed its extension. Rather, at his popular festivals he caused dramas to be performed not only in Latin and Greek but also in other languages, presumably Phoenician, Aramaic, Syrian, and Spanish.

But if Caesar consciously accepted the existing fundamental character of the capital, he yet worked energetically to improve the lamentable and disgraceful conditions prevailing there. Unhappily, the basic evils were the most difficult to eradicate. Caesar could not abolish slavery, and it must remain an open question whether he might eventually have attempted at least to limit the number of slaves in the capital, as he undertook in another field. As little could he create a free industry in Rome. Yet his great building program partly remedied the lack of employment there, and offered the proletariat a source of small but honorable gain.

At the same time Caesar labored energetically to shrink the free proletariat. The constant influx brought to Rome by the grain distribution was materially restricted, if not wholly stopped, by converting this distribution into a provision for a fixed number of the poor. The ranks of the existing proletariat were thinned by the tribunals instructed to proceed rigorously against the rabble, and also by comprehensive transmarine colonization. Of the 80,000 colonists whom Caesar sent overseas in his few years of rule, a great majority must have come from the capital's proletariat. Indeed, most of the Corinthian settlers were freedmen. Though freedmen were traditionally excluded from any urban honorary office, Caesar opened the senate house to them in his colonies, doubtless to encourage emigration by the better-situated freedmen.

This emigration must have been more than a mere temporary arrangement. Caesar, convinced like every sensible man that the proletariat's misery could really be remedied only by a well-regulated system of colonization, and put in a position to realize it to an almost unlimited extent, must have intended to continue the process by keeping open a constant means of abating a constantly recurring evil. Measures were also taken to limit the market fluctuations of the most important means of subsistence in the capital. The reorganized and liberally administered state treasury furnished the means for this purpose, and two new magistrates, the grain aediles, were charged with supervising the contractors and the markets of the capital.

The club system was checked by constitutional change more effectually than was possible through prohibitive laws, since the corruption and violence of the electioneering automatically ended along with republican elections and the republic itself. Moreover, the combinations which grew up under the Clodian law were broken up, and the whole system of association was placed under supervision of the government. Except for the ancient guilds and associations, the religious unions of the Jews, and other specially exempted categories, for which a simple intimation to the Senate seems to have sufficed, permission to organize a permanent society with fixed dues and meetings was made a concession to be granted by the Senate, and, as a rule, doubtless only with the monarch's consent.

To this was added a stricter policing and administration of justice. The laws, especially as regards violence, were strengthened, and the irrational republican law which permitted the convicted criminal to avoid a part of his penalty by self-banishment was set aside. Caesar's detailed police regulations are in great part still preserved; they include regulations requiring house proprietors to put the streets into repair and pave the footpath in its whole breadth with hewn stones, as well as appropriate enactments regarding the movement of litters and wagons, which were allowed to move freely through the capital's narrow streets only in the evening and at night. Supervision of the police remained as before chiefly in the hands of four aediles, each of whom now superintended a distinctly marked-off police district.

Lastly, public building in the capital received from Caesar, who combined in himself the Roman and the organizer's love of building, a stimulus which not merely put to shame the mismanagement of recent times, but also left the best efforts of the Roman aristocracy as far behind as Caesar's genius surpassed the honest talents of the Marcii and Aemilii. Caesar excelled his predecessors not merely by the extent of his buildings and the magnitude of his expenditures, but by a genuine statesmanly perception of the public good. Instead of building temples and other splendid structures, as did his successors, he relieved the market place of Rome, where the citizen-assemblies, the chief courts, the exchange, and the daily traffic of both business and idleness still were crowded together, by constructing a new place of assembly, the Saepta Julia in the Campus Martius, a new courthouse, and the Forum Julium, between the Capitol and the Palatine.[4]

But these achievements were but the first steps toward a complete remodeling of Rome. Projects were already formed for a new senate house, for a new magnificent bazaar, for a theater to rival that of Pompey, for a public Latin and Greek library modeled on that recently destroyed at Alexandria (the first institution of its sort in Rome), and for a temple of Mars intended to surpass all earlier rivals in riches and glory. Still more brilliant was the idea of draining the Pomptine marshes, and altering the lower course of the Tiber by leading it through a new

■

4. The original notes that he also supplied the public baths yearly with three million pounds of oil, so necessary to ancient concepts of hygiene.

channel to an adequate artificial harbor. By this gigantic plan the capital's most dangerous enemy, malaria, would be banished; the extremely limited building space would be vastly enlarged; and the city would at the same time obtain a safe seaport, so long and painfully needed. It seemed as if the Imperator could remove mountains and rivers, and contend with nature herself.

However, much as Rome gained in commodiousness and magnificence by the new order of things, its political supremacy was irretrievably lost through that very change. The idea that the Roman state should coincide with the city had indeed gradually become preposterous, but the maxim was so central to the Roman republic that it could not perish before the republic itself. Only in Caesar's new state was it completely set aside (except perhaps for some legal fictions), and the capital was placed on a level with other municipalities. Indeed, Caesar—here as always endeavoring not merely to regulate the thing, but also to call it by its right name—issued his Italian municipal ordinance both for the capital and for other urban communities. The Rome of the imperial period, just because it was incapable of a living as a community, was essentially inferior to other major municipalities. Republican Rome was a den of robbers, but it was also the state; the Rome of the monarchy, although beginning to embellish itself with all the glories of three continents and to glitter in gold and marble, was nothing more than a royal residence appended to a poorhouse—in other words, a necessary evil.

While Caesar's only object in the capital was to get rid of palpable evils by massive police action, it was far more difficult to remedy the deep economic disorganization. Its radical misfortunes were those already noted—the disappearance of the agricultural and the unnatural increase of the mercantile population. The reader will not fail to remember the wretched state of Italian agriculture. Despite the most earnest attempts to check the annihilation of small holdings, farm husbandry was no longer the predominant economy in any Italian region in this period, except perhaps for the Apennine and Abruzzi valleys.

As for the management of estates, there is no material difference between the Catonian system already described and that pictured for us by Varro, except that the latter shows the traces for better or for worse of the progress of city life on a great scale in Rome. "Formerly," says Varro, "the barn on the estate was larger than the manor-house; now it is wont to be the reverse." In Tusculum and Tibur, on the shores of Tarracina and Baiae, where the old Latin and Italian farmers had sown and reaped, there now rose in barren splendor the villas of Roman nobles, some covering the space of a fair-sized town with their gardens and aqueducts, fresh and salt water ponds for breeding and keeping river and marine fish, nurseries of snails and slugs, game preserves for hares, rabbits, stags, roes, and wild boars, and aviaries containing even cranes and peacocks.

But the luxury of a great city also enriches many an industrious hand, and supports more poor than philanthropy. Those noble aviaries and fishponds were of course a very costly indulgence. The system was carried to such an extent that the stock of a pigeon house was valued at 100,000 sesterces. A methodical system of fattening had sprung up, and manure from the aviaries became important in agriculture. A single bird-dealer was able to furnish at once 5,000 fieldfares at three denarii each, a single fish-breeder 2,000 *muraenae;* and the fishes left behind by Lucius Lucullus brought 40,000 sesterces. As may readily be conceived, under such circumstances any one who followed this occupation industriously and intelligently might earn very large profits on little capital. A small bee-breeder of this period sold from his one-acre thyme-garden near Falerii an average of 10,000 sesterces worth of honey each year.

The rivalry among growers of fruit went so far that the marble-lined fruit-chamber in elegant villas was often fitted out as a dining room, with fine fruit acquired by purchase sometimes exhibited there as homegrown. At this period the cherry from Asia Minor and other foreign fruit trees were first planted in Italy. The vegetable gardens, the beds of roses and violets in Latium and Campania, yielded rich produce, and the "market for dainties" by the side of the Via Sacra, where fruits, honey, and chaplets were sold, played an important part in the life of the capital.

Generally the management of estates, worked on the planter system, had reached an economic level scarcely to be surpassed. The valley of Rieti, the region round the Fucine lake, the districts on the Liris and Volturnus, and indeed Central Italy in general, were in the most flourishing condition. Even certain branches of industry, which were suitable adjuncts to an estate cultivated by slaves, were taken up by intelligent landlords, and under favorable circumstances inns, weaving factories, and especially brickworks were constructed on the estate. The Italian producers of wine and oil not only supplied the Italian market but also carried on a considerable export trade.

A homely professional treatise of this period compares Italy to a great fruit garden; and a contemporary poet pictures his beautiful native land as a place where well-watered meadows, luxuriant grain fields, and pleasant vine-covered hills are fringed by the dark line of the olive trees, where the "ornament" of the land, smiling in varied charms, cherishes the loveliest gardens in its bosom and is itself wreathed round by food-producing trees. These descriptions, evidently faithful pictures of the landscape daily presented to the eye of the poet, transplant us into the most flourishing districts of Tuscany and Terra di Lavoro.

It is true that the pastoral husbandry, which for reasons formerly explained was always spreading especially in southern and southeastern Italy, was in every respect a backward step; but it too participated in the general progress of agriculture. Much was done for improvement of breeds, and asses for breeding brought 60,000, 100,000, and even 400,000 sesterces. The solid Italian husbandry of this period, when the general development of intelligence and abundance of capital rendered it fruitful, achieved far more brilliant results than the old system of small cultivators could ever have done. It was even carried beyond the bounds of Italy, for the Italian agriculturist reared cattle and even cultivated grain on large tracts in the provinces.

Alongside this estate husbandry unnaturally prospering over the ruin of the small farmers, private banking also assumed enormous proportions, as the Italian merchants vying with the Jews spread over all the provinces and protectorates of the empire. However, to demonstrate how all capital ultimately flowed to Rome, it will be sufficient to point to the single fact that in the money market of the capital the regular rate of interest at this time was six per cent—cheaper by a half than it was on an average elsewhere in antiquity.

Out of this economic system, based both in its agrarian and mercantile aspects on masses of capital and on speculation, there arose a most fearful maldistribution of wealth. The often-used and often-abused phrase of a nation of millionaires and beggars applies perhaps nowhere so aptly as to Rome at the end of the republic. The essential maxim of the slave state—that the rich man who lives on his slaves is necessarily respectable, while the poor man who lives by his own labors is necessarily vulgar—has perhaps never again been recognized with such terrible precision as the principle underlying all public and private intercourse. There was no middle class in our sense, as indeed no such class can exist in any fully developed slave state. What appears to be a middle class is composed of those rich business men and landholders who are so uncultivated, or so highly cultivated, as to stay within their own sphere and keep aloof from public life. Of the men of business—a class among whom numerous freedmen and other upstarts were often seized with the giddy fancy of playing the man of quality—there were not many who showed so much judgment.

A model of this sort was Titus Pomponius Atticus, frequently mentioned in accounts of this period. He acquired an immense fortune partly through estate farming in Italy and Epirus, partly from money transactions throughout Italy, Greece, Macedonia, and Asia Minor. But at the same time he remained the simple man of business, refusing to be seduced into soliciting office or even into monetary transactions with the state. Equally remote from avaricious niggardliness or the prodigal and burdensome luxury of his time (his table, for instance, was maintained at a daily cost of 100 sesterces), he contented himself with an easy existence including the charms of both country and city life, the pleasures of intercourse with the best society of Rome and Greece, and all the enjoyments of literature and art.

More numerous and more solid were the Italian landholders of the old type. Contemporary literature preserves the description of one such rural nobleman, Sextus Roscius, who was murdered amid the proscriptions of 81 B.C. His wealth, estimated at 6,000,000 sesterces, is mainly invested in his thirteen landed estates; he manages it in person systematically and with enthusiasm; he seldom or never comes to the capital, and when he does, his clownish manners contrast not less with those of the polished senator than his hosts of uncouth rural slaves with the elegant domestic slaves of the capital. Far more than the circles of the cosmopolitan nobility, and the mercantile lords at home everywhere and nowhere, these landlords and their country homes preserved the discipline and manners as well as the pure and noble language of their fathers.

This landlord class was regarded as the flower of the nation. The speculator who has made his fortune, and who aspires to ultimate respectability, buys an estate and seeks, if not to become a squire himself, at any rate to rear his son with that view. We find traces of this landlord class wherever a national movement appears in politics, and wherever literature puts forth any fresh growth. From it the patriotic opposition to the new monarchy drew its best strength; to it belonged Varro, Lucretius, Catullus; and nowhere perhaps is the comparative freshness of this landlord-life more clearly revealed than in the graceful Arpinate introduction to the second book of Cicero's treatise *De Legibus*—a green oasis amidst the fearful desert of that equally empty and voluminous writer.

But the cultivated class of merchants and the vigorous order of landlords were far overshadowed by the two classes that gave the society its tone—the mass of beggars and the world of quality. We have no figures to indicate precisely the relative proportions of poor and rich in this epoch, yet we may again recall the expression of a Roman statesman some fifty years earlier, that the number of solidly rich families among the Roman citizens did not number 2,000. The body of citizens had changed since then, but the clear indications are that the disproportion between poor and rich had remained at least as great. The impoverishment of the multitude shows itself only too plainly in the grain distributions and army enlistments. The corresponding increase of riches is expressly attested by an author of this generation, when, speaking of the Marian period, he describes an estate of 2,000,000 sesterces as "riches according to the circumstances of that day"; and the statements which we find as to individual wealth support the same conclusion. The very rich Lucius Domitius Ahenobarbus promised four acres of land out of his own property to each of twenty thousand soldiers. Pompey's estate amounted to 70,000,000 sesterces, that of Aesopus the actor to 20,000,000. Marcus Crassus, the richest of the rich, possessed 7,000,000 sesterces at the outset of his career, and at its close, after spending enormous sums, 170,000,000.

The effect of such poverty and such riches was on both sides an economic and moral disorganization outwardly different, but at bottom the same. If the common man was saved from starvation only by the state, it was the necessary consequence of this mendicant misery (although it also reciprocally appears as a cause of it) that he addicted himself to the beggar's laziness and the beggar's good cheer. The Roman plebeian was fonder of looking at the theater than of working, and the taverns and brothels were so frequented that the demagogues found it to their special interest to win over the proprietors of such establishments.

The gladiatorial games, which both revealed and fostered the worst demoralization of ancient times, had become so flourishing that a lucrative business was done in the sale of the programs for them. This age introduced the horrible innovation whereby the life or death of the vanquished gladiator depended not on the law of duel or on the pleasure of the victor, but on the caprice of the onlooking public; and according to its signal the victor either spared or transfixed his prostrate antagonist. The trade of fighting had so risen, or freedom had so fallen in value, that the intrepidity and emulation lacking on the battlefields of this age were universal in the arena, where the law of the duel required that every gladiator allow himself to be stabbed mutely and without shrinking. In fact, free men not unfrequently sold themselves to contractors for board and wages as gladiatorial slaves. The plebeians of the third century B.C. also suffered want and famine, but they did not sell their freedom; and still less would the jurists of that period have approved as lawful the equally immoral and illegal contract of such a gladiatorial slave "to let himself be chained, scourged, burnt or killed without opposition, if the laws of the institution should so require."

In the world of quality such things did not occur, but at base it was hardly different, and least of all better. The aristocrat boldly competed with the proletarian in indolence: if the latter lounged on the pavement, the former lay in bed till late in the day. Extravagance was as unbounded as it was tasteless. It was lavished on politics and on the theater, of course to the corruption of both. The consular office was purchased at an incredible price— in the summer of 54 B.C. the first voting-division alone was paid 10,000,000 sesterces. And any pleasure a cultured man might take in the drama was spoiled by the mania for decoration.

Rents in Rome appear to have averaged four times as high as in the country-towns, and a house in the capital once sold for 15,000,000 sesterces. The house of Marcus Lepidus (consul in 78 B.C.), which at the time of Sulla's death was the finest in Rome, a generation afterwards was not even in the first hundred Roman palaces. We have already mentioned the extravagance in country houses, one of which brought 4,000,000 sesterces, chiefly because of its fishpond. A fashionable grandee now needed at least two villas—one in the Sabine or Alban mountains near the capital, and a second in the vicinity of the Campanian baths—and preferably also a garden immediately outside Rome. Still more irrational than these palaces were the palatial sepulchres, several of which still attest how lofty a pile of masonry the rich Roman needed in order to die in style.

Fanciers of horses and dogs too were not wanting,

24,000 sesterces being a not uncommon price for a showy horse. The rich also indulged in fine furniture, such as tables of African cypress-wood costing 1,000,000 sesterces; in dresses of purple stuffs or transparent gauzes accompanied by an elegant adjustment of their folds before the mirror (the orator Hortensius is said to have brought a damage suit against a colleague because he ruffled his dress in a crowd); and in precious stones and pearls, which in this period first took the place of the far more beautiful and artistic ornaments of gold. It was already utter barbarism, when at Pompey's triumph over Mithradates the image of the victor appeared wrought wholly of pearls, and when the sofas and the shelves in the dining hall were silver-mounted and even the kitchen utensils were made of silver. In a similar spirit the collectors of this period took out the artistic medallions from old silver cups, to set them anew in vessels of gold.

There was also no lack of luxury in travelling. "When the governor travelled," Cicero tells us of a Sicilian governor, "which of course he did not in winter, but only at the beginning of spring—not the spring of the calendar but the beginning of the season of roses—he had himself conveyed, as was the custom with the kings of Bithynia, in a litter with eight bearers, sitting on a cushion of Maltese gauze stuffed with rose leaves, with one garland on his head and a second twined round his neck, applying to his nose a little smelling-bag of fine linen, with minute meshes, filled with roses; and thus he had himself carried even to his bedchamber."

But no luxury flourished more than the coarsest of all —the luxury of the table. The whole arrangement and life of the villa ultimately revolved around dining. There were not only different dining rooms for winter and summer, but dinner was served in the picture gallery, in the fruit-chamber, in the aviary, or on a platform erected in the deer park, around which, when the bespoken "Orpheus" appeared in theatrical costume and blew his flourish, the duly-trained roes and wild boars congregated. Amid all this care bestowed on decoration, the reality was by no means forgotten. Not only was the cook a graduate in gastronomy, but the master himself often acted as the instructor of his cooks. The roast had long ago been overshadowed by marine fishes and oysters, but now the Italian river-fishes were utterly banished from good tables, and Italian delicacies and wines were looked on as almost vulgar. Even at the popular festivals three foreign wines—Sicilian, Lesbian, and Chian—were distributed in addition to Italian Falerian, while a generation before it had been sufficient even at great banquets to send round Greek wine once. In the cellar of the orator Hortensius were found 10,000 jars of foreign wine, at 33 quarts each. It was no wonder that Italian winegrowers began to complain of the competition from the Greek islands.

No naturalist could ransack land and sea more zealously for new animals and plants than the epicures of that day ransacked them for new culinary dainties. The practice of the guest taking an emetic after a banquet, to avoid the consequences of the varied fare set before him, no longer created surprise. Debauchery of every sort became so systematic and aggravated that it found its professors, who earned a livelihood by instructing the youth of quality in the theory and practice of vice.

There is no need to dwell longer on this confused picture, so monotonous in its variety, especially since the far-from-original Romans confined themselves to an exaggerated and stupid copy of Helleno-Asiatic luxury. But Plutus devours his children as well as Kronos. The competition for these worthless objects of fashionable longing so forced up prices that those who swam with the stream saw the most colossal estate melt away, and even those who only joined in what was most necessary saw their inherited and firmly established wealth rapidly undermined. The race for the consulship was the usual road to ruin for noble houses, but much the same applies to the games, the great buildings, and all those other pleasant but expensive pursuits.

The princely wealth of that period was surpassed only by its still more princely liabilities. Around 62 B.C. Caesar owed 25,000,000 sesterces, after deducting his assets. Marcus Antonius owed 6,000,000 sesterces at the age of twenty-four, and 40,000,000 fourteen years afterwards. Curio owed 60,000,000, Milo 70,000,000. That the extravagant habits of the Roman world of quality rested solely on credit is shown by the fact that the monthly interest rate once rose suddenly from four to eight per cent, through the borrowing of different competitors for the consulship. Insolvency, instead of leading in due time to a meeting of creditors or at any rate to a liquidation which might at least clear up matters, was ordinarily prolonged by the debtor as much as possible. Instead of selling his property and especially his landed estates, he continued to borrow and to present the semblance of riches till the crash only became the worse, and the winding-up yielded a result as in Milo's case, where the creditors obtained something like four per cent.

Amid this rapid transition from riches to ruin and this systematic swindling, nobody of course profited so much as the cool banker who knew when to give or refuse credit. Debtor-creditor relations thus reverted almost to the point where they had stood during the worst of the social crises of the third century B.C. The nominal owners held their lands virtually at the sufferance of their creditors. The debtors were either in servile subjection to their creditors, so that the humbler of them appeared like freedmen in the creditor's train, and those of higher rank spoke and voted even in the Senate at the nod of their creditor lord; or they threatened to declare war on property itself, to intimidate their creditors or get rid of them by conspiracy and civil war. On such relations was based the power of Crassus. Out of them arose the insurrections of Cinna, and still more definitely those of Catiline, of Coelius, and of Dolabella, closely resembling the Hellenic world's battles of a century before between those who had and those who had not. That in so rotten an economy every financial or political crisis should occasion the most dreadful confusion was merely to be expected. We need hardly mention that the usual phenomena—the flight of capital, the sudden depreciation of landed estates, innumerable bankruptcies, and an almost universal insolvency—made their appearance during the civil war just as during the Social and Mithradatic wars.

Under such circumstances morality and family life were treated as outmoded among all ranks of society. To be poor was not merely the sorest disgrace and the worst crime, but the only disgrace and the only crime. For money the statesman sold the state, and the citizen his freedom. The officer's post and the judge's vote were to be had for money, and for money the lady of quality surrendered her person like the common courtesan. Perjury and falsification of documents had become so common that a popular poet of this age referred to an oath as "the plaster for debts." Men had so forgotten what honesty was that a person who refused a bribe was regarded not as an upright man, but as a personal foe. The criminal statistics of all times and countries will hardly furnish a parallel to the dreadful picture of crimes—so varied, so horrible, and so unnatural—which the trial of Aulus Cluentius unrolled in the bosom of one of the most respected families of an Italian country town.

But while the slime was thus accumulating ever more deleteriously and deeply underneath the national life, the more smooth and glittering was the surface, overlaid with the varnish of polished manners and universal friendship. All the world interchanged visits, so that in the houses of quality it was necessary to admit the persons presenting themselves in a certain order fixed by the master or occasionally by the attendant in waiting, and to give audience only to the more notable one by one, while the rest were summarily admitted partly in groups, and partly *en masse* at the close. (This practice Gaius Gracchus, here too paving the way for the new monarchy, is said to have introduced.) The interchange of courtesy letters was as common as courtesy visits; "friendly" letters flew over land and sea between persons who had neither personal relations nor business with each other, whereas proper and formal business letters scarcely occur except where the letter is addressed to a corporation.

In like manner invitations to dinner, the customary new year's presents, and the domestic festivals were divested of meaning and almost transformed into public ceremonials. Even death did not release the Roman from obligation to his countless "neighbors," for in order to die respectably he had to provide each of them at least with a keepsake. Just as in certain circles of our mercantile world, genuine family intimacy and friendship had so totally vanished from the Rome of that day that the whole intercourse of business and acquaintance could be garnished with forms and flourishes of affections which had lost all meaning. Thus the reality gradually came to be superseded by that spectral shadow of "friendship," which holds by no means the least place among the various evil spirits brooding over the proscriptions and civil wars of this age.

Equally characteristic of the brilliant decay of this period was the emancipation of women. Economically, women had long since made themselves independent. In the present epoch we even meet with solicitors acting specially for women, who officiously lend their aid to solitary rich ladies in managing their property and their lawsuits, impress them with their knowledge of business and law, and thereby procure for themselves ampler perquisites and legacies than other loungers on the exchange.

But it was not merely from the economic guardianship of father or husband that women felt themselves emancipated. Love intrigues of all sorts were constantly in progress. The ballet dancers (*mimae*) were easily a match for those of the present day in the variety and skill of their pursuits, and prima donnas like Cytheris pollute even the pages of history. But their virtually licensed trade was materially injured by the free art of aristocratic ladies. Liaisons in the first houses had become so frequent that only an exceptional scandal could cause any special talk, and legal action now seemed almost ridiculous. The unparalleled scandal created by Publius Clodius in 61 B.C. at the women's festival in the house of the pontifex maximus, although a thousand times worse than the occurrences which fifty years before had led to a series of capital sentences, passed wholly without punishment and almost without investigation. The watering-place season —in April, when political business was suspended and the world of quality congregated in Baiae and Puteoli—derived its chief charm from the relations licit and illicit which, along with music and song and elegant breakfasts on board or on shore, enlivened the gondola voyages.

The ladies, however, were by no means content with this domain which rightfully belonged to them. They also acted as politicians, appeared in party conferences, and took part with their money and their intrigues in the wild machinations of the time. Any one who beheld these female statesmen performing on the stage of Scipio and Cato, and saw at their side the young fop—as with smooth chin, delicate voice, and mincing gait, with headdress and neckerchiefs, frilled robe, and women's sandals, he copied the loose courtesan—might well have recoiled in horror from this unnatural world, in which the sexes seemingly wished to change parts.

The aristocracy's ideas on divorce may be judged from the conduct of their best and most moral hero, Marcus Cato, who did not hesitate to give up his wife to a friend desirous of marrying her, nor on the death of this friend to marry the same wife a second time. Celibacy and childlessness became common, especially among the upper classes. While these had long regarded marriage as a burden shouldered only in the public interest, we now encounter even in Cato and his followers the maxim to which Polybius a century before traced the decay of Greece, that it is the duty of a citizen to keep great wealth together and therefore not to beget too many children. Where were the days when the designation "children-producer" (*proletarius*) had been a term of honor for the Roman?

In such circumstances the Latin stock in Italy diminished alarmingly, and its fair provinces were overspread partly by parasitic immigrants and partly by desolation. Much of the population of Italy flocked to foreign lands. Already the total talent and working power needed to supply Italian magistrates and Italian garrisons for the whole Mediterranean world exceeded the resources of the peninsula, especially since the elements thus sent abroad were often lost forever to the nation. The more Rome grew to be a multi-nationed empire, the less the governing aristocracy looked on Italy as their exclusive home; while a considerable portion of the soldiers perished in the many wars, especially in the bloody civil war, and another portion became wholly estranged from their native country by the long term of service, which sometimes lasted for a generation. In like manner a portion of the landholders and almost the whole body of merchants spent all or much of their lives out of the country, and the itinerant trading life in particular estranged the latter altogether from the mother country and from the conditions of family life.

In return for these, Italy obtained on the one hand the proletariat of slaves and freedmen, and on the other the craftsmen and traders flocking thither from Asia Minor, Syria, and Egypt, who flourished chiefly in the capital and still more in the seaport towns of Ostia, Puteoli, and Brundisium. In the largest and most important part of Italy however, there was not even a replacement by impure elements, but an absolute decline in population. Especially was this true of such pastoral districts as Apulia, the chosen land of cattle-breeding, which contemporaries call the most deserted part of Italy, and of the region around Rome, where the Campagna was annually becoming more desolate under the reciprocal action of declining agriculture and increasing malaria. Labici, Gabii, and Bovillae, once cheerful little country towns, were so decayed that it was difficult to find representatives of them for the ceremony of the Latin festival. Tusculum, although still one of the most esteemed communities of Latium, consisted almost solely of some genteel families who lived in the capital but retained their native Tusculian franchise, and had fewer citizens entitled to vote than even small communities in the interior of Italy. The stock of men capable of arms in this district, on which Rome's ability to defend herself had once mainly depended, had so totally vanished that people read with astonishment and perhaps with horror the accounts—so fantastic in comparison with the current state of affairs—of the Aequian and Volscian wars. Matters were not so bad everywhere, especially in the other portions of Central Italy and in Campania. Nevertheless, as Varro complains, "the once populous cities of Italy" in general "stood desolate."

It is a dreadful picture, this picture of Italy under the oligarchy. There was nothing to soften the fatal contrast between the two worlds of beggary and riches. The more clearly this contrast was felt, the giddier the height of wealth and the abyss of poverty, the more frequently were individuals tossed from the bottom to the top of this hazardous world, and from top to the bottom again. The wider the chasm between the two worlds, the more completely they coincided in undermining family life (which is the germ and core of all nationality), in laziness and luxury, unsubstantial economy, unmanly dependence, corruption differing only in its price, criminal demoralization, and longing to begin the war with property.

Riches and misery in close league drove the Italians out of Italy, and filled the peninsula partly with swarms of slaves, partly with awful silence. It is a terrible picture, but not one peculiar to Italy. Wherever the government of capitalists in a slave state has fully developed, it has desolated God's fair world in the same way. As rivers glisten in different colors, but a common sewer looks everywhere the same, so the Italy of the Ciceronian epoch resembles the Hellas of Polybius and still more closely the Carthage of Hannibal's time, where in exactly similar fashion the all-powerful rule of capital ruined the middle class, raised trade and estate-farming to the highest prosperity, and ultimately led to a hypocritically whitewashed moral and political corruption of the nation. All the arrant sins of capital against nation and civilization in modern times remain as far inferior to the abominations of the ancient capitalist states as the free man, be he ever so poor, remains superior to the slave. Not until the dragonseed of North America ripens will the world again have similar fruits to reap.

These evils, under which the national economy of Italy lay prostrate, were in their deepest essence irremediable, and those capable of remedy depended largely on the people and on time. For the wisest government, like the most skilful physician, cannot give freshness to the corrupt juices of the organism, or do more in the case of deeprooted evils than to prevent those accidents which obstruct the remedial power of nature. The peaceful energy of the new rule furnished some such preventive, for by it some of the worst excrescences were done away with, such as the pampering of the proletariat, the failure to punish crimes, and the purchase of offices. But the government could do more than simply abstain from harm. Caesar was not one of those people who refuse to embank the sea, because no dike can defy some sudden influx. It is better if a nation and its economy follow spontaneously the natural path; but seeing that they had got out of this path, Caesar applied all his energies to bring the nation back to its home and family life by special intervention, and to reform the economy by law and decree.

With a view to checking the desertion of Italy by the Italians, and to induce the world of quality and the merchants to make their homes in their native land, the term of service for soldiers was shortened; men of senatorial rank were prohibited altogether from settling outside Italy, except on public business; and other Italians of marriageable age (from the twentieth to the fortieth year) were forbidden to be absent from Italy for more than three consecutive years. In his first consulship Caesar had on founding the colony of Capua given preference to fathers with several children. Now as Imperator he proposed special rewards for fathers of large families, while as supreme judge of the nation he treated divorce and adultery with unparalleled rigor.

He even issued a detailed law on luxury—which among other points, cut down at least one irrational extravagance in building, that of sepulchral monuments; restricted the use of purple robes and pearls to certain times, ages, and classes, and totally prohibited it in grown-up men; fixed a maximum for table expenditures; and directly forbade a number of luxurious dishes. Such ordinances were admittedly not new, but it was new when the "master of morals" seriously insisted on their observance, stationed paid inspectors at the provision markets, and ordered that the tables of men of rank be examined and the forbidden dishes on them confiscated. It is true that these police lessons in moderation did little more than compel luxury to retire somewhat into concealment. But if hypocrisy is the homage which vice pays to virtue, under the circumstances even a semblance of propriety was an improvement not to be despised.

Caesar's measures regulating Italian monetary and agricultural relations were of a graver character and promised greater results. The first move here related to the scarcity of money and the debt crisis generally. The law called forth by the outcry as to hidden capital—that no one should have on hand more than 60,000 sesterces in gold and silver—was probably issued only to allay the public's blind indignation against the usurers. The form of publication, based on the fiction that this was merely the renewed enforcement of an earlier law, shows that Caesar was ashamed of this enactment, and it can hardly have been put into practice.

Far more serious was the treatment of pending claims for debt, whose complete remission was vehemently demanded from Caesar by the party which carried his name. We have already mentioned that he did not yield to this demand, but two important concessions to debtors were made as early as 49 B.C. First, arrears of interest were cancelled, and interest already paid was deducted from the principal. Second, the creditor was compelled to accept the debtor's moveable and immoveable property in lieu of payment at their estimated value before the civil war.

The latter enactment was not unreasonable. If the creditor was to be looked on *de facto* as the owner of the property to the amount of the sum due him, it was proper that he should bear his share in the general depreciation. On the other hand the canceling of interest payments made or oustanding—which practically meant that creditors lost the interest itself plus an average of 25 per cent of their capital—was in fact a partial cancellation of creditors' claims, for which the democrats had clamored so vehemently. But however bad may have been the conduct of the usurers, it is not possible thereby to justify the retroactive abolition of all claims for interest.

In order at least to understand this agitation we must recollect how the democratic party stood on the question of interest. The legal prohibition against taking interest, which the old plebeian opposition had extorted in 342

B.C., had been practically disregarded by the nobility (which controlled the civil procedure by means of the praetorship) but had remained formally valid since that period. The democrats of the first century B.C., who regarded themselves as inheritors of that old agitation as to social privilege, had maintained the position of the illegality of all interest, and temporarily even had enforced that principle during the confusion of the Marian period.

It is not credible that Caesar shared his party's crude views on the interest question. The fact that his account of the matter of liquidation mentions the surrender of the debtor's property in lieu of payment, but is silent as to the cancellation of interest, in perhaps a tacit self-reproach. But like every party leader, he could not directly repudiate the traditional maxims of his party—especially when he had to decide this question even before his departure for Epirus, rather than as the all-powerful conqueror of Pharsalus. But while he perhaps permitted rather than originated this violation of legal order and of property, it is certainly to his credit that the monstrous demand for wiping out all debts was rejected; and it may perhaps be looked on as a saving of his honor, that the debtors were far more indignant at this extremely unsatisfactory (according to their view) concession than the injured creditors, and made under Caelius and Dolabella those foolish and speedily suppressed attempts to extort by riot and civil war what Caesar had refused.

But Caesar did not confine himself to temporary help for the debtor; he did as legislator what he could to reduce the fearful power of capital. First of all, the great legal maxim was proclaimed that freedom is not a possession commensurable with property but an eternal right of man, of which the state alone, and not the debtor, is judicially entitled to deprive the criminal. It was Caesar, perhaps stimulated here also by the more humane Egyptian and Greek legislation, who introduced this principle

—diametrically opposed to the earlier ordinances on bank-ruptcy—into the common law, where it has remained ever since.

According to earlier Roman law the debtor unable to pay became the serf of his creditor. To be sure, the Poe-telian law had allowed a debtor who had become unable to pay because of temporary embarrassment, rather than genuine insolvency, to save his personal freedom by the cession of his property. Nevertheless, for the truly insol-vent that principle of law, though modified in minor ways, had remained substantially unaltered for five hundred years. Direct recourse to the debtor's estate occurred only exceptionally, when the debtor had died, or had forfeited his citizenship, or could not be found. It was Caesar who first gave an insolvent the right—on which our modern bankruptcy regulations are based—of formally ceding his estate to his creditors, whether it sufficed to satisfy them or not. Thus he might save at best his personal freedom (though with diminished honorary and political rights), and begin a new financial existence in which he could be sued only for claims proceeding from the earlier period and not protected in the liquidation, if he could pay them without renewed financial ruin.

While the great democrat thus had the imperishable honor of emancipating personal freedom in principle from capital, he attempted moreover to limit the exces-sive power of capital by usury laws. He did not affect to disown the democratic antipathy for interest as such. For Italian money-dealing there was fixed a maximum amount of loans the individual capitalist might make, apparently proportionate to the size of his Italian landed estate, and perhaps amounting to half its value. Transgressions of this enactment were, after the procedure prescribed in the republican usury laws, treated as criminal offences and sent before a special jury commission.

If these regulations were successfully carried into ef-fect, every Italian man of business would be compelled to become at the same time an Italian landholder, and the class of capitalists subsisting entirely on their interest would disappear wholly from Italy. Indirectly, too, the no less degraded group of insolvent landowners who practically managed their estates for their creditors was by this same means materially curtailed, inasmuch as their creditors, if they wished to keep their lending business, were compelled to buy for themselves. From this very fact besides it is plain that Caesar by no means simply wished to renew the old naive prohibition of interest, but on the contrary to allow it within certain limits.

It is quite probable, however, that he did not confine himself merely to specifying for Italy a loan maximum, but also, especially with respect to the provinces, prescribed maximum interest rates. The enactments that it was illegal to take more than 1 per cent per month, or to charge interest on arrears of interest, or to sue for arrears of interest exceeding the original loan, were (probably also after the Graeco-Egyptian model) first introduced in the empire by Lucius Lucullus in Asia Minor, and retained there by his better successors. Soon afterwards they were transferred to other provinces by edicts of the governors, and ultimately at least some of them were given the force of law in all provinces by a senatorial decree of 50 B.C. The fact that these Lucullan enactments afterwards appeared intact as imperial law, and have thus become the basis of both Roman and modern legislation as to interest, may also perhaps be traced back to an ordinance of Caesar.

Hand in hand with these efforts to limit the ascendancy of capital went Caesar's endeavors to restore agriculture to the status most advantageous for the commonwealth. For this purpose better policing and administration of justice was essential. Hitherto nobody in Italy had felt secure of his person or property: Roman *condottieri,* when their gangs were not helping to manage the politics of the capital, applied themselves to robbery in the forests of Etruria or rounded off the country estates of their paymasters by fresh acquisitions. This sort of club law was now at an end, and the change must have benefitted especially the agricultural population of all classes. Caesar's plans for public works were also of similar intent. For instance, the construction of a convenient highway from Rome through the Apennine passes to the Adriatic was designed to stimulate the internal traffic of Italy, and the lowering of the level of the Fucine lake to benefit the Marsian farmers. But Caesar also sought to benefit Italian husbandry by more direct measures. Thus, Italian graziers were required to take at least a third of their herdsmen from freeborn adults, whereby brigandage was checked and at the same time a source of gain was opened to the free proletariat.

In the agrarian question Caesar, already experienced from his first consulship, was more judicious than Tiberius Gracchus. He did not seek to restore the small farmers at any price, even including a revolution (concealed under juristic clauses) directed against property. On the contrary, like every other genuine statesman, he regarded the security of property, or what is at any rate regarded by the public as property, as the first and most inviolable of all political maxims; and only within the limits of this maxim did he seek to improve the lot of the Italian small holders, which also appeared to him as a vital question for the nation.

Even so, there was much still left for him to do. Every private right, whether it was called property or entitled heritable possession, whether traceable to Gracchus or to Sulla, was unconditionally respected by him. On the other hand Caesar, after instituting in his strictly economical fashion (which tolerated no waste or negligence even on a small scale) a general revision of Italian land titles by the revived commission of Twenty, earmarked all the public land of Italy, including a considerable portion of the estates in the hands of religious groups but legally belonging to the state, for distribution in the Gracchan fashion insofar as it was fitted for agriculture. The Apulian summer pastures and the Samnite winter pastures belonging to the state were retained as public domain; and it was at least the design of the Imperator, if these lands should not suffice, to procure the necessary additional land by buying Italian estates with public funds.

In selecting the new farmers provision was naturally made first for veteran soldiers; thus the burden which the levy imposed on the nation was converted as far as possible into a benefit by the fact that Caesar took the proletarian as a recruit, but gave him back as a farmer. (It is noteworthy also that desolate Latin communities such as Veii and Capena seem to have been preferentially provided with new colonists.) Caesar's regulation that the new owners could not alienate their lands for twenty years was a happy medium between giving full right of sale, which would have soon brought most of the distributed land back into the hands of the great capitalists, and the permanent restrictions which Tiberius Gracchus and Sulla had enacted, both equally in vain.

Lastly, while the government thus energetically applied itself to remove the diseased and strengthen the sound elements of Italian national life, the newly regulated municipal system—which had but recently developed out of the Social War alongside the state framework—was intended to give the new monarchy a fitting communal life, and to enliven again the best elements of the nation. The leading principles in the two municipal ordinances issued in 49 B.C. for Cisalpine Gaul and in 45 B.C. for Italy, the latter of which remained the fundamental law for the future, are apparently, first, the strict purifying of the urban corporations from all immoral elements, though no trace of a political police yet occurs; and second, the utmost restriction of centralization and the utmost freedom of movement in the communities, which even now were granted the right to elect their own magistrates and a definite though limited civil and criminal jurisdiction. It is true, however, that the general police enactments such as the restrictions on the right of association came into play here.

Such were the ordinances by which Caesar attempted to reform the Italian national economy. It is easy both to show their insufficiency, seeing that they allowed a multitude of evils to remain, and to prove that they operated injuriously in various respects by severely restricting freedom of dealing. It is still easier to show that the general ills of the Italian economy were incurable. But in spite of this the practical statesman will admire the work as well as the master workman. It was already no small achievement merely to recognize and grapple with the evil, where a man like Sulla had despaired of remedy and contented himself with a mere formal reorganization; and we may well conclude that Caesar's reforms achieved as much as it was given to a statesman and a Roman to achieve. He could not and did not expect them to regenerate Italy. On the contrary, he sought to attain this in a very different way, for the understanding of which it is necessary first to review the condition of the provinces as Caesar found them.

There were fourteen such provinces: seven European —Further and Hither Spain, Transalpine Gaul, Italian Gaul with Illyricum, Macedonia with Greece, Sicily, Sardinia with Corsica; five Asiatic—Asia, Bithynia and Pontus, Cilicia with Cyprus, Syria, and Crete; and two African—Cyrene and Africa. To these Caesar added three new ones by establishing the two new governorships of Lugdunese Gaul and Belgica, and by constituting Illyricum a separate province.

The misrule of these provinces by the oligarchy had reached a point which, notwithstanding various noteworthy efforts, no other government, at least in the West, has ever attained. Certainly the responsibility for this rests not on the Romans alone. Almost everywhere before their day the Greek, Phoenician, or Asiatic rule had crushed the higher spirit and the sense of right and liberty inherited from better times. It was doubtless bad that every accused provincial was required, upon demand, to defend himself in person in Rome; that the Roman governor interfered at pleasure in the administration of justice and the management of dependent communities, pronounced capital sentences, and cancelled transactions of the municipal council; and that in case of war he treated the militia as he chose and often infamously, as when Cotta at the siege of the Pontic Heraclea assigned to the militia all the posts of danger in order to spare his Italians, and when the siege went badly, ordered the heads of his engineers to be laid at his feet. It was doubtless bad that no rule of moral or criminal law bound either the Roman administrators or their retinue, and that outrages, rapes, and murders with or without legal pretext were daily occurrences in the provinces. But these things at least were nothing new. Most men had long been accustomed to be treated like slaves, and it signified little in the long run whether a Carthaginian overseer, a Syrian satrap, or a Roman proconsul acted as the local tyrant. Almost the only thing for which the provincials still cared, their material well-being, was far less disturbed by such occurrences, which however numerous merely affected isolated individuals, than by the financial exactions which pressed heavily on all, and which had never before been prosecuted with such vigor.

In this area the Romans gave fearful proof of their old mastery of money matters. From its original modest and rational foundations, the Roman system of provincial oppression increased both in size and in corruption. The ordinary taxes became far more oppressive from their inequality and from the preposterous system of levying them than from their exhorbitant level. As to the burden of quartering troops, Roman statesmen themselves expressed the opinion that a town suffered nearly as much when a Roman army took up winter quarters in it as when an enemy took it by storm. While originally the taxation had been an indemnification for the burden of military defense undertaken by Rome, with the community paying tribute thus being exempt from ordinary service, now garrison duty—as is attested in the case of Sardinia—was performed mostly by the provincials; and even in the regular armies, the whole burden of the cavalry-service, besides other duties, devolved upon them.

The extraordinary exactions—such as the deliveries of grain for little or no compensation to benefit the proletariat of the capital, the frequent and costly naval armaments and coast-defenses in order to check piracy, the task of supplying works of art, wild beasts, or other demands of the insane Roman luxury in the theatre and the chase, and the military requisitions in case of war—were as frequent as they were oppressive and incalculable. A single instance may show how far things were carried. During the three years' administration of Sicily by Gaius Verres, the number of farmers in Leontini fell from 84 to 32, in Motuca from 187 to 86, in Herbita from 252 to 120, in Agyrium from 250 to 80. Thus in four of the most fertile districts of Sicily, 59 per cent of the landholders preferred to let their fields lie fallow rather than cultivate them under such a government. And these landholders, as their small number shows and is expressly stated, were by no means small farmers, but respectable planters and in large part Roman citizens!

In the protectorates the forms of taxation were somewhat different, but the burdens were if possible still worse, since in addition to the exactions of the Romans there came those of the native rulers. In Cappadocia and Egypt, the farmer as well as the king was bankrupt, the former being unable to satisfy the tax collector, the latter his Roman creditor. To these must be added the exactions not merely of the governor himself but also of his "friends," each of whom fancied that he had as it were a draft on the governor and accordingly the right to come back from the province a made man.

The Roman oligarchy in this respect resembled a gang of robbers who carried on the plundering of the provincials in a professional and businesslike manner. Capable members of the gang worked not too nicely, for they had to share the spoil with the advocates and the jurymen, and the more they stole the more secure they were. The notion of honor in theft was already developed; the great robber looked down on the small, and the latter on the mere thief, with contempt. Any one who for a wonder had been condemned boasted of the vast sums which he was proved to have extorted. Such was the behavior in the provinces of the men whose ancestors had been accustomed to bring home nothing from their governorships but the thanks of the subjects and the approbation of their fellow citizens.

But still worse, if possible, and still less subject to any control, was the havoc committed by the Italian business men among the unhappy provincials. The richest lands and the whole commercial and monetary business in the provinces were concentrated in their hands. The estates which Italian grandees owned in overseas regions were exposed to all the misery of management by stewards, and never saw their owners, excepting perhaps for the hunting-parks which even now had begun to appear in Transalpine Gaul with an area amounting to nearly twenty square miles.

Usury flourished as never before. The small landowners in Illyricum, Asia, and Egypt managed their estates even in Varro's time in large part practically as the debtor-slaves of their Roman or non-Roman creditors, just as the plebeians in former days had for their patrician lords. Cases occurred of capital being lent to urban communities at four per cent per month. It was not unusual for an energetic and influential man of business to get either the title of envoy given to him by the Senate or

that of officer by the governor, and, if possible, to have
soldiers put at his service for the better prosecution of
his affairs. A case is told on credible authority where one
of these honorable martial bankers prosecuted a claim
against the town of Salamis in Cyprus by keeping its municipal council blockaded in the town hall, until five of the
members had died of hunger.

To these two modes of oppression, each of which by
itself was intolerable and which were always being better
arranged to supplement each other, were added the general calamities for which the Roman government was also
in considerable part at least indirectly responsible. In the
various wars a large amount of capital was siphoned away
from the country and a larger amount destroyed, sometimes by the barbarians and sometimes by the Roman
armies. Due to the worthlessness of the Roman land and
maritime police, brigands and pirates swarmed everywhere. In Sardinia and the interior of Asia Minor brigandage was endemic. In Africa and Further Spain it
became necessary to fortify with walls and towers all
buildings constructed outside of cities. The panaceas
which the Roman governor was wont to interpose when
the inevitable scarcity of money or famine occurred—the
prohibition of the export of gold or grain from the province—did not help matters. Communal affairs were almost
everywhere embarrassed, in addition to the general distress, by local disorders and the frauds of public officials.

Where such grievances afflicted communities and individuals not temporarily but for generations with an inevitable, steady, and ever-growing oppression, the best
regulated public or private economy could not but suc-
cumb to them, and the most unspeakable misery could not
but extend over all the nations from the Tagus to the
Euphrates. "All the communities," says a treatise published as early as 70 B.C., "are ruined." The same truth
is specially attested as regards Spain and Narbonese Gaul,
the very provinces which, comparatively speaking, were

still in the most tolerable economic position. In Asia Minor even towns like Samos and Halicarnassus stood almost empty. Legal slavery seemed here a haven of rest compared with the torments to which the free provincial succumbed, and even the patient Asiatic had become, according to the descriptions of Roman statesmen, weary of life. Any one who desires to fathom the depths to which man can sink in the criminal infliction of all conceivable injustice, and in its no less criminal endurance, might gather together from the criminal records of this era the wrongs which Roman grandees could perpetrate and Greeks, Syrians, and Phoenicians could suffer. Even the statesmen of Rome publicly and frankly conceded that the Roman name was unutterably odious through all Greece and Asia; and when the citizens of the Pontic Heraclea on one occasion put to death the whole of the Roman tax collectors, the only occasion for regret was that such things did not occur oftener.

The Optimates scoffed at the new master who went in person to inspect his "farms" one after the other. In reality, the condition of the provinces demanded all the earnestness and wisdom of one of those rare men who redeem the name of king from being regarded as merely a conspicuous example of human insufficiency. The wounds inflicted had to be healed by time, but Caesar took care that they might be so healed, and that there should be no fresh inflictions.

The system of administration was thoroughly remodelled. The Sullan proconsuls and propraetors had been in their provinces essentially sovereign and subject to no control. Those of Caesar were the well-disciplined servants of a stern master, who from the very unity and life-tenure of his power sustained a more natural and more tolerable relation to the subjects than those annually changing petty tyrants. The governorships were no doubt still distributed among the two retiring consuls and the sixteen praetors; but as the Imperator directly nominated eight of the latter, and the distribution of the provinces among the competitors depended solely on him, they were in reality bestowed by the Imperator.

The functions of the governors were also practically restricted. The superintendence of justice and the administrative control of the communities remained in their hands, but their command was paralyzed by the new supreme command in Rome and its adjutants associated with the governor. The levying of taxes was probably even now committed substantially to imperial officials, so that the governor was thenceforward surrounded with an auxiliary staff which was absolutely dependent on the Imperator by virtue either of the laws of the military hierarchy or of the still stricter laws of domestic discipline. While hitherto the proconsul and his quaestor had appeared as if they were members of a gang of robbers dispatched to levy contributions, the magistrates of Caesar were present to protect the weak against the strong. Instead of the previous worse than useless equestrian or senatorian tribunals, the proconsul and his staff had to answer for themselves at the bar of a just and unyielding monarch. The law as to extortions, which Caesar had already in his first consulate made more stringent, was applied by him against the chief commandants in the provinces with an inexorable severity going even beyond its letter; and the tax officers, if indeed they ventured to indulge in an injustice, atoned for it to their master as slaves and freedmen according to the cruel domestic law of that time.

The extraordinary public burdens were reduced to the right proportion and the actual necessity, while the ordinary burdens were materially lessened. In addition to the comprehensive regulation of taxation already mentioned, the extension of the exemptions from tribute, the general lowering of the direct taxes, the limitation of the system of *decumae* to Africa and Sardinia, and the complete setting aside of middlemen in the collection of the direct taxes, were most beneficial reforms for the provincials. It cannot be proved that Caesar, after the example of one of his great democratic predecessors Sertorius, sought to free the subjects from the burden of quartering troops, or that he insisted on the soldiers erecting permanent encampments for themselves. But he was not the man to abandon the subject to the soldier, at least after he had exchanged the part of pretender for that of king. It was quite in keeping with his spirit when the heirs of his policy created such military camps, and then converted them into towns which formed rallying points for Italian civilization amid the barbarian frontier districts.

It was a task far less difficult to check official irregularities than to deliver the provincials from the oppressive ascendency of Roman capital, whose power could not be directly broken without applying remedies still more dangerous than the evil. For the time being the government could abolish only isolated abuses (as when Caesar prohibited the use of the title of state envoy for financial purposes) and meet manifest acts of violence and usury by a sharp application of the general penal and usury laws which also applied to the provinces. But a more radical cure of the evil was only to be expected from reviving the prosperity of the provincials under a better administration.

Temporary enactments to relieve the insolvency of particular provinces had been issued on several earlier occasions. Caesar himself in 60 B.C. as governor of Further Spain had assigned to creditors two-thirds of the income of their debtors in order to pay themselves from that source. Lucius Lucullus likewise when governor of Asia Minor had directly cancelled a portion of the arrears of interest which had swelled beyond measure, and had for the remaining portion assigned the creditors a fourth part of the produce of the lands of their debtors, as well as a suitable proportion of the profits accruing from house rents or slave labor. We are not expressly informed that

Caesar after the civil war instituted similar general liquidations of debt in the provinces. Yet from what has just been remarked, and from what was done in the case of Italy, it can hardly be doubted that Caesar likewise directed his efforts towards this object, or at least that it formed part of his plan.

While thus the Imperator, as far as lay within human power, relieved the provincials from the oppressions of the magistrates and capitalists of Rome, it could certainly be expected that the reinvigorated government would scare off the wild border-peoples, and disperse the freebooters by land and sea, as the rising sun chases away the mist. However the old wounds might still smart, with Caesar there appeared for the sorely tortured subjects the dawn of a more tolerable epoch, the first intelligent and humane government that had appeared for centuries, and a policy of peace which rested not on cowardice but on strength. Well might the subjects above all mourn along with the best Romans by the bier of the great liberator.

But this abolition of existing abuses was not the main objective in Caesar's provincial reform. In the Roman republic, according to the views of aristocrats and democrats alike, the provinces had been nothing but (as they were frequently called) country estates of the Roman people, to be employed and worked as such. This view now passed away. The provinces as such were gradually to disappear, in order to prepare a new and more spacious home for the renovated Helleno-Italic nation, no one of whose component parts existed merely for the sake of another, but all for each and each for all. The new existence in the renovated home, the fresher, broader, grander national life, was of itself to overcome the sorrows and wrongs of the nation for which there was no help in the old Italy.

These ideas, as is well known, were not new. The emigration from Italy to the provinces that had been going on for centuries had long since (though unconsciously on the part of the emigrants themselves) paved the way for such an extension of Italy. The first man who in a systematic way guided the Italians to settle beyond the bounds of Italy was Gaius Gracchus, creator of the Roman democratic monarchy, author of the Transalpine conquests, and founder of the colonies of Carthage and Narbo. The second Roman democratic statesman of genius, Quintus Sertorius, began to introduce the barbarous Occidentals to Latin civilization, teaching the Spanish youth of rank to wear Roman dress, and urging them to speak Latin and to acquire the higher Italian culture at the training institute founded by him in Osca. When Caesar founded his government a large Italian population, though lacking much in stability and concentration, already existed in all the provinces and protectorates. In addition to the formally Italian towns in Spain and southern Gaul, we need only recall the numerous legions of citizens raised by Sertorius and Pompey in Spain, by Caesar in Gaul, by Juba in Numidia, and by the constitutional party in Africa, Macedonia, Greece, Asia Minor, and Crete; the Latin lyre (doubtless ill-tuned) on which the town poets of Corduba as early as the Sertorian war sang the praises of the Roman generals; and the translations of Greek poetry, valued for their very elegance of language, which the earliest non-Italian poet of note, the Transalpine Publius Terrentius Varro of the Aude, published shortly after Caesar's death.

On the other hand, the interpenetration of Latin and Greek culture was as old as Rome. In the unification of Italy the conquering Latin nation had assimilated all the other conquered nationalities except the Greek, which was received just as it stood without any attempt at amalgamation. Wherever the Roman legionary went the Greek schoolmaster, no less a conqueror in his own way, followed; at an early date we find famous teachers of the Greek language settled on the Guadalquivir, and Greek

as well as Latin was taught in the institute of Osca. The
higher Roman culture itself was in fact nothing else than
the proclamation of the great gospel of Hellenic manners
and art in the Italian idiom; and the Hellene could hardly
protest if the civilizing conquerors chose to proclaim it
first of all in their own language to the barbarians of the
West. Already the Greek everywhere (and especially
where the national feeling was purest and strongest, on
the frontiers threatened by barbaric denationalization)
saw in Rome the protector and avenger of Hellenism. In
fact, the founding of towns by Pompey in the East resumed the beneficent work of Alexander after an interruption of centuries.

The idea of an Italo-Hellenic empire with two languages and a single nationality was not new, for otherwise it would have been a blunder. But its development
from isolated projects to a firmly grasped conception,
from scattered initial efforts to the laying of a firm foundation, was the work of the third and greatest of the
Roman democratic statesmen.

The first and most essential condition for the political
levelling of the empire was the preservation and extension of the two dominant nations, along with the absorption as rapidly as possible of the barbarian peoples (or
those termed barbarian) existing by their side. In a certain sense we might name along with Romans and Greeks
a third nationality, which was also omnipresent in the
world of that day, and which was destined to play no
insignificant part in the new state of Caesar. We speak of
the Jews. This remarkable people, yielding yet tenacious,
was then as now everywhere and nowhere at home, and
everywhere and nowhere powerful. The successors of David and Solomon were of hardly more significance for the
Jews of that age than Jerusalem for those of the present
day. The nation doubtless found for its religious and intellectual unity a visible symbol in the petty kingdom of
Jerusalem; but the nation itself consisted not merely of

its subjects, but of the innumerable bodies of Jews scattered through the whole Parthian and Roman empires.

Especially within the cities of Alexandria and Cyrene the Jews formed special communities that were administratively and even locally distinct, not unlike the "Jews' quarters" of our towns, but with a freer position and superintended by a "master of the people" as superior judge and administrator. How numerous was the Jewish population in Rome before Caesar's time, and how closely the Jews even then kept together as fellow countrymen, is shown by the remark of an author of this period, that it was dangerous for a governor to offend the Jews in his province, because he might then certainly reckon on being hissed after his return by the populace of the capital. Even at this time the predominant business of the Jews was trade. The Jewish trader moved everywhere with the conquering Roman merchant just as he later accompanied the Genoese and the Venetian, and on all sides capital flowed into the hands of the Jewish as well as the Roman merchants.

At this period too we encounter the peculiar antipathy of the Occidentals towards this so thoroughly Oriental race and their foreign opinions and customs. This Judaism, though not the most pleasing feature of the nowhere pleasing mixture of nations which then prevailed, was nevertheless a historical fact which the statesman could neither ignore nor combat, and which Caesar, like his predecessor Alexander, with correct discernment fostered as far as possible. While Alexander's founding of Alexandrian Judaism did almost as much for the nation as King David's planning the temple of Jerusalem, Caesar also advanced the interests of the Jews in Alexandria and in Rome by special favors and privileges, protecting their peculiar worship against the Roman and Greek local priests.

These two great rulers of course did not contemplate placing the Jewish nationality on an equal footing with the Hellenic or Italo-Hellenic. But the Jew, who has not received like the Occidental the Pandora's gift of political organization, and who is substantially indifferent to the state; who is as reluctant to give up the essence of his nationality as he is ready to adapt himself to any nationality up to a certain degree—for this very reason the Jew was particularly suited for a state built on the ruins of a hundred living states and endowed from the outset with a somewhat abstract and toned-down nationality. Even in the ancient world Judaism was an effective leaven of cosmopolitanism and to that extent a specially privileged member in the Caesarian state, whose citizenship was strictly speaking world citizenship, and whose nationality was at bottom nothing but humanity.

But the Latin and Hellenic nationalities continued exclusively as the positive elements of the new citizenship. The distinctively Italian state of the republic was thus at an end; but the rumor that Caesar was purposely ruining Italy and Rome in order to transfer the center of the empire to the Greek east, and to make Ilion or Alexandria its capital, was nothing but a piece of talk (equally explicable and silly) by the angry nobility. On the contrary, in Caesar's framework the Latin nationality always remained predominant, as is indicated in the fact that he issued all his enactments in Latin, although those destined for Greek-speaking countries were also issued in Greek. In general he arranged the relations of the two great nations in his monarchy just as his republican predecessors had arranged them in the united Italy: the Hellenic nationality was protected where it existed, the Italian was extended as far as circumstances permitted, and the Italian was destined to inherit the races to be absorbed.

This last was necessary because a complete equalization of Greek and Latin elements would probably have soon occasioned the catastrophe which Byzantinism produced several centuries later. For the Greek element was not only intellectually markedly superior to the Roman, but also had hosts of Hellene and half-Hellene missionaries who had migrated compulsorily or voluntarily to Italy, and whose influence could not be overestimated. The rule of Greek lackeys over the Roman monarchs is as old as the monarchy. The first in the equally long and repulsive list of such personages is Pompey's confidential servant, Theophanes of Mytilene, who by his power over his weak master contributed probably more than any one else to the outbreak of the war between Pompey and Caesar. Not without reason was he treated with divine honors by his countrymen after his death, for he commenced the *valet de chambre* government of the imperial period.

The government accordingly had every reason not to encourage the spread of Hellenism at least in the West. If Sicily was not simply relieved of the pressure of the *decumae* but had its communities invested with Latin rights, this was presumably meant to be followed in due course by full equalization with Italy. For it must have been Caesar's design to merge into Italy this glorious island, which, though desolate at that time under the rule of predominantly Italian speculators, was by nature destined to be not so much a neighboring land as rather the finest of Italy's provinces. But otherwise the Greek element was preserved and protected wherever it existed. However political crises might tempt the Imperator to demolish the strong pillars of Hellenism in the West and in Egypt, Massilia and Alexandria were neither destroyed nor denationalized.

On the other hand the Roman element was promoted by the government through colonization and Latinizing with all vigor throughout the empire. The principle that all the soil in the provinces not ceded by special act of the government to communities or private persons was the property of the state, and that its holders had merely an heritable possession revocable at any time, no doubt originated from a bad combination of formal law and brute force. But it was inevitably necessary in order to deal expeditiously with the nations destined to destruction, and thus was retained by Caesar and raised from a democratic party-theory to a fundamental principle of monarchical law.

Gaul, of course, was the immediate arena for the extension of Roman nationality. In 49 B.C. Cisalpine Gaul obtained throughout what many of its inhabitants had long enjoyed, political equality with the mother country by the formal admission of the Transpadane communities into the Roman citizens union. Practically this province had already become completely Latinized during the forty years since the bestowal of Latin rights. The exclusives might ridicule the broad and gurgling accent of the Celtic Latin, or miss "an undefined something of the grace of the capital" in the Insubrian or Venetian who as Caesar's legionary had won by his sword a place in the Roman Forum and even in the Roman senate-house. Nevertheless, Cisalpine Gaul with its dense agricultural population was even before Caesar's time a predominantly Italian country, and remained for centuries the true asylum of Italian manners and culture. Indeed, the teachers of Latin literature found nowhere else outside the capital so much encouragement and approbation. While Cisalpine Gaul was thus substantially merged into Italy, its former place was occupied by the Transalpine province, which Caesar's conquests had converted from a frontier into an inland province, and which by location as well as climate was fitted beyond all other regions to become in due course an Italian land.[1]

In the other non-Greek and non-Latin regions of the empire, which were still more remote from the influence of Italy and the process of assimilation, Caesar confined himself to establishing several centers of Italian civilization in order to pave the way for a future complete equali-

---

1. A brief section of the original, here omitted, describes a few of the new Transalpine colonies.

zation. Such steps can be pointed out in every province except for the poorest and least important of all, Sardinia. In northern Gaul the Latin language obtained official recognition throughout, though it was not yet employed for all branches of public intercourse; and the colony of Noviodunum (Nyon) arose on Lake Leman as the most northerly town with an Italian constitution.

In Spain, at that time presumably the most densely peopled country of the Roman empire, Caesarian colonists were settled in the important Helleno-Iberian seaport town of Emporiae alongside the old population. Moreover, as recently discovered records have shown, a number of colonists probably taken predominantly from the proletariat of the capital were located in the town of Urso (Osuna), not far from Seville in the heart of Andalusia, and perhaps also in several other townships of this province. The ancient and wealthy mercantile city of Gades, whose municipal system Caesar as praetor had remodeled, obtained from the Imperator in 49 B.C. the full rights of the Italian *municipia,* thus becoming what Tusculum had been in Italy, the first extra-Italian community not founded by Rome to receive full Roman citizenship. Some years afterwards, similar rights were conferred also on some other Spanish communities, and Latin rights presumably on still more.

In Africa the project which Gaius Gracchus had initiated was now carried out. On the spot where once stood the city of the hereditary foes of Rome, 3,000 Italian colonists and a great number of the tenants on lease and sufferance in the Carthaginian territory were settled. The new "Venus-colony," the Roman Carthage, throve with amazing rapidity in its incomparably favorable location. Utica, hitherto the capital and first commercial town in the province, had already been partly compensated beforehand, apparently by the bestowal of Latin rights. In the Numidian territory newly annexed to the empire, Cirta and other communities assigned to the Roman *con-*

dottiere Publius Sittius for himself and his bands obtained
the legal status of Roman military colonies. The stately
provincial towns, which the insane fury of Juba and the
desperate remnant of the constitutional party had reduced
to ruins, did not revive so rapidly as they had been demolished, and many a desolate site long recalled this fatal
period. But the two new Julian colonies, Carthage and
Cirta, became and continued to be the centers of Afro-
Roman civilization.

In desolate Greece Caesar, besides other plans such
as founding a Roman colony in Buthrotum (opposite
Corfu), busied himself above all with the restoration of
Corinth. Not only was a considerable colony of citizens
settled there, but a plan was projected for cutting through
the isthmus so as to avoid the dangerous circumnaviga-
tion of the Peloponnesus and to make the whole traffic between Italy and Asia pass through the Corintho-Saronic
gulf. Lastly, even in the remote Hellenic east the monarch
created Italian settlements, such as those at Heraclea and
Sinope on the Black Sea, where the Italian colonists
shared the towns with the old inhabitants, and the important port of Berytus on the Syrian coast, which like Sinope
obtained an Italian constitution. Even in Egypt a Roman
station was established on the lighthouse-island commanding the harbor of Alexandria.

Through these ordinances Italian municipal freedom
was widely disseminated over the provinces. The communities of full citizens—that is, all the towns of the Cisalpine province, and the citizen-colonies and *municipia* scattered in Transalpine Gaul and elsewhere—were on an
equal footing with the Italian, insofar as they administered their own affairs. On the other hand the more important questions came before the Roman authorities competent to deal with them, usually the governor of the
province. The formally autonomous Latin and the other
emancipated communities (including all those of Sicily
and of Narbonese Gaul, so far as they were not citizen-

communities, and a considerable number also in the other provinces) had such broad municipal freedom that the governor was only entitled to interfere by virtue of his administrative powers. No doubt there had already been communities of full citizens within the provinces of governors, such as Aquileia and Narbo; and whole governors' provinces, such as Cisalpine Gaul, had consisted of communities with Italian constitutions. But it was politically if not legally singularly important that there was now a province as well as Italy peopled solely by Roman citizens, and that others promised to become so.

With this disappeared the first great practical distinction that separated Italy from the provinces. The second—that ordinarily no troops were stationed in Italy—was likewise in the process of disappearing. Troops were now stationed only where there was a frontier to be defended, and the commandants of the provinces in which this was not the case, such as Narbo and Sicily, were officers only in name. The formal contrast between Italy and the provinces continued certainly even now to exist, for Italy was the sphere of civil jurisdiction and of consuls and praetors, while the provinces were districts under martial law and subject to proconsuls and propraetors. But procedures under civil and martial law had long been practically coincident, and the different titles of the magistrates signified little after one Imperator was over all.

In these various municipal foundations and ordinances —which are traceable at least in plan, if not perhaps all in execution, to Caesar—a definite system is apparent. Italy was converted from the mistress of the subject peoples into the mother of the renovated Italo-Hellenic nation. The complete equalization of the Cisalpine province with the mother country was a promise and a guarantee that, in Caesar's monarchy just as in the healthier days of the republic, every Latinized district might expect to achieve equal footing alongside its elder sisters and the mother herself. On the threshold of full national and political

equality with Italy stood the adjoining lands, such as the
Greek Sicily and the south of Gaul, which were rapidly
becoming Latinized. In a more remote stage of preparation were the other provinces of the empire, in which (just
as hitherto Narbo in Southern Gaul had been a Roman
colony) the great maritime cities of Emporiae, Gades,
Carthage, Corinth, Heraclea in Pontus, Sinope, Berytus,
and Alexandria now became Italian or Helleno-Italian
communities, the centers of Italian civilization even in the
Greek East and the fundamental base of the future national and political leveling of the empire.

The rule of the urban community of Rome over the
shores of the Mediterranean was at an end. In its stead
came the new Mediterranean state, and its first act was
to atone for the two worst outrages which that urban
community had perpetrated on civilization. While the destruction of the two greatest marts of commerce in the
Roman dominions marked the turning-point at which the
Roman protectorate degenerated into political tyranny
and financial oppression, the prompt and brilliant restoration of Carthage and Corinth marked the foundation of
the great new commonwealth which was to lead all the
Mediterranean regions to national and political equality
in a single state. Well might Caesar add to the far-
famed ancient name of Corinth the new one of "Honor
to Julius" (LAVS JVLI).

While the new empire was thus furnished with a national character, which doubtless lacked individuality because necessarily it was an inanimate product of art rather
than a natural growth, it also needed unity in those institutions which express the general life of nations—in constitution and administration, in religion and jurisprudence,
in money, measures, and weights—in all of which, of
course, extensive local diversities were quite compatible
with essential union. In all these departments we can only
speak of the initial steps, for the completion of Caesar's
monarchy was the work of the future, and all that he did

was to lay the foundation for the building of centuries. But several of the lines which the great man drew can still be recognized, and it is more pleasing to follow him here than in his building on the ruins of the past.

As to constitution and administration, we have already noted the most important elements of the new unity—the transition of the sovereignty from the municipal council of Rome to the sole ruler of the Mediterranean monarchy; the conversion of that municipal council into a supreme imperial council representing Italy and the provinces; and above all, the transference of the Roman, and generally of the Italian, municipal organization to the provincial communities. This bestowal of Latin, and thereafter of Roman, rights on the communities ripe for full admission to the united state gradually of itself brought about uniform communal arrangements.

In one respect alone, however, this process could not be waited for. The new empire needed immediately an institution which should place before the government at a glance the proportions of population and property in the different communities—in other words, an improved census. First the census of Italy was reformed. According to Caesar's ordinance—which probably, indeed, only carried out the arrangements which were at least in principle adopted as a result of the Social War—when a census took place in the Roman community, there were to be simultaneously registered by the highest authority in each Italian community the name of every citizen and that of his father or manumitter, his district, his age, and his property. These lists were to be furnished to the Roman censor early enough to enable him to complete in due time the general list of Roman citizens and property.

That it was also Caesar's intention to introduce similar institutions in the provinces is attested partly by the measurement and survey of the whole empire ordered by him, partly by the nature of the arrangement itself; for it furnished the general instrument for securing the information needed for the central administration. Evidently here too Caesar intended to revert to the earlier republican practice, and to reintroduce the republican census of the empire in essentially the same way as he effected the Italian—by extending the institution of the urban censorship to all the subject communities of Italy and Sicily. This had been one of the first institutions which the torpid aristocracy allowed to drop, thus depriving the supreme administrative authority of any concept of its resources in men and money, and consequently of any possibility of effective control. The indications show irrefutably that Caesar intended to renew the general census that had been obsolete for centuries.

We need scarcely say that in religion and in jurisprudence no thorough levelling could be thought of. Yet with all toleration towards local faiths and laws, the new state needed a common worship corresponding to the Italo-Hellenic nationality and a general code of law superior to the municipal statutes. The need for them is shown by their *de facto* existence. In the field of religion men had for centuries been busy fusing together the Italian and Hellenic worships, partly by external adoption and partly by internal adjustment of their respective conceptions of the gods. Owing to the pliant formless character of the Italian deities, there had been no great difficulty in resolving Jupiter into Zeus, Venus into Aphrodite, and every essential idea of the Latin faith into its Hellenic counterpart. The Italo-Hellenic religion already existed in broad outline. How conscious men were of having gone beyond the Roman point of view towards an Italo-Hellenic quasi-nationality is shown by the distinction, made in the already mentioned theology of Varro, between the "common" gods acknowledged by Romans and Greeks alike, and the special gods of the Roman community.

As concerns criminal law, where the government interferes more directly and where judicious legislation will suffice, there was no difficulty in attaining needed uniformity for the unity of the empire. In civil law, where the initiative belongs to commercial intercourse and merely the formal shape to the legislator, the code for the united empire had been already long since developed in a natural way through commercial intercourse itself. Roman urban law was indeed still legally based on the embodiment of the Latin national law contained in the Twelve Tables. Later laws had doubtless introduced various improvements of detail, among which the most important was probably the abolition of the old inconvenient mode of commencing a lawsuit, and the substitution for it of an instruction drawn up in writing by the presiding magistrate for the single juryman. But in the main the popular legislation had only piled upon that venerable foundation an endless chaos of special laws long since in great part antiquated and forgotten, which can only be compared to the English statute-law. The attempts to impart scientific shape and system to them had certainly rendered the tortuous paths of the old civil law accessible; but no Roman Blackstone could remedy the fundamental defect that an urban code composed four hundred years earlier, with its equally diffuse and confused supplements, was now to serve as the law of a great state.

Commercial intercourse provided for itself a more thorough remedy. The lively intercourse between Romans and non-Romans had long ago developed in Rome an international private law—that is to say, a body of maxims especially relating to commercial matters. Roman judges made decisions based on these, when a case could not be decided either according to their own or any other national code, and they were thus compelled to revert to the common views of right underlying all dealings. The formation of the newer law proceeded on this basis. In the first place, as a standard for the legal dealings of Roman citizens with each other, it substituted *de facto* for the old and practically useless urban law a new code based in substance on a compromise between the national law of the Twelve Tables and the international code. The former was essentially adhered to (though of course with modifications suited to the times) in the law of marriage, family, and inheritance; whereas the international law was standard in all matters regarding property, ownership, and contracts.[2]

Lastly, in money, measures, and weights the substantial equalization of the Latin and Hellenic systems had long been in progress. It was very ancient so far as concerned the definitions of weight and measures indispensable for trade and commerce, and in the monetary system little more recent than the introduction of silver coinage. But these older equations were not sufficient, because in the Hellenic world itself the most varied metrical and monetary systems existed side by side. It was necessary, and doubtless formed part of Caesar's plan, to introduce Roman money, Roman measures, and Roman weights everywhere in the new united empire in such a manner that they alone should be used in official intercourse, and that the non-Roman systems should be restricted to local currency or placed in specified ratio to the Roman. The action of Caesar, however, can only be discerned in two of the most important of these, the monetary system and the calendar.

The Roman monetary system was based on the two precious metals circulating side by side and in a fixed relation to each other, gold being given and taken according to weight, silver in the form of coin. But in the extensive foreign trade gold far preponderated over silver. It is uncertain whether the acceptance of Roman silver money was not even at an earlier period obligatory throughout the empire. At any rate, uncoined gold essentially performed the function of imperial money throughout Ro-

■

2. Mommsen's discussion of the spread of this new code is here omitted.

man territory, the more so as the Romans had prohibited
the coining of gold in all the provinces and protectorates.
Thus the denarius had, in addition to Italy, naturalized itself *de jure* or *de facto* in Cisalpine Gaul, in Sicily, in
Spain, and in various other places, especially in the West.
But the imperial coinage begins with Caesar. Exactly like
Alexander, he marked the foundation of the new monarchy embracing the civilized world by the fact that the
only universally accepted metal obtained the first place in
coinage. The scale on which the new Caesarian gold piece
was immediately coined is shown by the fact that in a single treasure buried seven years after Caesar's death 80,-
000 of these pieces were found together, though financial
speculations may have exercised a collateral influence in
this respect.

As for silver money, the exclusive rule of the Roman
denarius in the West, for which the foundation had previously been laid, was finally established by Caesar when he
closed the only Occidental mint that still competed with
the Roman, that of Massilia. The coining of silver or copper small money was still permitted to a number of Occidental communities; three-quarter denarii were struck by
some Latin communities of southern Gaul, half denarii by
several cantons in northern Gaul, and copper small coins
even after Caesar's time by various communes of the west.
But this small money was throughout coined after the Roman standard, and its acceptance was probably obligatory
only in local dealings.

Caesar, like the earlier government, does not seem to
have contemplated unifying the monetary system of the
East, where great masses of coarse silver money (much
of it too easily debased or worn away) and to some extent even, as in Egypt, a copper coinage akin to our paper
money were in circulation, and where the Syrian commercial cities would have felt severely the loss of their previous national coinage corresponding to the Mesopotamian

currency. We find here subsequently the arrangement that the denarius is legal currency everywhere and is the only medium of official reckoning, while the local coins circulate within their limited range but on an unfavorable exchange rate as compared with the denarius. This was probably not introduced all at once, and in part may have preceded Caesar. But it was at any rate the essential complement to the Caesarian imperial coinage, whose new gold piece was modeled on the almost equally heavy coin of Alexander and was doubtless designed especially for circulation in the East.

Of a kindred nature was the reform of the calendar. The republican calendar, which strangely enough was still the old decemviral calendar, had come by a combination of wretched mathematics and wretched administration to anticipate the true time by 67 whole days, so that the festival of Flora, for example, was celebrated on July 11 instead of April 28. Caesar finally removed this evil, and with the help of the Greek mathematician Sosigenes officially introduced the Italian farmer's year regulated according to the Egyptian calendar of Eudoxus, as well as a rational system of intercalation. At the same time the old beginning of the year on March 1 was abolished, and the date of January 1—fixed at first as the official time for changing the supreme magistrates, and therefore long since prevailing in civil life—was assumed also as commencing the calendar year. Both changes came into effect on January 1, 45 B.C., and along with them the use of the Julian calendar so named after its author, which long after the fall of the monarchy of Caesar remained the regulative standard of the civilized world and in the main is so still. By way of explanation there was added in a detailed edict a star calendar derived from the Egyptian astronomical observations and transferred—though not very skillfully—to Italy, which fixed the rising and setting of the stars named according to days of the calendar. In this domain also the Roman and Greek worlds were thus placed on a par.

Such were the foundations of the Mediterranean monarchy of Caesar. For the second time in Roman history the social question had reached a crisis whose antagonisms were actually insoluble. On the former occasion Rome had been saved by being merged into Italy, and in the new and enlarged home the old antagonisms fell into abeyance. Now Rome was once more saved by the fact that the countries of the Mediterranean were merged in it or became prepared for merging. The war between the Italian poor and rich, which in the old Italy could only end with the destruction of the nation, no longer had a battlefield or a meaning in the Italy of three continents. The Latin colonies closed the gap which threatened to swallow up the Roman community in the third century B.C.; the deeper chasm two hundred years later was filled by the Transalpine and overseas colonizations of Gaius Gracchus and Julius Caesar.

For Rome alone history not only performed miracles but repeated them, and twice cured the internal crisis, which within the state itself was incurable, by regenerating the state. There was doubtless much evil in this regeneration. As the union of Italy was accomplished over the ruins of the Samnite and Etruscan nations, so the Mediterranean monarchy built itself on the ruins of countless once living and vigorous states and tribes. But it was a corruption out of which sprang a fresh growth, part of which remains green to this day. What was pulled down were merely the secondary nationalities long since marked for destruction by the leveling hand of civilization.

Caesar, wherever he acted as a destroyer, only carried out the pronounced verdict of historical development. But he protected the germs of culture where and as he found them, in his own land as well as among the sister nation of the Hellenes. He saved and renewed the Roman type; and not only did he spare the Greek type, but with the same self-reliant genius that accomplished the regeneration of Rome he undertook also the regeneration of the Hellenes, and resumed the interrupted work of the great Alexander whose image, we may well believe, was never absent from Caesar's soul. He solved these two great tasks not merely side by side, but the one by means of the other. The two great essentials of humanity—general and individual development, or state and culture—once united in embryo in those old Graeco-Italians feeding their flocks in primeval simplicity far from the coasts and islands of the Mediterranean, had become severed when they were parted into Italians and Hellenes, and had remained apart for many centuries. Now the descendant of the Trojan prince and the Latin king's daughter created, out of a state without distinctive culture or cosmopolitan civilization, a new whole in which culture and state again met in the rich fullness of blessed maturity.

These are the outlines which Caesar drew for this work, according to which he himself labored, and according to which posterity—for many centuries confined to the paths which this great man marked out—endeavored to work generally in accordance with the intentions of the illustrious master, if not with his intellect and energy. Little was finished, much was merely begun. Whether the plan was complete, those who venture to vie in thought with such a man may decide. We observe no material defect in what lies before us. Every single stone of the building is enough to make a man immortal, yet all combine to form one harmonious whole. Caesar's reign as king of Rome was five and a half years, not half as long as Alexander's. In the intervals of seven great campaigns, which allowed him to stay no more than fifteen months altogether in the capital, he regulated the destinies of the world for the present and the future, from the establishment of the boundary line between civilization and barbarism down to the removal of the pools of rain in the streets of the capital, and yet retained time and composure enough to follow attentively the prize pieces in the theater and to confer the chaplet on the victor with improvised verses.

The rapidity and precision with which his plan was executed prove that it had long been meditated and all its parts settled in detail, but they still remain not much less wonderful than the plan itself. The outlines of the new state was defined for all coming time, leaving to the boundless future the completion of the structure. To this extent Caesar might say that his aim was attained, and this was probably what he meant when he sometimes said that he had "lived enough." But precisely because the building was endless, as long as he lived the master restlessly added stone to stone, always with the same dexterity and elasticity busy at his work, never overturning or postponing, just as if there were for him no tomorrow but only today. Thus he worked and created as never any mortal before or since. As worker and creator, after wellnigh two thousand years he still lives in the memory of nations as the first and only Imperator Caesar.

*　　*　　*　　*　　*　　*　　*

We have reached the end of the Roman republic. After five hundred years' rule in Italy and in the countries on the Mediterranean, we have seen it brought to ruin in politics and morals, religion and literature, not through outward violence but through inward decay, thereby making room for the new monarchy of Caesar. There was in that world, as Caesar found it, much of the noble heritage of past centuries and an infinite abundance of pomp and glory, but little spirit, less taste, and least of all true delight in life. It was indeed an old world, and even the richly gifted patriotism of Caesar could not make it young again. The dawn does not return till after the night has run its course. But with him there came, to the sorely harassed peoples on the Mediterranean, a tolerable evening after the sultry noon. And when at length after a long historical night the new day dawned, and fresh, free nations commenced their race towards new and higher goals, there were among them not a few which were sprung from seed sown by Caesar, and which owed and still owe to him their national individuality.

GLOSSARY

AEDILE: Four aediles were elected annually by the *comitia tributa* (see below). Their duties included supervision of the public markets, general policing of the capital, and particularly the management of public games and festivals. In this last capacity the aedile was expected to procure wild animals and gladiators at his own expense for the celebrations. Only men of wealth or large credit could maintain themselves in the office. The reward for lavish outlay came years later, when election to the praetorship, followed by a year as provincial governor, finally placed a man in a position to reap substantial profits.

CENSOR: Two censors were elected every five years from former consuls. The censors' duties were to maintain and revise the citizenship rolls and assign each citizen his proper tribe, class, and century. The censors also had a general supervision over public morals, and were empowered to remove senators or equites from their classes for scandalous conduct.

COMITIUM, COMITIA: The Latin word *comitium*, though it occurs in the singular, most frequently appears in the plural, *comitia*. The singular comitium meant the place of an election or popular meeting, usually the Forum. The plural comitia meant the assembling of the people for the purpose of voting, and hence in most contexts is practically equivalent to election, plebiscite, or electoral assembly. There were three types of comitia:

1. *Comitia tributa:* This is most commonly meant when Mommsen speaks of "a vote of the people," or "a popular assembly." Each Roman citizen was assigned to a "tribe," originally a geographical term like "ward." In the last age of the republic there were thirty-five tribes. An assembly of the tribes, comitia tributa, could be summoned at any time by a consul, a praetor, or a tribune. The meeting place was the Forum. The vote was taken by tribes. This comitia elected the quaestors, aediles, and tribunes. It could also accept or reject any proposed law (rogatio), and thus became the most important legislative body. Down to the time of the Gracchi, laws were rarely offered for approval that had not previously been discussed and recommended by the Senate, and in this earlier period the comitia tributa was little more than a ratifying body for senatorial decrees. In the later period, the possibility of using the comitia tributa independently to by-pass the Senate was recognized and exploited by various demagogues known as *populares*, and this development of the power of the comitia became a leading issue in the political agitations of the republic's last century. The comitia tributa was attended chiefly by the idle city rabble, and fell increasingly under the influence of bribery and rioting. The power of the tribunes (see below) rested chiefly on their right to convoke and lead the comitia tributa.

2. *Comitia centuriata:* This was the oldest and, in a sense, the most authoritative of the popular assemblies. It was organized by "centuries," originally a military division, but by the time of the late republic a purely formal division for the purpose of voting. It was summoned annually to

elect the higher ranking magistrates (consuls, praetors). It met in the *Campus Martius.* It was attended by citizens from all Italy, as well as by the city populace; consequently it had a somewhat more representative character than the comitia tributa, and was less easily influenced by demagogic agitation. It was also, like the comitia tributa, competent to pass upon legislation, but as it was less easily convoked and more dominated by property interest than the tribal assembly, it was not often called for legislative purposes.

3. *Comitia curiata:* This ancient assembly had lost all political power by the last century of the republic, but was still summoned annually to confer the formal *imperium,* or full military authority, upon the consuls.

CONSUL, CONSULSHIP: The executive power of the Roman republic was vested in two consuls, elected annually by the comitia centuriata. The consuls normally presided over meetings of the senate, and held the titular command of the army (*imperium*). Election to the consulship conferred the equivalent of a title of nobility, and those who counted consuls in their ancestry were called *nobiles.* The principal material reward of election to the consulship, however, was the rich province which fell to each consul in the year following his consulship, a province which he administered as proconsul.

CURULE CHAIR, CURULE OFFICE: Higher ranking officials (censors, consuls, praetors, and two of the aediles—the so-called "curule" aediles) were entitled to sit in a ceremonial chair inlaid with ivory. Accordingly the term "curule chairs" may be used metaphorically to denote simply the higher aristocracy.

EQUITES, EQUESTRIAN ORDER: A Roman *eques* (plural, *equites*) meant, in the last century of the republic, simply a citizen of nonsenatorial rank whose property amounted to 400,000 sesterces or more. The equites or equestrian order thus formed a middle class of wealth between the senatorial order and the vast propertyless commons. The term once designated a man wealthy enough to furnish his own horse for military service, but it had long lost its original connotation. The closest English equivalent, the word "knight," is so misleading and unsatisfactory that the terms "capitalists," "the rich," and "the business interests" have been substituted wherever possible.

FORUM: The central market place in Rome, where the populace gathered for meetings of the comitia tributa, where major public speeches were delivered, and where, on ordinary days, upper-class Romans met their friends and retainers and learned the news of the hour.

IMPERATOR: After a significant victory, a successful general would be hailed "Imperator!" by his troops, and thereafter would be entitled to decorate his fasces with wreaths of laurel, and to be addressed by the honorary title. The word may also be used simply for "supreme commander" or "general-in-chief."

PONTIFEX MAXIMUS: In the complicated organization of the Roman religion, an important position was held by the College of Priests (*collegium pontificum*) presided over by a pontifex maximus or chief priest. Priesthoods were held for life. They were, however, purely political offices, as the Roman religion had, by the last century of the republic, lost all spiritual or moral meaning.

PRAETOR: Eight praetors were elected annually by the comitia centuriata. Their principal duties were presiding over the standing courts. After serving a year as judge, a praetor would normally be sent to govern one of the lesser provinces as *propraetor*. In this capacity he had many opportunities for enrichment, and was thus commonly able to recoup the heavy expenses he had incurred in advancing up the political ladder.

PROCONSUL, PROPRAETOR: After their year of office in Rome, the consuls and praetors were normally appointed to a military command in the provinces, where they served as proconsuls or propraetors. Before leaving the city, they were formally invested with the *imperium*, or full military authority. While exercising their duties in the city in time of peace, the imperium was considered as held in abeyance, and only after a formal investiture by the comitia curiata were the axes unsheathed on the fasces, symbolizing the life-and-death power of the command.

QUAESTOR: The quaestors were younger officials elected by the comitia tributa as assistants to the higher magistrates. After Sulla, the quaestors numbered twenty, most of whom served as aides-de-camp on the staff of a provincial governor. Two special quaestors, called *quaestores urbani*, were in charge of the treasury and the public archives at Rome. The quaestorship was the first step in the so-called *cursus honorum*, or succession of magistracies, and was chiefly sought by young men of senatorial family at the beginning of their political careers.

SESTERCES: This English plural is derived from the Latin *sestertius*, a small silver coin. In Cicero's day it was the standard unit for stating sums of money. It is impossible, except very roughly, to state its modern value. As a rule of thumb, the sestertius may be taken as five cents. Thus, the minimum net worth for equites was $20,000 (400,000 sesterces). The sestertius was equal to one-fourth of a *denarius*.

TRIBUNE: The tribunes, numbering ten in the later republic, were elected annually by the comitia tributa. The full title, "tribune of the people," reflects the origin of the office as a guardian of popular rights. The tribunes had the power of veto or intercession against the acts of other magistrates. Their persons were sacrosanct. The powers inherent in the office were little used from the times of the patrician-plebeian struggles of the early republic down to the age of the Gracchi, who revived the early revolutionary tradition. In the hands of able demagogues, the tribunate became a very powerful office in the last century of the republic, often overshadowing even the consulship. The powers of the tribunes were much curtailed by Sulla, but were fully restored a few years after his death.

TRIUMPH, TRIUMPHATOR: On his return from a successful military campaign of major importance, the general and his army were honored by a great parade through the streets called a triumph, roughly equivalent to New York's modern ticker-tape welcomes. A general who had celebrated a triumph was called triumphator. The honor of a triumph was given by a formal vote of the Senate, and accordingly involved all the usual political maneuvering and wire-pulling.

NOTE: Roman practice with proper names is the indexer's despair. A Roman ordinarily bore three names—a *praenomen* (first name), a *nomen* (family or *gentile* name), and a *cognomen* (branch of family name). Unfortunately there was no uniformity in the *commonly* used name—it might be the *nomen*, the *cognomen*, or a nickname which a man acquired and passed on to his descendants like a true family name. To confound confusion more, there were constant adoptions from one family to another, the adopted individual carrying both his original and adopted family names. Thus the great general and statesman of the second century B.C. is often called Scipio Africanus Minor, but equally often Scipio Aemilianus (because he was adopted into the Scipio family from the Aemilian gens), or Scipio Numantinus (because he conquered Numantia). In technical works on Roman history, consistency is obtained by listing all persons alphabetically by *nomen*. This system has its advantages, but it can hardly be applied in a work intended for the general reader. It results in listing Caesar, for example, under "Julius," and Cicero under "Tullius," Scipio Africanus Minor would not be listed under *any* of the names above, but under "Cornelius," his adopted gentile *nomen*. The following index aims at usefulness rather than consistency. The better-known persons are listed under their most commonly used names, *e.g.*, Caesar, Catiline, Pompey. Less well-known persons are generally listed under the name Mommsen uses in speaking of them, usually (but not always) the *cognomen*. The following standard Roman abbreviations are used for the common *praenomina*: A. — Aulus; Ap. — Appius; C. — Gaius; Cn. — Gnaeus; D. — Decimus; L. — Lucius; M. — Marcus; M'. — Manius; N. — Numerius; P. — Publius; Q. — Quintus; Ser. — Servius; Sex. — Sextus; Sp. — Spurius; T. — Titus; Ti. — Tiberius.

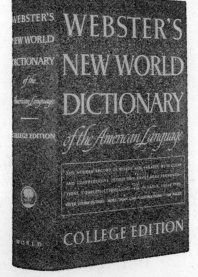